D0881366

Literature In America

LITERATURE IN

GLOUCESTER, MASS.

PETER SMITH

1973

an anthology of

literary criticism selected

and introduced by

PHILIP RAHV

America

Philip Rahv

Philip Rahv, the editor of LITERATURE IN AMERICA, is presently
Visiting Professor of Comparative Literature at Brandeis University.
He is one of the founders of *The Partisan Review,* the author of
Image and Idea, The Discovery of Europe, and a forthcoming study
of Dostoevsky.

M

AN ORIGINAL MERIDIAN BOOK
First published by Meridian Books, Inc. September 1957
First printing August 1957
Second printing May 1958
Third printing April 1960

Copyright 1957 by Meridian Books, Inc.

Library of Congress catalog card number: 57-10840

ISBN: 0-8446-2776-3

Reprinted, 1973, by Permission of
WORLD PUBLISHING
Times Mirror

Contents

5

Foreword

This anthology is not a collection of critical "gems" or of aesthetic judgments pure and simple, nor is it meant to represent American criticism in toto or even to exhibit its finest achievements as a self-defined medium of writing regulated by methods of its own and pursuing standards of value proper to itself. Such criticism, though written by Americans, is under no obligation to deal with American authors or it may deal with them from a purely literary standpoint, without significantly touching upon their native affiliations, background, qualities and meanings. Critical work of that type, however excellent in itself, is necessarily excluded by the principle of selection I have exercised in this book, this principle being that of concentrating only upon those observations and analyses of American writers and writing in which the emphasis, as a whole or in part, is on national characteristics and relation to the national experience. Thus every item in this collection has been chosen with an eye to what it contributes to our understanding of the literary process at work under New World conditions.

Some of the pieces, such as the two essays, so directly contradictory of each other, on "Nationality in Literature" (by E. A. Duyckinck and James Russell Lowell respectively), I have included chiefly for documentary reasons, illustrating the highly controversial character which the very notion of an *American* literature assumed

8

even as late as 1847, in the very period when our literature entered into its state of high germination, readying itself for the production within a few years of some of its greatest works, such as *The Scarlet Letter, Representative Men, Leaves of Grass,* and *Moby Dick.* Most of the other pieces in this volume are evaluative in intent, defining the creative accomplishment or failure, as the case may be, of our writers in the light of their response to the multiple challenges of American life. When, in the essay re-printed in this book, Randall Jarrell finds it possible to say of three poets so strongly marked in their individual traits as W. C. Williams, Marianne Moore, and Wallace Stevens, that "their reproduction of things, in their empirical gaiety, its clear abstract refinement of presentation, has something peculiarly and paradoxically American about it," he defines at one stroke the theme and unifying idea of this anthology.

There has been an immense amount of writing, both here and abroad, on the subject of American literature in which it is approached precisely from the standpoint of its essential Americanness, and I may add that the main difficulty that confronted me as an anthologist was this luxuriant abundance of material, a veritable *embarras de richesse*. Because of inevitable restrictions of space I was forced to exclude a good many fine and perspicuous statements. Inevitably, too, the stress in my selection has been on essays treating those American writers whose importance is inseparable from their native bias and/or integral use of indigenous materials.

The organization of the anthology is, I trust, apparent. No artificial separation of the contents into parts or sections seemed justified or feasible. I have chosen rather to organize the selections chronologically, interposing where it was relevant the assessments of later critics. Thus Cooper's essay on *American Literature* is followed by D. H. Lawrence's discussion of Cooper; as is Emerson's by that of John Jay Chapman.

P. R.
New York, April 15, 1957

Introduction: THE NATIVE BIAS

"Characteristically American" is the phrase that crops up with virtually compulsive regularity in a good many of the texts assembled in this volume. Inevitably it occurs and recurs in all the intensive discussions of the prospects and condition of the national letters conducted since the earliest years of the Republic. Quite often the phrase carries with it the suggestion that the user of it is far from certain in his own mind as to what the "characteristically American" actually comes to and that he is in fact looking to the literary expression of his countrymen to provide him with the key to the enigma. Thus it would seem that one of the principal functions of literature in America has been to serve as a vademecum of Americanness, if not of Americanism. The latter term has by now acquired an unction compelling its surrender to the politicians; it is with Americanness, a category more existential than political, that our writers and critics have been concerned.

There is little to be wondered at in the uncertainty that has prevailed from the start as to the actual constituents of the "characteristically American." Henry James saw complexity in the very fate of being an American, and among the recognitions that this complexity entails is the fact that as a national entity we are uniquely composed of diverse and sometimes clashing ethnic and regional strains. Even more important is the fact that as a nation we are

11

afloat in history without moorings in pre-history. Americans have
no organic past, only ambiguous memories of European derivations.
The decisive factor in the forming of American civilization, as one
cultural historian put it, is that "the American community had a
beginning at a particular moment in history in contrast with the
traditional communities that, far from having a precise historical
origin, rose out of the bottomless darkness of time in that epoch of
pre-history which is history, if at all, only in its latent and undevel-
oped stage."● Hence American society has the startling look about
it of a human artifact, constructed for specific socio-political and
economic purposes in a given period, a period well known and
thoroughly documented. It is a society established on contractual
rather than traditional foundations, the very existence of which
makes for the impression that in the New World the legend of the
"social contract" has finally been brought to visible life. And this
very perceptibility, so to speak, of the national origins is not the
least of the elements making for a profound sense of the problematical in the American awareness of cultural identity.

This sense of the problematical, this sense of always verging on
a definition yet somehow missing it, enters significantly into many
of the critical approaches that Americans have made to their own
literature—approaches tending to turn into a search for America
that takes on the aura of a spiritual adventure or mythic quest. Now
the problematical is surely not so far apart from the fascinating; and
the more committed minds among those who embarked on this
search form a vital band of native spokesmen to whom the American character presents itself as a fascinating problem. The effects
of this fascination, of this tall measure of devotion, are writ large
in our criticism. Most of the famous testaments of our cultural
history owe to it their verve in undertaking successively fresh
appraisals of the national experience. Its operation is everywhere
manifest in such works as Emerson's "American Scholar," Whitman's various prefaces and *Democratic Vistas,* James's biography
of Hawthorne, Adams's *Education,* the letters and essays of Randolph
Bourne, and the books full of passionate indictment that Van
Wyck Brooks issued year after year before the change of front
made evident in his *Makers and Finders* series. Yet even this voluminous record of filio-pietistic indulgence is quickened and given
its rationale by the lasting fascination with the American character,

● *F. G. Friedmann, "America: A Country without a Pre-History,"*
Partisan Review, *March-April 1952.*

a fascination which continues to serve at once as the goad and the charm of even such relatively late and sober-minded studies as F. O. Matthiessen's *American Renaissance* and Alfred Kazin's *On Native Grounds*. In the latter work Mr. Kazin alludes with insight to some of the consequences of this absorbing commitment on the part of American critics when he observes that "from Emerson and Thoreau to Mencken and Brooks, criticism has been the great American lay philosophy, the intellectual carryall. It had been a study of literature inherently concerned with ideals of citizenship, and often less a study of literary texts than a search for some imperative moral order within which American writing could live and grow. . . . It has even been the secret intermediary . . . between literature and society in America."

Among the earliest tasks that American critics set for themselves was that of locating and defining the differences between American and European writing. All through the past century and, in fact, until the renaissance that transformed the American literary consciousness in the earlier part of this century, this effort at definition met with resistance from the more genteel and agreeable writers and critics. These worthies, from Irving and Lowell to Brownell and Woodberry, entertained expurgated notions of the creative life, and they were unable to countenance "the snapping asunder," in Poe's phrase, "of the leading strings of our British Grandmamma." This prolonged resistance is to be explained by the fear of learning that the differences between the literature of the Old and the New World were indeed acute and real. "It is hard to hear a new voice," wrote D. H. Lawrence, "as hard as it is to listen to a new language; and there is a new voice in the old American classics." This new feeling originated in the psychic shift that occurred in the movement to the Western hemisphere. Lawrence called it a displacement, adding that "displacements hurt. This hurts. So we try to tie it up, like a cut finger, to put a rag round it." Whitman and Emerson exalted in the displacement; Hawthorne brooded about it and made what he could of it by searching for its beginnings in the annals of New England; Melville was heroic in his striving to do it justice but soon suffered a breakdown because he could not sustain the pitch of intensity at which he expended himself. A more easeful or complacent reaction was evolved by Longfellow, Lowell, Holmes and the other distinguished authors of a tame reflective literature. They recoiled in paleface fashion from the tensions and hazards of the fresh experience thrown up by the dynamism of American life; and in so far as this experience came within their purview at all they saw it in its crude, exposed state, judging it to be unfit for imaginative treatment.

Barrett Wendell, the Harvard professor who published *A Literary History of America* in 1900, was among the foremost exponents of the Genteel Tradition and one of those luminaries of the academy in America who could not bring themselves to treat American writers as anything but poor relations of the towering British figures to whom they looked up with reverence.• Yet even so, though ignoring Melville and disdaining Whitman in his book, Wendell somehow hit upon the formula that accounts for the feebleness that affects us so discouragingly in studying the pre-modern period in American letters. (It has become habitual among us to regard Melville and Whitman as the representative creative types of that period. But this view indicates a loss of perspective on the past, for both were signally unsuccessful in gaining the esteem of the public of their time and in influencing the creative practice of their contemporaries. Whitman survived by making a fight of it, while Melville went under, his best work scarcely known.) Wendell's formula is that this literature is in essence "a record of the national inexperience," and its "refinement of temper, conscientious sense of form and instinctive disregard of actual fact" are its most characteristic traits. Thus he accurately noted, though with no objecion on his part, the overriding fault—that of innocuousness—against which Melville warned in declaring that "the visible world of experience . . . is that procreative thing which impregnates the Muses." And if a novelist like Howells is virtually unread today, then surely it is because of the lack in him of "that procreative thing." Hence the failure of the recent efforts to stage his "revival." Evidently the absence of the "procreative thing" cannot be made up for by the clarity of design of his fiction and by the considerable intelligence and attractiveness of the personality that informs it. It is plain that whatever interest we may have in Howells today is not actual but falls somewhere on the borderline between the historical and and the antiquarian; that is equally true of Longfellow, Whittier, Simms and others whose names are still honored in the textbooks. Now modern American literature has attempted to overcome the fault so fatal to Howells and his prede-

---

• *In his* Days of the Phoenix (*1957*), *Van Wyck Brooks recalls that even as late as 1920, when American writing had come to seem important, it was "still ignored in academic circles where Thackeray and Tennyson were treated as twin kings of our literature and all the American writers as poor relations. It was regarded as 'a pale and obedient provincial cousin about which the less said the better,' in the phrase of Ernest Boyd, and Christian Gauss at Princeton, as Edmund Wilson pointed out, chimed in with Woodberry at Columbia and Wendell at Harvard."*

cessors by at long last seizing upon what the native genius had long been deprived of, by finding, in other words, its major stimulus in the urge toward and immersion in experience.* American writers were able to accomplish this transformation, however, not merely by accepting experience in all its indigenousness but also by overturning the tradition of the palefaces and by frequently making the most, in true redskin fashion, of experience precisely in its crude, exposed state, thus turning what had long been taken as a defect into a virtue. The law of over-compensation is as operative in art as in life.

It seems to me that it is only by facing up to the fact of the enfeeblement of the greater part of the older American literature by its negative relation to experience that we can properly evaluate the complaint against the native environment typically voiced by so many of the worst as well as the best of our nineteenth-century writers. Let us attend only to the best of them, noting the virtual identity of the terms in which they state the case against their country's capacity to provide them with imaginative substance. There is Cooper, for instance, asserting back in 1828 that among the main obstacles against which the native writer has to contend is sheer "poverty of materials." "There is scarcely an ore which contributes to the wealth of the author, that is found, here, in veins in rich as in Europe. There are no annals for the historian; no follies (beyond the most vulgar and commonplace) for the satirist; no manners for the dramatist; no obscure fictions for the writer of romance . . . nor any of the rich auxiliaries of poetry . . . no costume for the peasant . . . no wig for the judge, no baton for the general, no diadem for the magistrate."* This complaint is substantially repeated by Hawthorne some three decades later in his preface to *The Marble Faun,* where he remarks upon the difficulty of "writing a romance about a country where there is no shadow, no antiquity, no mystery, no picturesque and gloomy wrong, nor anything but a commonplace prosperity, in broad and simple daylight, as is happily the case with our dear native land." James, quoting these words in his biography of Hawthorne, is powerfully moved to enlarge upon them, and it is

As I argue in the essay re-printed in this collection, the true initiators of the line of modernity in American writing are Whitman and James because both adopted a positive approach to experience, even while defining its value and content in diametrically opposite ways. Hence the specifically modern in the national letters cannot be said to have had its start, as is usually assumed, in this century, with the onset of the "new" poetry and the movement toward realism in fiction.

See Cooper's essay "American Literature" in this volume.

at this point in his book that the famous passage comes in ("No sovereign, no court, no personal loyalty, no aristocracy, no church, no clergy, no army," etc., etc.) enumerating the items of high civilization absent from American life. It is important to observe that James's version, by stretching Hawthorne's statement to the limit, no longer refers to "romance" alone but to artistic creation in general. Essentially he is duplicating Cooper's complaint in a more elaborate and conscious manner; and where Cooper speaks of "the poverty of materials" available to the American writer, James speaks of "the paucity of ingredients."

The justice and pathos of this standing complaint have been more or less recognized by our critics and historians of letters. No doubt it is justified in so far as we cannot but accept in some sense the Jamesian dictum that it takes "an accumulation of history and custom . . . to form a suggestion for the novelist." But there is none the less a fallacy in the argument so strikingly concurred in by Cooper, Hawthorne, and James. For what they are saying, intrinsically, is that it is impossible to write European literature in America; the necessary ingredients are missing. And so they were if we are thinking in terms of a Walter Scott romance or a Jane Austen novel or the poems of Byron; no part of the United States was then a center of high civilization. Still, what is wrong is the tacit assumption that the ingredients are of a fixed kind, given once and for all. But is it really true that the relationship between literature and high civilization is so completely binding? If that were strictly the case, we would be utterly at a loss to explain the appearance in backward Russia, and so early in the nineteenth century at that, of so great a poet as Pushkin and a master of narrative-prose like Gogol. Whitman's "Song of Myself" is in no sense a poem of high civilization, but it is a magnificent poem nevertheless. Is it not more to the point to acknowledge that the genuinely new and venturesome in literary art emerges from a fresh selection of the materials at hand, from an assimilation, that is, to imaginative forms of that which life newly offers but which the conventions of past literature are too rigid to let through? And in the earlier as well as the latter part of the nineteenth century, life in America certainly offered sufficient experience for imaginative treatment, though not the sort of experience marked by richness and complexity of historical reference and safely certified for literary use by the past conventions of authorship. Actually, in creating the character of Leatherstocking, Cooper did break through those conventions; as Lowell wrote in his *Fable for Critics*: "He has drawn you one character, though, that is new/ One wild-flower he's plucked that is wet with the dew/ Of this fresh western world"; where Cooper failed in his Leatherstocking tales, however, is in being far too obedient to the established conventions in point of style and technique.

As for Hawthorne, he appears to have attached a disproportionate importance to the question of "romance," plainly because of his incapacity to come to terms with the kind of subject-matter which is novelistic in essence. The fact is that in his time "romance" was a genre already far gone in obsolescence; it was the novel that was then full of promise and vitality. Let us recall, too, that some of "the follies" disdained by Cooper as much too "vulgar and commonplace" for literary exploitation, served the French novel very well in the work of Balzac, Flaubert, and Zola. In his *Comédie humaine* Balzac intended to treat all strata of society, but in practice he assigned the major role to the trading and professional classes. There was no lack of such classes in the United States, and yet no indigenous version of a novel comparable to *César Birotteau* was ever produced by a writer who knew his New York, Boston, or Philadelphia. A subject so lowly as Balzac tackled in his commercial saga of a Parisian linen-draper was entirely at variance with the "abnormal dignity" which then prevailed in American letters. Another example would be *Madame Bovary*. Can it really be claimed that the material fashioned by Flaubert into a work of art was unavailable a hundred years ago in America? After all, a pretty woman's boredom, adultery, and suicide are scarcely a monopoly of French life. Yet the sort of imaginative transaction represented by the story of Emma Bovary is unthinkable in mid-nineteenth century America. It was not the absence of materials but the absence of writers prepared to cope with the materials actually at hand that decided the issue, and it is in this sense that the standing complaint cited above was misdirected. Allowing for Whitman and in part for Melville as formidable exceptions, what stood in the way was the fixed stance of the writers, their lack of inner 'freedom to break with tradition so as to be able to say the seemingly unsayable. "The immense and vague cloud-canopy of idealism," in Brooks's phrase, which then hung over the national culture made any such attempts prohibitive. The truth is that there were no real novelists in America until the 'eighties and 'nineties, only pre-novelists and romancers. A conspicuous instance attesting to this fact is Melville's *Pierre,* the one work in which he undertook to possess himself of the forms of realism developed by his European contemporaries and in which he failed dismally. I am stressing this point in order to reinforce my contention in the essay, "The Cult of Experience in American Writing," that in that period American literature was not yet in position to adapt for itself "the vitally new principle of realism by which the art of fiction in Europe was at that time evolving toward an hitherto inconceivable condition of objectivity and familiarity with existence." This principle of realism—which Erich Auerbach defines in his *Mimesis* as "a serious representation of contemporary social reality against the background of a constant historical movement"—requires above all a give-and-take relation between the ego and experience. It is only with the appearance of narratives like *Washington Square* (1881) and *The Bostonians* (1886) that we sense that this relation is perceptibly beginning to come into being. And if the former narrative, in its recreation of old New York focusing on the house in Washington Square with its chintz-covered parlor where Catherine Sloper is courted by Morris Townsend, still puts us under a spell, it is hardly because those young people are especially memorable or their case compelling but because earlier American fiction is so poor in evocations of the actual in its time and place. It is a matter of the Americanness of a past age coming through as an aesthetic impression by virtue of the precision with which it is conveyed. But James was soon to settle in London, taking his American characters with him. It was to be a question for him of becoming either a novelist of high civilization, even if mainly of its impact on his countrymen, or nothing at all. He removed himself from the scene, exerting an uncertain influence from afar. Not till after the turn of the century, when the qualities of national existence changed radically and a native intelligentsia rose to the surface of social life, did American literature succeed in liberating itself from its past inhibitions.

Of course, all through the nineteenth century the ideologues of nativity bent every effort to nullify the complaint against America's "poverty of materials." Whitman's prose is one long counterargument. And at an earlier date, apart from the Young America group in New York, led by the Duyckincks and Cornelius Mathews, of whom a thorough and entertaining account has recently been given by Professor Perry Miller in his study *The Raven and the Whale,* powerful voices were raised in defence of America's creative possibilities. There is Emerson, for example, writing in 1842 that "we have as yet no genius in America, with tyrannous eye, which knew the value of our incomparable materials, and saw, in the barbarism and materialism of the times, another carnival of the same gods he so much admires in Homer. . . . Banks and tariffs, the newspaper and caucus, Methodism and Unitarianism, are flat and dull to dull people, but rest on the same foundations of wonder as the town of Troy and the temple of Delphi. . . . Our log-rolling, our stumps and their politics, our fisheries, our Negroes and Indians . . . the northern trades, the southern planting, the western clearing, Oregon and Texas, are yet unsung. Yet America is a poem in our eyes; its ample geography dazzles the imagination, and it will not wait long for metres." As usual Emerson is being beautifully eloquent. His catalogue of materials is impressive, a splendid retort to disparagers and complainers. But a catalogue is one thing; the personal appropriation of materials is something else again. Only writers of a truly Balzacian grossness of appetite could conceivably have digested them. What was needed was not a "tyrannous eye" but a strong stomach above all; but unfortunately the men of letters of that period were typically inclined either toward a morbid type of spirituality or toward a propitiatory and at bottom escapist jocosity.

Whitman alone responded in programmatic fashion to Emerson's challenge, though his master was sometimes depressed by his want of metres. Moreover the master, along with the lesser partisans of nativity, was not content to submit his inventory of materials without at the same time prescribing an attitude of patriotic glow as the condition of their assimilation. Note that Emerson says of America that it is "a poem in our eyes," just as Whitman was to say in the 1855 preface to *Leaves of Grass* that "the United States are themselves the greatest poem." Thus dogmatic patriotism is turned into a prerequisite of artistic creation. Historically speaking, this is indeed the vulnerable side of nativism in literature, that it cannot advocate the use of the American subject-matter without at once demanding of the writer that he declare himself in advance to stand in an affirmative relation to it. Nativists can never understand that any attempt to enlist literature "in the cause of America" is bound to impose an intolerable strain on the imaginative faculty. The real issue in the times of Emerson and Whitman was not between love of America and disdain of it; neither Cooper nor Hawthorne nor James disdained it. The issue was rather the availability at home of creatively usable materials; their availability was the point, and the writer's readiness to benefit from it according to his lights, not the political or moral or philosophical valuation to be put upon them. It is through his achievement in his own medium that the important writer contributes to the spiritual development of his people. To ask that he commit himself to flattering the national ego is a proceeding as simple-minded as it is vicious. And it is a false idea of what affirmation comes to in the long run to believe that the literary artist who brings to his people not peace but a sword has failed in his spiritual task. As isolable qualities neither pessimism nor optimism are definable as values in art.

At the present time, when the issue of "poverty of materials" can no longer arise in America, the habit of demanding affirmation still persists. We are living in a period of renewed national belligerency when pessimism is again regarded as "unAmerican." In many circles so recent a lesson as that taught us in the 'twenties, when American writing showed far more creative force than it does now even while engaging in a bitter assault on the national pieties, has been conveniently forgotten. As in the old days, so now the appeal to "the sanely and wholesomely American" is taken up as a weapon against the moral freedom of literature.

It is true, as Mr. Henry Bamford Parkes points out in his essay in this volume, that a good deal of American writing, in the classic as in the modern period, is dominated by forms of flight from the organized pressures of society. Mr. Parkes brilliantly marshals the evidence to show that the Leatherstocking type of hero who may be seen as a fugitive from society reappears again and again in our fiction, which carries with it a specific emotion of disappointment in the consequences of civilization. In *Huckleberry Finn* as in some of the novels of Anderson, Dos Passos, Hemingway and Fitzgerald, an antagonism is demonstrated between individual integrity and institutional disciplines and mores. To the texts cited by Mr. Parkes one might add so signal an expression of the same tendency as Faulkner's long story, "The Bear," in which the principal character, Isaac McCaslin, relinquishes the land he has inherited in the belief that rapacity was the prime motive-power of subduing the wilderness and that civilization represents a fall from goodness and innocence requiring the strictest expiation.

One wonders, however, whether Mr. Parkes is right in the interpretation he puts upon the evidence at his disposal. Is not the pessimism which he perceives to be so strikingly characteristic of modern American literature to be found in even stronger ideological doses, though not expressed with the same heedless violence, in modern European writing? Are we justified in absolving civilization of sin and guilt while convicting writers of an impossible idealism derived from a Rousseauistic faith in natural virtue and natural religion? Is not discontent with civilization one of the major sources of the virulence of modernity? Literature, here as in Europe, has so long made a specialty of the depiction of evil in man that it can scarcely be said to tell us that he is good; but neither does it tell us that social institutions are admirable, endowed with "prescriptive" rights which the individual does wrong to challenge. Institutions are made and unmade by particular men under particular circumstances, and to confer a sacrosanct character upon their own handiwork is to turn them into idolaters and slaves.

A close observer of the creative process once finely remarked that the honor of a literature lies in its capacity to develop "a great quarrel within the national consciousness." One has only to think of the outstanding Victorian figures who decried the state of England, or of the French and particularly the Russian novel in the past century, to realize the truth of that statement. In a somewhat different way the modern American novel is likewise implicated in a "great quarrel within the national consciousness." To my mind, the principal theme of this novel, from Dreiser and Anderson to Fitzgerald and Faulkner, has been the discrepancy between the high promise of the American dream and what history has made of it. The inner feeling of this novel is one of nostalgic love of nativity combined with baffled (and sometimes angry) disenchantment. That is what comes so tellingly through to us, with plangent lyrical force, in the wonderful closing paragraphs of *The Great Gatsby,* when the narrator, Nick Carraway, wanders down to the beach at night:

Most of the big shore places were closed now and there were hardly any lights except the shadowy, moving glow of a ferryboat across the Sound. And as the moon rose higher the inessential houses began to melt away until gradually I became aware of the old island that flowered once for Dutch sailors' eyes—a fresh, green breast of the new world. Its vanished trees, the trees that had made way for Gatsby's house, had once pandered in whispers to the last and greatest of all human dreams; for a transitory enchanted moment man must have held his breath in the presence of this continent, compelled into an aesthetic contemplation he neither understood nor desired, face to face for the last time in history with something commensurate to his capacity for wonder.

And as I sat there brooding on the old, unknown world, I thought of Gatsby's wonder when he first picked out the green light at the end of Daisy's dock. He had come a long way to this blue dawn, and his dream must have seemed so close that he could hardly fail to grasp it. He did not know that it was already behind him, somewhere back in that vast obscurity beyond the city, where the dark fields of the republic rolled on under night.

Gatsby believed in the green light, the orgastic future that year by year recedes before us. It eluded us then, but that's no matter—tomorrow we will run faster, stretch our arms further. . . . And one fine morning——

So we beat on, boats against the current, borne back ceaselessly into the past.

Art has always fed on the contradiction between the reality of the world and the image of glory and orgastic happiness and harmony and goodness and fulfilment which the self cherishes as it aspires to live even while daily dying. If reality ever measures up to that image, art would witness its own dissolution in a beautiful world. But the world is what it is, in the New as in the Old. And in transposing this reflection into a national key, one feels compelled to say that America, whatever it looked like in its fresh flowering to Dutch sailors' eyes, is far more what its best artists have made it out to be than it is the achieved Utopia invoked in our mass-media and by officialdom in politics as in culture. In their relation to their native land those artists have never lost their capacity for wonder, and they are in no danger of losing it so long as they do not degrade wonder into submission, acquiescence or an allegiance simple, uniform, and thoughtless.

Philip Rahv

1

Alexis de Tocqueville: LITERARY CHARACTERISTICS
OF DEMOCRATIC TIMES [1835]

When a traveler goes into a bookseller's shop in the United States and examines the American books on the shelves, the number of works appears very great, while that of known authors seems, on the contrary, extremely small. He will first find a multitude of elementary treatises, destined to teach the rudiments of human knowledge. Most of these books were written in Europe; the Americans reprint them, adapting them to their own use. Next comes an enormous quantity of religious works, Bibles, sermons, edifying anecdotes, controversial divinity, and reports of charitable societies; lastly appears the long catalogue of political pamphlets. In America parties do not write books to combat each other's opinions, but pamphlets, which are circulated for a day with incredible rapidity and then expire.

In the midst of all these obscure productions of the human brain appear the more remarkable works of a small number of authors whose names are, or ought to be, known to Europeans.

Although America is perhaps in our days the civilized country in which literature is least attended to, still a large number of persons there take an interest in the productions of the mind and make them, if not the study of their lives, at least the charm of their leisure hours. But England supplies these readers with most of the books that they require. Almost all important English books are republished in the United States. The literary genius of Great Britain still darts its rays into the recesses of the forests of the New World. There is hardly a pioneer's hut that does not contain a few odd volumes of Shakespeare. I remember that I read the feudal drama of *Henry V* for the first time in a log cabin.

Not only do the Americans constantly draw upon the treasures of English literature, but it may be said with truth that they find the literature of England growing on their own soil. The larger part of that small number of men in the United States who are engaged in the composition of literary works are English in substance and still more so in form. Thus they transport into the midst of democracy the ideas and literary fashions that are current among the aristocratic nation they have taken for their model. They paint with colors borrowed from foreign manners; and as they hardly ever represent the country they were born in as it really is, they are seldom popular there.

The citizens of the United States are themselves so convinced that it is not for them that books are published, that before they can make up their minds upon the merit of one of their authors, they generally wait till his fame has been ratified in England; just as in pictures the author of an original is held entitled to judge of the merit of a copy.

The inhabitants of the United States have, then, at present, properly speaking, no literature. The only authors whom I acknowledge as American are the journalists. They indeed are not great writers, but they speak the language of their country and make themselves heard. Other authors are aliens; they are to the Americans what the imitators of the Greeks and Romans were to us at the revival of learning, an object of curiosity, not of general sympathy. They amuse the mind, but they do not act upon the manners of the people.

I have already said that this state of things is far from originating in democracy alone, and that the causes of it must be sought for in several peculiar circumstances independent of the democratic principle. If the Americans, retaining the same laws and social condition, had had a different origin and had been transported into another country, I do not question that they would have a literature. Even as they are, I am convinced that they will ultimately have one; but its character will be different from that which marks the American literary productions of our time, and that character will be peculiarly its own. Nor is it impossible to trace this character beforehand.

In an aristocratic people, among whom letters are cultivated, I suppose that intellectual occupations, as well as the affairs of government, are concentrated in a ruling class. The literary as well as the political career is almost entirely confined to this class, or to those nearest to it in rank. These premises suffice for a key to all the rest.

When a small number of the same men are engaged at the same time upon the same objects, they easily concert with one another and agree upon certain leading rules that are to govern them each and all. If the object that attracts the attention of these men is literature, the productions of the mind will soon be subjected by them to precise canons, from which it will no longer be allowable to depart. If these men occupy a hereditary position in the country, they will be naturally inclined, not only to adopt a certain number of fixed rules for themselves, but to follow those which their forefathers laid down for their own guidance; their code will be at once strict and traditional. As they are not necessarily engrossed by the cares of daily life, as they have never been so, any more than their fathers were before them, they have learned to take an interest, for several generations back, in the labors of mind. They have learned to understand literature as an art, to love it in the end for its own sake, and to feel a scholar-like satisfaction in seeing men conform to its rules. Nor is this all: the men of whom I speak began and will end their lives in easy or affluent circumstances; hence they have naturally conceived a taste for carefully chosen gratifications and a love of refined and delicate pleasures. Moreover, a kind of softness of mind and heart, which they frequently contract in the midst of this long and peaceful enjoyment of so much welfare, leads them to put aside, even from their pleasures, whatever might be too startling or too acute. They had rather be amused than intensely excited; they wish to be interested, but not to be carried away.

Now let us fancy a great number of literary performances executed by the men, or for the men, whom I have just described, and we shall readily conceive a style of literature in which everything will be regular and prearranged. The slightest work will be carefully wrought in its least details; art and labor will be conspicuous in everything; each kind of writing will have rules of its own, from which it will not be allowed to swerve and which distinguish it from all others. Style will be thought of almost as much importance as thought, and the form will be no less considered than the matter; the diction will be polished, measured, and uniform. The tone of the mind will be always dignified, seldom very animated, and writers will care more to perfect what they produce than to multiply their productions. It will sometimes happen that the members of the literary class, always living among themselves and writing for themselves alone, will entirely lose sight of the rest of the world, which will infect them with a false and labored style; they will lay down minute literary rules for their exclusive use, which will insensibly lead them to deviate from common sense and finally to transgress the bounds of nature. By dint of striving after a mode of parlance different from the popular, they will arrive at a sort of aristocratic jargon which is hardly less remote from pure language than is the coarse dialect of the people. Such are the natural perils of literature among aristocracies. Every aristocracy that keeps itself entirely aloof from the people becomes impotent, a fact which is as true in literature as it is in politics.●

Let us now turn the picture and consider the other side of it: let us transport ourselves into the midst of a democracy not unprepared by ancient traditions and present culture to partake in the pleasures of mind. Ranks are there intermingled and identified; knowledge and power are both infinitely subdivided and, if I may use the expression, scattered on every side. Here, then, is a motley multitude whose intellectual wants are to be supplied. These new votaries of the pleasures of mind have not all received the same education; they do not resemble their fathers; nay, they perpetually differ from themselves, for they live in a state of incessant change of place, feelings, and fortunes. The mind of each is therefore unattached to that of his fellows by tradition or common habits; and they have never had the power, the inclination, or the time to act together. It is from the bosom of this heterogeneous and agitated mass, however, that authors spring; and from the same source their profits and their fame are distributed.

I can without difficulty understand that under these circumstances I must expect to meet in the literature of such a people with but few of those strict conventional rules which are admitted by readers and writers in aristocratic times. If it should happen that the men of some one period were agreed upon any such rules, that would prove nothing for the following period; for among democratic nations each new generation is a new people. Among such nations, then, literature will not easily be subjected to strict rules, and it is impossible that any such rules should ever be permanent.

In democracies it is by no means the case that all who cultivate literature have received a literary education; and most of those who have some tinge of belles-lettres are engaged either in politics or in a profession that only allows them to taste occasionally and by stealth the pleasures of mind. These pleasures, therefore, do not con-

---

● *All this is especially true of the aristocratic countries that have been long and peacefully subject to a monarchical government. When liberty prevails in an aristocracy, the higher ranks are constantly obliged to make use of the lower classes; and when they use, they approach them. This frequently introduces something of a democratic spirit into an aristocratic community. There springs up, moreover, in a governing privileged body an energy and habitually bold policy, a taste for stir and excitement, which must infallibly affect all literary performances.*

stitute the principal charm of their lives, but they are considered as a transient and necessary recreation amid the serious labors of life. Such men can never acquire a sufficiently intimate knowledge of the art of literature to appreciate its more delicate beauties; and the minor shades of expression must escape them. As the time they can devote to letters is very short, they seek to make the best use of the whole of it. They prefer books which may be easily procured, quickly read, and which require no learned researches to be understood. They ask for beauties self-proffered and easily enjoyed; above all, they must have what is unexpected and new. Accustomed to the struggle, the crosses, and the monotony of practical life, they require strong and rapid emotions, startling passages, truths or errors brilliant enough to rouse them up and to plunge them at once, as if by violence, into the midst of the subject.

Why should I say more, or who does not understand what is about to follow before I have expressed it? Taken as a whole, literature in democratic ages can never present, as it does in the periods of aristocracy, an aspect of order, regularity, science, and art; its form, on the contrary, will ordinarily be slighted, sometimes despised. Style will frequently be fantastic, incorrect, overburdened, and loose, almost always vehement and bold. Authors will aim at rapidity of execution more than at perfection of detail. Small productions will be more common than bulky books; there will be more wit than erudition, more imagination than profundity; and literary performances will bear marks of an untutored and rude vigor of thought, frequently of great variety and singular fecundity. The object of authors will be to astonish rather than to please, and to stir the passions more than to charm the taste.

Here and there, indeed, writers will doubtless occur who will choose a different track and who, if they are gifted with superior abilities, will succeed in finding readers in spite of their defects or their better qualities; but these exceptions will be rare, and even the authors who so depart from the received practice in the main subject of their works will always relapse into it in some lesser details.

I have just depicted two extreme conditions, but nations never leap from the first to the second; they reach it only by stages and through infinite gradation. In the progress that an educated people makes from the one to the other, there is almost always a moment when the literary genius of democratic nations coinciding with that of aristocratic nations, both seek to establish their sway jointly over the human mind. Such epochs are transient, but very brilliant; they are fertile without exuberance, and animated without confusion. The French literature of the eighteenth century may serve as an example.

I should say more than I mean if I were to assert that the literature of a nation is always subordinate to its social state and its political constitution. I am aware that, independently of these causes, there are several others which confer certain characteristics on literary productions; but these appear to me to be the chief. The relations that exist between the social and political condition of a people and the genius of its authors are always numerous; whoever knows the one is never completely ignorant of the other.

2

James Fenimore Cooper:
AMERICAN LITERATURE [1828]

. . . The Americans have been placed, as respects moral and intellectual advancement, different from all other infant nations. They have never been without the wants of civilization, nor have they ever been entirely without the means of a supply. Thus pictures, and books, and statuary, and everything else which appertains to elegant life, have always been known to them in an abundance, and of a quality exactly proportioned to their cost. Books, being the cheapest, and the nation having great leisure and prodigious zest for information, are not only the most common, as you will readily suppose, but they are probably more common than among any other people. I scarcely remember ever to have entered an American dwelling, however humble, without finding fewer or more books. As they form the most essential division of the subject, not only on account of their greater frequency, but on account of their far greater importance, I shall give them the first notice in this letter.

Unlike the progress of the two professions in the countries of our hemisphere, in America the printer came into existence before the author. Reprints of English works gave the first employment to the press. Then came almanacs, psalm-books, religious tracts, sermons, journals, political essays, and even rude attempts at poetry. All these preceded the revolution. The first journal was established in Boston at the commencement of the last century. There are several original polemical works of great originality and power that belong to the same period. I do not know that more learning and talents existed at that early day in the States of New England than in Virginia, Maryland, and the Carolinas, but there was certainly a stronger desire to exhibit them. . . .

As respects authorship there is not much to be said. Compared to the books that are printed and read, those of native origin are few indeed. The principal reason of this poverty of original writers is owing to the circumstance that men are not yet driven to their wits for bread. The United States is the first nation that possessed institutions, and, of course, distinctive opinions of its own, that was ever dependent on a foreign people for its literature. Speaking the same language as the English, and long in the habit of importing their books from the mother country, the revolution effected no immediate change in the nature of their studies, or mental amusements. The works were reprinted, it is true, for the purposes of economy but they still continued English. Had the latter nation used this powerful engine with tolerable address, I think they would have secured such an ally in this country as would have engendered their own decline not only more secure, but as illustrious as had been their rise. There are many theories entertained as to the effect produced in this country by the falsehoods and jealous calumnies which have been undeniably uttered in the mother country, by means of the press, concerning her republican descendant. It is my own opinion that, like all other ridiculous absurdities, they have defeated themselves, and that they are now more laughed at and derided, even here, than resented. By all that I can learn, twenty years ago, the Americans were, perhaps, far too much disposed to receive the opinions and to adopt the prejudices of their relatives; whereas, I think it is very apparent that they are now beginning to receive them with singular distrust. It is not worth our while to enter further into this subject, except as it has had, and is likely to have, an influence on the national literature.

It is quite obvious, that, so far as taste and forms alone are concerned, the literature of England and that of America must be fashioned after the same models. The authors, previously to the revolution, are common property, and it is quite idle to say that the American has not just as good a right to claim Milton, and Shakespeare, and all the old masters of the language, for his countrymen, as an Englishman. The Americans having continued to cultivate, and to cultivate extensively, an acquaintance with the writers of the mother country, since the separation, it is evident they must have kept pace with the trifling changes of the day. The only peculiarity that can, or ought to be expected in their literature, is that which is connected with the promulgation of their distinctive political opinions. They have not been remiss in this duty, as any one may see, who chooses to examine their books. . . .

The literature of the United States has, indeed, two powerful obstacles to conquer before (to use a mercantile expression) it can ever enter the markets of its own country on terms of perfect equality with that of England. Solitary and individual works of genius may, indeed, be occasionally brought to light, under the impulses of the high feeling which has conceived them; but, I fear, a good, wholesome, profitable and continued pecuniary support is the applause that talent most craves. The fact that an American publisher can get an English work without money must for a few years longer (unless legislative protection shall be extended to their own authors) have a tendency to repress a national literature. No man will pay a writer for an epic, a tragedy, a sonnet, a history, or a romance, when he can get a work of equal merit for nothing. I have conversed with those who are conversant on the subject, and, I confess, I have been astonished at the information they imparted.

A capital American publisher has assured me that there are not a dozen writers in this country whose works he should feel confidence in publishing at all, while he reprints hundreds of English books without the least hesitation. This preference is by no means so much owing to any difference in merit, as to the fact that, when the price of the original author is to be added to the uniform hazard which accompanies all literary speculations, the risk becomes too great. The general taste of the reading world in this country is better than that of England. The fact is both proved and explained by the circumstances that thousands of works that are printed and read in the mother country are not printed and read here. The publisher on this side of the Atlantic has the advantage of seeing the reviews of every book he wishes to reprint, and, what is of far more importance, he knows, with the exception of books that he is sure of selling, by means of a name, the decision of the English critics before he makes his choice. Nine times in ten, popularity, which is all he looks for, is a sufficient test of general merit. Thus, while you find every English work of character, or notoriety, on the shelves of an American bookstore, you may ask in vain for most of the trash that is so greedily devoured in the circulating libraries of the mother country, and which would be just as eagerly devoured here, had not a better taste been created by a compelled abstinence. That taste must now be overcome before such works could be sold at all.

When I say that books are not rejected here, from any want of talent in the writers, perhaps I ought to explain. I wish to express something a little different. Talent is sure of too many avenues to wealth and honor in America, to seek, unnecessarily, an unknown and hazardous path. It is better paid in the ordinary pursuits of life than it would be likely to be paid by an adventure in which an extraordinary and skillful, because practiced, foreign competition is certain. Perhaps high talent does not often make the trial with the American bookseller; but it is precisely for the reason I have named.

The second obstacle against which American literature has to contend is in the poverty of materials. There is scarcely an ore which contributes to the wealth of the author that is found here in veins as rich as in Europe. There are no annals for the historian; no follies (beyond the most vulgar and commonplace) for the satirist; no manners for the dramatist; no obscure fictions for the writer of romance; no gross and hardy offences against decorum for the moralist; nor any of the rich artificial auxiliaries of poetry. The weakest hand can extract a spark from the flint, but it would baffle the strength of a giant to attempt kindling a flame with a pudding-stone. I very well know there are theorists who assume that the society and institutions of this country are, or ought to be, particularly favorable to novelties and variety. But the experience of one month, in these States, is sufficient to show any observant man the falsity of their position. The effect of a promiscuous assemblage any where is to create a standard of deportment; and great liberty permits every one to aim at its attainment. I have never seen a nation so much alike in my life, as the people of the United States, and what is more, they are not only like each other, but they are remarkably like that which common sense tells them they ought to resemble. No doubt, traits of character that are a little peculiar, without, however, being either very poetical, or very rich, are to be found in remote districts; but they are rare, and not always happy exceptions. In short, it is not possible to conceive a state of society in which more of the attributes of plain good sense, or fewer of the artificial absurdities of life, are to be found, than here. There is no costume for the peasant (there is scarcely a peasant at all), no wig for the judge, no baton for the general, no diadem for the chief magistrate. The darkest ages of their history are illuminated by the light of truth; the utmost efforts of their chivalry are limited by the laws of God; and even the deeds of their sages and heroes are to be sung in a language that would differ but little from a version of the ten commandments. However useful and respectable all this may be in actual life, it indicates but one direction to the man of genius.

It is very true there are a few young poets now living in this country, who have known how to extract sweets from even these wholesome but scentless native plants. They have, however, been compelled to seek their inspiration in the universal laws of nature, and they have succeeded precisely in proportion as they have been most general in their application. Among these gifted young men, there is one (Halleck) who is remarkable for an exquisite vein of ironical wit, mingled with a fine, poetical, and, frequently, a lofty expression. This gentleman commenced his career as a satirist in one of the journals of New York. Heaven knows, his materials were none of the richest and yet the melody of his verse, the quaintness and force of his comparisons, and the exceeding humor of his strong points, brought him instantly into notice. He then attempted a general satire, by giving the history of the early days of a *belle*. He was again successful, though everybody, at least everybody of any talent, felt that he wrote in leading-strings. But he happened, shortly after the appearance of the little volume just named (*Fanny*), to visit England. Here his spirit was properly excited, and probably on a rainy day, he was induced to try his hand at a *jeu d'esprit* in the mother country. The result was one of the finest semi-heroic ironical descriptions to be found in the English language. This simple fact, in itself, proves the truth of a great deal of what I have just been writing, since it shows the effect a superiority of material can produce on the efforts of a man of true genius.

Notwithstanding the difficulties of the subject, talent has even done more than in the instance of Mr. Halleck. I could mention several other young poets of this country of rare merit. By mentioning Bryant, Percival, and Sprague, I shall direct your attention to the names of those whose works would be most likely to give you pleassure. . . .

The next, though certainly an inferior branch of imaginative writing, is fictitious composition. From the facts just named, you cannot expect that the novelists, or romance writers of the United States, should be very successful. The same reason will be likely, for a long time to come, to repress the ardor of dramatic genius. Still, tales and plays are no novelties in the literature of this country. Of the former, there are many as old as soon after the revolution, and a vast number have been published within the last five years. One of their authors of romance, who curbed his talents by as few allusions as possible to actual society, is distinguished for power and comprehensiveness of thought. I remember to have read one of his books (*Wieland*) when a boy, and I take it to be a never failing evidence of genius that, amid a thousand similar pictures which have succeeded, the images it has left still stand distinct and prominent in my recollection. This author (Mr. Brockden Brown) enjoys a high reputation among his countrymen, whose opinions are sufficiently impartial, since he flattered no particular prejudice of the nation in any of his works.

The reputation of Irving is well known to you. He is an author distinguished for a quality (humor) that has been denied his countrymen; and his merit is the more rare, that it has been shown in a state of society so cold and so restrained. Besides these writers, there are many others of a similar character, who enjoy a greater or less degree of favor in their own country. The works of two or three have been translated (in French) in Europe, and a great many are reprinted in England. Though every writer of fiction in America has to contend against the difficulties I have named, there is a certain interest in the novelty of the subject, which is not without its charm. I think, however, it will be found that they have all been successful, or the reverse, just as they have drawn warily, or freely, on the distinctive habits of their own country. I now speak of their success purely as writers of romance. It certainly would be impossible for an American to give a description of the manners of his own country, in a book that he might choose to call a romance, which should be read, because the world is curious on the subject, but which would certainly never be read for that nearly indefinable poetical interest which attaches itself to a description of manners less bad and uniform. All the attempts to blend history with romance in America have been comparatively failures (and perhaps fortunately) since the subjects are too familiar to be treated with the freedom that the imagination absolutely requires. Some of the descriptions of the progress of society on the borders have had a rather better success, since there is a positive, though not very poetical, novelty in the subject; but, on the whole, the books which have been best received are those in which the authors have trusted most to their own conceptions of character and to qualities that are common to the rest of the world and to human nature. This fact, if its truth be admitted, will serve to prove that the American writer must seek his renown in the exhibition of qualities that are general, while he is confessedly compelled to limit his observations to a state of society that has a wonderful tendency not only to repress passion but to equalize humours. . . .

3

D. H. *Lawrence:* FENIMORE COOPER'S LEATHERSTOCKING NOVELS

In his Leatherstocking books, Fenimore is off on another track. He is no longer concerned with social white Americans that buzz with pins through them, buzz loudly against every mortal thing except the pin itself. The pin of the Great Ideal.

One gets irritated with Cooper because he never for once snarls at the Great Ideal Pin which transfixes him. No, indeed. Rather he tries to push it through the very heart of the Continent.

But I have loved the Leatherstocking books so dearly. Wish-fulfilment!

Anyhow one is not supposed to take LOVE seriously, in these books. Eve Effingham [in *Homeward Bound*] impaled on the social pin, conscious all the time of her own ego and of nothing else, suddenly fluttering in throes of love: no, it makes me sick. Love is never LOVE until it has a pin pushed through it and becomes an IDEAL. The ego turning on a pin is wildly IN LOVE, always. Because that's the thing to be.

Cooper was a GENTLEMAN, in the worst sense of the word. In the Nineteenth Century sense of the word. A correct, clock-work man.

Not altogether, of course.

The great National Grouch was grinding inside him. Probably he called it COSMIC URGE. Americans usually do: in capital letters. Best stick to National Grouch. The great American grouch.

Cooper had it, gentleman as he was. That is why he flitted round Europe so uneasily. Of course in Europe he could be, and was, a gentleman to his heart's content.

"In short," he says in one of his letters, "we were at table two counts, one monsignore, an English Lord, an Ambassador, and my humble self."

Were we really!

How nice it must have been to know that one self, at least, was humble.

And he felt the democratic American tomahawk wheeling over his uncomfortable scalp all the time.

The great American grouch.

Two monsters loomed on Cooper's horizon.

MRS. COOPER	MY WORK
MY WORK	MY WIFE
MY WIFE	MY WORK

THE DEAR CHILDREN
MY WORK! ! !

There you have the essential keyboard of Cooper's soul.

If there is one thing that annoys me more than a business man and his BUSINESS, it is an artist, a writer, painter, musician, and MY WORK. When an artist says MY WORK, the flesh goes tired on my bones. When he says MY WIFE, I want to hit him.

Cooper grizzled about his work. Oh, heaven, he cared so much whether it was good or bad, and what the French thought, and what Mr. Snippy Knowall said, and how Mrs. Cooper took it. The pin, the pin!

But he was truly an artist: then an American: then a gentleman. And the grouch grouched inside him, through all.

They seemed to have been specially fertile in imagining themselves "under the wigwam," do these Americans, just when their knees were comfortably under the mahogany, in Paris, along with the knees of

4 Counts
2 Cardinals
1 Milord
5 Cocottes
1 Humble self.

You bet, though, that when the cocottes were being raffled off, Fenimore went home to his WIFE.

Wish Fulfilment		Actuality
THE WIGWAM	*vs.*	MY HOTEL
CHINGACHGOOK	*vs.*	MY WIFE
NATTY BUMPPO	*vs.*	MY HUMBLE SELF

Fenimore lying in his *Louis Quartorze* hôtel in Paris, passionately musing about Natty Bumppo and the pathless forest, and mixing his imagination with the Cupids and Butterflies on the painted ceiling, while Mrs. Cooper was struggling with her latest gown in the next room, and *déjeuner* was with the Countess at eleven. . . .

Men live by lies.

In actuality, Fenimore loved the genteel continent of Europe, and waited gasping for the newspapers to praise his WORK.

In another actuality, he loved the tomahawking continent of America, and imagined himself Natty Bumppo.

His actual desire was to be: *Monsieur Fenimore Cooper, le grand écrivain américain.*

His innermost wish was to be: Natty Bumppo.

Now Natty and Fenimore arm-in-arm are an odd couple.

You can see Fenimore: blue coat, silver buttons, silver-and-diamond buckle shoes, ruffles.

You see Natty Bumppo: a grizzled, uncouth old renegade, with gaps in his old teeth and a drop on the end of his nose.

But Natty was Fenimore's great Wish: his wish-fulfilment.

"It was a matter of course," says Mrs. Cooper, "that he should dwell on the better traits of the picture rather than on the coarser and more revolting, though more common points. Like West, he could see Apollo in the young Mohawk."

The coarser and more revolting, though more common points.

You see now why he depended so absolutely on MY WIFE. She had to look things in the face for him. The coarser and more revolting, and certainly more common points, she had to see.

He himself did so love seeing pretty-pretty, with the thrill of a red scalp now and then.

Fenimore, in his imagination, wanted to be Natty Bumppo, who, I am sure, belched after he had eaten his dinner. At the same time Mr. Cooper was nothing if not a gentleman. So he decided to stay in France and have it all his own way.

In France, Natty would not belch after eating, and Chingachgook could be all the Apollo he liked.

As if ever any Indian was like Apollo. The Indians, with their curious female quality, their archaic figures, with high shoulders and deep, archaic waists, like a sort of woman! And their natural devilishness, their natural insidiousness.

But men see what they want to see: especially if they look from a long distance, across the ocean, for example.

Yet the Leatherstocking books are lovely. Lovely half-lies.

They form a sort of American Odyssey, with Natty Bumppo for Odysseus.

Only, in the original Odyssey, there is plenty of devil, Circes and swine and all. And Ithacus is devil enough to outwit the devils. But Natty is a saint with a gun, and the Indians are gentlemen through and through, though they may take an occasional scalp.

There are five Leatherstocking novels: a *decrescendo* of reality, and a crescendo of beauty.

1. *Pioneers:* A raw frontier-village on Lake Champlain, at the end of the eighteenth century. Must be a picture of Cooper's home, as he knew it when a boy. A very lovely book. Natty Bumppo an old man, an old hunter, half-civilized.

2. *The Last of the Mohicans:* A historical fight between the British and the French, with Indians on both sides, at a Fort by Lake Champlain. Romantic flight of the British general's two daughters, conducted by the scout, Natty, who is in the prime of life; romantic death of the last of the Delawares.

3. *The Prairie:* A wagon of some huge, sinister Kentuckians trekking west into the unbroken prairie. Prairie Indians, and Natty, an old, old man; he dies, seated on a chair on the Rocky Mountains, looking east.

4. *The Pathfinder:* The Great Lakes. Natty, a man of about thirty-five, makes an abortive proposal to a bouncing damsel, daughter of the Sergeant of the Fort.

5. *Deerslayer:* Natty and Hurry Harry, both quite young, are hunting in the virgin wild. They meet two white women. Lake Champlain again.

These are the five Leatherstocking novels: Natty Bumppo being Leatherstocking, Pathfinder, Deerslayer, according to his ages.

Now let me put aside my impatience at the unreality of this vision, and accept it as a wish-fulfilment vision, a kind of yearning myth. Because it seems to me that the things in Cooper that make one so savage, when one compares them with actuality, are perhaps, when one considers them as presentations of a deep subjective desire, real in their way, and almost prophetic.

The passionate love for America, for the soil of America, for example. As I say, it is perhaps easier to love America passionately, when you look at it through the wrong end of the telescope, across all the Atlantic water, as Cooper did so often, than when you are right there. When you are actually *in* America, America hurts, because it has a powerful disintegrative influence upon the white psyche. It is full of grinning, unappeased aboriginal demons, too, ghosts, and it persecutes the white men like some Eumenides, until the white men give up their absolute whiteness. America is tense with latent violence and resistance. The very common sense of white Americans has a tinge of helplessness in it, and deep fear of what might be if they were not common-sensical.

Yet one day the demons of America must be placated, the ghosts must be appeased, the Spirit of Place atoned for. Then the true passionate love for American Soil will appear. As yet, there is too much menace in the landscape.

But probably, one day America will be as beautiful in actuality as it is in Cooper. Not yet, however. When the factories have fallen down again.

And again, this perpetual blood-brother theme of the Leatherstocking novels, Natty and Chingachgook, the Great Seprent. At present it is a sheer myth. The Red Man and the White Man are not blood-brothers: even when they are most friendly. When they are most friendly, it is as a rule the one betraying his race-spirit to the other. In the white man—rather highbrow—who "loves" the Indian, one feels the white man betraying his own race. There is something unproud, underhand in it. Renegade. The same with the Americanized Indian who believes absolutely in the white mode. It is a betrayal. Renegade again.

In the actual flesh, it seems to me the white man and the red man cause a feeling of oppression, the one to the other, no matter what the good will. The red life flows in a different direction from the white life. You can't make two streams that flow in opposite directions meet and mingle soothingly.

Certainly, if Cooper had had to spend his whole life in the backwoods, side by side with a Noble Red Brother, he would have screamed with the oppression of suffocation. He had to have Mrs. Cooper, a straight strong, pillar of society, to hang on to. And he had to have the culture of France to turn back to, or he would just have been stifled. The Noble Red Brother would have smothered him and driven him mad.

So that the Natty and Chingachgook myth must remain a myth. It is a wish-fulfilment, an evasion of actuality. As we have said before, the folds of the Great Serpent would have been heavy, very heavy, too heavy, on any white man. Unless the white man were a true renegade, hating himself and his own race-spirit, as sometimes happens.

It seems there can be no fusion in the flesh. But the spirit can change. The white man's spirit can never become as the red man's spirit. It doesn't want to. But it can cease to be the opposite and the negative of the red man's spirit. It can open out a new great area of consciousness, in which there is room for the red spirit too.

To open out a new wide area of consciousness means to slough the old consciousness. The old consciousness has become a tight-fitting prison to us, in which we are going rotten.

You can't have a new, easy skin before you have sloughed the old, tight skin.

You can't.

And you just can't, so you may as well leave off pretending.

Now the essential history of the people of the United States seems to me just this: At the Renaissance the old consciousness was becoming a little tight. Europe sloughed her last skin, and started a new, final phase.

But some Europeans recoiled from the last final phase. They wouldn't enter the *cul de sac* of post-Renaissance, "liberal" Europe. They came to America.

They came to America for two reasons:

1. To slough the old European consciousness completely.

2. To grow a new skin underneath, a new form. This second is a hidden process.

The two processes go on, of course, simultaneously. The slow forming of the new skin underneath is the slow sloughing of the old skin. And sometimes this immortal serpent feels very happy, feeling a new golden glow of a strangely patterned skin envelop him: and sometimes he feels very sick, as if his very entrails were being torn out of him, as he wrenches once more at his old skin, to get out of it.

Out! Out! he cries, in all kinds of euphemisms.

He's got to have his new skin on him before ever he can get out.

And he's got to get out before his new skin can ever be his own skin.

So there he is, a torn, divided monster.

The true American, who writhes and writhes like a snake that is long in sloughing.

Sometimes snakes can't slough. They can't burst their old skin. Then they go sick and die inside the old skin, and nobody ever sees the new pattern.

It needs a real desperate recklessness to burst your old skin at last. You simply don't care what happens to you, if you rip yourself in two, so long as you do get out.

It also needs a real belief in the new skin. Otherwise you are likely never to make the effort. Then you gradually sicken and go rotten and die in the old skin.

Now Fenimore stayed very safe inside the old skin: a gentleman, almost a European, as proper as proper can be. And, safe inside the old skin, he *imagined* the gorgeous American pattern of a new skin.

He hated democracy. So he evaded it, and had a nice dream of something beyond democracy. But he belonged to democracy all the while.

Evasion!—Yet even that doesn't make the dream worthless.

Democracy in America was never the same as Liberty in Europe. In Europe Liberty was a great life-throb. But in America Democracy was always something anti-life. The greatest democrats, like Abraham Lincoln, had always a sacrificial, self-murdering note in their voices. American Democracy was a form of self-murder, always. Or of murdering somebody else.

Necessarily. It was a *pis aller*. It was the *pis aller* to European Liberty. It was a cruel form of sloughing. Men murdered themselves into this democracy. Democracy is the utter hardening of the old skin, the old form, the old psyche. It hardens till it is tight and fixed and inorganic. Then it *must* burst, like a chrysalis shell. And out must come the soft grub, or the soft damp butterfly of the American-at-last.

America has gone the *pis aller* of her democracy. Now she must slough even that, chiefly that, indeed.

What did Cooper dream beyond democracy? Why, in his immortal friendship of Chingachgook and Natty Bumppo he dreamed the nucleus of a new society. That is, he dreamed a new human relationship. A stark, stripped human relationship of two men, deeper than the deeps of sex. Deeper than property, deeper than fatherhood, deeper than marriage, deeper than love. So deep that it is loveless. The stark, loveless, wordless unison of two men who have come to the bottom of themselves. This is the new nucleus of a new society, the clue to a new world-epoch. It asks for a great and cruel sloughing first of all. Then it finds a great release into a new world, a new moral, a new landscape.

Natty and the Great Seprent are neither equals nor unequals. Each obeys the other when the moment arrives. And each is stark and dumb in the other's presence, starkly himself, without illusion created. Each is just the crude pillar of a man, the crude living column of his own manhood. And each knows the godhead of this crude column of manhood. A new relationship.

The Leatherstocking novels create the myth of this new relation. And they go backwards, from old age to golden youth. That is the true myth of America. She starts old, old, wrinkled and writhing in an old skin. And there is a gradual sloughing of the old skin, towards a new youth. It is the myth of America.

You start with actuality. *Pioneers* is no doubt Cooperstown, when

Cooperstown was in the stage of inception: a village of one wild street of log cabins under the forest hills by Lake Champlain: a village of crude, wild frontiersmen, reacting against civilization.

Towards this frontier-village, in the winter time, a Negro slave drives a sledge through the mountains, over deep snow. In the sledge sits a fair damsel, Miss Temple, with her handsome pioneer father, Judge Temple. They hear a shot in the trees. It is the old hunter and backwoodsman, Natty Bumppo, long and lean and uncouth, with a long rifle and gaps in his teeth.

Judge Temple is "squire" of the village, and he has a ridiculous, commodious "hall" for his residence. It is still the old English form. Miss Temple is a pattern young lady, like Eve Effingham: in fact she gets a young and very genteel but impoverished Effingham for a husband. The old world holding its own on the edge of the wild. A bit tiresomely too, with rather more prunes and prisms than one can digest. Too romantic.

Against the "hall" and the gentry, the real frontiers-folk, the rebels. The two groups meet at the village inn, and at the frozen church, and at the Christmas sports, and on the ice of the lake, and at the great pigeon shoot. It is a beautiful, resplendent picture of life. Fenimore puts in only the glamour.

Perhaps my taste is childish, but these scenes in *Pioneers* seem to me marvelously beautiful. The raw village street, with woodfires blinking through the unglazed window-chinks, on a winter's night. The inn, with the rough woodsmen and the drunken Indian John; the church, with the snowy congregation crowding to the fire. Then the lavish abundance of Christmas cheer, and turkey shooting in the snow. Spring coming, forests all green, maple sugar taken from the trees; and clouds of pigeons flying from the south, myriads of pigeons, shot in heaps; and night fishing on the teeming, virgin lake; and deer hunting.

Pictures! Some of the loveliest, most glamorous pictures in all literature.

Alas, without the cruel iron of reality. It is all real enough. Except that one realizes that Fenimore was writing from a safe distance, where he would idealize and have his wish-fulfilment.

Because, when one comes to America, one finds that there is always a certain slightly devilish resistance in the American landscape, and a certain slightly bitter resistance in the white man's heart. Hawthorne gives this. But Cooper glosses it over.

The American landscape has never been at one with the white man. Never. And white men have probably never felt so bitter anywhere, as here in America, where the very landscape, in its very beauty, seems a bit devilish and grinning, opposed to us.

Cooper, however, glosses over this resistance, which in actuality can never quite be glossed over. He *wants* the landscape to be at one with him. So he goes away to Europe and sees it as such. It is a sort of vision.

And, nevertheless, the oneing will surely take place—some day.

The myth is the story of Natty. The old, lean hunter and back-woodsman lives with his friend, the gray-haired Indian John, an old Delaware chief, in a hut within reach of the village. The Delaware is christianized and bears the Christian name of John. He is tribeless and lost. He humiliates his gray hairs in drunkenness, and dies, thankful to be dead, in a forest fire, passing back to the fire whence he derived.

And this is Chingachgook, the splendid Great Serpent of the later novels.

No doubt Cooper, as a boy, knew both Natty and the Indian John. No doubt they fired his imagination even then. When he is a man, crystallized in society and sheltering behind the safe pillar of Mrs. Cooper, these two old fellows become a myth to his soul. He traces himself to a new youth in them.

As for the story: Judge Temple has just been instrumental in passing the wise game laws. But Natty has lived by his gun all his life in the wild woods, and simply childishly cannot understand how he can be poaching on the Judge's land among the pine trees. He shoots a deer in the closed season. The Judge is all sympathy, but the law *must* be enforced. Bewildered Natty, an old man of seventy, is put in stocks and in prison. They release him as soon as possible. But the thing was done.

The letter killeth.

Natty's last connection with his own race is broken. John, the Indian, is dead. The old hunter disappears, lonely and severed, into the forest, away, away from his race.

In the new epoch that is coming, there will be no Letter of the Law.

Chronologically, *The Last of the Mohicans* follows *Pioneers*. But in the myth, *The Prairie* comes next.

Cooper of course knew his own America. He travelled west and saw the prairies, and camped with the Indians on the prairie.

The Prairie, like *Pioneers,* bears a good deal the stamp of actuality. It is a strange, splendid book, full of sense of doom. The figures of the great Kentuckian men, with their wolf-women, loom colossal on the vast prairie, as they camp with their wagons. These are different pioneers from Judge Temple. Lurid, brutal, tinged with the sinister-ness of crime these are the gaunt white men who push west, push on and on against the natural opposition of the continent. On towards a doom. Great wings of vengeful doom seem spread over the west, grim against the intruder. You feel them again in Frank Norris' novel, *The Octopus*. While in the West of Bret Harte there is a very devil in the air, and beneath him are sentimental self-conscious people being wicked and goody by evasion.

In *The Prairie* there is a shadow of violence and dark cruelty flickering in the air. It is the aboriginal demon hovering over the core of the content. It hovers still, and the dread is still there.

Into such a prairie enters the huge figure of Ishmael, ponderous, pariah-like Ishmael and his huge sons and his were-wolf wife. With their wagons they roll on from the frontiers of Kentucky, like Cyclops into the savage wilderness. Day after day they seem to force their way into oblivion. But their force of penetration ebbs. They are brought to a stop. They recoil in the throes of murder and entrench themselves in isolation on a hillock in the midst of the prairie. There they hold out like demi-gods against the elements and the subtle Indian.

The pioneering brute invasion of the West, crime-tinged!

And into this setting, as a sort of minister of peace, enters the old, old hunter Natty, and his suave, horse-riding Sioux Indians. But he seems like a shadow.

The hills rise softly west, to the Rockies. There seems a new peace: or is it only suspense, abstraction, waiting? Is it only a sort of beyond?

Natty lives in these hills, in a village of the suave, horse-riding Sioux. They revere him as an old wise father.

In these hills he dies, sitting in his chair and looking far east, to the forest and great sweet waters, whence he came. He dies gently, in physical peace with the land and the Indians. He is an old, old man.

Cooper could see no further than the foothills where Natty died, beyond the prairie.

The other novels bring us back east.

The Last of the Mohicans is divided between real historical narrative and true "romance." For myself, I prefer the romance. It has a myth meaning, whereas the narrative is chiefly record.

For the first time, we get actual women: the dark, handsome Cora and her frail sister, the White Lily. The good old division, the dark sensual woman and the clinging, submissive little blonde, who is so "pure."

These sisters are fugitives through the forest, under the protection of a Major Heyward, a young American officer and Englishman. He is just a "white" man, very good and brave and generous, etc., but limited, most definitely *borné*. He would probably love Cora, if he dared, but he finds it safer to adore the clinging White Lily of a younger sister.

This trio is escorted by Natty, now Leatherstocking, a hunter and scout in the prime of life, accompanied by his inseparable friend Chingachgook, and the Delaware's beautiful son—Adonis rather than Apollo—Uncas, the Last of the Mohicans.

There is also a "wicked" Indian, Magua, handsome and injured incarnation of evil.

Cora is the scarlet flower of womanhood, fierce, passionate off-spring of some mysterious union between the British officer and a Creole woman in the West Indies. Cora loves Uncas. Uncas loves Cora. But Magua also desires Cora, violently desires her. A lurid little circle of sensual fire. So Fenimore kills them all off, Cora, Uncas, and Magua, and leaves the White Lily to carry on the race. She will breed plenty of white children to Major Heyward. These tiresome "lilies that fester" of our day.

Evidently Cooper—or the artist in him—has decided that there can be no blood-mixing of the two races, white and red. He kills 'em off.

Beyond all this heart-beating stand the figures of Natty and Chingachgook: the two childless womanless men of opposite races. They are the abiding thing. Each of them is alone, and final in his race. And they stand side by side, stark, abstract, beyond emotion, yet eternally together. All the other loves seem frivolous. This is the new great thing, the clue, the inception of a new humanity.

And Natty, what sort of a white man is he? Why, he is a man with a gun. He is a killer, a slayer. Patient and gentle as he is, he is a slayer. Self-effacing, self-forgetting, still he is a killer.

Twice, in the book, he brings an enemy down hurling in death through the air, downwards. Once it is the beautiful, wicked Magua —shot from a height, and hurtling down ghastly through space, into death.

This is Natty, the white forerunner. A killer. As in *Deerslayer,* he shoots the bird that flies in the high, high sky, so that the bird falls out of the invisible into the visible, dead, he symbolizes himself. He will bring the bird of the spirit out of the high air. He is the stoic American killer of the old great life. But he kills, as he says, only to live.

Pathfinder takes us to the Great Lakes, and the glamour and beauty of sailing the great sweet waters. Natty is now called Pathfinder. He is about thirty-five years old, and he falls in love. The damsel is Mabel Dunham, daughter of Sergeant Dunham of the Fort garrison. She is blonde and in all things admirable. No doubt Mrs. Cooper was very much like Mabel.

And Pathfinder doesn't marry her. She won't have him. She wisely prefers a more comfortable Jasper. So Natty goes off to grouch, and to end by thanking his stars. When he had got right clear, and sat by the campfire with Chingachgook, in the forest, didn't he just thank his stars! A lucky escape!

Men of an uncertain age are liable to these infatuations. They aren't always lucky enough to be rejected.

Whatever would poor Mabel have done, had she been Mrs. Bumppo?

Natty had no business marrying. His mission was elsewhere.

The most fascinating Leatherstocking book is the last, *Deerslayer*. Natty is now a fresh youth, called Deerslayer. But the kind of silent prim youth who is never quite young, but reserves himself for different things.

It is a gem of a book. Or a bit of perfect paste. And myself, I like a bit of perfect paste in a perfect setting, so long as I am not fooled by pretense of reality. And the setting of Deerslayer *could* not be more exquisite. Lake Champlain again.

Of course it never rains: it is never cold and muddy and dreary: no one ever has wet feet or toothache: no one ever feels filthy, when they can't wash for a week. God knows what the women would really have looked like, for they fled through the wilds without soap, comb, or towel. They breakfasted off a chunk of meat, or nothing, lunched the same, and supped the same.

Yet at every moment they are elegant, perfect ladies, in correct toilet.

Which isn't quite fair. You need only go camping for a week, and you'll see.

But it is a myth, not a realistic tale. Read it as a lovely myth. Lake Glimmerglass.

Deerslayer, the youth with the long rifle, is found in the woods with a big, handsome, blond-bearded backwoodsman called Hurry Harry. Deerslayer seems to have been born under a hemlock tree out of a pine cone: a young man of the woods. He is silent, simple, philosophic, moralistic, and an unerring shot. His simplicity is the simplicity of age rather than of youth. He is race-old. All his reactions and impulses are fixed, static. Almost he is sexless, so race-old. Yet intelligent, hard, dauntless.

Hurry Harry is a big blusterer, just the opposite of Deerslayer. Deerslayer keeps the center of his own consciousness steady and unperturbed. Hurry Harry is one of those floundering people who bluster from one emotion to another, very self-conscious, without any center to them.

These two young men are making their way to a lovely, smallish lake, Lake Glimmerglass. On this water the Hutter family has established itself. Old Hutter, it is suggested, has a criminal, coarse, buccaneering past, and is a sort of fugitive from justice. But he is a good enough father to his two grown-up girls. The family lives in a log hut "castle," built on piles in the water, and the old man has also constructed an "ark," a sort of house-boat, in which he can take his daughters when he goes on his rounds to trap the beaver.

The two girls are the inevitable dark and light. Judith, dark, fearless, passionate, a little lurid with sin, is the scarlet-and-black blossom. Hetty, the younger, blond, frail and innocent, is the white lily again. But alas, the lily has begun to fester. She is slightly imbecile.

The two hunters arrive at the lake among the woods just as war has been declared. The Hutters are unaware of the fact. And hostile Indians are on the lake already. So, the story of thrills and perils.

Thomas Hardy's inevitable division of women into dark and fair, sinful and innocent, sensual and pure, is Cooper's division too. It is indicative of the desire in the man. He wants sensuality and sin, and he wants purity and "innocence." If the innocence goes a little rotten, slightly imbecile, bad luck!

Hurry Harry, of course, like a handsome impetuous meat-fly, at once wants Judith, the lurid poppy-blossom. Judith rejects him with scorn.

Judith, the sensual woman, at once wants the quiet, reserved, unmastered Deerslayer. She wants to master him. And Deerslayer is half tempted, but never more than half. He is not going to be mastered. A philosophic old soul, he does not give much for the temptations of sex. Probably he dies virgin.

And he is right of it. Rather than be dragged into a false heat of deliberate sensuality, he will remain alone. His soul is alone, for ever alone. So he will preserve his integrity, and remain alone in the flesh. It is a stoicism which is honest and fearless, and from which Deerslayer never lapses, except when, approaching middle age, he proposes to the buxom Mabel.

He lets his consciousness pentrate in loneliness into the new continent. His contacts are not human. He wrestles with the spirits of the forest and the American wild, as a hermit wrestles with God and Satan. His one meeting is with Chingachgook, and this meeting is silent, reserved, across an unpassable distance.

Hetty, the White Lily, being imbecile, although full of vaporous religion and the dear, good God, "who governs all things by his providence," is hopelessly infatuated with Hurry Harry. Being innocence gone imbecile, like Dostoevsky's Idiot, she longs to give herself to the handsome meatfly. Of course he doesn't want her.

And so nothing happens: in that direction. Deerslayer goes off to meet Chingachgook and help him woo an Indian maid. Vicarious.

It is the miserable story of the collapse of the white psyche. The white man's mind and soul are divided between these two things: innocence and lust, the Spirit and Sensuality. Sensuality always carries a stigma, and is therefore more deeply desired, or lusted after. But spirituality alone gives the sense of uplift, exaltation, and "winged life," with the inevitable reaction into sin and spite. So the white man is divided against himself. He plays off one side of himself against the other side, till it is really a tale told by an idiot, and nauseating.

Against this, one is forced to admire the stark, enduring figure of Deerslayer. He is neither spiritual nor sensual. He is a moralizer, but he always tries to moralize from actual experience, not from theory. He says: "Hurt nothing unless you're forced to." Yet he gets his deepest thrill of gratification, perhaps, when he puts a bullet through the heart of a beautiful buck, as it stoops to drink at the lake. Or when he brings the invisible bird fluttering down in death, out of the high blue. "Hurt nothing unless you're forced to." And yet he lives by death, by killing the wild things of the air and earth.

It's not good enough.

But you have there the myth of the essential white America. All the other stuff, the love, the democracy, the floundering into lust, is a sort of byplay. The essential American soul is hard, isolate, stoic, and a killer. It has never yet melted.

Of course the soul often breaks down into disintegration, and you have lurid sin and Judith, imbecile innocence lusting in Hetty, and bluster, bragging, and self-conscious strength in Harry. But there are the disintegration products.

What true myth concerns itself with is not the disintegration product. True myth concerns itself centrally with the onward adventure of the integral soul. And this, for America, is Deerslayer. A man who turns his back on white society. A man who keeps his moral integrity hard and intact. An isolate, almost selfless, stoic, enduring man, who lives by death, by killing, but who is pure white.

This is the very intrinsic-most American. He is at the core of all the other flux and fluff. And when *this* man breaks from his static isolation, and makes a new move, then look out, something will be happening.

Ralph Waldo Emerson: THE AMERICAN SCHOLAR—Two Excerpts [1837]

I greet you on the recommencement of our literary year. Our anniversary is one of hope, and, perhaps, not enough of labor. We do not meet for games of strength or skill, for the recitation of histories, tragedies, and odes, like the ancient Greeks; for parliaments of love and poesy, like the Troubadours; nor for the advancement of science, like our contemporaries in the British and European capitals. Thus far, our holiday has been simply a friendly sign of the survival of the love of letters amongst a people too busy to give to letters any more. As such it is precious as the sign of an indestructible instinct. Perhaps the time is already come when it ought to be, and will be, something else; when the sluggard intellect of this continent will look from under its iron lids and fill the postponed expectation of the world with something better than the exertions of mechanical skill. Our day of dependence, our long apprenticeship to the learning of other lands, draws to a close. The millions that around us are rushing into life, cannot always be fed on the sere remains of foreign harvests. Events, actions arise, that must be sung, that will sing themselves. Who can doubt that poetry will revive and lead in a new age, as the star in the constellation Harp, which now flames in our zenith, astronomers announce, shall one day be the polestar for a thousand years?

But I have dwelt perhaps tediously upon this abstraction of the Scholar. I ought not to delay longer to add what I have to say of nearer reference to the time and to this country.

Historically, there is thought to be a difference in the ideas which predominate over successive epochs, and there are data for marking the genius of the Classic, of the Romantic, and now of the Reflective or Philosophical age. With the views I have intimated of the oneness or the identity of the mind through all individuals, I do not much dwell on these differences. In fact, I believe each individual passes through all three. The boy is a Greek; the youth, romantic; the adult, reflective. I deny not, however, that a revolution in the leading idea may be distinctly enough traced.

Our age is bewailed as the age of Introversion. Must that needs be evil? We, it seems, are critical; we are embarrassed with second thoughts; we cannot enjoy anything for hankering to know whereof the pleasure consists; we are lined with eyes; we see with our feet; the time is infected with Hamlet's unhappiness—

"Sicklied o'er with the pale cast of thought." It is so bad then? Sight is the last thing to be pitied. Would we be blind? Do we fear lest we should outsee nature and God, and drink truth dry? I look upon the discontent of the literary class as a mere announcement of the fact that they find themselves not in the state of mind of their fathers, and regret the coming state as untried; as a boy dreads the water before he has learned that he can swim. If there is any period one would desire to be born in, it is not the age of Revolution; when the old and the new stand side by side and admit of being compared; when the energies of all men are searched by fear and by hope; when the historic glories of the old can be compensated by the rich possibilities of the new era? This time, like all times, is a very good one, if we but know what to do with it.

I read with some joy of the auspicious signs of the coming days, as they glimmer already with poetry and art, through philosophy and science, through church and state.

One of these signs is the fact that the same movement which effected the elevation of what was called the lowest class in the state, assumed in literature a very marked and as benign an aspect. Instead of the sublime and beautiful, the near, the low, the common, was explored and poetized. That which had been negligently trodden under foot by those who were harnessing and provisioning themselves for long journeys into far countries, is suddenly found to be richer than all foreign parts. The literature of the poor, the feelings of the child, the philosophy of the street, the meaning of household life, are the topics of the time. It is a great stride. It is a sign—is it not? —of new vigor when the extremities are made active, when currents of warm life run into the hands and the feet. I ask not for the great, the remote, the romantic; what is doing in Italy or Arabia; what is Greek art, or Provençal minstrelsy; I embrace the common, I explore and sit at the feet of the familiar, the low. Give me insight into today, and you may have the antique and future world. What would we really know the meaning of? The meal in the firkin; the milk in the pan; the ballad in the street; the news of the boat; the glance of the eye; the form and the gait of the body; show me the ultimate reason of these matters; show me the sublime presence of the highest spiritual cause lurking, as always it does lurk, in these suburbs and extremities of nature; let me see every trifle bristling with the polarity that ranges it instantly on an eternal law; and the shop, the plough, and the ledger referred to the like cause by which light undulates and poets sing; and the world lies no longer a dull miscellany and lumber-room, but has form and order; there is no trifle, there is no puzzle, but one design unites and animates the farthest pinnacle and the lowest trench.

This idea has inspired the genius of Goldsmith, Burns, Cowper, and, in a newer time, of Goethe, Wordsworth, and Carlyle. This idea they have differently followed and with various success. In contrast with their writing, the style of Pope, of Johnson, of Gibbon looks cold and pedantic. This writing is blood-warm. Man is surprised to find that things near are not less beautiful, and wondrous than things remote. The near explains the far. The drop is a small ocean. A man is related to all nature. This perception of the worth of the vulgar is fruitful in discoveries. Goethe, in this very thing the most modern of the moderns, has shown me, as none ever did, the genius of the ancients. . . .

Another sign of our times, also marked by an analogous political movement, is the new importance given to the single person. Everything that tends to insulate the individual—to surround him with barriers of natural respect, so that each man shall feel the world is his, and man shall treat with man as a sovereign state with a sovereign state—tends to true union as well as greatness. "I learned," said the melancholy Pestalozzi, "that no man in God's wide earth is either willing or able to help any other man." Help must come from the bosom alone. The scholar is that man who must take up into himself all the ability of the time, all the contributions of the past, all the hopes of the future. He must be a university of knowledges.

If there be one lesson more than another which should pierce his ear, it is: The world is nothing, the man is all; in yourself is the law of all nature, and you know not yet how a globule of sap ascends; in yourself slumbers the whole of Reason; it is for you to know all; it is for you to dare all. Mr. President and Gentlemen, this confidence in the unsearched might of man belongs, by all motives, by all prophecy, by all preparation, to the American Scholar. We have listened too long to the courtly muses of Europe. The spirit of the American freeman is already suspected to be timid, imitative, tame. Public and private avarice make the air we breathe thick and fat. The scholar is decent, indolent, complaisant. See already the tragic consequence. The mind of this country, taught to aim at low objects, eats upon itself. There is no work for any but the decorous and the complaisant. Young men of the fairest promise, who begin life upon our shores, inflated by the mountain winds, shined upon by all the stars of God, find the earth below not in unison with these, but are hindered from action by the disgust which the principles on which business is managed inspire, and turn drudges, or die of disgust, some of them suicides. What is the remedy? They did not yet see, and thousands of young men as hopeful now crowding to the barriers for the career do not yet see, that if the single man plant himself indomitably on his instincts, and there abide, the huge world will come round to him. Patience—patience; with the shades of all the good and great for company; and for solace the perspective of your own infinite life; and for work the study and the communication of principles, the making those instincts prevalent, the conversion of the world. Is it not the chief disgrace in the world, not to be a unit; not to be reckoned one character; not to yield that peculiar fruit which each man was created to bear, but to be reckoned in the gross, in the hundred, or the thousand, of the party, the section, to which we belong; and our opinion predicted geographically, as the north, or the south? Not so, brothers and friends—please God, ours shall not be so. We will walk on our own feet; we will work with our own hands; we will speak our own minds. The study of letters shall be no longer a name for pity, for doubt, and for sensual indulgence. The dread of man and the love of man shall be a wall of defense and a wreath of joy around all. A nation of men will for the first time exist, because each believes himself inspired by the Divine Soul which also inspires all men.

John Jay Chapman: EMERSON [1897]

Leave this hypocritical prating about the masses. Masses are rude, lame, unmade, pernicious in their demands and influence, and need not to be flattered, but to be schooled. I wish not to concede anything to them, but to tame, drill, divide, and break them up, and draw individuals out of them. The worst of charity is that the lives you are asked to preserve are not worth preserving. Masses! The calamity is the masses. I do not wish any mass at all, but honest men only, lovely, sweet, accomplished women only, and no shovel-handed, narrow-brained, gin-drinking million stockingers or *lazzaroni* at all. If government knew how, I should like to see it check, not multiply the population. When it reaches its true law of action, every man that is born will be hailed as essential. Away with this hurrah of masses, and let us have the considerate vote of single men spoken on their honor and their conscience.

This extract from *The Conduct of Life* gives fairly enough the leading thought of Emerson's life. The unending warfare between the individual and society shows us in each generation a poet or two, a dramatist or a musician who exalts and deifies the individual, and leads us back again to the only object which is really worthy of enthusiasm or which can permanently excite it—the character of a man. It is surprising to find this identity of content in all great deliverances. The only thing we really admire is personal liberty. Those who fought for it and those who enjoyed it are our heroes.

But the hero may enslave his race by bringing in a system of tyranny; the battle-cry of freedom may become a dogma which crushes the soul; one good custom may corrupt the world. And so the inspiration of one age becomes the damnation of the next. This crystallizing of life into death has occurred so often that it may almost be regarded as one of the laws of progress.

Emerson represents a protest against the tyranny of democracy. He is the most recent example of elemental hero-worship. His opinions are absolutely unqualified except by his temperament. He expresses a form of belief in the importance of the individual which is independent of any personal relations he has with the world. It is as if a man had been withdrawn from the earth and dedicated to condensing and embodying this eternal idea—the value of the individual soul—so vividly, so vitally, that his words could not die, yet in such illusive and abstract forms that by no chance and by no power could his creed be used for purposes of tyranny. Dogma cannot be extracted from it. Schools cannot be built on it. It either lives as the spirit lives, or else it evaporates and leaves nothing. Emerson was so afraid of the letter that killeth that he would hardly trust his words to print. He was assured there was no such thing as literal truth, but only literal falsehood. He therefore resorted to metaphors which could by no chance be taken literally. And he has probably succeeded in leaving a body of work which cannot be made to operate to any other end than that for which he designed it. If this be true, he has accomplished the inconceivable feat of eluding misconception. If it be true, he stands alone in the history of teachers; he has circumvented fate, he has left an unmixed blessing behind him.

The signs of those times which brought forth Emerson are not wholly undecipherable. They are the same times which gave rise to every character of significance during the period before the war. Emerson is indeed the easiest to understand of all the men of his time, because his life is freest from the tangles and qualifications of circumstance. He is a sheer and pure type and creature of destiny, and the unconsciousness that marks his development allies him to the deepest phenomena. It is convenient, in describing him, to use language which implies consciousness of his part, but he himself had no purpose, no theory of himself; he was a product.

The years between 1820 and 1830 were the most pitiable through which this country has ever passed. The conscience of the North was pledged to the Missouri Compromise, and that Compromise neither slumbered nor slept. In New England, where the old theocratical oligarchy of the colonies had survived the Revolution and kept under its own water-locks the new flood of trade, the conservatism of politics reinforced the conservatism of religion; and as if these two inquisitions were not enough to stifle the soul of man, the conservatism of business self-interest was superimposed. The history of the conflicts which followed has been written by the radicals, who negligently charge up to self-interest all the resistance which establishments offer to change. But it was not solely self-interest, it was conscience that backed the Missouri Compromise, nowhere else, naturally, so strongly as in New England. It was conscience that made cowards of us all. The white-lipped generation of Edward Everett were victims, one might even say martyrs, to conscience. They suffered the most terrible martyrdom that can fall to man, a martyrdom which injured their immortal volition and dried up the springs of life. If it were not that our poets have too seldom deigned to dip into real life, I do not know what more awful subject for a poem could have been found than that of the New England judge enforcing the Fugitive Slave Law. For lack of such a poem the heroism of these men has been forgotten, the losing heroism of conservatism. It was this spiritual power of a committed conscience which met the new forces as they arose, and it deserves a better name than these new forces afterward gave it. In 1830 the social fruits of these heavy conditions could be seen in the life of the people. Free speech was lost.

"I know no country," says Tocqueville, who was here in 1831, "in which there is so little independence of mind and freedom of discussion as in America." Tocqueville recurs to the point again and again. He cannot disguise his surprise at it, and it tinged his whole philosophy and his book. The timidity of the Americans of this era was a thing which intelligent foreigners could not understand. Miss Martineau wrote in her *Autobiography*:

> It was not till months afterwards that I was told that there were two reasons why I was not invited there [Chelsea] as elsewhere. One reason was that I had avowed, in reply to urgent questions, that I was disappointed in an oration of Mr. Everett's; and another was that I had publicly condemned the institution of slavery. I hope the Boston people have outgrown the childishness of sulking at opinions not in either case volunteered, but obtained by pressure. But really, the subservience to opinion at that time seemed a sort of mania.

The mania was by no means confined to Boston, but qualified this period of our history throughout the Northern States. There was no literature. "If great writers have not at present existed in America, the reason is very simply given in the fact that there can be no literary genius without freedom of opinion, and freedom of opinion does not exist in America," wrote Tocqueville. There were no amusements, neither music nor sport nor pastime, indoors or out-of-doors. The whole life of the community was a life of the intelligence, and upon the intelligence lay the weight of intellectual tyranny. The pressure kept on increasing, and the suppressed forces kept on increasing, till at last, as if to show what gigantic power was needed to keep conservatism dominant, the Merchant Province put forward Daniel Webster.

The worst period of panic seems to have preceded the antislavery agitations of 1831, because these agitations soon demonstrated that the sky did not fall nor the earth yawn and swallow Massachusetts because of Mr. Garrison's opinions, as most people had sincerely believed would be the case. Some semblance of free speech was therefore gradually regained.

Let us remember the world upon which the young Emerson's eyes opened. The South was a plantation. The North crooked the hinges of the knee where thrift might follow fawning. It was the era of *Martin Chuzzlewit,* a malicious caricature—founded on fact. This time of humiliation, when there was no free speech, no literature, little manliness, no reality, no simplicity, no accomplishment, was the era of American brag. We flattered the foreigner and we boasted of ourselves. We were oversensitive, insolent, and cringing. As late as 1845, G. P. Putnam, a most sensible and modest man, published a book to show what the country had done in the field of culture. The book is a monument of the age. With all its good sense and good humor, it justifies foreign contempt because it is explanatory. Underneath everything lay a feeling of unrest, an instinct—"this country cannot permanently endure half slave and half free"—which was the truth, but which could not be uttered.

So long as there is any subject which men may not freely discuss, they are timid upon all subjects. They wear an iron crown and talk in whispers. Such social conditions crush and maim the individual, and throughout New England, as throughout the whole North, the individual was crushed and maimed.

The generous youths who came to manhood between 1820 and 1830, while this deadly era was maturing, seem to have undergone a revulsion against the world almost before touching it; at least two of them suffered, revolted, and condemned, while still boys sitting on benches in school, and came forth advancing upon this old society like gladiators. The activity of William Lloyd Garrison, the man of action, preceded by several years that of Emerson, who is his prophet. Both of them were parts of one revolution. One of Emerson's articles of faith was that a man's thoughts spring from his actions rather than his actions from his thoughts, and possibly the same thing holds good for society at large. Perhaps all truths, whether moral or economic, must be worked out in real life before they are discovered by the student, and it was therefore necessary that Garrison should be evolved earlier than Emerson.

The silent years of early manhood, during which Emerson passed through the Divinity School and to his ministry, known by few, understood by none, least of all by himself, were years in which the revolting spirit of an archangel thought out his creed. He came forth perfect, with that serenity of which we have scarce another example in history—that union of the man himself, his beliefs, and his vehicle of expression that makes men great because it makes them comprehensible. The philosophy into which he had already transmuted all his earlier theology at the time we first meet him consisted of a very simple drawing together of a few ideas, all of which had long been familiar to the world. It is the wonderful use he made of these ideas, the closeness with which they fitted his soul, the tact with which he took what he needed, like a bird building its nest, that makes the originality, the man.

The conclusion of Berkeley, that the external world is known to us only through our impressions, and that therefore, for aught we know, the whole universe exists only in our own consciousness, cannot be disproved. It is so simple a conception that a child may understand it; and it has probably been passed before the attention of every thinking man since Plato's time. The notion is in itself a mere philosophical catch or crux to which there is no answer. It may be true. The mystics made this doctrine useful. They were not content to doubt the independent existence of the external world. They imagined that this external world, the earth, the planets, the phenomena of nature, bore some relation to the emotions and destiny of the soul. The soul and the cosmos were somehow related, and related so intimately that the cosmos might be regarded as a sort of projection or diagram of the soul.

Plato was the first man who perceived that this idea could be made to provide the philosopher with a vehicle of expression more powerful than any other. If a man will once plant himself firmly on the proposition that *he is* the universe, that every emotion or expression of his mind is correlated in some way to phenomena in the external world, and that he shall say how correlated, he is in a position where the power of speech is at a maximum. His figures of speech, his tropes, his witticisms, take rank with the law of gravity and the precession of the equinoxes. Philosophical exaltation of the individual cannot go beyond this point. It is the climax.

This is the school of thought to which Emerson belonged. The sun and moon, the planets, are mere symbols. They signify what-ever the poet chooses. The planets for the most part stay in con-junction just long enough to flash his thought through their sym-bolism, and no permanent relation is established between the soul and the zodiac. There is, however, one link of correlation between the external and internal world which Emerson considered estab-lished, and in which he believed almost literally, namely, the moral law. This idea he drew from Kant through Coleridge and Words-worth, and it is so familiar to us all that it hardly needs stating. The fancy that the good, the true, the beautiful—all things of which we instinctively approve—are somehow connected together and are really one thing; that our appreciation of them is in its essence the recognition of a law; that this law, in fact all law and the very idea of law, is a mere subjective experience; and that hence any external sequence which we co-ordinate and name, like the law of gravity, is really intimately connected with our moral nature—this fancy has probably some basis of truth. Emerson adopted it as a cornerstone of his thought.

Such are the ideas at the basis of Emerson's philosophy, and it is fair to speak of them in this place because they antedate everything else which we know of him. They had been for years in his mind before he spoke at all. It was in the armor of this invulnerable ideal-ism and with weapons like shafts of light that he came forth to fight.

In 1836, at the age of thirty-three, Emerson published the little pamphlet called *Nature,* which was an attempt to state his creed. Although still young, he was not without experience of life. He had been assistant minister to the Rev. Dr. Ware from 1829 to 1832, when he resigned his ministry on account of his views regarding the Lord's Supper. He had married and lost his first wife in the same interval. He had been abroad and had visited Carlyle in 1833. He had returned and settled in Concord, and had taken up the pro-fession of lecturing, upon which he in part supported himself ever after. It is unnecessary to review these early lectures. "Large por-tions of them," says Mr. Cabot, his biographer, "appeared after-wards in the *Essays,* especially those of the first series." Suffice it that through them Emerson had become so well known that although *Nature* was published anonymously, he was recognized as the author. Many people had heard of him at the time he resigned his charge, and the story went abroad that the young minister of the Second Church had gone mad. The lectures had not discredited the story, and *Nature* seemed to corroborate it. Such was the impression which the book made upon Boston in 1836. As we read it today, we are struck by its extraordinary beauty of language. It is a supersensuous, lyrical, and sincere rhapsody, written evidently by a man of genius. It reveals a nature compelling respect—a Shelley, and yet a sort of Yankee Shelley, who is mad only when the wind is nor'-nor'west; a mature nature which must have been nourished for years upon its own thoughts, to speak this new language so eloquently, to stand so calmly on its feet. The deliverance of his thought is so perfect that this work adapts itself to our mood and has the quality of poetry. This fluency Emerson soon lost; it is the quality missing in his poetry. It is the efflorescence of youth.

In good health, the air is a cordial of incredible virtue. Crossing a bare common in snow puddles, at twilight, under a clouded sky, without having in my thoughts any occurrence of special good fortune, I have enjoyed a perfect exhilaration. I am glad to the brink of fear. In the woods, too, a man casts off his years, as the snake his slough, and at what period soever of life is always a child. In the woods is perpetual youth. Within these plantations of God, a decorum and sanctity reign, a perennial festival is dressed, and the guest sees not how he should tire of them in a thousand years. . . . It is the uniform effect of culture on the human mind, not to shake our faith in the stability of particular phenomena, as heat, water, azote, but to lead us to regard nature as phenomenon, not a substance; to attribute necessary existence to spirit; to esteem nature as an accident and an effect.

Perhaps these quotations from the pamphlet called *Nature* are enough to show the clouds of speculation in which Emerson had been walking. With what lightning they were charged was soon seen.

In 1837 he was asked to deliver the Phi Beta Kappa oration at Cambridge. This was the opportunity for which he had been waiting. The mystic and eccentric young poet-preacher now speaks his mind, and he turns out to be a man exclusively interested in real life. This recluse, too tender for contact with the rough facts of the world, whose conscience has retired him to rural Concord, pours out a vial of wrath. This cub puts forth the paw of a full-grown lion.

Emerson has left behind him nothing stronger than this address, *The American Scholar.* It was the first application of his views to the events of his day, written and delivered in the heat of early manhood while his extraordinary powers were at their height. It moves with a logical progression of which he soon lost the habit. The subject of it, the scholar's relation to the world, was the passion of his life. The body of his belief is to be found in this address, and in any adequate account of him the whole address ought to be given.

Thus far, our holiday has been simply a friendly sign of the survival of the love of letters amongst a people too busy to give to letters any more. As such it is precious as the sign of an indestructible instinct. Perhaps the time is already come when it ought to be, and will be, something else; when the sluggard intellect of this continent will look from under its iron lids and fill the postponed expectation of the world with something better than the exertions of mechanical skill. . . . The theory of books is noble. The scholar of the first age received into him the world around; brooded thereon; gave it the new arrangement of his own mind, and uttered it again. It came into him life; it went out of him truth. . . . Yet hence arises a grave mischief. The sacredness which attaches to the act of creation, the act of thought, is transferred to the record. The poet chanting was felt to be a divine man: henceforth the chant is divine, also. The writer was a just and wise spirit: henceforward it is settled the book is perfect; as love of the hero corrupts into worship of his statue. Instantly the book becomes noxious: the guide is a tyrant. . . . Books are the best of things, well used; abused, among the worst. What is the right use? What is the one end which all means go to effect? They are for nothing but to inspire. . . . The one thing in the world, of value, is the active soul. This every man is entitled to; this every man contains within him, although in almost all men obstructed, and as yet unborn. The soul active sees absolute truth and utters truth, or creates. In this action it is genius; not the privilege of here and there a favorite, but the sound estate of every man. . . . Genius is always sufficiently the enemy of genius by overinfluence. The literature of every nation bears me witness. The English dramatic poets have Shakespearized now for two hundred years. . . . These being his functions, it becomes him to feel all confidence in himself, and to defer never to the popular cry. He, and he only, knows the world. The world of any moment is the merest appearance. Some great decorum, some fetish of a government, some ephemeral trade, or war, or man, is cried up by half mankind and cried down by the other half, as if all depended on this particular up or down. The odds are that the whole question is not worth the poorest thought which the scholar has lost in listening to the controversy. Let him not quit his belief that a popgun is a popgun, though the ancient and honorable of the earth affirm it to be the crack of doom.

Dr. Holmes called this speech of Emerson's our "intellectual Declaration of Independence," and indeed it was. "The Phi Beta Kappa speech," says Mr. Lowell, "was an event without any former parallel in our literary annals,—a scene always to be treasured in the memory for its picturesqueness and its inspiration. What crowded and breathless aisles, what windows clustering with eager heads, what enthusiasm of approval, what grim silence of foregone dissent!"

The authorities of the Divinity School can hardly have been very careful readers of *Nature* and *The American Scholar,* or they would not have invited Emerson, in 1838, to deliver the address to the graduating class. This was Emerson's second opportunity to apply his beliefs directly to society. A few lines out of the famous address are enough to show that he saw in the church of his day signs of the same decadence that he saw in the letters:

The prayers and even the dogmas of our church are like the zodiac of Denderah and the astronomical monuments of the Hindoos, wholly insulated from anything now extant in the life and business of the people. They mark the height to which the waters once rose. . . . It is the office of a true teacher to show us that God is, not was; that he speaketh, not spake. The true Christianity—a faith like Christ's in the infinitude of man —is lost. None believeth in the soul of man, but only in some man or person old and departed. Ah me! no man goeth alone. All men go in flocks to this saint or that poet, avoiding the God who seeth in secret. They cannot see in secret; they love to be blind in public. They think society wiser than their soul, and know not that one soul, and their soul, is wiser than the whole world.

It is almost misleading to speak of the lofty utterances of these early addresses as attacks upon society, but their reception explains them. The element of absolute courage is the same in all natures. Emerson himself was not unconscious of what function he was performing.

The "storm in our wash-bowl" which followed this Divinity School address, the letters of remonstrance from friends, the advertisements by the Divinity School of "no complicity," must have been cheering to Emerson. His unseen yet dominating ambition is shown throughout the address, and in this note in his diary of the following year:

August 31. Yesterday at the Phi Beta Kappa anniversary. Steady, steady. I am convinced that if a man will be a true scholar he shall have perfect freedom. The young people and the mature hint at odium and the aversion of forces to be presently encountered in society. I say No; I fear it not.

The lectures and addresses which form the latter half of the first volume in the collected edition show the early Emerson in the ripeness of his powers. These writings have a lyrical sweep and a beauty which the later works often lack. Passages in them remind us of Hamlet:

How silent, how spacious, what room for all, yet without space to insert an atom;—in graceful succession, in equal fullness, in balanced beauty, the dance of the hours goes forward still. Like an odor of incense, like a strain of music, like a sleep, it is inexact and boundless. It will not be dissected, nor unraveled, nor shown. . . . The great Pan of old, who was clothed in a leopard skin to signify the beautiful variety of things and the firmament, his coat of stars—was but the representative of thee, O rich and various men! thou palace of sight and sound, carrying in thy senses the morning and the night and the unfathomable galaxy; in thy brain, the geometry of the City of God; in thy heart, the bower of love and the realms of right and wrong. . . . Every star in heaven is discontent and insatiable. Gravitation and chemistry cannot content them. Ever they woo and court the eye of the beholder. Every man who comes into the world they seek to fascinate and possess, to pass into his mind, for they desire to republish themselves in a more delicate world than that they occupy. . . . So it is with all immaterial objects. These beautiful basilisks set their brute glorious eyes on the eye of every child, and, if they can, cause their nature to pass through his wondering eyes into him, and so all things are mixed.

Emerson is never far from his main thought: "The universe does not attract us till it is housed in an individual." "A man, a personal ascendancy, is the only great phenomenon." "I cannot find language of sufficient energy to convey my sense of the sacredness of private integrity."

On the other hand, he is never far from his great fear: "But Truth is such a fly-away, such a sly-boots, so untransportable and unbarrelable a commodity, that it is as bad to catch as light." "Let him beware of proposing to himself any end. . . . I say to you plainly, there is no end so sacred or so large that if pursued for itself will not become carrion and an offense to the nostril."

There can be nothing finer than Emerson's knowledge of the world, his sympathy with young men and with the practical difficulties of applying his teachings. We can see in his early lectures before students and mechanics how much he had learned about the structure of society from his own short contact with the organized church.

Each finds a tender and very intelligent conscience a disqualification for success. Each requires of the practitioner a certain shutting of the eyes, a certain dapperness and compliance, an acceptance of customs, a sequestration from the sentiments of generosity and love, a compromise of private opinion and lofty integrity. . . . The fact that a new thought and hope have dawned in your breast, should apprise you that in the same hour a new light broke in upon a thousand private hearts. . . . And further I will not dissemble my hope that each person whom I address has felt his own call to cast aside all evil customs, timidity, and limitations, and to be in his place a free and helpful man, a reformer, a benefactor, not content to slip along through the world like a footman or a spy, escaping by his nimbleness and apologies as many knocks as he can, but a brave and upright man who must find or cut a straight road to everything excellent in the earth, and not only go honorably himself, but make it easier for all who follow him to go in honor and with benefit. . . .

Beneath all lay a greater matter—Emerson's grasp of the forms and conditions of progress, his reach of intellect, which could afford fair play to everyone.

His lecture on *The Conservative* is not a puzzling *jeu d'esprit,* like *Bishop Blougram's Apology,* but an honest attempt to set up the opposing chessmen of conservatism and reform so as to represent real life. Hardly can such a brilliant statement of the case be found elsewhere in literature. It is not necessary to quote here the reformer's side of the question, for Emerson's whole life was devoted to it. The conservatives' attitude he gives with such accuracy and such justice that the very bankers of State Street seem to be speaking:

> The order of things is as good as the character of the population permits. Consider it as the work of a great and beneficent and progressive necessity, which, from the first pulsation in the first animal life up to the present high culture of the best nations, has advanced thus far. . . .
>
> The conservative party in the universe concedes that the radical would talk sufficiently to the purpose if we were still in the garden of Eden; he legislates for man as he ought to be; his theory is right, but he makes no allowance for friction, and this omission makes his whole doctrine false. The idealist retorts that the conservative falls into a far more noxious error in the other extreme. The conservative assumes sickness as a necessity, and his social frame is a hospital, his total legislation is for the present distress, a universe in slippers and flannels, with bib and papspoon, swallowing pills and herb tea. Sickness gets organized as well as health, the vice as well as the virtue.

It is unnecessary to go, one by one, through the familiar essays and lectures which Emerson published between 1838 and 1875. They are in everybody's hands and in everybody's thoughts. In 1840 he wrote in his diary:

> In all my lectures I have taught one doctrine, namely, the infinitude of the private man. This the people accept readily enough, and even with commendation, as long as I call the lecture Art or Politics, or Literature or the Household; but the moment I call it Religion they are shocked, though it be only the application of the same truth which they receive elsewhere to a new class of facts.

To the platform he returned, and left it only once or twice during the remainder of his life.

His writings vary in coherence. In his early occasional pieces, like the Phi Beta Kappa address, coherence is at a maximum. They were written for a purpose, and were perhaps struck off all at once. But he earned his living by lecturing, and a lecturer is always recasting his work and using it in different forms. A lecturer has no prejudice against repetition. It is noticeable that in some of Emerson's important lectures the logical scheme is more perfect than in his essays.

The truth seems to be that in the process of working up and perfecting his writings, in revising and filing his sentences, the logical scheme became more and more obliterated. Another circumstance helped make his style fragmentary. He was by nature a man of inspirations and exalted moods. He was subject to ecstasies, during which his mind worked with phenomenal brilliancy. Throughout his works and in his diary we find constant reference to these moods, and to his own inability to control or recover them. "But what we want is consecutiveness. 'Tis with us a flash of light, then a long darkness, then a flash again. Ah! could we turn these fugitive sparkles into an astronomy of Copernican worlds!"

In order to take advantage of these periods of divination, he used to write down the thoughts that came to him at such times. From boyhood onward he kept journals and commonplace books, and in the course of his reading and meditation he collected innumerable notes and quotations which he indexed for ready use. In these mines he "quarried," as Mr. Cabot says, for his lectures and essays. When he needed a lecture he went to the repository, threw together what seemed to have a bearing on some subject, and gave it a title. If any other man should adopt this method of composition, the result would be incomprehensible chaos; because most men have many interests, many moods, many and conflicting ideas. But with Emerson it was otherwise. There was only one thought which could set him aflame, and that was the thought of the unfathomed might of man. This thought was his religion, his politics, his ethics, his philosophy. One moment of inspiration was in him brother to the next moment of inspiration, although they might be separated by six weeks. When he came to put together his star-born ideas, they fitted well, no matter in what order he placed them, because they were all part of the same idea.

His works are all one single attack on the vice of the age, moral cowardice. He assails it not by railings and scorn, but by positive and stimulating suggestion. The imagination of the reader is touched by every device which can awaken the admiration for heroism, the consciousness of moral courage. Wit, quotation, anecdote, eloquence, exhortation, rhetoric, sarcasm, and very rarely denunciation, are launched at the reader, till he feels little lambent flames beginning to kindle in him. He is perhaps unable to see the exact logical connection between two paragraphs of an essay, yet he feels they are germane. He takes up Emerson tired and apathetic, but presently he feels himself growing heady and truculent, strengthened in his most inward vitality, surprised to find himself again master in his own house.

The difference between Emerson and the other moralists is that all these stimulating pictures and suggestions are not given by him in illustration of a general proposition. They have never been through the mill of generalization in his own mind. He himself could not have told you their logical bearing on one another. They have all the vividness of disconnected fragments of life, and yet they all throw light on one another, like the facets of a jewel. But whatever cause it was that led him to adopt his method of writing, it is certain that he succeeded in delivering himself of his thought with an initial velocity and carrying power such as few men ever attained. He has the force at his command of the thrower of the discus.

His style is American, and beats with the pulse of the climate. He is the only writer we have had who writes as he speaks, who makes no literary parade, has no pretensions of any sort. He is the only writer we have had who has wholly subdued his vehicle to his temperament. It is impossible to name his style without naming his character: they are one thing.

Both in language and in elocution Emerson was a practiced and consummate artist, who knew how both to command his effects and to conceal his means. The casual, practical, disarming directness with which he writes puts any honest man at his mercy. What difference does it make whether a man who can talk like this is following an argument or not? You cannot always see Emerson clearly; he is hidden by a high wall; but you always know exactly on what spot he is standing. You judge it by the flight of the objects he throws over the wall—a bootjack, an apple, a crown, a razor, a volume of verse. With one or other of these missiles, all delivered with a very tolerable aim, he is pretty sure to hit you. These catchwords stick in the mind. People are not in general influenced by long books or discourses, but by odd fragments of observation which they overhear, sentences or headlines which they read while turning over a book at random or while waiting for dinner to be announced. These are the oracles and orphic words that get lodged in the mind and bend a man's most stubborn will. Emerson called them the Police of the Universe. His works are a treasury of such things. They sparkle in the mine, or you may carry them off in your pocket. They get driven into your mind like nails, and on them catch and hang your own experiences, till what was once his thought has become your character.

"God offers to every mind its choice between truth and repose. Take which you please; you can never have both." "Discontent is want of self-reliance; it is infirmity of will." "It is impossible for a man to be cheated by anyone but himself."

The orchestration with which Emerson introduces and sustains these notes from the spheres is as remarkable as the winged things themselves. Open his works at a hazard. You hear a man talking.

A garden is like those pernicious machineries we read of every month in the newspapers, which catch a man's coat-skirt cr his hand, and draw in his arm, his leg, and his whole body to irresistible destruction. In an evil hour he pulled down his wall and added a field to his homestead. No land is bad, but land is worse. If a man own land, the land owns him. Now let him leave home if he dare. Every tree and graft, every hill of melons, row of corn, or quickset hedge, all he has done and all he means to do, stand in his way like duns, when he would go out of his gate.

Your attention is arrested by the reality of this gentleman in his garden, by the firsthand quality of his mind. It matters not on what subject he talks. While you are musing, still pleased and patronizing, he has picked up the bow of Ulysses, bent it with the ease of Ulysses, and sent a shaft clear through the twelve axes, nor missed one of them. But this, it seems, was mere byplay and marksmanship; for before you have done wondering, Ulysses rises to his feet in anger, and pours flight after flight, arrow after arrow, from the great bow. The shafts sing and strike, the suitors fall in heaps. The brow of Ulysses shines with unearthly splendor. The air is filled with lightning. After a little, without shock or transition, without apparent change of tone, Mr. Emerson is offering you a biscuit before you leave, and bidding you mind the last step at the garden end. If the man who can do these things be not an artist, then must we have a new vocabulary and rename the professions.

There is, in all this effectiveness of Emerson, no pose, no literary art; nothing that corresponds even remotely to the pretended modesty and ignorance with which Socrates lays pitfalls for our admiration in Plato's dialogues.

It was the platform which determined Emerson's style. He was not a writer, but a speaker. On the platform his manner of speech was a living part of his words. The pauses and hesitation, the abstraction, the searching, the balancing, the turning forward and back of the leaves of his lecture, and then the discovery, the illumination, the gleam of lightning which you saw before your eyes descend into a man of genius—all this was Emerson. He invented this style of speaking, and made it express the supersensuous, the incommunicable. Lowell wrote, while still under the spell of the magician:

Emerson's oration was more disjointed than usual, even with him. It began nowhere, and ended everywhere, and yet, as always with that divine man, it left you feeling that something beautiful had passed that way, something more beautiful than anything else, like the rising and setting of stars. Every possible criticism might have been made on it but one

—that it was not noble. There was a tone in it that awakened all elevating associations. He boggled, he lost his place, he had to put on his glasses; but it was as if a creature from some fairer world had lost his way in our fogs, and it was *our* fault, not his. It was chaotic, but it was all such stuff as stars are made of, and you couldn't help feeling that, if you waited awhile, all that was nebulous would be whirled into planets, and would assume the mathematical gravity of system. All through it I felt something in me that cried, "Ha! ha!" to the sound of the trumpets.

It is nothing for any man sitting in his chair to be overcome with the sense of the immediacy of life, to feel the spur of courage, the victory of good over evil, the value, now and forever, of all great-hearted endeavor. Such moments come to us all. But for a man to sit in his chair and write what shall call up these forces in the bosoms of others—that is desert, that is greatness. To do this was the gift of Emerson. The whole earth is enriched by every moment of converse with him. The shows and shams of life become transparent, the lost kingdoms are brought back, the shutters of the spirit are opened, and provinces and realms of our own existence lie gleaming before us.

It has been necessary to reduce the living soul of Emerson to mere dead attributes like "moral courage" in order that we might talk about him at all. His effectiveness comes from his character; not from his philosophy, nor from his rhetoric nor his wit, nor from any of the accidents of his education. He might never have heard of Berkeley or Plato. A slightly different education might have led him to throw his teaching into the form of historical essays or of stump speeches. He might, perhaps, have been bred a stonemason, and have done his work in the world by traveling with a panorama. But he would always have been Emerson. His weight and his power would always have been the same. It is solely as character that he is important. He discovered nothing; he bears no relation whatever to the history of philosophy. We must regard him and deal with him simply as a man.

Strangely enough, the world has always insisted upon accepting him as a thinker: and hence a great coil of misunderstanding. As a thinker, Emerson is difficult to classify. Before you begin to assign him a place, you must clear the ground by a disquisition as to what is meant by "a thinker," and how Emerson differs from other thinkers. As a man, Emerson is as plain as Ben Franklin.

People have accused him of inconsistency; they say that he teaches one thing one day, and another the next day. But from the point of view of Emerson there is no such thing as inconsistency. Every man is each day a new man. Let him be today what he is today. It is immaterial and waste of time to consider what he once was or what he may be.

His picturesque speech delights in fact and anecdote, and a public which is used to treatises and deduction cares always to be told the moral. It wants everything reduced to a generalization. All generalizations are partial truths, but we are used to them, and we ourselves mentally make the proper allowance. Emerson's method is, not to give a generalization and trust to our making the allowance, but to give two conflicting statements and leave the balance of truth to be struck in our own minds on the facts. There is no inconsistency in this. It is a vivid and very legitimate method of procedure. But he is much more than a theorist: he is a practitioner. He does not merely state a theory of agitation: he proceeds to agitate. "Do not," he says, "set the least value on what I do, or the least discredit on what I do not, as if I pretended to settle anything as false or true. I unsettle all things. No facts are to me sacred, none are profane. I simply experiment, an endless seeker with no past at my back." He was not engaged in teaching many things, but one thing—Courage. Sometimes he inspires it by pointing to great characters—Fox, Milton, Alcibiades; sometimes he inspires it by bidding us beware of imitating such men, and, in the ardor of his rhetoric, even seems to regard them as hindrances and dangers to our development. There is no inconsistency here. Emerson might logically have gone one step further and raised inconsistency into a jewel. For what is so useful, so educational, so inspiring, to a timid and conservative man, as to do something inconsistent and regrettable? It lends character to him at once. He breathes freer and is stronger for the experience.

Emerson is no cosmopolitan. He is a patriot. He is not like Goethe, whose sympathies did not run on national lines. Emerson has America in his mind's eye all the time. There is to be a new religion, and it is to come from America; a new and better type of man, and he is to be an American. He not only cared little or nothing for Europe, but he cared not much for the world at large. His thought was for the future of this country. You cannot get into any chamber in his mind which is below this chamber of patriotism. He loves the valor of Alexander and the grace of the Oxford athlete; but he loves them not for themselves. He has a use for them. They are grist to his mill and powder to his gun. His admiration of them he subordinates to his main purpose—they are his blackboard and diagrams. His patriotism is the backbone of his significance. He came to his countrymen at a time when they lacked, not thoughts, but manliness. The needs of his own particular public are always before him.

It is odd that our people should have, not water on the brain, but a little gas there. A shrewd foreigner said of the Americans that "whatever they say has a little the air of a speech."

I shall not need to go into an enumeration of our national defects and vices which require this Order of Censors in the State. . . . . The timidity of our public opinion is our disease, or, shall I say, the publicness of opinion, the absence of private opinion.

Our measure of success is the moderation and low level of an individual's judgment. Dr. Channing's piety and wisdom had such weight in Boston that the popular idea of religion was whatever this eminent divine held.

Let us affront and reprimand the smooth mediocrity, the squalid contentment of the times.

The politicians he scores constantly.

"Who that sees the meanness of our politics but congratulates Washington that he is long already wrapped in his shroud and forever safe." The following is his description of the social world of his day: "If any man consider the present aspects of what is called by distinction *society,* he will see the need of these ethics. The sinew and heart of man seem to be drawn out, and we are become timorous, desponding whimperers."

It is the same wherever we open his books. He must spur on, feed up, bring forward the dormant character of his countrymen. When he goes to England, he sees in English life nothing except those elements which are deficient in American life. If you wish a catalogue of what America has not, read *English Traits.* Emerson's patriotism had the effect of expanding his philosophy. Today we know the value of physique, for science has taught it, but it was hardly discovered in his day, and his philosophy affords no basis for it. Emerson in this matter transcends his philosophy. When in England, he was fairly made drunk with the physical life he found there. He is like Caspar Hauser gazing for the first time on green fields. *English Traits* is the ruddiest book he ever wrote. It is a hymn to force, honesty, and physical well-being, and ends with the dominant note of his belief: "By this general activity and by this sacredness of individuals, they [the English] have in seven hundred years evolved the principles of freedom. It is the land of patriots, martyrs, sages, and bards, and if the ocean out of which it emerged should wash it away, it will be remembered as an island famous for immortal laws, for the announcements of original right which make the stone tables of liberty."

He had found in England free speech, personal courage, and reverence for the individual.

No convulsion could shake Emerson or make his view unsteady even for an instant. What no one else saw, he saw, and he saw nothing else. Not a boy in the land welcomed the outbreak of the war so fiercely as did this shy village philosopher, then at the age of fifty-eight. He saw that war was the cure for cowardice, moral as well as physical. It was not the cause of the slave that moved him; it was not the cause of the Union for which he cared a farthing. It was something deeper than either of these things for which he had been battling all his life. It was the cause of character against convention. Whatever else the war might bring, it was sure to bring in character, to leave behind it a file of heroes; if not heroes, then villains, but in any case strong men. On the ninth of April 1861, three days before Fort Sumter was bombarded, he had spoken with equanimity of "the downfall of our character-destroying civilization. . . . We find that civilization crowed too soon, that our triumphs were treacheries; we had opened the wrong door and let the enemy into the castle."

"Ah," he said, when the firing began, "sometimes gunpowder smells good." Soon after the attack on Sumter he said in a public address, "We have been very homeless for some years past, say since 1850; but now we have a country again. . . . The war was an eye opener, and showed men of all parties and opinions the value of those primary forces that lie beneath all political action." And it was almost a personal pledge when he said at the Harvard Commemmoration in 1865, "We shall not again disparage America, now that we have seen what men it will bear."

The place which Emerson forever occupies as a great critic is defined by the same sharp outlines that mark his work, in whatever light and from whatever side we approach it. A critic in the modern sense he was not, for his point of view is fixed, and he reviews the world like a searchlight placed on the top of a tall tower. He lived too early and at too great a distance from the forum of European thought to absorb the ideas of evolution and give place to them in this philosophy. Evolution does not graft well upon the Platonic Idealism, nor are physiology and the kindred sciences sympathetic. Nothing aroused Emerson's indignation more than the attempts of the medical faculty and of phrenologists to classify, and therefore limit individuals. "The grossest ignorance does not disgust me like this ignorant knowingness."

We miss in Emerson the underlying conception of growth, of development, so characteristic of the thought of our own day, and which, for instance, is found everywhere latent in Browning's poetry. Browning regards character as the result of experience and as an ever changing growth. To Emerson, character is rather an entity complete and eternal from the beginning. He is probably the last great writer to look at life from a stationary standpoint. There is a certain lack of the historic sense in all he has written. The ethical assumption that all men are exactly alike permeates his work. In his mind, Socrates, Marco Polo, and General Jackson stand surrounded by the same atmosphere, or rather stand as mere naked characters surrounded by no atmosphere at all. He is probably the last great writer who will fling about classic anecdotes as if they were club gossip. In the discussion of morals, this assumption does little harm. The stories and proverbs which illustrate the thought of the moralist generally concern only those simple relations of life which are common to all ages. There is charm in this familiar dealing with antiquity. The classics are thus domesticated and made real to us. What matter if Aesop appear a little too much like an American citizen, so long as his points tell?

It is in Emerson's treatment of the fine arts that we begin to notice his want of historic sense. Art endeavors to express subtle and ever changing feelings by means of conventions which are as protean as the forms of a cloud; and the man who in speaking on the plastic arts makes the assumption that all men are alike will reveal before he has uttered three sentences that he does not know what art is, that he has never experienced any form of sensation from it. Emerson lived in a time and clime where there was no plastic art, and he was obliged to arrive at his ideas about art by means of a highly complex process of reasoning. He dwelt constantly in a spiritual place which was the very focus of high moral fervor. This was his enthusiasm, this was his revelation, and from it he reasoned out the probable meaning of the fine arts. "This," thought Emerson, his eye rolling in a fine frenzy of moral feeling, "this must be what Apelles experienced, this fervor is the passion of Bramante. I understand the Parthenon." And so he projected his feelings about morality into the field of the plastic arts. He deals very freely and rather indiscriminately with the names of artists—Phidias, Raphael, Salvator Rosa—and he speaks always in such a way that it is impossible to connect what he says with any impression we have ever received from the works of those masters.

In fact, Emerson has never in his life felt the normal appeal of any painting, or any sculpture, or any architecture, or any music. These things, of which he does not know the meaning in real life, he yet uses, and uses constantly as symbols to convey ethical truths. The result is that his books are full of blind places, like the notes which will not strike on a sick piano.

It is interesting to find that the one art of which Emerson did have a direct understanding, the art of poetry, gave him some insight into the relation of the artist to his vehicle. In his essay on Shakespeare there is a full recognition of the debt of Shakespeare to his times. This essay is filled with the historic sense. We ought not to accuse Emerson because he lacked appreciation of the fine arts, but rather admire the truly Goethean spirit in which he insisted upon the reality of arts of which he had no understanding. This is the same spirit which led him to insist on the value of the Eastern poets. Perhaps there exist a few scholars who can tell us how far Emerson understood or misunderstood Saadi and Firdusi, and the Koran. But we need not be disturbed for his learning. It is enough that he makes us recognize that these men were men, too, and that their writings mean something not unknowable to us. The East added nothing to Emerson, but gave him a few trappings of speech. The whole of his mysticism is to be found in *Nature,* written before he knew the sages of the Orient, and it is not improbable that there is some real connection between his own mysticism and the mysticism of the Eastern poets.

Emerson's criticism on men and books is like the test of a great chemist who seeks one or two elements. He burns a bit of the stuff in his incandescent light, shows the lines of it in his spectrum, and there an end.

It was a thought of genius that led him to write *Representative Men.* The scheme of this book gave play to every illumination of his mind, and it pinned him down to the objective, to the field of vision under his microscope. The table of contents of *Representative Men* is the dial of his education. It is as follows: Uses of Great Men; Plato, or The Philosopher; Plato, New Readings; Swedenborg, or The Mystic; Montaigne, or The Skeptic; Shakespeare, or The Poet; Napoleon, or The Man of the World; Goethe, or The Writer. The predominance of the writers over all other types of men is not cited to show Emerson's interest in The Writer, for we know his interest centered in the practical man—even his ideal scholar is a practical man—but to show the sources of his illustration. Emerson's library was the old-fashioned gentleman's library. His mines of thought were the world's classics. This is one reason why he so quickly gained an international currency. His very subjects in *Representative Men* are of universal interest, and he is limited only by certain inevitable local conditions. *Representative Men* is thought by many persons to be his best book. It is certainly filled with the strokes of a master. There exists no more profound criticism than Emerson's analysis of Goethe and of Napoleon, by both of whom he was at once fascinated and repelled. . . .

E. A. Duyckinck: NATIONALITY IN LITERATURE [1847]

We are a nation of readers, thirty millions strong; but what are our books, and who are our writers?

There are many persons who have not yet tasted of death, who were living when Edmund Burke, on the floor of the British Parliament, described America as having been, within the lifetime of the then Lord Bathurst, "a little speck, scarce visible in the mass of the national interest; a small seminal principle, rather than a formed body." That infant people, then "but in the gristle, and not yet hardened into the bone of manhood"—struggling with the vicissitudes of life in a new country, and subduing the wilderness and the savage tribes who peopled it—thirteen feeble colonies, "growing by the neglect of their parent state—have, within the threescore years and ten which have since elapsed, achieved their National Independence, through the fiery ordeal of a long and bloody war—erected new institutions of government, a new civil polity and social condition—become the first political power in the Western hemisphere, and the second commercial power in the world—and is beginning to exert an influence upon human affairs, which, if wisely directed, seems likely to change the destinies of our race, through all future time, and over the entire surface of the globe. Our Republic occupies a land, suited to the grand part which seems to be allotted to it on the great stage of time. Its shores washed by two oceans—its interior penetrated by noble rivers, and dotted over with vast lakes and inland seas—its mountains rich with the most useful and valuable minerals—its fertile soil teeming with all the productions of the temperate zone, and thickly studded with broad prairies and nobly-timbered forests—a domain equal in extent to the whole of southern and western Europe, adequate to the government of fifty independent states, and the maintenance of the hundreds of millions, who are advancing from the future to occupy it—present elements of growth, of strength, and of greatness, which give assurance of the most splendid career to be traced in the annals of the human race. . . .

And yet this great country that is—this greater country that is to be; this nation of churches and schoolhouses, as well as canals and railroads—"pliant and prone to seek after knowledge," has no native literature, but is, in letters, in a state of colonial and provincial dependency upon the old world.

It is not difficult to point out the causes which have retarded the literary growth of this country. The settlers of a new country have neither the leisure to enjoy, nor the wealth to procure the means of enjoying the delights of literature. An inhospitable climate, a rude wilderness, savage enemies, privation and sickness, all had to be borne or overcome by the founders of the American States. And as if these were not sufficient to crush those who here planted the seeds of our civilization and freedom, the despotic hand of the parent government was laid heavily upon them. They gave what time they could to religious worship, to the instruction of the young in the necessary rudiments of knowledge—to brief household endearments, to the government and order of the settlement, to necessary repose, and the rest was painfully devoted to toil. The forest had to be cleared, the crop sown and harvested—the hut, the dwelling, and the log fort reared and defended from the fierce onslaught of savage foes, and the despotic authority of England to be watched and resisted. It can excite no surprise that letters were not cultivated under such adverse circumstances. Again, the loyalty of the colonists to the parent government operated in the same direction. They resisted exaction and oppression as infractions of the British Constitution, but they loved their country, and submitted cheerfully to the exercise of legitimate authority over themselves and their property. They were Englishmen, and English literature was the common heritage of Englishmen wherever their lot might be cast. Speaking the English tongue, deeply imbued with English tastes and prejudices, reared in the admiration of English writers, and acknowledging nothing as superior to English models, nothing is more natural than that whatever was attempted in composition in this country, should be a close imitation of, and bear a marked resemblance to, the literature of the old country.

And when the colonies finally asserted their independence, it was only against the political power of the mother country. They retained her language, her letters, and the frame of her great writers, as their birthright as Englishmen, or the descendants of Englishmen; their young career in letters was commenced under all the influences of old habits, old associations, and old prejudices in favor of English models, and the mind of the country has not yet cast off this old literary domination. . . .

Overmastered by the literature of England, we have consented to remain in a state of pupilage, instead of aspiring to be masters in the vocation of letters. "The parents have eaten sour grapes, and the children's teeth are set on edge." We have gone on from generation to generation, imitating old English authors, and working by old critical rules. "The imitation of our own antiquities," says Sir James Mackintosh, "may be as artificial as the copy of a foreign literature." In every department of literary composition, we have come to consider that which is but one mode of writing to be *the* mode, and the only permissible one. Instead of regarding the drama as comprehending an unlimited range of passion and of modes of manifestation, Shakespeare's plays are received by us as bounding the horizon of dramatic composition. So Milton is accepted as the only standard of sublimity, and Addison as the perfect measure of ease and grace. We are to make the metals, torn from the virgin soil of a new country, flow into these old molds, and harden into these antique forms. We must take these shapes, or not be at all. . . .

Something will be gained for the cause of an indigenous literature by a clear development of the idea and the necessity of nationality. First and foremost, nationality involves the idea of home writers. Secondly, the choice of a due proportion of home themes, affording opportunity for descriptions of our scenery, for the illustration of passing events, and the preservation of what tradition has rescued from the past, and for the exhibition of the manners of the people, and the circumstances which give form and pressure to the time and the spirit of the country; and all these penetrated and vivified by an intense and enlightened patriotism. The literature of a country should, as from a faithful mirror, reflect the physical, moral and intellectual aspects of the nation. Other nations and later ages should look to the writers of the land for the lineaments of its people, and to trace the influence of institutions, of civil and religious polity, upon the condition, the manners and the happiness of individuals, and upon the strength, the power and the permanency of the state. The Scriptures represent man as speaking "out of the abundance of the heart." The literature of a people should be its written thought, uttered "out of the abundance of its heart," and exhibiting its interior as well as exterior life. . . .

What cultivated mind fails to distinguish between the literature of Greece and that of Rome; of Italy and that of Spain; of Germany and that of France and England? Undoubtedly, there are many things common to them all; but there are strongly marked and characteristic differences, which constitute the individuality of each. The dissimilarity of Homer and Virgil; of Camoëns, Dante, and Milton; of Goethe, Racine, and Shakespeare, is not more sharply cut and strongly defined, than that between the general literature of the countries to which they respectively belonged. Referring to Madame de Staël's brilliant observations on the Greek drama, and the prodigious effects produced by the representation of the Greek tragedies, Jeffrey says: "A great part of the effect of these representations must have depended on *the exclusive nationality of their subjects, and the extreme nationality of their auditors.*" And the same eminent critic expresses the opinion that Shakespeare could not have written his great dramas—could not have been Shakespeare—if he had been born in any other country than England. Indeed, Shakespeare, notwithstanding his infinite variety, and those "touches of nature which make the whole world kin," is a thorough Briton, and his writings are surcharged with the spirit of nationality. Could Milton have written the *Iliad,* or Homer *Paradise Lost*? Could Goethe have wrought the *Heart of Midlothian,* or Scott the tragedy of *Faust*? Are not these works distinct with the characteristics of the country and age in which they were produced? . . .

It will thus be seen that our view of nationality is conceived in no narrow spirit. Illiberality and exclusiveness have no part in our creed. We would burn no books, banish no authors, shut our hearts against no appeal which speaks to them in the voice of nature. We would not narrow, but enlarge, the horizon of letters; we would not restrict the empire of thought, but annex our noble domain to it. A writer in the last October number of the *North American Review* says that "an intense national self-consciousness, though the shallow may name it patriotism, is the worst foe to the true and generous unfolding of national genius." Against the opinion of this learned Theban, we set the high authorities we have already cited. . . .

The *North American* reviewer before referred to, says that "the advocates of nationality seem to think that American authors ought to limit themselves to American subjects, and hear none but American criticism." This is erroneous. They have nowhere intimated such an opinion. We say that Shakespeare, Milton, Dante, Goethe and Racine, were all writers who wrote in a truly national spirit, and yet they did not limit themselves to subjects belonging exclusively to their own country or times. As we are men, whatever is common to humanity falls fairly within the range of the American author; but as we are Americans, whatever is peculiar to our country and characteristic of our countrymen is especially deserving of his regard. Is there any lack of home themes that our authors should lack home thoughts? Is there not the same variety in the play of human passions in the new world as in the old—in the present as in the past ages—under free as under despotic institutions? We would set no limits to the subjects on which our authors should write. We would leave to them the whole range of nature and humanity. We would wish them to strike every key in the grand scale of human passion. But we would have them true to their country. If there is anything peculiar in our institutions and condition, we would have some native bard to sing, some native historian to record it. We would have those who are born upon our soil, who have faith in republican governments, who cherish noble hopes and aspirations for our country, whose hearts beat in unison with our countrymen, to manifest their faith, their hopes, their sympathies, in some suitable manner. What we complain of is the unnational spirit of our writers; that they slavishly adhere to old and foreign models; that alike in their subjects, and in their method of handling them, they are British, or German, or something else than American. We are not ungrateful for what some of our writers have done; but we ask, if the American people were suddenly destroyed by some great convulsions of nature, what fitting memorial of our national existence would be left, to instruct and delight, centuries hence, the nations which are yet in the womb of time? . . .

7

James Russell Lowell: NATIONALITY IN
LITERATURE [1849]

. . . After the United States had achieved their independence, it was
forthwith decided that they could not properly be a nation without
a literature of their own. As if we had been without one! As if Shakespeare, sprung from the race and the class which colonized New
England, had not been also ours! As if we had no share in the puritan and republican Milton, we who had cherished in secret for more
than a century the idea of the great puritan effort, and at last embodied it in a living commonwealth! But this ownership in common
was not enough for us, and, as partition was out of the question, we
must have a drama and an epos of our own. It must be national, too;
we must have it all to ourselves. Other nations kept their poets, and
so must we. We were to set up a literature as people set up a carriage, in order to be as good as our neighbors. It was even seriously
proposed to have a new language. Why not, since we could afford it?
Beside, the existing ones were all too small to contain our literature
whenever we should get it. One enthusiast suggested the ancient Hebrew, another a fire-new tongue of his own invention. Meanwhile, we
were busy growing a literature. We watered so freely, and sheltered
so carefully, as to make a soil too damp and shaded for anything

but mushrooms; wondered a little why no oaks came up, and ended by voting the mushroom an oak, an American variety. Joel Barlow made the lowest bid for the construction of our epos, got the contract, and delivered in due season the *Columbiad,* concerning which we can only regret that it had not been entitled to a still higher praise of nationality by being written in one of the proposed new languages.

One would think that the Barlow experiment should have been enough. But we are still requested by critics, both native and foreign, to produce a national literature, as if it were some school exercise in composition to be handed in by a certain day. The sharp struggle of a day or a year may settle the question of a nation's political independence, but even for that, there must be a long moral preparation. The first furrow drawn by an English plow in the thin soil of Plymouth was truly the first line in our Declaration of Independence. Jefferson was not the prophet looking forth into the future, but the scribe sitting at the feet of the past. But nationality is not a thing to be won by the sword. We may safely trust to the influence of our institutions to produce all of it that is valuable. Let us be content that, if we have been to blame for a *Columbiad,* we have also given form, life, and the opportunity of entire development to social ideas ever reacting with more and more force upon the thought and the literature of the Old World.

The poetry and romance of other nations are assumed to be national, inasmuch as they occupy themselves about local traditions or objects. But we, who never had any proper youth as a nation, never had our mythic period either. We had no cradle and no nursery to be haunted with such bugaboos. One great element of external and immediate influence is therefore wanting to our poets. They cannot, as did Goethe in his *Faust,* imbue an old legend, which already has a hold upon the fancy and early associations of their countrymen, with a modern and philosophical meaning which shall make it interesting to their mature understandings and cultivated imaginations. Whatever be the cause, no race into whose composition so large a Teutonic element has entered, is divided by such an impassable chasm of oblivion and unbelief from the ancestral mythology as the English. Their poets accordingly are not popular in any true sense of the word, and have influenced the thought and action of their countrymen less than those of any other nation except those of ancient Rome. Poets in other countries have mainly contributed to the creating and keeping alive of national sentiment; but the English owe theirs wholly to the sea which islands them. Chaucer and Spenser are Normans, and their minds open most fairly southward. Skelton, the Swift of his day, a purely English poet, is forgotten. Shakespeare, thoroughly English as he is, has chosen foreign subjects for the greatest of his dramas, as if to show that genius is cosmopolitan. The first thorough study, criticism, and consequent appreciation of him we owe to the Germans; and he can in no sense be called national except by accident of birth. Even if we grant that he drew his fairy mythology from any then living faith among his countrymen, this formed no bond of union between him and them, and was even regarded as an uncouthness and barbarism till long after every vestige of such faith was obliterated. If we concede any nationality to Milton's great poem, we must at the same time allow to the English an exclusive title to the localities where the scene is laid, a title which they would hardly be anxious to put forward in respect, at least, to one of them. When he was meditating a national poem, it was, he tells us, on the legend of Arthur, who, if he had ever existed at all, would have been English only in the same sense that Tecumseh is American. Coleridge, among his thousand reveries, hovered over the same theme, but settled at last upon the siege of Jerusalem by Titus as the best epical subject remaining. Byron, in his greatest poem, alludes only to England in a rather contemptuous farewell. Those strains of Wordsworth, which have entitled his name to a place on the selecter list of English poets, are precisely the ones in which England has only a common property with the rest of mankind. He could never have swum over Lethe with the sonnets to the river Duddon in his pocket. Whether we look for the cause in the origin of the people, or in their insular position, the English mind has always been characterized by an emigrating tendency. Their most truly national epic was the colonizing of America.

If we admit that it is meritorious in an author to seek for a subject in the superstitions, legends, and historical events of his own peculiar country or district, yet these (unless delocalized by their own intrinsic meaning) are by nature ephemeral, and a wide tract of intervening years makes them as truly foreign as oceans, mountains, or deserts could. Distance of time passes its silent statute of outlawry and alienage against them, as effectually as distance of space. . . .

This demand for a nationality bounded historically and geographically by the independent existence and territory of a particular race or fraction of a race, would debar us of our rightful share in the past and the ideal. It was happily illustrated by that parochially national Gascon, who would have been edified by the sermon had it been his good fortune to belong to the parish. Let us be thankful that there is no court by which we can be excluded from our share in the inheritance of the great poets of all ages and countries, to which our simple humanity entitles us. No great poet has ever sung but the whole human race has been, sooner or later, the wiser and better for it. Above all, let us not tolerate in our criticism a principle which would operate as a prohibitory tariff of ideas. The intellect is a diœcious plant, and books are the bees which carry the quickening pollen from one to another mind. It detracts nothing from Chaucer that we can trace in him the influences of Dante and Boccaccio; nothing from Spenser that he calls Chaucer master; nothing from Shakespeare that he acknowledges how dear Spenser was to him; nothing from Milton that he brought fire from Hebrew and Greek altars. There is no degradation in such indebtedness. Venerable rather is this apostolic succession, and inspiring to see the *vitai lampada* passed thus from consecrated hand to hand.

Nationality, then, is only a less narrow form of provincialism, a sublimer sort of clownishness and ill-manners. It deals in jokes, anecdotes, and allusions of such purely local character that a majority of the company are shut out from all approach to an understanding of them. Yet so universal a demand must have for its basis a more or less solid substratum of truth. There are undoubtedly national, as truly as family, idiosyncrasies, though we think that these will get displayed without any special schooling for that end. The substances with which a nation is compelled to work will modify its results, as well intellectual as material. The still renewing struggle with the unstable desert sands gave to the idea of durability in the Egyptian imagination a preponderance still further increased by the necessity of using granite, whose toughness of fiber and vagueness of coloring yielded unwillingly to fineness of outline, but seemed the natural helpmates of massiveness and repose. The out-of-door life of the Greeks, conducing at once to health and an unconscious education of the eye, and the perfection of physical development resulting from their palæstral exercises and constantly displayed in them, made the Greeks the first to perceive the noble symmetry of the human figure, for embodying the highest types of which Pentelicus supplied the fittest material. Corporeal beauty and strength, therefore, entered largely into their idea of the heroic, and perhaps it was rather policy than dandyism which hindered Alcibiades from learning to play the flute. With us, on the other hand, clothed to the chin in the least graceful costume ever invented by man, and baked half the year with stoves and furnaces, beauty of person has gradually receded from view, and wealth or brain is the essential of the modern novelist's hero. It may not be fanciful to seek in climate, and its resultant effects upon art, the more remote cause of that fate-element which entered so largely into the Greek drama. In proportion as sculpture became more perfect, the images of the gods became less and less merely symbolical, and at last presented to the popular mind nothing more than actual representations of an idealized humanity. Before this degradation had taken place, and the divinities had been vulgarized in marble to the common eye, the ideas of the unseen and supernatural came to the assistance of the poet in giving interest to the struggles or connivances between heroes and gods. But presently a new and deeper chord of the imagination must be touched, and the unembodiable shadow of Destiny was summoned up, to move awe and pity as long as the human mind is incapable of familiarizing by precise definition the fearful and the vague. In that more purely objective age, the conflict must be with something external, and the struggles of the mind with itself afforded no sufficient theme for the poet. With us introspection has become a disease, and a poem is a self-dissection.

That Art in America will be modified by circumstances, we have no doubt, though it is impossible to predict the precise form of the molds into which it will run. New conditions of life will stimulate thought and give new forms to its expression. It may not be our destiny to produce a great literature, as, indeed, our genius seems to find its kindliest development in practicalizing simpler and more perfect forms of social organization. We have yet many problems of this kind to work out, and a continent to subdue with the plow and the railroad, before we are at leisure for æsthetics. Our spirit of adventure will first take a material and practical direction, but will gradually be forced to seek outlet and scope in unoccupied territories of the intellect. In the meantime we may fairly demand of our literature that it should be national to the extent of being as free from outworn conventionailties, and as thoroughly impregnated with humane and manly sentiment, as is the idea on which our political fabric rests. Let it give a true reflection of our social, political, and household life. The *Poems on Man in the Republic,* by Cornelius Mathews, disfigured as they were by gross faults of dialect and meter, had the great merit of presenting the prominent features of our civilization in an American light. The story of *Margaret* is the most emphatically *American* book ever written. The want of plan and slovenliness of construction are characteristic of a new country. The scenery, character, dialect, and incidents mirror New England life as truly as Fresh Pond reflects the sky. The moral, also, pointing forward to a new social order, is the intellectual antitype of that restlessness of disposition, and facility of migration which are among our chief idiosyncrasies. This mistake of our imaginative writers generally is that, though they make take an American subject, they *costume* it in a foreign or antique fashion. The consequence is a painful vagueness and unreality. It is like putting Roman drapery upon a statue of Washington, the absurdity of which does not strike us so forcibly because we are accustomed to it, but which we should recognize at once were the same treatment applied to Franklin. The old masters did exactly the reverse of this. They took ancient or foreign subjects, but selected their models from their own immediate neighborhood. When Shakespeare conceived his Athenian mechanics, he did not cram with Grecian antiquities in order to make them real in speech and manners. Their unconscious prototypes were doubtless walking Stratford streets, and demonstrating to any one who had clear enough eyes, that stupidity and conceit were precisely the same things on the banks of the Avon and those of the Ilissus. Here we arrive at the truth which is wrapped up and concealed in the demand for nationality in literature. It is neither more nor less than this, that authors should use their own eyes and ears, and not those of other people. We ask of them human nature as it appears in man, not in books; and scenery not at second hand from the canvas of painter or poet, but from that unmatched landscape painted by the Great Master upon the retina of their own eyes. Though a poet should make the bobolink sing in Attica, the *anachronism* is nothing, provided he can only make it truly sing so that we can hear it. He will have no difficulty in making his peace with posterity. The error of our advocates of nationality lies in their assigning geographical limits to the poet's range of historical characters as well as to his natural scenery. There is no time or place in human nature, and Prometheus, Coriolanus, Tasso and Tell are ours if we can use them, as truly as Washington or Daniel Boone. Let an American author make a living character, even if it be antediluvian, and nationality will take care of itself. . . .

8

Henry James: HAWTHORNE:
EARLY MANHOOD [1879]

The twelve years that followed• were not the happiest or most brilliant phase of Hawthorne's life; they strike me indeed as having had
an altogether peculiar dreariness. They had their uses; they were the
period of incubation of the admirable compositions which eventually
brought him reputation and prosperity. But of their actual aridity the
young man must have had a painful consciousness; he never lost the
impression of it. Mr. Lathrop quotes a phrase to this effect from one
of his letters, late in life: "I am disposed to thank God for the gloom
and chill of my early life, in the hope that my share of adversity came
then, when I bore it alone." And the same writer alludes to a touching
passage in the English *Note-Books,* which I shall quote entire:

I think I have been happier this Christmas [1854] than ever before
—by my own fireside, and with my wife and children about me—more
content to enjoy what I have, less anxious for anything beyond it, in this
life. My early life was perhaps a good preparation for the declining half
of life; it having been such a blank that any thereafter would compare

• *After leaving Bowdoin College in 1825 and going back to live in
Salem.* [*Editor*]

favorably with it. For a long, long while, I have occasionally been visited with a singular dream; and I have an impression that I have dreamed it ever since I have been in England. It is, that I am still at college, or, sometimes, even, at school—and there is a sense that I have been there unconscionably long, and have quite failed to make such progress as my contemporaries have done; and I seem to meet some of them with a feeling of shame and depression that broods over me as I think of it, even when awake. This dream, recurring all through these twenty or thirty years, must be one of the effects of that heavy seclusion in which I shut myself up for twelve years after leaving college, when everybody moved onward and left me behind. How strange that it should come now, when I may call myself famous and prosperous!—when I am happy too.

The allusion here is to a state of solitude which was the young man's positive choice at the time—or into which he drifted at least under the pressure of his natural shyness and reserve. He was not expansive, he was not addicted to experiments and adventures of intercourse, he was not, personally, in a word, what is called sociable. The general impression of this silence-loving and shade-seeking side of his character is doubtless exaggerated, and, in so far as it points to him as a somber and sinister figure, is almost ludicrously at fault. He was silent, diffident, more inclined to hesitate, to watch and wait and meditate, than to produce himself, and fonder, on almost any occasion, of being absent than of being present. This quality betrays itself in all his writings. There is in all of them something cold and light and thin, something belonging to the imagination alone, which indicates a man but little disposed to multiply his relations, his points of contact, with society. If we read the six volumes of *Note-Books* with an eye to the evidence of this unsocial side of his life, we find it in sufficient abundance. But we find at the same time that there was nothing unamiable or invidious in his shyness, and above all that there was nothing preponderantly gloomy. The qualities to which the *Note-Books* most testify are, on the whole, his serenity and amenity of mind. They reveal these characteristics indeed in an almost phenomenal degree. The serenity, the simplicity, seem in certain portions almost childlike; of brilliant gaiety, of high spirits, there is little; but the placidity and evenness of temper, the cheerful and contented view of the things he notes, never belie themselves. I know not what else he may have written in this copious record, and what passages of gloom and melancholy may have been suppressed; but as his diaries stand, they offer in a remarkable degree the reflection of a mind whose development was not in the direction of sadness. A very clever French critic, whose fancy is often more lively than his observation is deep, M. Emile Montégut, writing in the *Revue des Deux Mondes,* in the year 1860, invents for our author the appellation of *"Un Romancier Pessimiste."* Superficially speaking, perhaps, the title is a happy one; but only superficially. Pessimism consists in having morbid and bitter views and theories about human nature; not in indulging in shadowy fancies and conceits. There is nothing whatever to show that Hawthorne had any such doctrines or convictions; certainly, the note of depression, of despair, of the disposition to undervalue the human race, is never sounded in his diaries. These volumes contain the record of very few convictions or theories of any kind; they move with curious evenness, with a charming, graceful flow, on a level which lies above that of a man's philosophy. They adhere with such persistence to this upper level that they prompt the reader to believe that Hawthorne had no appreciable philosophy at all—no general views that were in the least uncomfortable. They are the exhibition of an unperplexed intellect. I said just now that the development of Hawthorne's mind was not towards sadness; and I should be inclined to go still further, and say that his mind proper —his mind in so far as it was a repository of opinions and articles of faith—had no development that it is of especial importance to look into. What had a development was his imagination—that delicate and penetrating imagination which was always at play, always entertaining itself, always engaged in a game of hide and seek in the region in which it seemed to him that the game could best be played—among the shadows and substructions, the dark-based pillars and supports, of our moral nature. Beneath this movement and ripple of his imagination—as free and spontaneous as that of the sea surface—lay directly his personal affections. These were solid and strong, but, according to my impression, they had the place very much to themselves.

His innocent reserve, then, and his exaggerated, but by no means cynical, relish for solitude, imposed themselves upon him, in a great measure, with a persistency which helped to make the time a tolerably arid one—so arid a one indeed that we have seen that in the light of later happiness he pronounced it a blank. But in truth, if these were dull years, it was not all Hawthorne's fault. His situation was intrinsically poor—poor with a poverty that one almost hesitates to look into. When we think of what the conditions of intellectual life, of taste, must have been in a small New England town fifty years ago; and when we think of a young man of beautiful genius, with a love of literature and romance, of the picturesque, of style and form and color, trying to make a career for himself in the midst of them, compassion for the young man becomes our dominant sentiment, and we see the large dry village picture in perhaps almost too hard a light. It seems to me then that it was possibly a blessing for Hawthorne that he was not expansive and inquisitive, that he lived much to himself and asked but little of his *milieu*. If he had been exacting and ambitious, if his appetite had been large and his knowledge various, he would probably have found the bounds of Salem intolerably narrow. But his culture had been of a simple sort—there was little of any other sort to be obtained in America in those days, and though he was doubtless haunted by visions of more suggestive opportunities, we may safely assume that he was not to his own perception the object of compassion that he appears to a critic who judges him after half a century's civilization has filtered into the twilight of that earlier time. If New England was socially a very small place in those days, Salem was a still smaller one; and if the American tone at large was intensely provincial, that of New England was not greatly helped by having the best of it. The state of things was extremely natural, and there could be now no greater mistake than to speak of it with a redundancy of irony. American life had begun to constitute itself from the foundations it had begun to *be,* simply; it was at an immeasurable distance from having begun to enjoy. I imagine there was no appreciable group of people in New England at that time proposing to itself to enjoy life; this was not an undertaking for which any provision had been made, or to which any encouragement was offered. Hawthorne must have vaguely entertained some such design upon destiny; but he must have felt that his success would have to depend wholly upon his own ingenuity. I say he must have proposed to himself to enjoy, simply because he proposed to be an artist, and because this enters inevitably into the artist's scheme. There are a thousand ways of enjoying life, and that of the artist is one of the most innocent. But for all that, it connects itself with the idea of pleasure. He proposed to give pleasure, and to give it he must first get it. Where he gets it will depend upon circumstances, and circumstances were not encouraging to Hawthorne.

He was poor, he was solitary, and he undertook to devote himself to literature in a community in which the interest in literature was as yet of the smallest. It is not too much to say that even to the present day it is a considerable discomfort in the United States not to be "in business." The young man who attempts to launch himself in a career that does not belong to the so-called practical order; the young man who has not, in a word, an office in the business quarter of the town, with his name painted on the door, has but a limited place in the social system, finds no particular bough to perch upon. He is not looked at askance, he is not regarded as an idler; literature and the arts have always been held in extreme honor in the American world, and those who practice them are received on easier terms than in other countries. If the tone of the American world is in some respects provincial, it is in none more so than in this matter of the exaggerated homage rendered to authorship. The gentleman or the lady who has written a book is in many circles the object of an admiration too indiscriminating to operate as an encouragement to good writing. There is no reason to suppose that this was less the case fifty years ago; but fifty years ago, greatly more than now, the literary man must have lacked the comfort and inspiration of belonging to a class. The best things come, as a general thing, from the talents that are members of a group; every man works better when he has companions working in the same line, and yielding the stimulus of suggestion, comparison, emulation. Great things of course have been done by solitary workers; but they have usually been done with double the pains they would have cost if they had been produced in more genial circumstances. The solitary worker loses the profit of example and discussion; he is apt to make awkward experiments; he is in the nature of the case more or less of an empiric. The empiric may, as I say, be treated by the world as an expert; but the drawbacks and discomforts of empiricism remain to him, and are in fact increased by the suspicion that is mingled with his gratitude, of a want in the public taste of a sense of the proportions of things. Poor Hawthorne, beginning to write subtle short tales at Salem, was empirical enough; he was one of, at most, some dozen Americans who had taken up literature as a profession. The profession in the United States is still very young, and of diminutive stature; but in the year 1830 its head could hardly have been seen above ground. It strikes the observer of today that Hawthorne showed great courage in entering a field in which the honors and emoluments were so scanty as the profits of authorship must have been at that time. I have said that in the United States at present authorship is a pedestal, and literature is the fashion; but Hawthorne's history is a proof that it was possible, fifty years ago, to write a great many little masterpieces without becoming known. He begins the preface to the *Twice-Told Tales* by remarking that he was "for many years the obscurest man of letters in America." When once this work obtained recognition, the recognition left little to be desired. Hawthorne never, I believe, made large sums of money by his writings, and the early profits of these charming sketches could not have been considerable; for many of them, indeed, as they appeared in journals and magazines, he had never been paid at all; but the honor, when once it dawned—and it dawned tolerably early in the author's career—was never thereafter wanting. Hawthorne's countrymen are solidly proud of him, and the tone of Mr. Lathrop's *Study* is in itself sufficient evidence of the manner in which an American storyteller may in some cases look to have his eulogy pronounced.

Hawthorne's early attempt to support himself by his pen appears to have been deliberate; we hear nothing of those experiments in countinghouses or lawyers' offices, of which a permanent invocation to the Muse is often the inconsequent sequel. He began to write, and to try and dispose of his writings; and he remained at Salem apparently only because his family, his mother and his two sisters lived there. His mother had a house, of which during the twelve years that elapsed until 1838 he appears to have been an inmate. Mr. Lathrop learned from his surviving sister that after publishing *Fanshawe* he produced a group of short stories entitled *Seven Tales of My Native Land,* and that this lady retained a very favorable recollection of the work, which her brother had given her to read. But it never saw the light; his attempts to get it published were unsuccessful, and at last, in a fit of irritation and despair, the young author burned the manuscript.

There is probably something autobiographic in the striking little tale of *The Devil in Manuscript.* "They have been offered to seventeen publishers," says the hero of that sketch in regard to a pile of his own lucubrations.

It would make you stare to read their answers. . . . One man publishes nothing but schoolbooks, another has five novels already under examination; . . . another gentleman is just giving up business, on purpose, I verily believe, to avoid publishing my book. In short, of all the seventeen publishers, only one has vouchsafed even to read my tales; and he—a literary dabbler himself, I should judge—has the impertinence to criticize them, proposing what he calls vast improvements, and concluding, after a general sentence of condemnation, with the definitive assurance that he will not be concerned on any terms. . . . [But there does seem to be one righteous man among these seventeen unrighteous ones, and he tells me, fairly, that no American publisher will meddle with an American work—seldom if by a known writer, and never if by a new one—unless at the writer's risk.

But though the *Seven Tales* were not printed, Hawthorne proceeded to write others that were; the two collections of the *Twice-Told Tales* and the *Snow Image* are gathered from a series of contributions to the local journals and the annuals of that day. To make these three volumes, he picked out the things he thought the best. "Some very small part," he says of what remains, "might yet be rummaged out (but it would not be worth the trouble) among the dingy pages of fifteen- or twenty-year-old periodicals, or within the shabby morocco covers of faded *Souvenirs.*" These three volumes represent no large amount of literary labor for so long a period, and the author admits that there is little to show "for the thought and industry of that portion of his life." He attributes the paucity of his productions to a "total lack of sympathy at the age when his mind would naturally have been most effervescent." "He had no incitement to literary effort in a reasonable prospect of reputation or profit; nothing but the pleasure itself of composition, an enjoyment not at all amiss in its way, and perhaps essential to the merit of the work in hand, but which in the long run will hardly keep the chill out of a writer's heart, or the numbness out of his fingers." These words occur in the preface attached in 1851 to the second edition of the *Twice-Told Tales; à propos* of which I may say that there is always a charm in Hawthorne's prefaces which makes one grateful for a pretext to quote from them. At this time *The Scarlet Letter* had just made his fame, and the short tales were certain of a large welcome; but the account he gives of the failure of the earlier edition to produce a sensation (it had been published in two volumes, at four years apart) may appear to contradict my assertion that, though he was not recognized immediately, he was recognized betimes. In 1850, when *The Scarlet Letter* appeared, Hawthorne was forty-six years old, and this may certainly seem a long-delayed popularity. On the other hand, it must be remembered that he had not appealed to the world with any great energy. The *Twice-Told Tales,* charming as they are, do not constitute a very massive literary pedestal. As soon as the author, resorting to severer measures, put forth *The Scarlet Letter,* the public ear was touched and charmed, and after that it was held to the end. "Well it might have been!" The reader will exclaim. "But what a grievous pity that the dulness of this same organ should have operated so long as a deterrent, and by making Hawthorne wait till he was nearly fifty to publish his first novel, have abbreviated by so much his productive career!" The truth is, he cannot have been in any very high degree ambitious; he was not an abundant producer, and there was manifestly a strain of generous indolence in his composition. There was a lovable want of eagerness about him. Let the encouragement offered have been what it might, he had waited till he was lapsing from middle life to strike his first noticeable blow; and during the last ten years of his career he put forth but two complete works, and the fragment of a third.

It is very true, however, that during this early period he seems to have been very glad to do whatever came to his hand. Certain of his tales found their way into one of the annuals of the time, a publication endowed with the brilliant title of *The Boston Token and Atlantic Souvenir.* The editor of this graceful repository was S. G. Goodrich, a gentleman who, I suppose, may be called one of the pioneers of American periodical literature. He is better known to the world as Mr. Peter Parley, a name under which he produced a

multitude of popular schoolbooks, storybooks, and other attempts
to vulgarize human knowledge and adapt it to the infant mind. This
enterprising purveyor of literary wares appears, incongruously
enough, to have been Hawthorne's earliest protector, if protection
is the proper word for the treatment that the young author received
from him. Mr. Goodrich induced him in 1836 to go to Boston to
edit a periodical in which he was interested, *The American Magazine of Useful and Entertaining Knowledge.* I have never seen the
work in question, but Hawthorne's biographer gives a sorry account
of it. It was managed by the so-called Bewick Company, which "took
its name from Thomas Bewick, the English restorer of the art of
wood engraving, and the magazine was to do his memory honor by
his admirable illustrations. But in fact it never did anyone honor,
nor brought anyone profit. It was a penny popular affair, containing
condensed information about innumerable subjects, no fiction, and
little poetry. The woodcuts were of the crudest and most frightful
sort. It passed through the hands of several editors and several publishers. Hawthorne was engaged at a salary of five hundred dollars
a year; but it appears that he got next to nothing, and did not stay
in the position long." Hawthorne wrote from Boston in the winter
of 1836: "I came here trusting to Goodrich's positive promise to pay
me forty-five dollars as soon as I arrived; and he has kept promising
from one day to another, till I do not see that he means to pay at
all. I have now broke off all intercourse with him, and never think
of going near him. . . . I don't feel at all obliged to him about the
editorship, for he is a stockholder and director in the Bewick Company . . . and I defy them to get another to do for a thousand dollars what I do for five hundred."—"I make nothing," he says in another letter, "of writing a history or biography before dinner."
Goodrich proposed to him to write a *Universal History* for the use
of schools, offering him a hundred dollars for his share in the work.
Hawthorne accepted the offer and took a hand—I know not how
large a one—in the job. His biographer has been able to identify a
single phrase as our author's. He is speaking of George IV: "Even
when he was quite a young man this king cared as much about dress
as any young coxcomb. He had a great deal of taste in such matters,
and it is a pity that he was a king, for he might otherwise have made
an excellent tailor." The *Universal History* had a great vogue and
passed through hundreds of editions; but it does not appear that
Hawthorne ever received more than his hundred dollars. The writer
of these pages vividly remembers making its acquaintance at an early
stage of his education—a very fat, stumpy-looking book, bound in
boards covered with green paper, and having in the text very small

woodcuts of the most primitive sort. He associates it to this day with the names of Sesostris and Semiramis whenever he encounters them, there having been, he supposes, some account of the conquests of these potentates that would impress itself upon the imagination of a child. At the end of four months, Hawthorne had received but twenty dollars—four pounds—for his editorship of the *American Magazine*.

There is something pitiful in this episode, and something really touching in the sight of a delicate and superior genius obliged to concern himself with such paltry undertakings. The simple fact was that for a man attempting at that time in America to live by his pen, there were no larger openings; and to live at all Hawthorne had, as the phrase is, to make himself small. This cost him less, moreover, than it would have cost a more copius and strenuous genius, for his modesty was evidently extreme, and I doubt whether he had any very ardent consciousness of rare talent. He went back to Salem, and from this tranquil standpoint, in the spring of 1837, he watched the first volume of his *Twice-Told Tales* come into the world. He had by this time been living some ten years of his manhood in Salem, and an American commentator may be excused for feeling the desire to construct, from the very scanty material that offers itself, a slight picture of his life there. I have quoted his own allusions to its dulness and blankness, but I confess that these observations serve rather to quicken than to depress my curiosity. A biographer has of necessity a relish for detail; his business is to multiply points of characterization. Mr. Lathrop tells us that our author "had little communication with even the members of his family. Frequently his meals were brought and left at his locked door, and it was not often that the four inmates of the old Herbert Street mansion met in family circle. He never read his stories aloud to his mother and sisters. . . . It was the custom in this household for the several members to remain very much by themselves; the three ladies were perhaps nearly as rigorous recluses as himself, and, speaking of the isolation which reigned among them, Hawthorne once said, 'We do not even *live* at our house!' " It is added that he was not in the habit of going to church. This is not a lively picture, nor is that other sketch of his daily habits much more exhilarating, in which Mr. Lathrop affirms that though the statement that for several years "he never saw the sun" is entirely an error, yet it is true that he stirred little abroad all day and "seldom chose to walk in the town except at night." In the dusky hours he took walks of many miles along the coast, or else wandered about the sleeping streets of Salem. These were his pastimes, and these were apparently his most intimate occasions of contact with life. Life, on such occasions, was not very exuberant, as anyone will reflect who has been acquainted with the physiognomy of a small New England town after nine o'clock in the evening. Hawthorne, however, was an inveterate observer of small things, and he found a field for fancy among the trivial accidents. There could be no better example of this happy faculty than the little paper entitled *Night Sketches,* included among the *Twice-Told Tales.* This small dissertation is about nothing at all, and to call attention to it is almost to overrate its importance. This fact is equally true, indeed, of a great many of its companions, which give even the most appreciative critic a singular feeling of his own indiscretion—almost of his own cruelty. They are so slight, so slight, so tenderly trivial, that simply to mention them is to put them in a false position. The author's claim for them is barely audible, even to the most acute listener. They are things to take or leave—to enjoy, but not to talk about. Not to read them would be to do them an injustice (to read them is essentially to relish them), but to bring the machinery of criticism to bear upon them would be to do them a still greater wrong. I must remember, however, that to carry this principle too far would be to endanger the general validity of the present little work—a consummation which it can only be my desire to avert. Therefore it is that I think it permissible to remark that in Hawthorne, the whole class of little descriptive effusions directed upon common things, to which these just-mentioned *Night Sketches* belong, have a greater charm than there is any warrant for in their substance. The charm is made up of the spontaneity, the personal quality, of the fancy that plays through them, its mingled simplicity and subtlety, its purity and its *bonhomie.* The *Night Sketches* are simply the light, familiar record of a walk under an umbrella, at the end of a long, dull, rainy day, through the sloppy, ill-paved streets of a country town, where the rare gas lamps twinkle in the large puddles, and the blue jars in the druggist's window shine through the vulgar drizzle. One would say that the inspiration of such a theme could have had no great force, and such doubtless was the case; but out of the Salem puddles, nevertheless, springs, flowerlike, a charming and natural piece of prose.

I have said that Hawthorne was an observer of small things, and indeed he appears to have thought nothing too trivial to be suggestive. His *Note-Books* give us the measure of his perception of common and casual things, and of his habit of converting them into *memoranda.* These *Note-Books,* by the way—this seems as good a place as any other to say it—are a very singular series of volumes; I doubt whether there is anthing exactly corresponding to them in the whole body of literature. The were published—in six volumes, issued at intervals—some years after Hawthorne's death, and no person attempting to write an account of the romancer could afford to regret that they should have been given to the world. There is a point of view from which this may be regretted; but the attitude of the biographer is to desire as many documents as possible. I am thankful, then, as a biographer, for the *Note-Books,* but I am obliged to confess that, though I have just reread them carefully, I am still at a loss to perceive how they came to be written—what was Hawthorne's purpose in carrying on for so many years this minute and often trivial chronicle. For a person desiring information about him at any cost, it is valuable; it sheds a vivid light upon his character, his habits, the nature of his mind. But we find ourselves wondering what was its value to Hawthorne himself. It is in a very partial degree a register of impressions, and in a still smaller sense a record of emotions. Outward objects play much the larger part in it; opinions, convictions, ideas pure and simple, are almost absent. He rarely takes his note-book into his confidence or commits to its pages any reflections that might be adapted for publicity; the simplest way to describe the tone of these extremely objective journals is to say that they read like a series of very pleasant, though rather dullish and decidedly formal, letters, addressed to himself by a man who, having suspicions that they might be opened in the post, should have determined to insert nothing compromising. They contain much that is too futile for things intended for publicity; whereas, on the other hand, as a receptacle of private impressions and opinions, they are curiously cold and empty. They widen, as I have said, our glimpse of Hawthorne's mind (I do not say that they elevate our estimate of it), but they do so by what they fail to contain, as much as by what we find in them. Our business for the moment, however, is not with the light that they throw upon his intellect, but with the information they offer about his habits and his social circumstances.

I know not at what age he began to keep a diary; the first entries in the American volumes are of the summer of 1835. There is a phrase in the preface to his novel of *The Marble Faun* which must have lingered in the minds of many Americans who have tried to write novels and to lay the scene of them in the western world. "No author, without a trial, can conceive of the difficulty of writing a romance about a country where there is no shadow, no antiquity, no mystery, no picturesque and gloomy wrong, nor anything but a commonplace prosperity, in broad and simple daylight, as is happily the case with my dear native land." The perusal of Hawthorne's American *Note-Books* operates as a practical commentary upon this somewhat ominous text. It does so at least to my own mind; it would be too much perhaps to say that the effect would be the same for the usual English reader. An American reads between the lines—he completes the suggestions—he constructs a picture. I think I am not guilty of any gross injustice in saying that the picture he constructs from Hawthorne's American diaries, though by no means without charms of its own, is not, on the whole, an interesting one. It is characterized by an extraordinary blankness—a curious paleness of color and paucity of detail. Hawthorne, as I have said, has a large and healthy appetite for detail, and one is therefore the more struck with the lightness of the diet to which his observation was condemned. For myself, as I turn the pages of his journals, I seem to see the image of the crude and simple society in which he lived. I use these epithets, of course, not invidiously, but descriptively; if one desire to enter as closely as possible into Hawthorne's situation, one must endeavor to reproduce his circumstances. We are struck with the large number of elements that were absent from them, and the coldness, the thinness, the blankness, to repeat my epithet, present themselves so vividly that our foremost feeling is that of compassion for a romancer looking for subjects in such a field. It takes so many things, as Hawthorne must have felt later in life, when he made the acquaintance of the denser, richer, warmer European spectacle—it takes such an accumulation of history and custom, such a complexity of manners and types, to form a fund of suggestion for a novelist. If Hawthorne had been a young Englishman, or a young Frenchman of the same degree of genius, the same cast of mind, the same habits, his consciousness of the world around him would have been a very different affair; however obscure, however reserved, his own personal life, his sense of the life of his fellow-mortals would have been almost infinitely more various. The negative side of the spectacle on which Hawthorne looked out, in his contemplative saunterings and reveries, might, indeed, with a little ingenuity, be made almost ludicrous; one might enumerate the items of high civilization, as it exists in other countries, which are absent from the texture of American life, until it should become a wonder to know what was left. No State, in the European sense of the word, and indeed barely a specific national name. No sovereign, no court, no personal loyalty, no aristocracy, no church, no clergy, no army, no diplomatic service, no country gentlemen, no palaces, no castles, nor manors, nor old country houses, nor parsonages, nor thatched cottages, nor ivied ruins; no cathedrals, nor abbeys, nor little Norman churches; no great universities nor public schools—no Oxford, nor Eton, nor Harrow; no literature, no novels, no museums, no pictures, no political society, no sporting class—no Epsom nor Ascot! Some such list as that might be drawn up of the absent things in American life—especially in the American life of forty years ago, the effect of which, upon an English or a French imagination, would probably as a general thing be appalling. The natural remark, in the almost lurid light of such an indictment, would be that if these things are left out, everything is left out. The American knows that a good deal remains; what it is that remains—that is his secret, his joke, as one may say. It would be cruel, in this terrible denudation, to deny him the consolation of his national gift, that "American humor" of which of late years we have heard so much.

But in helping us to measure what remains, our author's diaries, as I have already intimated, would give comfort rather to persons who might have taken the alarm from the brief sketch I have just attempted of what I have called the negative side of the American social situation, than do those reminding themselves of its fine compensations. Hawthorne's entries are to a great degree accounts of walks in the country, drives in stage-coaches, people he met in taverns. The minuteness of the things that attract his attention and that he deems worthy of being commemorated is frequently extreme, and from this fact we get the impression of a general vacancy in the field of vision. "Sunday evening, going by the jail, the setting sun kindled up the windows most cheerfully; as if there were a bright, comfortable light within its darksome stone wall." "I went yesterday with Monsieur S— to pick raspberries. He fell through an old log bridge thrown over a hollow; looking back, only his head and shoulders appeared through the rotten logs and among the bushes.—A shower coming on, the rapid running of a little barefooted boy, coming up unheard, and dashing swiftly past us, and showing us the soles of his naked feet as he ran down the path and up the opposite side." In another place he devotes a page to a description of a dog whom he saw running round after its tail; in still another he remarks, in a paragraph by itself—"The aromatic odor of peat-smoke in the sunny autumnal air is very pleasant." The reader says to himself that when a man turned thirty gives a place in his mind—and his inkstand—to such trifles as these, it is because nothing else of superior importance demands admission. Everything in the notes indicates a simple, democratic, thinly composed society; there is no evidence of the writer finding himself in any variety or intimacy of relations with anyone or with anything. We find a good deal of warrant for believing that if we add that statement of Mr. Lathrop's about his meals being left at the door of his room, to rural rambles of which an impression of the temporary phases of the local apple-crop were the usual, and an encounter with an organ-grinder, or an eccentric dog, the rarer, outcome, we construct a rough image of our author's daily life during the several years that preceded his marriage. He appears to have read a good deal, and that he must have been familiar with the sources of good English we see from his charming, expressive, slightly self-conscious, cultivated, but not too cultivated, style. Yet neither in these early volumes of his *Note-Books* nor in the later is there any mention of his reading. There are no literary judgments or impressions—there is almost no allusion to works or to authors. The allusions to individuals of any kind are indeed much less numerous than one might have expected; there is little psychology, little description of manners. We are told by Mr. Lathrop that there existed at Salem during the early part of Hawthorne's life "a strong circle of wealthy families," which "maintained rigorously the distinctions of class," and whose "entertainments were splendid, their manners magnificent." This is a rather pictorial way of saying that there were a number of people in the place—the commercial and professional aristocracy, as it were—who lived in high comfort and respectability, and who, in their small provincial way, doubtless had pretensions to be exclusive. Into this delectable company Mr. Lathrop intimates that his hero was free to penetrate. It is easy to believe it, and it would be difficult to perceive why the privilege should have been denied to a young man of genius and culture, who was very good-looking (Hawthorne must have been in those days, judging by his appearance later in life, a strikingly handsome fellow), and whose American pedigree was virtually as long as the longest they could show. But in fact Hawthorne appears to have ignored the good society of his native place almost completely; no echo of its conversation is to be found in his tales or his journals. Such an echo would possibly not have been especially melodious, and if we regret the shyness and stiffness, the reserve, the timidity, the suspicion, or whatever it was, that kept him from knowing what there was to be known, it is not because we have any very definite assurance that his gains would have been great. Still, since a beautiful writer was growing up in Salem, it is a pity that he should not have given himself a chance to commemorate some of the types that flourished in the richest soil of the place. Like almost all people who possess in a strong degree the storytelling faculty, Hawthorne had a democratic strain in his composition and a relish for the commoner stuff of human nature. Thoroughly American in all ways, he was in none more so than in the vagueness of his sense of social distinctions and his readiness to forget them if a moral or intellectual sensation were to be gained by it. He liked to fraternize with plain people, to take them on their own terms, and put himself if possible into their shoes. His *Note-Books,* and even his tales, are full of evidence of this easy and natural feeling about all his unconventional fellow-mortals—this imaginative interest and contemplative curiosity—and it sometimes takes the most charming and graceful forms. Commingled as it is with his own subtlety and delicacy, his complete exemption from vulgarity, it is one of the points in his character which his reader comes most to appreciate—that reader I mean for whom he is not, as for some few, a dusky and malarious genius.

But even if he had had, personally, as many pretensions as he had few, he must in the nature of things have been more or less of a consenting democrat, for democracy was the very keystone of the simple social structure in which he played his part. The air of his journals and his tales alike is full of the genuine democratic feeling. This feeling has by no means passed out of New England life; it still flourishes in perfection in the great stock of the people, especially in rural communities; but it is probable that at the present hour a writer of Hawthorne's general fastidiousness would not express it quite so artlessly. "A shrewd gentlewoman, who kept a tavern in the town," he says, in *Chippings with a Chisel,* "was anxious to obtain two or three gravestones for the deceased members of her family, and to pay for these solemn commodities by taking the sculptor to board." This image of a gentlewoman keeping a tavern and looking out for boarders seems, from the point of view to which I allude, not at all incongruous. It will be observed that the lady in question was shrewd; it was probable that she was substantially educated, and of reputable life, and it is certain that she was energetic. These qualities would make it natural to Hawthorne to speak of her as a gentlewoman; the natural tendency in societies where the sense of equality prevails being to take for granted the high level rather than the low. Perhaps the most striking example of the democratic sentiment in all our author's tales, however, is the figure of Uncle Venner, in *The House of the Seven Gables.* Uncle Venner is a poor old man in a brimless hat and patched trousers, who picks up a precarious subsistence by rendering, for a compensation, in the houses and gardens of the good people of Salem, those services that are known in New England as "chores." He carries parcels, splits firewood, digs potatoes, collects refuse for the maintenance of his pigs, and looks forward with philosophic equanimity to the time when he shall end his days in the almshouse. But in spite of the very modest place that he occupies in the social scale, he is received on a footing of familiarity in the household of the far-descended Miss Pyncheon; and when this ancient lady and her companions take the air in the garden of a summer evening, he steps into the estimable circle and mingles the smoke of his pipe with their refined conversation. This obviously is rather imaginative—Uncle Venner is a creation with a purpose. He is an original, a natural moralist, a philosopher; and Hawthorne, who knew perfectly what he was about in introducing him—Hawthorne always knew perfectly what he was about—wished to give in his person an example of humorous resignation and of a life reduced to the simplest and homeliest elements, as opposed to the fantastic pretensions of the antiquated heroine of the story. He wished to strike a certain exclusively human and personal note. He knew that for this purpose he was taking a license; but the point is that he felt he was not indulging in any extravagant violation of reality. Giving in a letter, about 1830, an account of a little journey he was making in Connecticut, he says, of the end of a seventeen miles' stage, that "in the evening, however, I went to a Bible class with a very polite and agreeable gentleman, whom I afterwards discovered to be a strolling tailor of very questionable habits."

Hawthorne appears on various occasions to have absented himself from Salem, and to have wandered somewhat through the New England States. But the only one of these episodes of which there is a considerable account in the *Note-Books* is a visit that he paid in the summer of 1837 to his old college-mate, Horatio Bridge, who was living upon his father's property in Maine, in company with an eccentric young Frenchman, a teacher of his native tongue, who was looking for pupils among the northern forests. I have said that there was less psychology in Hawthorne's journals than might have been looked for; but there is nevertheless a certain amount of it, and nowhere more than in a number of pages relating to this remarkable "Monsieur S." (Hawthorne, intimate as he apparently became with him, always calls him "Monsieur," just as throughout all his diaries he invariably speaks of all his friends, even the most familiar, as "Mr." He confers the prefix upon the unconventional Thoreau, his fellow-woodsman at Concord, and upon the emancipated brethren at Brook Farm.) These pages are completely occupied with Monsieur S., who was evidently a man of character, with the full complement of his national vivacity. There is an elaborate effort to analyze the poor young Frenchman's disposition, something conscientious and painstaking, respectful, explicit, almost solemn. These passages are very curious as a reminder of the absence of the offhand element in the manner in which many Americans, and many New Englanders especially, make up their minds about people whom they meet. This, in turn, is a reminder of something that may be called the importance of the individual in the American world, which is a result of the newness and youthfulness of society and of the absence of keen competition. The individual counts for more, as it were, and, thanks to the absence of a variety of social types and of settled heads under which he may be easily and conveniently pigeonholed, he is to a certain extent a wonder and a mystery. An Englishman, a Frenchman —a Frenchman above all—judges quickly, easily, from his own social standpoint, and makes an end of it. He has not that rather chilly and isolated sense of moral responsibility which is apt to visit a New Englander in such processes; and he has the advantage that his standards are fixed by the general consent of the society in which he lives. A Frenchman, in this respect, is particularly happy and comfortable, happy and comfortable to a degree which I think is hardly to be overestimated; his standards being the most definite in the world, the most easily and promptly appealed to, and the most identical with what happens to be the practice of the French genius itself. The Englishman is not quite so well off, but he is better off than his poor interrogative and tentative cousin beyond the seas. He is blessed with a healthy mistrust of analysis, and hairsplitting is the occupation he most despises. There is always a little of the Dr. Johnson in him, and Dr. Johnson would have had woefully little patience with that tendency to weigh moonbeams which in Hawthorne was almost as much a quality of race as of genius; albeit that Hawthorne has paid to Boswell's hero (in the chapter on "Lichfield and Uttoxeter," in his volume on England) a tribute of the finest appreciation. American intellectual standards are vague, and Hawthorne's countrymen are apt to hold the scales with a rather uncertain hand and a somewhat agitated conscience.

9

Paul Elmer More: HAWTHORNE:
LOOKING BEFORE AND AFTER [1904]

Nathaniel Hawthorne was born just one hundred years ago, and, by a happy coincidence, the one artist who worked in materials thoroughly American and who is worthy to take a place among the great craftsmen of the world celebrates his nativity on the birthday of the nation.● By something more than a mere coincidence he lived and wrote at the only period in the history of the country which could have fostered worthily his peculiar genius; he came just when the moral ideas of New England were passing from the conscience to the imagination and just before the slow, withering process of decay set in. As I read his novels and tales today, with the thought of this centenary in my mind, the inevitable comparison arises with what preceded and what exists now; he stands as a connecting link be-

● *On the Fourth of July, 1904, the centenary of Hawthorne's birth was celebrated at Salem, Mass., at Bowdoin College and elsewhere. I was asked to write something in commemoration of the season for the* Independent, *and it seemed appropriate to consider Hawthorne's work historically, as the central point of a long development in New England literature.*

tween old Cotton Mather and—*magna cum parvis*—Mary Wilkins Freeman, and only by looking thus before and after can one get a clear idea of his work.

It seldom happens, in fact, that the history of a country shows so logical a development as that represented by these three names. To look backward, almost all of Hawthorne may be found in germ in the group of ecclesiastical writers among whom Cotton Mather rises pre-eminent, and he in turn is but a spokesman of that half-civilisation which migrated across the Atlantic under the pressure of the Laudian persecutions. I say half-civilisation, for the beginnings of New England took place when the mother country was split, as no people in the world ever before was divided, not by sectional but by moral differences into two hostile parties; nor do we always remember how largely the brilliant flowering and quick decay of New England depend on this incompleteness of her origins. Especially is this true in literature. Read through the critical essays that were written in the Elizabethan and Jacobean ages and you will be struck by the fact that the most serious debate was whether poetry had any right to exist at all. That discussion, of course, is as old as Plato and was taken up by the Italians of the Renaissance as part of their classical inheritance. But in England the question was not academic, but vital; it came to the actual test of battle. As early as 1579, in the very first bloom of that "perpetual spring of ever-growing invention," Stephen Gosson dedicated to Sir Philip Sidney his *School of Abuse,* which he aptly describes as "an invective against poets, pipers, players, jesters, and such-like caterpillars of a Commonwealth." "The fathers of lies, pipes of vanity, and schools of abuse," to use another of the crabbed Gosson's phrases, remained snugly in the mother country, along with those who thought it possible to worship God with the homage of the imagination, who made of religion, in fact, a fine sense of decorum in the ordering of the world. The wonder might seem to be that any literature at all ever sprang from the half-civilisation that came to New England, or that any sense of art found root among a people who contemned the imagination as evil and restricted the outpouring of emotion to the needs of a fervid but barren worship. The root was indeed long in coming to flower, yet there are passages in the *Magnalia* of Cotton Mather both magnificent in themselves and indispensable for a right understanding of what was to follow. There is, for example, that famous account of the death of John Cotton, worthy of repeated quotation:

> After this in that *study,* which had been *perfumed* with many such *days* before, he now spent a *day* in secret *humiliations* and *supplications* before the Lord; seeking the special assistances of the Holy Spirit, for the

great work of dying, that was now before him. What glorious *transactions* might one have heard passing between the Lord Jesus Christ, and an excellent servant of his, now coming unto him, if he could have had an *hearing place* behind the *hangings* of the chamber, in such a day! But having finished the duties of the day, he took his leave of his beloved *study,* saying to his consort, *I shall go into that room no more!*

That is the positive side of the ideal, and it is a dull heart today that can read this story of rapt holiness without a thrill of wonder and admiration. But the negative side is close at hand. The same annalist records of another of his family, Nathaniel Mather, a little incident that shows how inveterate was the suppression of the easy enjoyments and emotions of life. The quotation is from Nathaniel's diary:

When very *young* I went astray from God, and my mind was altogether taken with *vanities* and follies; such as the remembrance of them doth greatly abase my soul within me. Of the manifold sins which then I was guilty of, none so sticks upon me, as that being very young, I was *whittling on the Sabbath-day;* and for fear of being seen, I did it behind the door. A great reproach of God! a specimen of that *atheism* that I brought into the world with me!

One may be inclined to smile, perhaps, at this early intrusion into sacred literature of the Yankee's proverbial trick of whittling, but he will be more apt to marvel at the austerity of a discipline which could associate such a childish escapade with lifelong remorse. It is not strange that melancholy hovered over that chosen land. To quote from the *Magnalia* once again:

There are many men, who in the very constitution of their *bodies,* do afford a *bed,* wherein busy and bloody *devils,* have a sort of lodging provided for them. . . . 'Tis well if *self-murder* be not the sad end, into which these hurried people are thus precipitated. *New England,* a country where *splenetic* maladies are prevailing and pernicious, perhaps above any other, hath afforded numberless instances, of even *pious people,* who have contracted those *melancholy indispositions,* which have unhinged them from all service or comfort; yea not a few persons have been hurried thereby to lay *violent hands* upon themselves at the last. These are among the *unsearchable judgments* of God!

It is not fanciful, I think, to find in these three passages from the greatest of the early New England divines the ideas that were in due time to blossom into a true and peculiar literature. That isolation from the world and absorption in an ideal that signalised the death of John Cotton were to leave an echo in many lives through the following years. Nor did the inability to surrender to the common expansive emotions of human nature and the dark brooding on damnation utterly die out when the real cause ceased to act. They changed, but did not pass away. When, with the coming of the nineteenth century, the fierce democracy of those Northern States asserted itself against priestly control and at the same time shook off the bondage of orthodoxy; it only moved the burden from one shoulder to the other, and the inner tyranny of conscience became as exacting as the authority of the Church had been. But this shifting of the center of authority from without to within was at least fruitful in one important respect: it brought about that further transition from the conscience to the imagination which made possible the only serious literature this country has yet produced. In that shift from the conscience to the imagination lies the very source of Hawthorne's art. The awful voice of the old faith still reverberates in his stories of New England life and gives them their depth of consciousness; the dissolution of the commands of a sectarian conscience into the forms of a subtle symbolism lifts them from provincial importance merely to the sphere of universal art.

Nor is it at all difficult to follow the religion of the seventeenth into the art of the nineteenth century. In an earlier essay on *The Solitude of Nathaniel Hawthorne* I pointed out—what must be plain to every reader of that author—the central significance of his *Ethan Brand* in the circle of his works. So manifestly do the doctrines of Cotton Mather stalk through that tale under the transparent mask of fiction that it might almost seem as if Hawthorne had taken the passages just quoted from the *Magnalia* as a text for his fancy. For the first quotation, in place of the rigid theologian "perfuming" the bleak atmosphere of his study with meditations on the great work of dying orthodoxly, we have Ethan Brand, the lime-burner, dwelling in the fragrant solitude of the mountains, watching his kiln through the long revolutions of the sun and the stars, perplexing his mind with no problem of predestination and free-will, but with the meaning of life itself, with its tangle of motives and restraining intelligence. For the second quotation, in place of remorse over one act of surrender to impulse against the arbitrary dictates of religion, we have a strange reversal of Puritan faith through the lens of the imagination. Ethan Brand returns to his long-abandoned lime-kiln after wandering over the world, bringing with him the sense that he has sought and found at last in his own heart the Unpardonable Sin, the sin of banishing from the breast all those natural, spontaneous emotions in the pursuit of an idea. He bears the mark, not of an artificial atheism, like that which abased the soul of the young divine, but of that ananthropism (if I may use the word) which was the real sin of

New England, symbolized by the strange nature of his successful search. "He had lost his hold of the magnetic chain of humanity. He was no longer a brother-man, opening the chambers or the dungeons of our common nature by the key of holy sympathy, which gave him a right to share in all its secrets; he was now a cold observer, looking on mankind as the subject of his experiment." There lies the tragedy not of Ethan Brand alone, but of the later New England. The dogmas of faith had passed away and left this loneliness of an unmeaning idealism; the enthusiasm which had trampled on the kindly emotions of the day has succumbed, and the contempt of the human heart has given place to this intolerable loneliness.

And last of all there is the "splenetic malady," the melancholy that pursues this thwarting of nature and drives the wanderer to lay violent hands on himself. The burning of Ethan Brand in the lime-kiln, within the circle of whose crimson light he had pondered the Unpardonable Sin, is not, in the sense of Cotton Mather, one of the unsearchable judgments of God, but a cunningly devised symbol of literary art.

This is the second act of the New England drama, and the third proceeds from it as naturally as the second proceeded from the first. From the religious intolerance of Cotton Mather to the imaginative isolation of Hawthorne and from that to the nervous impotence of Mrs. Freeman's men and wmen, is a regular progress. The great preacher sought to suppress all worldly emotions; the artist made of the solitude which follows this suppression one of the tragic symbols of human destiny; the living novelist portrays a people in whom some native spring of action has been dried up, and who suffer in a dumb, unreasoning inability to express any outreaching passion of the heart or to surrender to any common impulse of the body. It is true, of course, that Mrs. Freeman describes only a single phase of New England character, just as Hawthorne did before her; but the very genealogy of her genius shows that she has laid hold of an essential trait of that character, and, indeed, it needs but little acquaintance with the stagnant towns of coast and mountains to have met more than one of the people of her books actual in the flesh. Her stories are not tragic in the ordinary sense of the word; they have no universal meaning and contain no problem of the struggle between human desires and the human will, or between the will and the burden of circumstances. They are, as it were, the echo of a tragedy long ago enacted; they touch the heart with the faint pathos of flowers pressed and withered in a book, which, found by chance, awaken the vague recollection of outlived emotions. They are very beautiful in their own way, but they are thoroughly provincial, just as the treatises of Cotton Mather were provincial; they have passed from the imagination to the nerves.

Already in Hawthorne we find the beginnings of this strangely repressed life. Hepzibah Pyncheon, struggling in an agony of shame and impotence to submit to the rude contact of the world, is the true parent of all those stiffened, lonely women that haunt the scenes of Mrs. Freeman's little stage. Only there is this signal difference: poor, blighted Hepzibah is part of a great drama of the conscience which in its brooding over the curse of ancestral sin can only be compared with the Atë of the Æschylean theatre. All the characters that move within the shadow of that *House of the Seven Gables* are involved in one tragic idea assimilated by the author's imagination from the religious inheritance of the society about him—the idea that pride, whether worldly or unworldly, works out its penalty in the separation of the possessor from the common heart of humanity. But in Mrs. Freeman's tales this moral has utterly vanished; they have no significance beyond the pathos of the lonely desolation depicted. Her first book, *A Humble Romance,* is made up of these frustrate lives, which are withheld by some incomprehensible paralysis of the heart from accepting the ordinary joys of humanity, and her latest book, *The Givers,* appeals to our sympathy by the same shadow of a foregone tragedy.

Very characteristic in the first book is the story of the *Two Old Lovers.* There was nothing to keep them apart, none of the well-used obstacles of romance in the shape of poverty or tyrannous parents or religious differences or an existing alliance—nothing save the ingrown inability of the man to yield to the simple call of his own bosom. For many years he visits the girl and, as time passes, the aged woman, as an accepted but curiously undemonstrative lover. There is, to me at least, a pathos like the nightly memory of tears in the watchfulness of the waiting woman over her diffident wooer:

She saw him growing an old man, and the lonely, uncared-for life that he led filled her heart with tender pity and sorrow for him. She did not confine her kind offices to the Saturday baking. Every week his little house was tidied and set to rights, and his mending looked after. Once, on a Sunday night, when she spied a rip in his coat, that had grown long from the want of womanly fingers constantly at hand, she had a good cry after he had left and she had gone to her room. There was something more pitiful to her, something that touched her heart more deeply, in that rip in her lover's Sunday coat, than in all her long years of waiting. As the years went on, it was sometimes with a sad heart that Maria stood and watched the poor lonely old figure moving slower than ever down the street to his lonely home; but the heart was sad for him always, and never for herself.

Only in the end, when he lies dying in his solitary house and she is summoned to his bedside, does the approach of the great silence of death unlock the dumbness of his breast:

> He looked up at her with a strange wonder in his glazing eyes. "Maria" —a thin, husky voice, that was more like a wind through dry cornstalks, said—"Maria, I'm dyin', an'—I allers meant to—have asked you—to—marry me."

Is it fanciful to say that this story has the shadowy pathos of emotions long ago fought against and overcome? The tragedy of New England came when Hawthorne wrought the self-denial of the ancient religion into a symbol of man's universal isolation, when out of the deliberate contemning of common affections he created the search for the Unpardonable Sin. In the pages of Mrs. Freeman we hear only an echo, we revive a fading memory, of that somber tragedy. *Ethan Brand* was a problem of the will, a question of morality; the tale of the *Two Old Lovers* is a sad picture of palsied nerves.

The latest volume of Mrs. Freeman's sketches treats the same theme, with this difference, however, that here it is the woman who abandons her lover for many years, returning to him only when both are grown old and past the age of spontaneous pleasures. There is perhaps some softening of tone, a kindlier feeling that into this strange desolation of the heart some consolation of the spirit may descend with chastened joy. Hardly in the earlier books, I think, will one find any picture of the possible mellowing effect of solitude comparable to this description of the waiting lover:

> He was a happy man, in spite of the unfulfilled natural depths of his life. His great sweetness of nature had made even of the legitimate hunger of humanity a blessing for the promoting of spiritual growth. It had fostered within him that grand acquiescence which is the essence of perfect freedom.

But beautiful as this *grand acquiescence* may be, it is not in that direction lies the real freedom of New England life or literature. Rather shall the deliverance come in the way hinted at in that other phrase, the *hunger of humanity*. The whole progress from Cotton Mather to Mrs. Freeman was determined by the original attempt to stamp out that legitimate hunger for the sake of an all-absorbing pride of the spirit. And now, when the spirit, after having been victorious in the long warfare, has itself starved away and left the barrenness of a dreary stagnation, the natural reversal may well be looked for, and we may expect the hunger of humanity to grow up out of the waste, untempered by spiritual ideals. Already in the New England of Hawthorne, in the exaggerated sentimentalism of the abolitionists and a thousand other reforming sects, this movement had begun. Hawthorne himself, despite his humorous insight and his aloofness from the currents of life about him, did not wholly escape its influence. Through the dark pages of *The House of Seven Gables* moves the hopeful figure of young Holgrave, the daguerreotypist. To him, says Hawthorne, thinking no doubt of the burden that weighed on his own imagination, it seemed "that in this age, more than ever before, the moss-grown and rotten Past is to be torn down, and lifeless institutions to be thrust out of the way, and their dead corpses buried, and everything to begin anew." There is a world of significance in the analysis which follows of Holgrave's restless and ardent nature, of his generous impulses, that might solidify him into the champion of some practical cause. He is the type of a whole race of men who were to take revenge on the despotism of the spirit by casting it out altogether for the idealised demands of the hunger of humanity.

But what was foreshadowed in Hawthorne becomes the one dominant human note of Mrs. Freeman's stories, heard through the desert silence that otherwise encompasses her characters. This vision of a growing humanitarianism that shall awaken new motives for healthy, active life and feed the hunger of the heart is the real theme of the best of her novels, *Jerome*. There is a scene in that book where the hero, beaten and marred by hard circumstance, suddenly gives vent in his awkward, unschooled manner to the late-born recalcitrance against the tyranny of Providence:

> What was it to the moon and all those shining swarms of stars, and that far star-dust in the Milky Way, whether he, Jerome Edwards, had shoes to close or not? Whether he and his mother starved or not, they would shine just the same. . . . He was maddened at the sting and despite of his own littleness in the face of that greatness. Suddenly a wild impulse of rebellion that was almost blasphemy seized him. He clinched a puny fist at a great star. "Wish I could make you stop shinin'," he cried out, in a loud, fierce voice; "wish I could do somethin'!"

And then, later, comes the companion scene, again under the cold eyes of the heavens, when the final determination takes shape before him and he sees at last the work which the world holds for him:

> A great passion of love and sympathy for the needy and oppressed of his kind, and an ardent defense of them, came upon Jerome Edwards, poor young shoemaker, going home with his sack of meal over his shoulder. Like a bird, which in the spring views every little straw and twig as toward his nest and purpose of love, Jerome would henceforth regard

all powers and instrumentalities that came in his way only in their bearing upon his great end of life.

We have followed the development of that half-civilization which molded New England from the religious enthusiasm of Cotton Mather, through the tragic art of Hawthorne, down to the pathetic paralysis portrayed in these stories of a living writer. We have seen a morbid spirituality, spurning the common nourishment of mankind, slowly starve itself into impotence. Now, as the hunger of humanity begins to assert itself unhampered by any vision beyond its own importunate needs, are we to behold a new ideal create in turn another half-civilization, blindly materialistic as its predecessor was harshly spiritual? That question may not be lightly answered. Only it is clear that, for the present, the way of growth for the literature of New England lies through the opening of this door of strictly human sympathies.

10

V. S. Pritchett: THE POE CENTENARY [1949]

A hundred years after his death what are we to make of Poe? He is a writer into whom large, inexact things may be read and from whom many things important to literature have been taken; a second-class writer, yet a fertilizing exclaimer. The paradox is that his genius was merely probable and narrow and yet his influence was wide. Read those poems again which Baudelaire compared to crystals; it is a strange comparison for verses so slack in their simplicity, so mechanical in their devices. And yet we are haunted by overtones of an exceptional experience. It is no ordinary tomb on which Poe weeps; there is more than loss in those tears. There is guilt and dismay. Afterwards, the mourner will be haunted not by the dead but by himself. When we turn to stories like "The Pit and the Pendulum," "The Murders of the Rue Morgue," "Ligeia," or "The Fall of the House of Usher," the accent is self-assured, but we are not, after two wars, bounded or interested by the rhetoric of suffering and sadism. D. H. Lawrence found the material conventional, meretricious and vulgar. The voice of incantation appears to be disguising the experience, is slurred and constructs the conventional nightmare of the drug addict or the facile alcoholic:

Not hear it;—yes, I hear it, and have heard it. Long—long—long— many minutes, many hours, many days, I have heard it—yet I dared not

—oh, pity me, miserable wretch that I am!—I dared not, *dared* not speak. *We have put her living in the tomb!* Said I not that my senses were acute? I *now* tell you that I heard her first feeble movements in the hollow coffin. I heard them—many, many days ago—and yet I dared not—*I dared not speak!* And now—tonight—Ethelred—ha! ha!—the breaking of the hermit's door, and the death cry of the dragon, and the clangour of the shield!—say, rather the rending of her coffin, and the grating of the iron hinges of her prison, and her struggles within the coppered archway of the vault.

Efficient, silly and yet its harangue can overpower. It is theatrical and yet not pure theater. If we set aside the skill of narration—and we ought not really to do so because part of Poe's gift to literature is his teaching and example of the conscious artist—there is more than the expert tale of mystery or horror; there is the sustained enacting in conditions amounting to claustrophobia, of a universal human pain. The redeeming thing is Poe's gift of generalizing morbid experience.

Poe's parents (it is well known) were actors; and one is obliged to see him as an actor-writer. Perhaps his technical genius in creating new literary forms came from the application of the actor's temperament to a medium that was alien to it. He comes on to the stage, among his grotesque properties—the pit of the Inquisitor, the rotting ancestral mansion, the luxurious Disraelian palace or the jeweled valley—and with the first oratorical words and the first hypnotic gesture, he has created an atmosphere. An atmosphere, the hostile must say, that one could cut with a knife. We suspect the old trouper and there is no doubt that his prose comes out of the catalogue; he goes from one cliché of Romance to the next; the names of his characters, the Lady Madeleine, Ligeia, Berenice, Lenore, are shamelessly stagy; and like the notorious "Nevermore," are made for the parodist. But what grips the reader is that Poe is evidently not acting an *alien* part; the story is *his* story, this is his pain, enlarged and generalized as poetry is, and it can suck us into its whirlpool just as, irresistibly, the death ship of "The MS. Found in a Bottle" was drawn down into the ocean. Suffering and guilt are his subjects: to magnify is his method.

There is a point at which the magnifying glass makes the object too large, when the close-up loses nature; and that is the point of vulgarity in Poe. But I do not believe there is a story in this assiduously inventive writer which is not taken from his own state. He was the first writer of any importance in English to take, possibly from Hoffmann and Vidocq, the notion of the tale of detection. He must have been one of the first writers of scientific romance. These are remarkable inventions. It is not merely by lucky chance that he saw the interest of these forms of writing, for both his extraordinary flair for literary genre and the peculiaity of his temperament predisposed him to them. They seem, when we speculate upon it, to be the natural interest of his divided nature and the fruit of personal guilt which has been turned to literary advantage. We can see the clever mind of the expert neurotic observing its own sensibility and its terrifying private fantasies. The mysterious, he sees, can be chemically split; explanation can be, he perceives, as exciting, sensationally, as the mysterious thing. In the tales of the dying woman prematurely buried, in the story of Ligeia rising from the dead to poison and annihilate her rival, we can see Poe dreading the death of his Virginia, wishing for it and willingly incurring remorse and punishment. One understands what such themes could suggest to Baudelaire and Dostoevsky; moreover, the writings reflect a life that seems itself to be a direct expression of Poe's own theory of "the unity of effect." His character is, in a sense, to be read at a sitting; it was constructed, we feel, from the end first; it was a suicide, the deliberate seeking of a preconceived fate. For Poe is steeped in pride; allowing for D. H. Lawrence's manias, his criticism that Poe blasphemed against the Holy Ghost within him is a true one.

Poe the alcoholic, Poe the incestuous, Poe the unconscious homosexual, Poe the Irishman, the Southerner, the derelict, Poe isolated in American life and ruined by the *odeur de magazine*—these versions are familiar. They have their share of truth. In a quietly provocative introduction to *The Centenary Poe,* Mr. Montagu Slater reminds us of the part played by simple financial misery in Poe's life. He got £2 for "The Raven." It seems doubtful whether writing for magazines ruined him: he was a magazine man. He was a brilliant lecturer. He was not a physical weakling: he had been a regimental sergeant major and a fine swimmer. Mr. Slater goes on to a vague argument of the kind that might be useful if it could be fully documented—and I do not see how it can be—that art for art's sake began with Poe, and has remained dominant in Western literature ever since. He links the doctrine with solipsism and with Poe's own doctrine, expressed in characteristic tones of incantation in "Eureka": that the soul is a particle of God that must return, annihilated, into His Oneness. Poe's famous proposal of the short poem, that long poems are merely short ones connected by prose, that works of art must be grasped at a sitting and that there must be unity of effect, is made to support Mr. Slater's argument. But to say that intensity and the love of beauty above all else have any special connection with art for art's sake is to force argument. Poe's doctrine of the instantaneous has, indeed, been realized, as Mr. Slater says, in many important forms of modern art; but that is far from meaning that copious works are more diverse, or that intense works are incapable of deep humanity. The personal voice and experience of Poe underlie his artificialities, and we now understand that what used to be called morbid experience is universal and has a direct bearing on spiritual life.

One great difference in kind between Poe and Sartre, Camus and Graham Greene, whom Mr. Slater regards as the latest if not the last of Poe's aesthetic line, is one of energy. In the sense that he carries within him the feeling of power which was felt in the early nineteenth century, Poe is electric: a positive neurotic, a willful madman, an aggressive suicide. His terrors, his pains, his guilt, his punishment, his melancholy itself, are represented as inflations and energies of the soul. They are not presented as maladies to be cured and he does not wish to lose them. He feels, romantically, all the larger and more powerful because of them as if they were a gift and a privilege. The Romantics felt all the greater for their cult of death and pain, whereas psychology has taught us to regard our sickness as multilation or a misleading of our powers. Poe is perfectly able to live his derelict and isolated life regardless of the community. A loquacious and throbbing pride enables him to do so; his sorrow runs a pipeline to the eternal. The later writers lack this aggressiveness. Pain is inflicted upon them. They are ciphers of passivity—as, indeed, the ordinary man is among the political horrors and farces, the double-faced institutions of our time, where persecutors and persecuted change places with the nullity of papers in a file. Though they attempt to dignify themselves with the belief that they are drifting to annihilation in the One, the Nothing, the Historical, or the Nevermore, they bob up and down on their way over Niagara with the feebleness of corks. Long ago they lost their bottles. They do not die: they blackout. Destruction is taken out of their own hands. They just run into it absurdly. Poe on the contrary did not believe life was a fraud; he believed it was an orchestrated tragedy; he had the Romantic afflatus. Loss and death were inevitable; pain was an action felt or done. It is pure speculation but, if he could be reborn, one imagines him writing his stories not about the victims of the Inquisition, but about the great repressed subject of our day: the morbid psychology of the Inquisitor and torturer and their guilt; simply because that is now the dominant, positive and energetic aspect of contemporary pain. The Inquisitor has had his romantic wish for power: what has *he* paid for it?

It is usually said that Poe is an un-American and cosmopolitan writer, and Baudelaire declared that America was Poe's prison. But

Poe was a natural prisoner. It seems to me he was very American and especially so of his time; intellectually aggressive and provincial, formed by journalism, a practical and exacting technician and critic —see his analyses of novels by Dickens and Hawthorne—as cranky in his way as Thoreau, Emerson and Hawthorne, for example, of rather wild personal independence in opinion. Above all, he is American in the capital hold that nostalgia has on his emotions. It is the melancholy, lonely dominant note in the feeling of American literature: from the Mark Twain of *Huckleberry Finn* to T. S. Eliot. It is indeed this feeling which encloses even the slack poems, that seem to us sentimental or merely pathetic; it is on a general and native longing, that he is able with all his power of rhetoric to play. The melody that runs through his writing, impure but sweeping and haunting, the loneliness of his incantations themselves seem to be designed to deploy that simple feeling; and the dream world which is not really a dream world, owes its effect to the fear and the longing it is meant to convey. We feel that a nation of lonely people is projecting his fantastic palaces or is considering his unlikely dungeons; for in a new and rapidly successful country, part of the human personality is a casualty, and in that injury is the desire that cannot be realized.

11

F. O. *Matthiessen:* POE'S INFLUENCE [1948]

Poe's final value may hardly be judged apart from the many traditions to which his work gave rise. French Symbolism, with its desire to attain the suggestiveness of music, began at the moment when Baudelaire recognized in Poe's logical formulas for a poem his own half-developed thoughts "combined to perfection." But Baudelaire was indebted to Poe for more than form. He took the title for his intimate journal from a phrase in *Marginalia,* "my heart laid bare," and attributed to Poe's reaffirmation of evil the recovery of human dignity from the shallowness of the optimistic reformers. Another note in *Marginalia,* "The orange ray of the spectrum and the buzz of the gnat . . . affect me with nearly similar sensations," led to Baudelaire's epoch-making sonnet, "Correspondences," and in turn to Rimbaud's further development of this same doctrine of the interpenetration of the senses. Rimbaud's masterpiece, *Le Bateau ivre,* also confirmed the degree to which Poe's image of man's destiny as a frail boat out of control on the flowing waters of life was to become a major symbol for the age. Meanwhile, Gautier and the Parnassian group had found in "The Philosophy of Composition" their conception that the form creates the idea. The relevance of all these complex developments to American poetry lies in the profound attraction that

T. S. Eliot and Wallace Stevens were to discover in Symbolism, and thence to bring Poe back to American art by way of France.

Poe's introspective heroes begat a long line of descendants. As Edmund Wilson demonstrated so brilliantly, the remote castle that Villiers de L'Isle-Adam's Axel inhabits was inherited from Roderick Usher; and when Huysmans voiced through his *Des Esseintes* the doctrines of decadence, almost every artificial detail of his shut-in paradise was borrowed from Poe's interiors, as was the disordered preoccupation with what Usher himself had called "a morbid acuteness of the senses." The furthest possible withdrawal of the hero from the responsibilities of a hostile world might seem to be that in Proust, and although nationalists in criticism now view with alarm any effect in America of such European influences, the feeling that the artist is at war with a business civilization was as much Hart Crane's as it was Poe's.

This may still seem to leave Poe remote from the main currents of American thought. And although Hawthorne admired the originality of his tales, and Lowell had been quick to recognize his double gift for imagination and analysis, the first generation of realists passed Poe by. Both Howells and Twain found his method as "mechanical" as Henry James did; and for that belated dedication of his tomb in 1875, Mallarmé wrote his great sonnet, but Whitman alone among important American writers attended—and Whitman judged Poe to belong finally "among the electric lights of imaginative literature, brilliant and dazzling, but with no heat." Yet his ultimate effect upon our most popular literature was enormous. As much as anyone ever invents a genre, Poe invented the detective story. He also inaugurated the vogue for the pseudoscientific romance and for that of adolescent adventure. Jules Verne, Stevenson, and Conan Doyle are equally in his debt. "The Gold Bug," "The Pit and the Pendulum," and "The Murders in the Rue Morgue" have now been read by millions oblivious of their author's aesthetic theories.

The notion has sometimes been advanced that the materialism of so many of Poe's interests, his fondness for inventions and hoaxes, and his special flair for journalism made him more "representative" than Emerson or Whitman of ordinary Americans. His more serious importance was noted by the Goncourt brothers, who declared in their journal for 1856 that here was "the literature of the twentieth century," an analytic literature that would be more given to what passes in the brain than in the heart. That distinction may be as brittle as some of Poe's own, but the intense investigation of the roots of Gothic horror in morbid states of mind has been part of American fiction from Brockden Brown and Poe through Ambrose Bierce and William Faulkner.

Poe wrote at a time when America was producing more real and alleged transcendental geniuses than maturely wrought poems or stories. In opposition to the romantic stress on the expression of personality, he insisted on the importance, not of the artist, but of the created work of art. He stands as one of the very few great innovators in American literature. Like Henry James and T. S. Eliot, he took his place, almost from the start, in international culture as an original creative force in contrast to the more superficial international vogue of Cooper and Irving.

12

Van Wyck Brooks: "OUR POETS" [1915]

It is a principle that shines impartially on the just and on the unjust that once you have a point of view all history will back you up. Everything no doubt depends upon evidence; and considering the case which has been outlined in the last chapter, an appeal to American literature, if literature really does record the spirit of a people, is an appeal that leads, I think, to evidence of a material sort.

Something, in American literature, has always been wanting— everyone, I think, feels that. Aside from the question of talent, there is not, excepting Walt Whitman, one American writer who comes home to a modern American with that deep, moving, shaking impact of personality for which one turns to the abiding poets and writers of the world. A certain density, weight, and richness, a certain poignancy, a "something far more deeply interfused," simply is not there.

Above all, the Americanism of our old writers appears to have had no faculty of development and adaptation. With the death of Emerson, Lowell, Holmes and their group something in the American mind really did come to an end. The generation which has gone by since then is a generation which has produced no indisputable leader of thought and letters, which has destroyed the coherence of the old American circle of ideas, and left us at the height of the second immigration among the chaotic raw materials of a perhaps altogether new attitude of mind.

It is, in fact, the plain, fresh, homely, impertinent, essentially innocent old America that has passed; and in its passing the allegory of Rip Van Winkle has been filled with a new meaning. Hendrik Hudson and his men, we see, have begun another game of bowls, and the reverberations are heard in many a summer thunderstorm; but they have been miraculously changed into Jews, Lithuanians, Magyars, and German socialists. Rip is that old innocent America which has fallen asleep and which hears and sees in a dream the movement of peoples, the thunder of alien wants. And when after twenty years he awakens again, stretches his cold rheumatic limbs, and discovers the long white beard, he will once more set out for home; but when he arrives will he be recognized?

What emotions pass through an hereditary American when he calls to mind the worthies who figured in that ubiquitous long paneled group of "Our Poets" which occupied once so prominent a place in so many domestic interiors? Our Poets were commonly six in number, kindly, gray-bearded, or otherwise grizzled old men. One recalls a prevailing six, with variations. Sometimes a venerable historian was included, a novelist or so, and even Bayard Taylor.

Nothing could make one feel so like a prodigal son as to look at the picture. So much for the first glance, the first quick impression after one has come home to it from the far wanderings of an ordinary profane existence. But more complicated emotions supervene. What a world within a world that picture summons up! Frankly, we feel in ourselves, we are no longer so fortunate as in those days. It could really have been said of us then, as it cannot now be said at all, that as a folk we had won a certain coherence, a certain sort of ripeness in the better part of ourselves, which was reflected in the coherence of our men of letters. Whittier, for example, was a common basis, and a very sweet and elevating basis, for a national programme of emotions the like of which no poet since his time has been able to compass. One recalls that fact, so full of meaning; and then, deep down, a forgotten world sweeps back over one, a world of memory, sentiment, and association, a world of influences the most benign— like a mournful autumn wind stirring in forsaken places. . . . But sooner or later the ordinary profane existence reasserts itself; and we have to put it to ourselves with equal frankness—has any one of these men, or any one of these influences, the power at bottom to make it any less profane? The most beautiful and benign sentiment in the world will not do so unless it has in it that which grips in some way at the root of personality. . . . Then it is we feel how inadequate, faded, and out of touch they are.

It is of no use to go off into a corner with American literature, as most of the historians have done—in a sulky, private sort of way, taking it for granted that if we give up world values we are entitled to our own little domestic rights and wrongs, criticism being out of place by the fireside. "But oh, wherever else I am accounted dull," wrote Cowper in one of his letters, "let me pass for a genius at Olney." This is the method of the old-fashioned camp in American criticism, just as the method of the contemporary camp is the method of depreciative comparison with better folk than our own.

The only fruitful approach is the personal approach, and to me at least Thoreau, Emerson, Poe, and Hawthorne are possessions forever. This does not alter the fact that if my soul were set on the accumulation of dollars not one of them would have the power to move me from it. And this I take to be a suggestive fact. Not one of them, not all of them, have had the power to move the soul of America from the accumulation of dollars; and when one has said this one has arrived at some sort of basis for literary criticism.

Plainly enough, during what has been called the classical period of American literature, the soul of America did not want to be moved from the accumulation of dollars; plainly enough the pioneering instinct of economic self-assertion was the law of the tribe. And if the New England writers were homogeneous with the American people as no other group, scarcely any other individual, has been since, it is equally plain that they themselves and all their works must have been accorded with the law of the tribe. The immense, vague cloud-canopy of idealism which hung over the American people during the nineteenth century was never permitted, in fact, to interfere with the practical conduct of life.

Never permitted, I say, though it is a more accurate explanation that, being essentially impersonal itself, the essence of this idealism lay in the very fact that it had and could have no connection with the practical conduct of life. The most successful and famous writers, Byrant and Longfellow, for example, promoted this idealism, being, so far as one can see, generally satisfied with the ordinary practices of society: they tacitly accepted the peculiar dualism that lies at the root of our national point of view. Emerson's really equivocal individualism on the one hand asserted the freedom and self-reliance of the spirit and on the other justified the unlimited private expediency of the business man. And as a suggestive corollary to all this, the two principal artists in American literature, Poe and Hawthorne, were out of touch with society as few other artists in the world had been before: to their contemporaries they seemed spectral and aloof, scarcely human, and it could easily be shown that the reaction upon their work of a world to them essentially unreal is equally marked.

Granting these facts, and granting the still more significant fact of the absence from our literature of that deep, moving, shaking impact of personality which would have brought it into more permanent touch with American life, I do not see how we can escape the general axiom: that a society whose end is impersonal and antisocial cannot produce an ideal reflex in literature which is personal and social, and, conversely, that the ideal reflex in literature by such a society will be unable to educate its own personal and social instincts. In effect, an examination of American literature will show, I think, that those of our writers who have possessed a vivid personal genius have been paralyzed by the want of a social background, while those who have possessed a vivid social genius have been equally unable to develop their own personalities.

II

And here at the outset a distinction must be drawn between what may be called the literature of necessity and absolute literature. It is perfectly plain that in one aspect literature is a simple cog in the machinery of life. The first generation of American writers were like prudent women who, having moved into a new house, energetically set to work laying down carpets, papering the walls, cutting and hanging the most appropriate window-curtains, and pruning the garden—making it, in short, a place of reasonable charm and contentment.

Than Washington Irving, for example, no one was ever more satisfied with things as they are; prosperity in others aroused in him the most benignant emotions, and there is a description by him of a smiling river farm with its fat hens and waddling pigs which rises to a sort of placid ecstasy—in recollection one confuses the pigs with little cherubim, and as to the farm itself one wonders why (or indeed whether) angels have not settled there.

The effect of this idyllic treatment is precisely that of the first warm blaze in a newly constructed hearth. It takes away the sense of chill; the room becomes at once cozy and cheerful, and we enjoy the prospect of spending an evening in it.

That is at least a principal element in the work of Irving, Cooper, Bryant, and Longfellow. When these men ceased writing, the towns, the woods, the wild flowers, even the bare and meager history of America were clothed with memories and associations. It was possible to feel them all, and even to muse upon them. The characters of Cooper lighted up a little fringe of the black uncut forest; they linked the wilderness with our own immemorial human world, just as the little figures Piranesi put in his engravings not only give the scale of his Roman ruins and relate them to the observer's eye but also arouse the sense of historical connections, the sense of pathos and of man's destiny.

When they wrote of Europe their essential motive was the same as when they wrote of America. Irving's English essays at bottom, as he himself declares, were deliberately intended to place England and America on a basis of mutual good will—a motive, in the proper sense, political. Longfellow never forgot in Europe that he was on leave of absence, and that in gathering specimens he was to bear in mind the soil to which they were to be transplanted. There was nothing in heaven or earth he was not able to prune and fertilize into harmony with the New England temperature; and who will deny that he in turn altered that temperature, warmed and gladdened it— that he came back as a kind of gulf stream to our frostbitten civilization, which has been kindlier ever since?

III

But out of this essential motive of the first generation of American writers a second motive arises. They were moralists, they were shot through and through with all manner of baccalaureate ideals; and this fact opens them to a different sort of treatment. For this let Longfellow and Bryant suffice, for they are typical.

Longfellow is to poetry what the barrel organ is to music; approached critically he simply runs on, and there is an end to the matter. But nobody dreams of criticizing Longfellow from the point of view of "mere literature": the human head and the human heart alike revolt from that. His personal sanction is rightly a traditional one, and the important thing is to see him as a beautifully typical figure and to see just what he typifies.

To Longfellow the world was a German picture-book, never detaching itself from the softly colored pages. He was a man of one continuous mood: it was that of a flaxen-haired German student on his *wanderjahr* along the Rhine, under the autumn sun—a sort of expurgated German student—ambling among ruined castles and reddening vines, and summoning up a thousand bright remnants of an always musical past. His was an eminently Teutonic nature of the old school, a pale-blue melting nature; and white hair and grandchildren still found him with all the confused emotion, the charming sadness, the indefinite high proposals of seventeen;—perhaps it was because they had never been opposed, never put to the test in that so innocently successful existence of his, that they persisted without one touch of disillusion, one moment of chagrin.

But frankly what preparation is a life like this for the poet whose work it is to revivify a people? The most telling thing I know about Longfellow is that, having remarked that "Carlyle was one of those men who sacrifice their happiness to their work," he himself was well content in later life to surrender the greater part of his time and energies to writing autographs and entertaining children. Here certainly the personal sanction oversteps the mark, just as it does in the case of indulgent politicians who exhibit their gratitude and warmheartedness by feathering the nests of all their friends and cousins. Though Longfellow had an unerring eye for the "practical application" that lurks in every shred of romance, totally unable to elude the agile moralist, the value of his moral promptings is just in proportion to the pressure behind them—and where was the pressure? His morals and ideals were, in fact, simply a part of the pretty picturebook, just as they are at seventeen: if they had not been so they would never have been laid on the shelf.

But the "practical application" cannot be dismissed in this way; and if the personal sanction is disarming in relation to Longfellow, the case is otherwise with Bryant, a virile, hardheaded man, whose memory can afford many a blow. To Bryant the moral ending was no half absent-minded flourish of the color brush—it was a tough Puritan reality; and Bryant's use of the moral ending is emblematic not merely, as in Longfellow's case, of the vacuity and impermanence of so much American idealism, but also of the corollary of these—the failure of Americans in general to develop and express their personality in and through their work.

Bluntly, the use of a moral ending means that the poet is unwilling to leave his effect to the emotion conveyed in the poem itself; he must needs intellectualize this emotion at the close, and show you that this emotion is only used, like cheese in a mousetrap, to entice the reader into a usually disagreeable fact, for which the whole exists. Now this procedure is full of meaning. For not the emotion, not the expression of personality, but the ulterior object is the essential issue in the mind of the poet: not life, but success, or salvation. And the same principle operates here, and renders the result equally barren, as in work which is done mainly for the ulterior object of making money, in religion which exists merely for the ulterior object of saving one's soul, in thought which exists merely for the ulterior object of proving something. The excellence and fruitfulness of anything consists in our loving and enjoying it, in our expressing our personality through it. Real poetry springs from the assumption that the spectacle is its own reward, that feeling, happy or unhappy, is final: it is concerned, as Shelley pointed out, not with effects and applications which are temporary, but with causes, which are permanent. The moral ending is simply a rigid and impersonal intellectualization of life, which is, consequently, out of touch with the motives that really determine men.

For this reason Bryant was never a personality; he was, to be exact, a somewhat eminent personage. After his eighteenth year he was miraculously changed, not into stone, but into wood—he was as bald, as plain, as immovable, so to say, as an old settee. He had no elasticity, no sense of play either in words, ideas, or emotions; two or three poetic forms sufficed him; even as a journalist he was abstract. One sees him during sixty years perambulating Broadway with that old blue cotton umbrella of his, the very picture of a spare old Puritan patriarch, with his big muscular joints, a hardy perennial. And all about him one sees that spry, flimsy New York of the forties and fifties and sixties—the New York of "Nothing to Wear" and N. P. Willis. It is these gulfs of contrast which let one into the secret of American humor.

Yes, this old man with his palsied gift, who had for two generations been pursued by glimpses of the grave but who had embalmed within him an incomparable vigor and who, past eighty, put Homer into English—this old man is himself Homeric (with a difference) amid that spawn of decadent Byronism which made up the so-called Knickerbocker school. New York has never possessed dignity—one loves the many-headed beast for a thousand other reasons than that; but it has achieved a sort of Napoleonic right to despise dignity, and it has come to possess its secrets. In the thirties and forties it possessed no secrets at all—it was the center of an ingenuous America which had only just learned to be worldly, which the lightest zephyr from London or Paris set fluttering, over which every ripple of fashion broke into a spray of tinsel.

IV

So much is necessary to give Poe what he badly needs, a naturalistic setting: Poe himself, who emerges from this New York of his time like a wreck at sea with its black spars etched against a sort of theatrical sunset. Ironical and sinister as he is, he is by no means "out of space, out of time," if by space we mean New York and by time the second quarter of the nineteenth century. The little imitation Byrons who swarmed about him wrote of haunted Gothic castles, Poe wrote "The House of Usher"; Bianca, Giordano, Ermengarde, Elfrida, Asthene, Zophiel were the human properties of their prose and verse, scarcely to be distinguished from the Madeleines and Eleanors, the Eulalies and Annabels, the Israfels and Al Aaraafs of Poe; they also lived in a world of moan and a world of moonlight; madness, irreparable farewells, dungeons, assignations, premature burials, hidden treasures, exotic musical instruments, prophetic night birds—these things were of the time and very particularly, since New York provided them with an additional unreality, of the place.

Poe took this bric-a-brac seriously—that is always a distinction and it is Poe's distinction. The tacit conventionalities of the Romantic epoch became in him objects of a fierce intellectual concentration. In the comfortable safety of good and abundant food, friendly talk, substantial occupation, his contemporaries amused themselves with specters, Oriental mysteries, hasheesh, and madness: Poe was the delirium which followed. He was a Byron without scope of action and without purging emotions.

Superficially at least he was not conscious of being out of his element. In those critical essays in which he is so accessible and so honest and has so many disagreeable things to say about his contemporaries it is never the false taste, never the epoch which displeases him. He likes *The Dying Rosebud's Lament* by Mrs. Fanny Osgood; what irritates him is bad grammar, bad rhymes, and plagiarism. Nor is there the least indication that he thought America provincial, or bourgeois, or depressing to a man of talent. That indeed is an element in the strength of all the American writers of the old school; an instinct of self-preservation kept them at home in spirit; so much of the missionary element was of the texture of what they had to say that a tinge of the cosmopolitan would have neutralized their best effects, would have rendered them personally, as it has certainly rendered Lowell, a little characterless, a little indistinct. But it is a rather disconcerting fact in relation to the theory that Poe is a kind of supersensual enigma, who might have lived with equal results in Babylon or Sioux City. At his second-best, in prose and verse, he is precisely at one, both in tone and execution, with his intellectual surroundings. At his best it is this outworn bric-a-brac which is transfigured, just as the suburban bibliolatry of England is transfigured in the drawings of Blake. The important thing is to consider what this bric-a-brac is transfigured into, and why, and what it means.

Since the days of the alchemists no one has produced more than Poe the effects of damnation, no one has been more conscious of being damned. In his pages the breath of life never stirs: crimes occur which do not reverberate in the human conscience, there is laughter which has no sound, there is weeping without tears, there is beauty without love, there is love without children, trees grow which bear no fruit, flowers which have no fragrance—it is a silent world, cold, blasted, moon-struck, sterile, a devil's heath. Only a sensation of intolerable remorse pervades it.

Poe is commonly called unreal; it is justly said of him that he never touches the general heart of man, that perhaps of all writers who have lived he has the least connection with human experience. Nothing is more sinister about Poe, for instance, than his tacit acceptance of common morals; you might even say that he is rigidly conventional, if you did not feel that he is conventional merely because the moral world no more exists for him than it exists for a black stone. If you could prove a vicious motive in him, as from certain points of view you can prove a vicious motive in Baudelaire, you might, even in that, establish some fusion between him and the common reason of humankind. Orchids are as much a part of the vegetable kingdom as potatoes, but Poe is an orchid made out of chemicals. Magic is always so; it has the sinister quality of a force operating outside nature, without any relation to human values.

No European can exist without a thousand subterranean relationships; but Americans can so exist, Americans do so exist. Edison, for example, resembles Poe as a purely inventive mathematical intellect, and with Edison, as with Poe, you feel that some electric fluid takes the place of blood; you feel that the greatest of inventors cannot be called a scientist at all, that his amazing powers over nature are not based in any philosophical grasp of the laws of nature, that he is in temperament a mechanic rather than a philosopher. His faculty is to that of Darwin, for example, what fish is to flesh—to the philosophical animal man he is more incomprehensible; and for all the beneficence of his faculty he is himself a kind of prodigious salamander. Poe is a mechanic of the same sort. He has discovered in literature the chemical secret of life. He has produced chemical men, chemical emotions, chemical landscapes; in "Eureka" he has produced even a chemical philosophy so much like real philosophy that until you try to feel it you will never guess it is the most sterile of illusions. For this reason the highly colored effects that light up his tales and his poems are lurid and metallic. The sinister greens and reds and yellows are not, you feel, the flames of honest wood and coal.

To explain all this is not enough to say that he had a spectral nature, that Emerson and Jonathan Edwards and Hawthorne had spectral natures, that theosophy and Christian Science suggest that this quality is a typical American quality. So much is probably true, but more is required; and to approach Poe is to approach those mysteriously fascinating thaumaturgic elements in nature which are responsible for most of the fraudulent science in the world. One treads warily on the outer edges of psychology, and I suppose it is not accurately known what sources of the mind were involved in medieval witchcraft, in alchemy, in the conception of Mephistopheles. But certainly to the Middle Ages the intelligence in and for itself was felt to be a maleficent force: Mephistopheles himself in the old legends is nothing other than pure intellect, irresponsible and operating independently of life. Necessarily therefore to him faith, love, and hope are illusions, and he is the negation of the soul. Above all, it is the secret of creating life for which in the medieval imagination souls were bartered to the devil: one obtained the power of competing with God at the price of a perpetual consciousness of one's own damnation. These are dark ways; but one emerges into the region of knowledge when one affirms that, by their mental twist, witches and alchemists were not convicted by society any more than they were convicted in themselves of having done the unpardonable and the irreparable. And certain it is that Poe experienced in his own imagination this power and this damnation. His haunted face, his driven life, the barren world which he has built and peopled, the horror of his accustomed mood, the inextinguishable obscure remorse that broods in him unite in this fact.

The power he still exerts is an hysterical rather than a literary power, and who can say what it signifies? But one thing seems true, with regard alike to witchcraft, alchemy, and Poe, that the mind can work healthily only when it is essentially in touch with the society of its own age. No matter into what unknown region it presses, it must have a point of relativity in the common reason of its time and place. Poe, having nothing in common with the world that produced him, constructed a little parallel world of his own, withered at the core, a silent comment. It is this that makes him so sterile and so inhuman; and he is himself, conversely, the most menacing indictment of a society which is not also an all-embracing organism.

V

Poe and Hawthorne, certainly, were much more of a common stock in temperament than the New York and New England of their time: the temperament which in Poe is at once vulgarized by vulgar circumstances and pressed up into the intellect is diffused in the character and work of Hawthorne; the harsher lights are neutralized, the familiar world reappears again—but is it the familiar world? Hawthorne's talent is like a phosphorescent pool; you touch it, you move your hand there and a thousand subdued elusive lights dance through it, but before you can fix your eye upon one it has retreated through the clear water, the still depths that in effect are so impenetrable.

No other talent is of so shining a purity as Hawthorne's—scarcely one other so light, so inevitable, so refined, so much a perfectly achieved intention. He models in mist as the Greeks modeled in marble; his beings take shape in the imagination with a sunlit perfection, but only for a moment; they melt and pass; the air is filled with a phantasmagorical movement of shapes, grouping themselves, putting on corporeality as a garment and at the same time dissolving into the nebulous background. It is a cloud pageant and the clouds are of opal dust. The Puritan conscience in Hawthorne is like some useful but inartistic Roman vessel of glass which has been buried for centuries in the earth and which comes forth at last fragile as a dragonfly's wing, shot through with all the most exquisite colors. He is the most opalescent of writers, and each of his books is an opal of a different type: crimson, purple, and emerald cross and recross *The Marble Faun*, and all the most fleeting tints of pale yellow, pale green, and pearly white shimmer through the *Blithedale Romance,* with a single strain of tragic red passing athwart it in the character of Zenobia. A hundred times the world of Hawthorne seems the familiar world, but just as we imagine we have gained a foothold there a wand passes over it, a wall is removed behind it—it has become a world within a world.

This leads one almost to forget that Hawthorne's range is limited, that his gift is meager and a little anaemic, that his poetry is not quite the same thing as wisdom. For if like the greatest poets he sees life as a fable, with a fable's infinitely multiplied correspondences, he feels it rather as a phantom than as a man. This being who passed twelve years of his youth in a solitary, close-curtained room, walking abroad only in the twilight or after the sun had set, was himself a phantom in a phantom world. Observe how he treats any one of his typical characters, the elfish little Priscilla, for example. He is describing the rumors current among her neighbors and how they believed that "the sun, at midday, would shine through her; in the first gray of the twilight, she lost all the distinctness of her outline; and, if you followed the dim thing into a dark corner, behold, she was not there." And he goes on in his own person: "There was a lack of human substance in her; it seemed as if, were she to stand up in a sunbeam, it would pass right through her figure, and trace out the cracked and dusty window-panes upon the naked floor." Could anything be more exquisite? Could anything more entirely fail to connect with reality in a practical Yankee world?

It is the natural corollary of all this that Hawthorne himself, as a social being (in his opinions especially—for he did not abstain from opinions), was more than commonly conventional. It is natural that this most deeply planted of American writers, who indicates more than any other the subterranean history of the American character, should have recoiled from every attempt to change, rectify, or spiritualize society; that he should have been incurious of every forward-looking impulse, a rather more than indifferent antiabolitionist, a much more than indifferent anti-Transcendentalist, and, though actively concerned with politics in one way or another through his middle and later years, always on the uninteresting side. His talent was a kind of Prospero's isle quite outside the world he lived in. It was *kept* outside that world by his own infallible instinct of artistic self-preservation. The comment he puts into the mouth of Miles Coverdale *à propos* of the "philanthropist" Hollingsworth is really his own comment on the society in which he found himself: "The moral which presents itself to my reflections, as drawn from Hollingsworth's character and errors, is simply this—that admitting what is called philanthropy, when adopted as a profession, to be often useful by its energetic impulse to society at large, it is perilous to the individual whose ruling passion, in one exclusive channel, it thus becomes. It ruins, or is fearfully apt to ruin, the heart, the rich juices of which God never meant should be pressed violently out, and distilled into alcoholic liquor, by an unnatural process, but should render life sweet, bland, and gently beneficent, and insensibly influence other hearts and other lives to the same blessed end."

Hawthorne was right with regard to the society of his day, but consider what he lost and what we lost by it. It is not the business of an artist as such to change society, and if Hawthorne held aloof from everything that stood for movement in his time that was the price of being sensitively organized in an age of rude, vague, boisterous, dyspeptic, incoherent causes. The fact that Hawthorne and Poe were the only two eminent minds of their age to which Transcendentalism was profoundly repugnant is the surest proof that they alone possessed the full and the right artistic instinct. They had to do what they could in society as it was—and what happened? Outwardly accepting it, but having nothing in common with it, they neither enriched society nor were enriched by it; they were driven to create and inhabit worlds of their own—diaphanous private worlds of mist and twilight.

VI

I find it impossible to approach the question of Transcendentalism—the thing itself, and Emerson, Margaret Fuller, the *Dial*, Brook Farm, and all the other permutations and combinations of it—without first of all expelling a persistent spleen, and then submitting myself to long explanations. So much truth, so much talent, so much of the American character is involved in that queer miasmatical group of lunar phenomena, in which philosophy, self-culture, politics, art, social reform, and religion were all mixed up and all felt to be, in some vague way, the same thing. One angel no doubt can stand quite comfortably on the point of a pin, but when a whole battalion of angels attempt to occupy this identical space there is war in heaven.

It is plain enough that the Transcendentalists had no sense of the relationship that exists between theory and practice, between the abstract and the concrete. The world they lived in was an excessively concrete world—a world of isolated facts. The white wooden houses, the farms, the patches of wood, the self-contained villages, each with its town-meeting, the politician, the minister, the lawyer, the merchant, were, in fact, very much what Emerson called his own sentences, "infinitely repellent particles"; they had, relatively speaking, nothing in common but the Yankee temperament—and the quality of this common temperament was to be as *un*-common, as individual and as different, as possible. There was no fusion, no operative background of social forces, no unwritten laws. The experience of New England was an experience of two extremes—bare facts and metaphysics: the machinery of self-preservation and the mystery of life. Experience of the world, of society, or art, the genial middle ground of human tradition, existed only as an appetite. Painting, sculpture, architecture were represented by engravings; history, travel, world politics, great affairs in general were represented by books. The habit of looking at things in the abstract, native to the old Calvinistic temper, was extended over the range of social and intellectual interests, partly as a result of isolation, partly because of the highly tenuous connection between these interests and the primitive actualities of life as New Englanders knew it.

German philosophy when it was released over the world inevitably came to port in this society, for above everything else it appeared to let one into the secret of universal experience. If, under the influence of this philosophy, you sat up late enough at night you could be an Alexander, a Plato, a Raphael, or (in Boston) a Washington Allston, without moving out of your chair. It is true you gained no territory and painted no pictures by this method, but you at least placed yourself at the seat of operations where all these wonderful things occur.

This accounts for the peculiar flavor of that old New England culture, so dry, so crisp, so dogmatic, so irritating. Having entered wholly through the brain in the form of general propositions, without any checking from observation or experience, it seems curiously inverted, curiously unreal. Witness for example that strange faraway tone in which Emerson so often and so characteristically refers to "Plato and Paul and Plutarch, Augustine, Spinoza, Chapman, Beaumont and Fletcher," or "the remains of Phidias, the Apollo, the works of Canova." There would be something quite ludicrous in this glimpse of St. Paul, Fletcher, Phidias and Spinoza arm in arm if you felt that Emerson had ever realistically pictured to himself these men as they individually were. To him they were all thrice-purified ghosts, ghosts of the printed page; the associations of the tavern, the synagogue, the drawing-room had fallen from their spirits in the mind of Emerson as utterly as from their bodies in the grave. To him they were exceptionally fine manifestations of the Over-Soul; philosophy like death had leveled them and had, as entirely, removed them from the region of terrestrial society, literature, and art. So also in effect when Margaret Fuller comes to the conclusion that "color is consecrate to passion and sculpture to thought." Having thus as it were removed the whole question to another planet, she is able to present us further with a jewel of criticism like this: "The Prophets and Sibyls are for the Michaelangelos. The Beautiful is Mr. Allston's dominion" (statements which make one feel a thousand years old). Yet this result is inevitable when works of art are approached not through the eye but through the mind: the element of taste, the perceptions of sense, once laid aside, there is no gulf between Phidias and Canova, between Michaelangelo and Washington Allston.

And then consider Emerson's style—that strange fine ventriloquism, that attenuated voice coming from a great distance, which so often strikes one as a continued falsetto. If it is extremely irritating —and I have known amiable and well-disposed persons to be exasperated by it—if it is filled with assertions that fairly insist upon being contradicted, it is because so often Emerson is abstract at the wrong times and concrete at the wrong times, because he has so little natural sense of the relation between the abstract and the concrete. Take, for instance, a typical sentence like this: "Archimedes will look through your Connecticut machine, at a glance, and judge of its fitness"—to which the inevitable reply is, that Archimedes will do nothing of the kind: I no more possess a Connecticut machine than Archimedes will put on mortality again to look through it. Is it unfair to literalize these metaphorical affirmations of Emerson? Of course I understand that to him "Archimedes" is merely a name for that particular aspect of the Over-Soul which broods over machinery, while my "Connecticut machine" means any human device that will serve to exhibit its powers of divination. But a prose which violates the actual overmuch, a prose in which the poetic effect is more than a heightened version of the actual is, I think, a prose one is entitled to find irritating. And furthermore his method of simply announcing as axiomatic what is in his mind is justified only by the possession of a faculty which Emerson does not possess, the faculty of hitting the nail inevitably on the head. Let one example suffice: "Shelley, though a poetic mind, is never a poet. His muse is uniformly imitative; all his poems composite. A good English scholar he is, with ear, taste, and memory; much more, he is a character full of noble and prophetic traits; but imagination, the original, authentic fire of the bard, he has not." Does this really suggest Shelley?

Emerson's artistic impressions are always of this hit-or-miss character; he can write page after page about a painter or a poet without one intelligibly apt utterance. Much the same is true of Carlyle and Ruskin, and for the same reason, that alike they all refer art to an extra-artistic standard. But Carlyle and Ruskin are concrete enough in their own willful ways, while Emerson is persistently abstract. He never lingers in the bodily world, he is always busy to be off again; and if he takes two or three paces on the earth they only serve to warm him for a fresh aerial adventure. Thus the essay on "Illusions" opens with an account of a day spent in the Mammoth Cave in Kentucky, and after the second sentence he continues in this way: "I lost the light of one day. I saw high domes, and bottomless pits; heard the voice of unseen waterfalls," &c. This is not the tone of descriptive writing; a glamour like that of oratory has fallen over it; phrase by phrase the effect is heightened and generalized under the reader's eye; we see how impatient he is to get to the real business and that the experience is already dimmed and evaporated by the approaching application.

The truth is that Emerson was not interested in human life; he cared nothing for experience or emotion, possessing so little himself. "He generally addressed me as if I were wholly impersonal," writes one of his disciples, who records an observation of Emerson that he "could never turn a dozen pages of *Don Quixote* or Dickens without a yawn." This accounts for the way in which his thoughts inevitably flew for refuge to capital letters, emerging as Demonology, Creeds,

Prudence, the Ideal, abstractions all. His point of view was formed very early; all his later books are sprouts from the first one, and there is no indication of growth, imbibition, or excursiveness beyond his original boundaries. If he remained open he was open as it were at the top; and before he was thirty-five he seems to have acquired that fixed, benignant, musing smile which implies the consciousness of having solved one's own problem and which is usually accompanied by a closure of the five senses.

I say all this without prejudice to Emerson's position in the world of the spirit. There he truly lived and lives, and of all American writers he alone appears to me to have proved the reality of that world and to have given some kind of basis to American idealism.

But Emerson's idealism was double-edged: it was concerned not merely with the spiritual life of the individual, but also with the individual in society, with the "conduct of life." This latter aspect of his teaching was in fact the secret of his contemporary influence. For if the logical result of a thoroughgoing, self-reliant individualism in the world of the spirit is to become a saint, it is no less true that the logical result of a thoroughgoing, self-reliant individualism in the world of the flesh is to become a millionaire. And in fact it would be hard to say whether Emerson more keenly relished saintliness or shrewdness. Both qualities he himself possessed in a high degree, as only an American can; and if on one side of his nature he was a most lonely and beautiful seer, the records of his life prove that he lacked none of the sagacity and caution of the true Yankee husbandman. He perfectly combined the temperaments of Jonathan Edwards and Benjamin Franklin;—the upper and lower levels of the American mind are fused in him and each becomes the sanction of the other.

In the long run there is a world of difference between individualism on the spiritual plane and individualism on the economic plane. Were it not so there would be no meaning in the phrase "Stone walls do not a prison make," there would be no meaning in Christianity. And therein consists the beauty and the permanence of Emersonianism. For as the scope of enterprise and self-reliance becomes with every generation more limited, as the generality of men are caught with both feet in the net of economic necessity and are led thereby to seek scope for their initiative in disinherited activity, just so the Emersonian doctrine comes into its own, the Emersonian virtues mount upward and create a self-reliance in the spirit itself. Emersonianism, in short, can only begin to be itself when it has taken its final place on the plane of poetry. In the nineteenth century it was economic as well; it was the voice of just those forces which moved, enlarged, created the American scene; it corresponded to a real freedom of movement and opportunity; pioneers, inventors, men of business, engineers, seekers of adventure found themselves expressed and justified in it. Emerson presided over and gave its tone to this world of infinite social fragmentation and unlimited free will, a world in which—as the presupposition was—every one started fresh, as if dropped from the sky, where entanglements of heredity and disposition, foreclosures of opportunity, desires and aims which require an already fertilized field for their development, where the whole welter of human history and social complexity had not yet as it were obscured the morning of time.

In all this Emerson was essentially passive. He was the child of his age, and what he did was to give his Yankee instincts free play under the sanction of his Transcendental idealism. He never dreamed of molding society, and he was incapable of an effective social ideal. Compare him in this respect with Carlyle. The social ideal of Carlyle was the Hero, and what Carlyle meant by the Hero was a particular kind of being whom all Englishmen understand: a creature of flesh and blood who leads men. No doubt Carlyle was absurd enough; but what made him nevertheless a mighty man was that he had the faculty of devising and making intensely real and contagious a social ideal the rudiments of which actually existed in the people he was addressing. The English admire heroism; Carlyle made the Hero a conscious and palpable objective; and his countrymen were stirred through and through. Carlyle counts his disciples from generation to generation; strong men and leaders of men, they go out conquering and ruling creation, and there is hardly a British governor who does not feel the apostolic hands of Carlyle upon his head. Preposterous no doubt they are, having so little of the science and humility that are proper to our late-sprung arboreal species. But who will deny that the doctrine itself has served to make them good human material— for a better doctrine?

What can Emerson show as a social ideal? *Representative Men.* Emerson has chosen six names, five of which are the names of writers, the sixth that of a man of action, Napoleon, whom, let us hope, Young America will not too closely emulate. The social idea of Emerson, as Froude pointed out, is a sort of composite of the philosopher, the mystic, the sceptic, the poet, the writer, and the man of the world. I wonder what passed through the mind of the American businessman of Emerson's day when he heard all these phrases, phrases so unrelated to the springs of action within himself? Did he feel that his profound instincts had been touched and unified, did he see opening before him the line of a disinterested career, lighted up by a sudden dramatization of his own finest latent possibilities, did he not rather, with a degree of reason, say to himself: "These papers will serve very well to improve my mind. I shall read them when I have time"? And did he not thereupon set to work accumulating all the more dollars in order that he might have the more time to cultivate his mind—in legal phrase—after the event?

Looked at from this side, Emerson has all the qualities of the typical baccalaureate sermon; and the baccalaureate sermon, as we know, beautiful as it often is, has never been found inconveniently inconsistent with the facts and requirements of business life. A glance at Young America after so many generations of being talked to might well convince one that something is wrong with the baccalaureate sermon. Since the day of Emerson's address on *The American Scholar* the whole of American literature has had the semblance of one vast, all-embracing baccalaureate sermon, addressed to the private virtues of young men. It has been one shining deluge of righteousness, purity, practical mysticism, the conduct of life, and at the end of ninety years the highest ambition of Young America is to be—do I exaggerate? —the owner of a shoe factory. As a result of this exclusive approach through the personal conscience (a conscience by no means connected with disinterested ends and the real development of personality), society in America has permanently stood for two things: in its private aspect as an immense preserve for the exercise of personal virtues like thrift, self-assertion, family provision, nest-feathering in general; in its public aspect as a thing to be coddled with rich gifts (Philanthropy) or scrubbed back to the political intentions of 1776 (Reform).

Emerson is the patron saint of every one of these diverse, chaotic impulses—the gentle, chimelike Emerson who in days to come will sound and shine over a better world.

13

Walt Whitman: PASSAGE FROM A PREFACE •

America does not repel the past or what it has produced under its forms or amid other politics or the idea of castes or the old religions . . . accepts the lesson with calmness . . . is not so impatient as has been supposed that the slough still sticks to opinions and manners and literature while the life which served its requirements has passed into the new life of the new forms . . . perceives that the corpse is slowly borne from the eating and sleeping rooms of the house . . . perceives that it waits a little while in the door . . . that it was fittest for its days . . . that its action has descended to the stalwart and well-shaped heir who approaches . . . and that he shall be fittest for his days.

The Americans of all nations at any time upon the earth have probably the fullest poetical nature. The United States themselves are essentially the greatest poem. In the history of the earth hitherto the largest and most stirring appear tame and orderly to their ampler largeness and stir. Here at last is something in the doings of man that corresponds with the broadcast doings of the day and night. Here is not merely a nation but a teeming nation of nations. Here is action

• *To* Leaves of Grass (*1855*).

untied from strings necessarily blind to particulars and details magnificently moving in vast masses. Here is the hospitality which forever indicates heroes. . . . Here are the roughs and beards and space and ruggedness and nonchalance that the soul loves. Here the performance disdaining the trivial unapproached in the tremendous audacity of its crowds and groupings and the push of its perspective spreads with crampless and flowing breadth and showers its prolific and splendid extravagance. One sees it must indeed own the riches of the summer and winter, and need never be bankrupt while corn grows from the ground or the orchards drop apples or the bays contain fish or men beget children upon women.

Other states indicate themselves in their deputies . . . but the genius of the United States is not best or most in its executives or legislatures, nor in its ambassadors or authors or colleges or churches or parlors, nor even in its newspapers or inventors . . . but always most in the common people. Their manners, speech, dress, friendships—the picturesque looseness of their carriage . . . their deathless attachment to freedom—their aversion to anything indecorous or soft or mean—the practical acknowledgment of the citizens of all other states—the fierceness of their roused resentment—their curiosity and welcome of novelty—their self-esteem and wonderful sympathy—their susceptibility to a slight—the air they have of persons who never knew how it felt to stand in the presence of superiors—the fluency of their speech—their delight in music, the sure symptom of manly tenderness and native elegance of soul . . . their good temper and openhandedness—the terrible significance of their elections—the President's taking off his hat to them not they to him—these too are unrhymed poetry. It awaits the gigantic and generous treatment worthy of it. . . .

14

Walt Whitman: TO EMERSON [1856]

Here are thirty-two poems, which I send you, dear Friend and Master, not having found how I could satisfy myself with sending any usual acknowledgment of your letter. The first edition, on which you mailed me that till now unanswered letter, was twelve poems—I printed a thousand copies, and they readily sold; these thirty-two Poems I stereotype, to print several thousand copies of. I much enjoy making poems. Other work I have set myself to do, to meet people and The States face to face, to confront them with an American rude tongue; but the work of my life is making poems. I keep on till I make a hundred, and then several hundred—perhaps a thousand. The way is clear to me. A few years, and the average annual call for my Poems is ten or twenty thousand copies—more, quite likely. Why should I hurry or compromise? In poems or in speeches I say the word or two that has got to be said, adhere to the body, step with the countless common footsteps, and remind every man and woman of something.

Master, I am a man who has perfect faith. Master, we have not come through centuries, caste, heroisms, fables, to halt in this land today. Or I think it is to collect a ten-fold impetus that any halt is made. As nature, inexorable, onward, resistless, impassive amid the threats and screams of disputants, so America. Let all defer. Let all attend respectfully the leisure of These States, their politics, poems, literature, manners, and their free-handed modes of training their own offspring. Their own comes, just matured, certain, numerous and capable enough, with egotistical tongues, with sinewed wrists, seizing openly what belongs to them. They resume Personality, too long left out of mind. Their shadows are projected in employments, in books, in the cities, in trade; their feet are on the flights of the steps of the Capitol; they dilate, a larger, brawnier, more candid, more democratic, lawless, positive native to The States, sweet-bodied, completer, dauntless, flowing, masterful, beard-faced, new race of men.

Swiftly, on limitless foundations, the United States too are founding a literature. It is all as well done, in my opinion, as could be practicable. Each element here is in condition. Every day I go among the people of Manhattan Island, Brooklyn, and other cities, and among the young men, to discover the spirit of them, and to refresh myself. These are to be attended to; I am myself more drawn here than to those authors, publishers, importations, reprints, and so forth. I pass coolly through those, understanding them perfectly well, and that they do the indispensable service, outside of men like me, which nothing else could do. In poems, the young men of The States shall be represented, for they outrival the best of the rest of the earth.

The lists of ready-made literature which America inherits by the mighty inheritance of the English language—all the rich repertoire of traditions, poems, histories, metaphysics, plays, classics, translations, have made, and still continue, magnificent preparations for that other plainly signified literature, to be our own, to be electric, fresh, lusty, to express the full-sized body, male and female—to give the modern meanings of things, to grow up beautiful, lasting, commensurate with America, with all the passions of home, with the inimitable sympathies of having been boys and girls together, and of parents who were with our parents.

What else can happen to The States, even in their own despite? That huge English flow, so sweet, so undeniable, has done incalculable good here, and is to be spoken of for its own sake with generous praise and with gratitude. Yet the price The States have had to lie under for the same has not been a small price. Payment prevails; a nation can never take the issues of the needs of other nations for nothing. America, grandest of lands in the theory of its politics, in popular reading, in hospitality, breadth, animal beauty, cities, ships, machines, money, credit, collapses quick as lightning at the repeated, admonishing, stern words. Where are any mental expressions from you, beyond what you have copied or stolen? Where the born throngs of poets, literates, orators, you promised? Will you but tag after other nations? They struggled long for their literature, painfully working their way, some with deficient languages, some with priestcraft, some in the endeavor just to live—yet achieved for their times, works, poems, perhaps the only solid consolation left to them through ages afterwards of shame and decay. You are young, have the perfectest of dialects, a free press, a free government, the world forwarding its best to be with you. As justice has been strictly done to you, from this hour do strict justice to yourself. Strangle the singers who will not sing you loud and strong. Open the doors of The West. Call for new great masters to comprehend new arts, new perfections, new wants. Submit to the most robust bard till he remedy your barrenness. Then you will not need to adopt the heirs of others; you will have true heirs, begotten of yourself, blooded with your own blood.

With composure I see such propositions, seeing more and more every day of the answers that serve. Expressions do not yet serve, for sufficient reasons; but that is getting ready, beyond what the earth has hitherto known, to take home the expressions when they come, and to identify them with the populace of The States, which is the schooling The States extract from the swarms of reprints, and from the current authors and editors. Such service and extract are done after enormous, reckless, free modes, characteristic of The States. Here are to be attained results never elsewhere thought possible; the modes are very grand too. The instincts of the American people are all perfect, and tend to make heroes. It is a rare thing in a man here to understand The States.

All current nourishments to literature serve. Of authors and editors I do not know how many there are in The States, but there are thousands, each one building his or her step to the stairs by which giants shall mount. Of the twenty-four modern mammoth two-double, three-double, and four-double cylinder presses now in the world, printing by steam, twenty-one of them are in These States. The twelve thousand large and small shops for dispensing books and newspapers —the same number of public libraries, any one of which has all the reading wanted to equip a man or woman for American reading—the three thousand different newspapers, the nutriment of the imperfect ones coming in just as usefully as any—the story papers, various, full of strong-flavored romances, widely circulated—the one-cent and two-cent journals—the political ones, no matter what side—the weeklies in the country—the sporting and pictorial papers—the monthly magazines, with plentiful imported feed—the sentimental novels, numberless copies of them—the low-priced flaring tales, adventures, biographies—all are prophetic; all waft rapidly on. I see that they swell tide, for reasons. I am not troubled at the movement of them, but greatly pleased. I see plying shuttles, the active ephemeral myriads of books also, faithfully weaving the garments of a generation of men, and a generation of women, they do not perceive or know. What a progress popular reading and writing has made in fifty years! What a progress fifty years hence! The time is at hand when inherent literature will be a main part of These States, as general and real as steam-power, iron, corn, beef, fish. First-rate American persons are to be supplied. Our perennial materials for fresh thoughts, histories, poems, music, orations, religions, recitations, amusements, will then not be disregarded, any more than our perennial fields, mines, rivers, seas. Certain things are established, and are immovable; in those things millions of years stand justified. The mothers and fathers of whom modern centuries have come, have not existed for nothing; they too had brains and hearts. Of course all literature, in all nations and years, will share marked attributes in common, as we all, of all ages, share the common human attributes. America is to be kept coarse and broad. What is to be done is to withdraw from precedents, and be directed to men and women—also to The States in their federalness; for the union of the parts of the body is not more necessary to their life than the union of These States is to their life.

A profound person can easily know more of the people than they know of themselves. Always waiting untold in the souls of the armies of common people, is stuff better than anything that can possibly appear in the leadership of the same. That gives final verdicts. In every department of These States, he who travels with a coterie, or with selected persons, or with imitators, or with infidels, or with the owners of slaves, or with that which is ashamed of the body of a man, or with that which is ashamed of the body of a woman, or with any thing less than the bravest and the openest, travels straight for the slopes of dissolution. The genius of all foreign literature is clipped and cut small, compared to our genius, and is essentially insulting to our usages, and to the organic compacts of These States. Old forms, old poems, majestic and proper in their own lands here in this land are exiles; the air here is very strong. Much that stands well and has a little enough place provided for it in the small scales of European kingdoms, empires, and the like, here stands haggard, dwarfed, ludicrous, or has no place little enough provided for it. Authorities, poems, models, laws, names, imported into America, are useful to America today to destroy them, and so move disencumbered to great works, great days.

Just so long, in our country or any country, as no revolutionists advance, and are backed by the people, sweeping off the swarms of routine representatives, officers in power, book-makers, teachers, ecclesiastics, politicians, just so long, I perceive, do they who are in power fairly represent that country, and remain of use, probably of very great use. To supersede them, when it is the pleasure of These States, full provision is made; and I say the time has arrived to use it with a strong hand. Here also the souls of the armies have not only overtaken the souls of the officers, but passed on, and left the souls of the officers behind out of sight many weeks' journey; and the souls of the armies now go en-masse without officers. Here also formulas, glosses, blanks, minutiae, are choking the throats of the spokesmen to death. Those things most listened for, certainly those are the things least said. There is not a single History of the World. There is not one of America, or of the organic compacts of These States, or of Washington, or of Jefferson, nor of Language, nor any Dictionary of the English Language. There is no great author; every one has demeaned himself to some etiquette or some impotence. There is no manhood or life-power in poems; there are shoats and geldings more like. Our literature will be dressed up, a fine gentleman, distasteful to our instinct, foreign to our soil. Its neck bends right and left wherever it goes. Its costumes and jewelry prove how little it knows Nature. Its flesh is soft; it shows less and less of the indefinable hard something that is Nature. Where is any thing but the shaved Nature of synods and schools? Where is a savage and luxuriant man? Where is an overseer? In lives, in poems, in codes of law, in Congress, in tuitions, theaters, conversations, argumentations, not a single head lifts itself clean out, with proof that it is their master, and has subordinated them to itself, and is ready to try their superiors. None believes in These States, boldly illustrating them in himself. Not a man faces round at the rest with terrible negative voice, refusing all terms to be bought off from his own eyesight, or from the soul that he is, or from friendship, or from the body that he is, or from the soil and seas. To creeds, literature, art, the army, the navy, the executive, life is hardly proposed, but the sick and dying are proposed to cure the sick and dying. The churches are one vast lie; the people do not believe them, and they do not believe themselves; the priests are continually telling what they know well enough is not so, and keeping back what they know is so. The spectacle is a pitiful one. I think there can never be again upon the festive earth more bad-disordered persons deliberately taking seats, as of late in These States, at the heads of the public tables—such corpses' eyes for judges—such a rascal and thief in the Presidency.

Up to the present, as helps best, the people, like a lot of large boys, have no determined tastes, are quite unaware of the grandeur of themselves, and of their destiny, and of their immense strides—

accept with voracity whatever is presented them in novels, histories, newspapers, poems, schools, lectures, every thing. Pretty soon through these and other means, their development makes the fiber that is capable of itself, and will assume determined tastes. The young men will be clear what they want, and will have it. They will follow none except him whose spirit leads them in the like spirit with themselves. Any such man will be welcome as the flowers of May. Others will be put out without ceremony. How much is there anyhow, to the young men of These States, in a parcel of helpless dandies, who can neither fight, work, shoot, ride, run, command—some of them devout, some quite insane, some castrated—all second-hand, or third, fourth, or fifth hand—waited upon by waiters, putting not this land first, but always other lands first, talking of art, doing the most ridiculous things for fear of being called ridiculous, smirking and skipping along, continually taking off their hats—no one behaving, dressing, writing, talking, loving, out of any natural and manly tastes of his own, but each one looking cautiously to see how the rest behave, dress, write, talk, love—pressing the noses of dead books upon themselves and upon their country—favoring no poets, philosophs, literates here, but dog-like danglers at the heels of the poets, philosophs, literates, of enemies' lands—favoring mental expressions, models of gentlemen and ladies, social habitudes in These States, to grow up in sneaking defiance of the popular substratums of The States? Of course they and the likes of them can never justify the strong poems of America. Of course no feed of theirs is to stop and be made welcome to muscle the bodies, male and female, for Manhattan Island, Brooklyn, Boston, Worcester, Hartford, Portland, Montreal, Detroit, Buffalo, Cleveland, Milwaukee, St. Louis, Indianapolis, Chicago, Cincinnati, Iowa City, Philadelphia, Baltimore, Raleigh, Savannah, Charleston, Mobile, New Orleans, Galveston, Brownsville, San Francisco, Havana, and a thousand equal cities, present and to come. Of course what they and the likes of them have been used for, draws toward its close, after which they will all be discharged, and not one of them will ever be heard of any more.

America, having duly conceived, bears out of herself offspring of her own to do the workmanship wanted. To freedom, to strength, to poems, to personal greatness, it is never permitted to rest, not a generation or part of a generation. To be ripe beyond further increase is to prepare to die. The architects of These States laid their foundations, and passed to further spheres. What they laid is a work done; as much more remains. Now are needed other architects, whose duty is not less difficult, but perhaps more difficult. Every age forever needs architects. America is not finished, perhaps never will be; now Amer-

ica is a divine true sketch. There are Thirty-Two States sketched—
the population thirty millions. In a few years there will be Fifty
States. Again in a few years there will be A Hundred States, the population hundreds of millions, the freshest and freest of men. Of
course such men stand for nothing less than the freshest and freest
expression.

Poets here, literates here, are to rest on organic different bases from
other countries; not a class set apart, circling only in the circle themselves, modest and pretty, desperately scratching for rhymes, pallid
with white paper, shut off, aware of the old pictures and traditions
of the race, but unaware of the actual race around them—not breed-
ing in and in among each other till they all have the scrofula. Lands
of ensemble, bards of ensemble! Walking freely out from the old
traditions, as our politics has walked out, American poets and literates recognize nothing behind them superior to what is present with
them—recognize with joy the sturdy living forms of the men and
women of These States, the divinity of sex, the perfect eligibility of
the female with the male, all The States, liberty and equality, real
articles, the different trades, mechanics, the young fellows of Manhattan Island, customs, instincts, slang, Wisconsin, Georgia, the noble Southern heart, the hot blood, the spirit that will be nothing less
than master, the filibuster spirit, the Western man, native-born perceptions, the eye for forms, the perfect models of made things, the
wild smack of freedom, California, money, electric-telegraphs, free-
trade, iron and the iron mines—recognize without demur those splendid resistless black poems, the steam-ships of the seaboard states, and
those other resistless splendid poems, the locomotives, followed
through the interior states by trains of rail-road cars.

A word remains to be said, as of one ever present, not yet permitted to be acknowledged, discharded or made dumb by literature,
and the results apparent. To the lack of an avowed, empowered, un-
abashed development of sex (the only salvation for the same), and
to the fact of speakers and writers fraudulently assuming as always
dead what every one knows to be always alive, is attributable the remarkable non-personality and indistinctness of modern productions
in books, art, talk; also that in the scanned lives of men and women
most of them appear to have been for some time past of the neuter
gender; and also the stinging fact that in orthodox society today, if
the dresses were changed, the men might easily pass for women and
the women for men.

Infidelism usurps most with foetid polite face; among the rest infidelism about sex. By silence or obedience the pens of savants, poets,
historians, biographers, and the rest, have long connived at the filthy

law, and books enslaved to it, that what makes the manhood of a man, that sex, womanhood, maternity, desires, lusty animations, organs, acts, are unmentionable and to be ashamed of, to be driven to skulk out of literature with whatever belongs to them. This filthy law has to be repealed—it stands in the way of great reforms. Of women just as much as men, it is the interest that there should not be infidelism about sex, but perfect faith. Women in These States approach the day of that organic equality with men, without which, I see, men cannot have organic equality among themselves. This empty dish, gallantry, will then be filled with something. This tepid wash, this diluted deferential love, as in songs, fictions, and so forth, is enough to make a man vomit; as to manly friendship, everywhere observed in The States, there is not the first breath of it to be observed in print. I say that the body of a man or woman, the main matter, is so far quite unexpressed in poems; but that the body is to be expressed, and sex is. Of bards for These States, if it come to a question, it is whether they shall celebrate in poems the eternal decency of the amativeness of Nature, the motherhood of all, or whether they shall be the bards of the fashionable delusion of the inherent nastiness of sex, and of the feeble and querulous modesty of deprivation. This is important in poems, because the whole of the other expressions of a nation are but flanges out of its great poems. To me, henceforth, that theory of anything, no matter what, stagnates in its vitals, cowardly and rotten, while it cannot publicly accept, and publicly name, with specific words, the things on which all existence, all souls, all realization, all decency, all health, all that is worth being here for, all of woman and of man, all beauty, all purity, all sweetness, all friendship, all strength, all life, all immortality depend. The courageous soul, for a year or two to come, may be proved by faith in sex, and by disdaining concessions.

To poets and literates—to every woman and man, today or any day, the conditions of the present, needs, dangers, prejudices, and the like, are the perfect conditions on which we are here, and the conditions for wording the future with undissuadable words. These States; receivers of the stamina of past ages and lands, initiate the outlines of repayment a thousand fold. They fetch the American great masters, waited for by old worlds and new, who accept evil as well as good, ignorance as well as erudition, black as soon as white, foreign-born materials as well as home-born, reject none, force discrepancies into range, surround the whole, concentrate them on present periods and places, show the application to each and any one's body and soul, and show the true sense of precedents. Always America will be agitated and turbulent. This day it is taking shape, not to be less so, but to be more so, stormily, capriciously, on native principles, with such vast proportions of parts! As for me, I love screaming, wrestling, boiling-hot days.

Of course, we shall have a national character, an identity. As it ought to be, and as soon as it ought to be, it will be. That, with much else, takes care of itself, is a result, and the cause of greater results. With Ohio, Illinois, Missouri, Oregon—and with the states around the Mexican sea—with cheerfully welcomed immigrants from Europe, Asia, Africa—with Connecticut, Vermont, New Hampshire, Rhode Island—with all varied interests, facts, beliefs, parties, genesis—there is being fused a determined character, fit for the broadest use for the freewomen and freemen of The States, accomplished and to be accomplished, without any exception whatever—each indeed free, each idiomatic, as becomes live states and men, but each adhering to one enclosing general form of politics, manners, talk, personal style, as the plenteous varieties of the race adhere to one physical form. Such character is the brain and spine to all, including literature, including poems. Such character, strong, limber, just, openmouthed, American-blooded, full of pride, full of ease, of passionate friendliness, is to stand compact upon that vast basis of the supremacy of Individuality—that new moral American continent without which, I see, the physical continent remaining incomplete, maybe a carcass, a bloat—that newer America, answering face to face with The States, with ever-satisfying and ever-unsurveyable seas and shores.

Those shores you found. I say you have led The States there—have led Me there. I say that none has ever done, or ever can do, a greater deed for The States, than your deed. Others may line out the lines, build cities, work mines, break up farms; it is yours to have been the original true Captain who put to sea, intuitive, positive, rendering the first report, to be told less by any report, and more by the mariners of a thousand bays, in each tack of their arriving and departing, many years after you.

Receive, dear Master, these statements and assurances through me, for all the young men, and for an earnest that we know none before you, but the best following you; and that we demand to take your name into our keeping, and that we understand what you have indicated, and find the same indicated in ourselves, and that we will stick to it and enlarge upon it through These States.

Ralph Waldo Emerson: LETTER TO WHITMAN

Concord, Massachusetts, July 21, 1855

Dear Sir—I am not blind to the worth of the wonderful gift of *Leaves of Grass.* I find it the most extraordinary piece of wit and wisdom that America has yet contributed. I am very happy in reading it, as great power makes us happy. It meets the demand I am always making of what seemed the sterile and stingy Nature, as if too much handiwork, or too much lymph in the temperament, were making our Western wits fat and mean.

I give you joy of your free and brave thought. I have great joy in it. I find comparable things said incomparably well, as they must be. I find the courage of treatment which so delights us, and which large perception only can inspire.

I greet you at the beginning of a great career, which yet must have had a long foreground somewhere, for such a start. I rubbed my eyes a little, to see if this sunbeam were no illusion; but the solid sense of the book is a sober certainty. It has the best merits, namely, of fortifying and encouraging.

I did not know until I last night saw the book advertised in a newspaper that I could trust the name as real and available for a post-office. I wish to see my benefactor, and have felt much like striking my tasks and visiting New York to pay you my respects.

R. W. EMERSON

Henry David Thoreau: CONCERNING
WALT WHITMAN (*A Letter to Harrison Blake*)

December 7, 1856

That Walt Whitman, of whom I wrote to you, is the most interesting
fact to me at present. I have read his second edition (which he gave
me), and it has done me more good than any reading for a long time.
Perhaps I remember best the poem of Walt Whitman, an American,
and the Sun-Down Poem. There are two or three pieces in the book
which are disagreeable, to say the least; simply sensual. He does not
celebrate love at all. It is as if the beasts spoke. I think that men
have not been ashamed of themselves without reason. No doubt
there have always been dens where such deeds were unblushingly re-
cited, and it is no merit to compete with their inhabitants. But even
on this side he has spoken more truth than any American or modern
that I know. I have found his poem exhilarating, encouraging. As for
its sensuality—and it may turn out to be less sensual than it appears
—I do not so much wish that those parts were not written, as that
men and women were so pure that they could read them without
harm, that is, without understanding them. One woman told me that
no woman could read it—as if a man could read what a woman could
not. Of course Walt Whitman can communicate to us no experience,

and if we are shocked, whose experience is it that we are reminded of?

On the whole, it sounds to me very brave and American, after whatever deductions. I do not believe that all the sermons, so called, that have been preached in this land put together are equal to it for preaching.

We ought to rejoice greatly in him. He occasionally suggests something a little more than human. You can't confound him with the other inhabitants of Brooklyn or New York. How they must shudder when they read him! He is awfully good.

To be sure I sometimes feel a little imposed on. By his heartiness and broad generalities he puts me in a liberal frame of mind prepared to see wonders—as it were, sets me upon a hill or in the midst of a plains—stirs me well up, and then—throws in a thousand of brick. Though rude and sometimes ineffectual, it is a great primitive poem —an alarm or trumpet-note ringing through the American camp. Wonderfully like the Orientals, too, considering that when I asked him if he had read them, he answered, "No: tell me about them."

I did not get far in conversation with him—two more being present —and among the few things which I chanced to say, I remember that one was, in answer to him as representing America, that I did not think much of America or of politics, and so on, which may have been somewhat of a damper to him.

Since I have seen him, I find that I am not disturbed by any brag or egoism in his book. He may turn out the least of a braggart of all, having a better right to be confident.

He is a great fellow.

17

Richard Chase: "ONE'S SELF I SING" [1955]

The main item in the 1855 edition of *Leaves of Grass* was, of course, "Song of Myself," the profound and lovely comic drama of the self which is Whitman's best poem and contains in essence nearly all, yet not quite all, there is to *Leaves of Grass*. The comic spirit of the poem is of the characteristic American sort, providing expression for a realism at once naturalistic and transcendental, for the wit, gaiety, and festive energy of all good comedy, and also for meditative soliloquy, at once intensely personal and strongly generic.

One circumstance that contributes to the general spontaneity of "Song of Myself" is, in fact, Whitman's unsuccessful attempt to be an Emersonian or Wordsworthian moralist. In his preface, he wrote that "of all mankind the poet is the equable man. Not in him but off from him things are grotesque or eccentric or fail of their sanity. . . . He is the arbiter of the diverse and he is the key. He is the equalizer of his age and land." Whitman tries, indeed, to install himself in his poem on this high moral ground: he will, he says, first regenerate himself by leaving the fallacious artificialities of modern life and getting back to fundamentals; then, having perfected himself as the norm, he will summon all the world to him to be freed of its abnormalities. But although in the poem the self remains pretty much at the center of things, Whitman finds it impossible to accept the idea that it is a norm. To the sententious prophet who "promulges" the normative self, the comic poet and ironic realist keep introducing other, disconcertingly eccentric selves.

> Who goes there? hankering, gross, mystical, nude. . . .

Whoever he is, he is not in a position to utter morality. The self in this poem *is* (to use Lawrence's phrase) "tricksy-tricksy"; it does "shy all sorts of ways" and is finally, as the poet says, "not a bit tamed," for "I too am untranslatable." So that as in all true, or high, comedy, the sententious, the too overtly insisted-on morality (if any) plays a losing game with ironical realism. In the social comedy of Molière, Congreve, or Jane Austen, moral senteniousness, like other deformities of comportment or personality, is corrected by society. But this attitude is, of course, foreign to Whitman, who has already wished to invite society to correct itself by comparing itself with him and who, furthermore, cannot even sustain this democratic inversion of an aristocratic idea. Whitman's comic poetry deflates pretensions and chides moral rigidity by opposing to them a diverse, vital, indeterminate reality.

"I resist anything better than my own diversity," says Whitman, and this is the characteristic note of "Song of Myself." Not that by referring to "Song of Myself" as a "comic" poem I wish too narrowly to limit the scope of discussion—nor do I suggest in using the term a special theory of Whitman or of American literature. I simply respond to my sense that "Song of Myself" is on the whole comic in tone and that although the poem's comic effects are of universal significance, they often take the specific form of American humor. If one finds "Song of Myself" enjoyable at all, it is because one is conscious of how much of the poem, though the feeling in many of its passages need not perhaps have been comic at all, nevertheless appeals to one, first and last, in its comic aspect. The poem is full of odd gestures and whimsical acts; it is written by a neo-Ovidian poet for whom self-metamorphosis is almost as free as free association, who can write "I am an old artillerist" or "I will go to the bank by the wood, and become undisguised and naked" as easily as he can write:

> Askers embody themselves in me and I am embodied in them,
> I project my hat, sit shame-faced, and beg.

The sense of incongruous diversity is very strong in "Song of Myself," and although one does not know how the sly beggar projecting his hat or the martial patriot is transformed into the "acme of things accomplish'd," and "encloser of things to be" who suddenly says:

> I find I incorporate gneiss, coal, long-threaded moss,
>   fruits, grains, esculent roots,
> And am stucco'd with quadrupeds and birds all over,

one is nevertheless charmed with the transformation.

Whitman conceives of the self, one might say, as James conceives of Christopher Newman in *The American*—as having the "look of being committed to nothing in particular, of standing in an attitude of general hospitality to the chances of life." In other words, the "self" who is the protagonist of Whitman's poem is a character portrayed in a recognizable American way; it illustrates the fluid, unformed personality exulting alternately in its provisional attempts to define itself and in its sense that it has no definition. The chief difference between "Song of Myself" and *The American* is, of course, the difference between the stages on which Whitman and James allow the self to act, James confining the action to his international scene and Whitman opening his stage out into an eventful universe which is a contradictory but witty collocation of the natural and the transcendent, the imperfect and the utopian, the personal and the generic—a dialectic world out of whose "dimness opposite equals advance" and in which there is "always a knot of identity" but "always distinction."

The very scope of Whitman's universe and the large freedom he assumes to move about in it allowed him to appropriate new areas of experience and thus to make of "Song of Myself" the original and influential poem it is. For one thing, this is the first American poem to invade that fruitful ground between lyric verse and prose fiction that so much of modern poetry cultivates, and one may suppose that "Song of Myself" has had at least as much effect on the novel as, let us say, *Moby Dick* or *The Golden Bowl* have had on poetry. The famous lines in Section 8 are, at any rate, both "imagistic" and novelistic:

> The little one sleeps in its cradle;
> I lift the gauze and look a long time, and silently brush
>   away flies with my hand.

> The youngster and the red-faced girl turn aside up the
>   bushy hill;
> I peeringly view them from the top.

> The suicide sprawls on the bloody floor of the bedroom;
> I witness the corpse with its dabbled hair, I note where
>   the pistol has fallen.

It is probably true that more than anyone else, more than Blake or Baudelaire, Whitman made the city poetically available to literature:

The blab of the pave, tires of carts, sluff of boot-soles,
    talk of the promenaders,
The heavy omnibus, the driver with his interrogating
    thumb, the clank of the shod horses on the granite
    floor. . . .

Such lines as these have been multitudinously echoed in modern prose and poetry, they have been endlessly recapitulated by the journey of the realistic movie camera up the city street. One might argue that Whitman's descriptions of the city made possible T. S. Eliot's *Waste Land*. The horror of Eliot's London, as of Baudelaire's *"cité pleine de rêves,"* is unknown in *Leaves of Grass,* but was not Whitman the first poet, so to speak, who put real typists and clerks in the imaginary city?

There can be no doubt that "Song of Myself" made sex a possible subject for American literature, and in this respect Whitman wrought a great revolution in, for example, his beautiful idyllic scene in which the "handsome and richly drest" woman imagines herself to join the "twenty-eight young men" who "bathe by the shore." In such a passage as this (as Henry Adams was to point out) American literature was moving toward the freedom and inclusiveness that came more naturally to Europeans—to Flaubert, or Chekhov, whose panoramic novelette *The Steppe* includes a similarly idyllic scene of bathing and sexuality. It is sex, too, although of an inverted kind, that allows Whitman to write the following unsurpassable lines in which love is at once so sublimely generalized and perfectly particularized:

And [I know] that a kelson of the creation is love,
And limitless are leaves stiff or drooping in the fields,
And brown ants in the little wells beneath them,
And mossy scabs of the worm fence, and heap'd stones,
    elder, mullein and poke-weed.

No summary view of "Song of Myself" would be complete without reference to the elegiac tone of the concluding lines. If, as we have been saying, Whitman's poem is remarkable for its gross inclusive scope, his elegiac verse is a great act of discrimination and nicety. Where else, in the generally grandiose nineteenth-century melodrama of love and death shall we find anything like the delicate precision of these incomparable lines?

The last scud of day holds back for me;
It flings my likeness after the rest and true as any, on
    the shadow'd wilds,
It coaxes me to the vapor and the dusk.

I depart as air, I shake my white locks at the runaway sun,
I effuse my flesh in eddies, and drift it in lacy jags.

I bequeathe myself to the dirt, to grow from the grass I love;
If you want me again look for me under your boot-soles

You will hardly know who I am or what I mean,
But I shall be good health to you nevertheless,
And filter and fibre your blood.

Failing to fetch me at first keep encouraged,
Missing me one place, search another,
I stop somewhere, waiting for you.

As every poet does, Whitman asks us provisionally to accept the imagined world of his poem. It is a fantastic world in which it is presumed that the self can become identical with all other selves in the universe, regardless of time and space. Not without precedent in Hindu poetry, this central metaphor is, as an artistic device, unique in American literature, as is the extraordinary collection of small imagist poems, versified short stories, realistic urban and rural genre paintings, inventories, homilies, philosophizings, farcical episodes, confessions, and lyric musings it encompasses in "Song of Myself." Yet as heavily taxing our powers of provisional credence, as inventing a highly idiosyncratic and illusory world, "Song of Myself" invites comparison with other curious works of the American imagination—*Moby Dick,* let us say, and *The Scarlet Letter* and *The Wings of the Dove.* It is of the first importance at any rate to see that Whitman's relation of the self to the rest of the universe is a successful aesthetic or compositional device, whatever we may think of it as a moral assertion.

If we look at Whitman's implicit metaphor more closely, we see that it consists in the paradox of "identity." The opening words of *Leaves of Grass,* placed there in 1867, state the paradox:

One's-self I sing, a simple separate person,
Yet utter the word Democratic, the word En-Masse.

In more general terms the opening lines of "Song of Myself" state the same paradox:

I celebrate myself and sing myself;
And what I assume you shall assume;
For every atom belonging to me, as good belongs to you.

Both politically and by nature man has "identity," in two senses of the word: on the one hand, he is integral in himself, unique, and separate; on the other hand, he is equal to, or even the same as, every-one else. Like the Concord transcendentalists, Whitman was easily led in prophetic moods to generalize the second term of the paradox of identity beyond the merely human world and with his ruthless equalitarianism to conceive the All, a vast cosmic democracy, placid, without episode, separation or conflict, though suffused, perhaps, with a bland illumination. More than anything else, it is this latter tendency which finally ruined Whitman as a poet, submerging as it did, his chief forte and glory—his entirely original, vividly realistic presentation of the comedy and pathos of "the simple separate person."

What finally happens is that Whitman loses his sense that his metaphor of self vs. en-masse is a *paradox,* that self and en-masse are in dialectic opposition. When this sense is lost the spontaneously eventful, flowing, and largely indeterminate universe of "Song of Myself" is replaced by a universe that is both mechanical and vaguely abstract. Whatever, in this universe, is in a state of becoming is moving toward the All, and the self becomes merely the vehicle by which the journey is made.

In some of his best as well as in some of his worst poems, Whitman actually conceives of the self as making a journey—for example, "Song of the Open Road," "Crossing Brooklyn Ferry," and "Passage to India." In others the self journeys, as it were, not forward and outward but backward and inward, back to the roots of its being, and discovers there a final mystery, or love, comradeship, or death—for example, the *Calamus* and *Sea Drift* poems. (Notable among the latter are "Out of the Cradle Endlessly Rocking" and "As I Ebb'd with the Ocean of Life.") In "Song of Myself," however, the self is not felt to be incomplete; it has no questing odyssey to make. It stands aggressively at the center of things, "Sure as the most certain sure, plumb in the uprights, well entretied, braced in the beams." It summons the universe, "syphons" universal experience through its dilating pores, calls "anything back again when I desire it." Or the self imagines itself to be infinitely expandable and contractible (like the web of the spider in Whitman's little poem called "A Noiseless Patient Spider"), so that there is no place where at any moment it may not be, no thing or person with whom it may not merge, no act in which it may not participate. Of great importance is the fact that most of "Song of Myself" has to do not with the self searching for a final identity but with the self escaping a series of identities which threaten to destroy its lively and various spontaneity. This combination of attitudes is what gives "Song of Myself" the alternately ecstatic and gravely musing, pastoral-godlike stability one feels at the center, around which, however, the poet is able to weave the most astonishing embellishments of wit and lyric song.

This is perhaps a valid way of feeling the shifting modes of sensibility in the poem. Yet it would be wrong to attribute any clear-cut structure to "Song of Myself." "The United States themselves are essentially the greatest poem," wrote Whitman in his preface. A Jacksonian Democrat, Whitman was not an admirer of federal unity, either in a nation or a poem. He was content to make his poem a loose congeries of states and half-settled territories. He was content that his poem should mirror that "freshness and candor of . . . physiognomy," that "picturesque looseness of carriage," and that "deathless attachment to freedom" which, in his preface, he attributed to his countrymen. His style would be organic; he would "speak in literature with the perfect rectitude and insouciance" of animals and growing things. Although capable of finely pictorial images, Whitman composed more by ear than by eye, and his ear being attuned to music of the looser, more variable sort, such as the Italian operas, he strung his poems together on a free melodic line and by means of motifs, voices, recapitulations, recitatives, rests, *crescendi* and *diminuendi*.

The motif of "Song of Myself" is the self taking on a bewildering variety of identities and with a truly virtuoso agility extricating itself from each one. The poem begins with the exhortation to leave the "rooms full of perfume," the "creeds and schools." Apart from conventions,

> Apart from the pulling and hauling stands what I am,
> Stands amused, complacent, compassionating, idle, unitary.

Having put society and convention behind, "What I am" finds itself in an Edenlike, early-morning world, wherein one easily observes the portentous dialectics of the universe:

> Urge and urge and urge,
> Always the procreant urge of the world.
> Out of the dimness opposite equals advance, always
>   substance and increase, always sex,
> Always a knit of identity, always distinction, always a
>   breed of life.

But of more importance is the fact that in this idyllic world the veil is lifted from the jaundiced eye, the cramped sensibility is set free, the senses and pores of the body receive the joyful intelligences dispatched to them by a friendly and providential nature. The self appears to be the offspring of a happy union of body and soul; sublime and delightful thoughts issue from the mind in the same miraculous way as the grass from the ground. Death itself is seen to be "lucky." And, in short, "what I am" can well afford to be complacent, to be certain that it is "unitary." Nor is the feeling of power denied to the self. It derives power from nature, as does the horse—"affectionate, haughty, electrical"—with which the poet compares himself. It derives power, too, from identification with others—the "runaway slave," "the butcher-boy," the "blacksmiths," "the boatmen and clam-diggers," the "trapper," the "red girl"—and finally with America itself.

> In me the caresser of life wherever moving, backward
>   as well as forward sluing,
> To niches aside and junior bending, not a person or
>   object missing,
> Absorbing all to myself and for this song.

Sections 24-28, though in places rather obscure, contain the essence of Whitman's drama of identity. The poet begins by proclaiming himself a Kosmos, and commanding us to "unscrew the locks from the doors! / Unscrew the doors themselves from their jambs!" so that the universe may flow through him—"through me the current and index" (that is, the undifferentiated flux and the "identities" that emerge therefrom). This proclamation announces not only the unshakable status and palpable reality but also the redemptive powers of the self. In a world which has been created by banishing social sanctions and social intelligence, what will keep man from being lost in idiocy, crime, squalor? What of that underground realm inhabited by

> . . . the deform'd, trivial, flat, foolish, despised,
> Fog in the air, beetles rolling balls of dung?

The threat of madness, crime, and obscenity is to be allayed by the curative powers of that Adamic world where wisdom consists in uttering "the pass-word primeval," "the sign of democracy." Siphoned through the haughty, electrical self or discussed frankly by persons not inhibited by prudery (the discourses seem perilously interchangeable), the crimes and obscenities will be redeemed:

> Voices indecent by me clarified and transfigur'd.

The poet then records a dreamlike idyl of auto-erotic experience, in which the parts of the body merge mysteriously with natural objects, and a great deal of diffuse and wistful love is generated. And, when dawn comes, the redemption is symbolized in these astonishing metaphors:

> Hefts of the moving world at innocent gambols silently
>   rising, freshly exuding,
> Scooting obliquely high and low.
>
> Something I cannot see puts upward libidinous prongs,
> Seas of bright juice suffuse heaven.

The poem then speaks anew of how the self may be distorted or destroyed. The poet's "identity" is said to be assailed and warped into other "identities" by agents referred to as "traitors," "wasters," and "marauders." Somewhat elusive in particular, these appear to have in common a quality of aggressiveness and imperiousness. They act as a radical individualist conceives society to act. They break down the self, they swagger, they assert convention, responsibility and reason, they dominate and impose passivity and furtiveness on the individual.

The beautiful, diffuse, kindly dawn is succeeded by a more formidable, a more imperious, apparition. The "dazzling and tremendous" sun leaps over the horizon and cries, "See then whether you shall be master!" The poet replies to this challenge by saying that the sunrise would indeed "kill me / If I could not now and always send sunrise out of me." The power with which the poet defeats what seeks to destroy him is asserted to be "my vision" and "my voice."

> My voice goes after what my eyes cannot reach,
> With the twirl of my tongue I encompass worlds.

In Section 26 both the metaphorical effects and the subject matter shift from the visual to the auditory. The "bravuras of birds, bustle of growing wheat, gossip of flames, clack of sticks cooking my meals" —these and myriad other sounds amplify into a symphonic orchestration. The crescendo and dying fall of the conclusion are rendered with full tone and exquisite wit.

> I hear the train'd soprano (what work, with hers, is this?)
> The orchestra whirls me wider than Uranus flies,
> It wrenches such ardors from me I did not know I
>   possess'd them,
> It sails me, I dab with bare feet, they are lick'd by the
>   indolent waves,
> I am cut by bitter and angry hail, I lose my breath,
> Steep'd amid honey'd morphine, my windpipe throttled
>   in fakes of death,
> At length let up again to feel the puzzle of puzzles,
> And that we call Being.

But again the poet is confronted with "Being"—that is, form or identity—and is not certain that this is the Being he wants to be. It is therefore dissipated and generalized, in Section 27, into a universal process of reincarnation.

In Section 28 there occurs the famous auto-erotic pastoral dream in which "prurient provokers," like nibbling cows, "graze at the edges of me." The "provokers," conceived as symbolic of the sense of touch, arouse and madden the dreaming poet and then they all unite "to stand on a headland and worry me." After touch has "quivered" him "to a new identity"—has left him confused, vexed, self-reproachful, and isolated—he proceeds in the following sections to resume a "true," "real," or "divine" identity. This act of restoration is accomplished through love, natural piety, pastoral and cosmic meditations, symbolic fusions of self with America, allegations of the "deific" nature of democratic man, ritual celebrations, and fatherly preachments, and finally, in the last Section, by the assertion that death is also merely an extrication of the self from an identity.

Everyone has noticed that the large, bland exterior of Walt Whitman concealed a Dionysus or Pan—one of the first was Moncure Conway, who visited Walt in Brooklyn in the summer of 1857, found him basking in the sun on a hill near the Whitman house, and later noticed that the only decorations in the poet's room were two engravings, "one of Silenus and the other of Bacchus." And surely no one can read "Song of Myself" without seeing that Whitman recreates there something of the spirit of the Greek cults out of which comedy evolved. Does he not summon us, his boon companions, to the outdoor revel, to "dance, laugh, and sing," to celebrate the phallic god? Are not masks donned and removed, "identities" concealed and exchanged? Do we not have a ritual celebration of "Nature without check with original energy," of the cycle of death and rebirth, the *agon,* sacrifice, and *gamos* of the protagonist, i.e. the self? Do we not have in Whitman's image of the diffusion of the self in nature a religious feeling akin to that engendered in the Dionysian mysteries by the dismemberment and assimilation of the sacrificial victim?

To be sure, the "mysticism" we ordinarily associate with Whitman is less akin to Dionysian than to Oriental and Quaker religion. His mode of religious contemplation, taking it by and large, tends toward passivity and quietism. There is much of this quietism even in "Song of Myself." But the poem as a whole takes its tone from something more vital, indeterminate, violent, and primitive. And it is only to find the most appropriate name for this that one hits on the word "Dionysian." The ritual submovement of comedy asserts itself with a brilliant if spasmodic energy in "Song of Myself." It provides a metaphorical foundation for even the most elaborately artificial of verbal fancies such as "I recline by the sills of the exquisite flexible doors" or "I depart as air. I shake my white locks at the runaway sun"—lines which in point of rococo refinement rival anything that Congreve's Millamant might say to Mirabell.

Historically, Whitman's "American humor" is indeed related, however remotely, to the Restoration comedy. Broadly speaking, there have been in English since 1660 three manifestations of the comic spirit: the aristocratic high comedy of Congreve, the bourgeois sentimental or genteel comedy (by far the most pervasive and influential sort ever since the Restoration), and that American humor which has been practiced in one way or another and at one time or another by nearly all of our best writers. This is not the place to attempt a history of comedy or an analysis of American humor—the latter has been done exquisitely, if a little impressionistically, by Constance Rourke. One may merely venture the idea that, historically, American humor is a radical modification of sentimental comedy. At its best—in Mark Twain, Melville, Thoreau, or Whitman—it retains the capacity of sentimental comedy for pathos but escapes its sentimentality and its hypocrisy. It achieved this by rejecting the cardinal ethical values of bourgeois comedy—money and domestic fidelity. American humor is contemptuous of, or at least feels remote from, the family and money as ethical norms. In this respect and in its tendency toward cruelty and sheer verbal brilliance it is akin to high comedy.

Considered as a comic poem, "Song of Myself" combines Dionysian gaiety and an impulse toward verbal artificiality with the tone and cultural presuppositions of American humor—a striking feat of hybridization certainly, yet no more so than that which produced *Moby Dick*. The intention here is not to deny the justice of Emerson's remark that Whitman's poem was "a remarkable mixture of the *Bhagvatgeeta* and the *New York Herald*" or of the voluminous but one-sided academic scholarship which, following Emerson's remark, has regarded "Song of Myself" as an amalgam of Oriental philosophy and American realism. The intention is rather to shift the ground of discourse toward a more strictly literary view—the view which Emerson also adumbrated in his remark that the first edition of *Leaves of Grass* was an "extraordinary piece of wit and wisdom."

In 1889 Whitman said to his Camden friends, "I pride myself on being a real humorist underneath everything else" and when it was suggested that he might after all go down in history as a "comedian" he replied that one "might easily end up worse." He will certainly not go down in history as, purely and simply, a comedian. But humor was always a strong part of his sensibility, and it is difficult to see how it ever came to be a cliché about Whitman that "he had no sense of humor." There is substantial evidence that in his early life his mind turned naturally toward comic writing. Much of his newspaper work, particularly the "Sun-Down Papers From the Desk of a School-master," which he wrote for the *Long Island Democrat* and the sketches he did for the New Orleans *Crescent* (1848) show that he had mastered at least the easier tricks of the native folk humor. At various times during the 1840's Whitman expressed in newspaper articles his partiality to Dickens and Carlyle—Dickens whom "I love and esteem . . . for what he has taught me through his writings"; Carlyle, whose *Sartor Resartus* exhibits in abundance the author's "strange wild way." From these two writers Whitman seems to have learned that a great book might be eloquent, crotchety, full of curious events and observations, or a humorous compound of realism, philosophy, and sentiment. He surely learned this even more directly from Emerson's essays. If indeed there are so many parallels between "Song of Myself" and "Self-Reliance" that we almost think the poem a versification of the essay, it is nevertheless true that the parallels are not confined to the philosophic or moral message. There is a good deal of humor in Emerson's essay of the spontaneous, odd, yeasty sort noticed by Santayana, who said that Emerson "was like a young god making experiments in creation: he botched the work and always began on a new and better plan. Every day he said, 'Let there be light,' and every day the light was new." More specifically, what Whitman may have sensed in "Self-Reliance" is the humorous touch-and-go between the self and the author, which underlies the elaborate web of portentous epigram. Surely, one of the Emersonian passages that brought the simmering Whitman to a boil (as the poet himself phrased it) was the one near the end of "Self-Reliance" where Emerson is speaking of the fatuity of foreign travel and says that although he should wake up in Naples, "there beside me is the stern fact, the sad self, unrelenting, identical, that I fled from."

But aside from the question of literary influences there is the more fundamental question of cultural influence. Whitman emulated our democratic American ideals to an extent unexampled among our great writers, and there can be no doubt that many of his moral ut-terances and even his poetic effects are produced by the sublime literalness of the democratic assumptions which were so faithfully registered on his plastic mind and temperament. Tocqueville . . . based a part of his discussion of language and literature in the United States upon his observation that

In democratic communities each citizen is habitually engaged in the con-templation of a very puny object, namely, himself. If he ever raises his looks higher, he then perceives nothing but the immense form of society at large, or the still more imposing aspect of mankind. His ideas are all either extremely minute and clear, or extremely general and vague; what lies between is an open void.

This habit of mind has induced in American writing a style capable of very great and sudden extremes and has drawn from such writers as Melville, Emerson, Thoreau, and Emily Dickinson their idiosyncratic styles—the common denominator among them being a tendency of the language to shift rapidly from the homely and the colloquial to a rhetoric at once highly self-conscious, highly abstract, and highly elaborate. Since such shifts of ground between incongruous extremes are of the essence of wit, it is proper to speak of wit, or as we say, of "American humor," as a central problem in any exact investigation of the language of American literature—so long as we keep in mind how very pervasive an attitude is American humor. For indeed this form of wit is not confined to rural hoe-downs, minstrel shows, or tall tales about Paul Bunyan. It is a style, a habit of thought which allows for the different combinations of the native vernacular and traditional English created by the American authors, as well as their common habit of shifting with such brilliant effect from the particular to the general, from the small to the great, from the concrete to the transcendent. To encompass such effects a language must be highly flexible, capable not of subtle and sustained modulations, as is the prose of Edmund Burke or the poetry of Shakespeare, but—as Selincourt observed in writing about Whitman's language—of rapid transpositions, rapid shifts of language and of levels of discourse. And if these remarks are generally true of all American authors, they seem more literally true of Whitman than of anyone else.

Thus Whitman's struggle for a language in the years before 1855 was not essentially different from that of his peers among American writers. It was easy to combine the literary with the vernacular as a joke, and Whitman often did this in his newspaper writings, as in (a sentence from one of his New Orleans sketches) "a beautiful, enameled, filigree, inlaid morceau of *bijouterie,* whose value intrinsically, *per se,* was perhaps about six bits," or "we will e'en just have to give the go-by." It was more difficult to learn the trick of producing similar transpositions without being silly or bathetic—such a trick as is

---

• *Shakespeare's style, wrote Whitman (sounding for the moment like Burke) is determined by "the exquisite and seductive transfiguration of caste."*

turned toward the end of "Song of Myself" where the last line of Section 43 and the first of 44 are:

Nor the present, nor the least wisp that is known.

It is time to explain myself—let us stand up.

And most difficult of all was to achieve the standard accomplishment of the poetry at its best—a style, that is, which is "literary" and conversational at the same time, a style which has one eye on the individual and the concrete and one eye on the general and the transcendent.

One had better hasten to admit that a good deal of caution is called for in arguments which adduce the culture a poet lives in to explain his aesthetics. For one thing, it is of course impossible to say just what American culture is or to be sure that one traces aright its manifold influences on poetry. Then, again, no culture is perfectly unique. France has had democratic poets, there are moments in Rabelais and Kafka which seem indistinguishable from "American humor," Heine and Arnold wrote relatively "free verse," Whitman's own ideals were not only national but international. Yet the fact remains that we do have an observable national culture as well as an inherited European one, and that a truly historical critique of Whitman's poetry must begin with a view of the spoken and unspoken assumptions, the myths and habits of mind, the manners and "sentiments," of the culture the poet lived in.

Read as autobiography "Song of Myself," like *Leaves of Grass* as a whole, seems remarkably ironic, covert, elusive, and given to skipping back and forth between the personal and the generic. Yet among Whitman's confusing attempts to describe the subject of *Leaves of Grass* there is the recurring idea that it "has been mainly the outcropping of my own emotional and other personal nature— an attempt from first to last, to put a *Person,* a human being (myself, in the latter half of the nineteenth century in America) freely, fully and truly on record." As early as the Brooklyn *Eagle* days Whitman had praised Goethe's autobiography for being a book of this sort and had held it up to his readers as an exemplary modern work. But to compare "Song of Myself" with *Dichtung und Wahrheit* or with Rousseau's *Confessions* or with Wordsworth's *Prelude* is to be struck with how sparsely Whitman has represented himself, how small is the volume of the concrete natural and social particularity of the author's life. Anyone who has read a life of Whitman can make up a long catalogue of interesting particulars which the poet never treats in his poetry. Modern readers tend to chide Wordsworth for leaving

sex out of the *Prelude;* yet there is infinitely more of concrete autobiography in the *Prelude* than there is in *Leaves of Grass.* Wordsworth moves from the personal and the particular to the general with
a massive inductive maneuver, Whitman leaps from the one to the
other and back again with the utmost agility. His native "humor,"
when it is not meditative or elegiac, is, in "Song of Myself," equivalent to what Nietzsche praised as the "presto" style and which he
found pre-eminently in the combined French and Latin temperament
of Stendhal.

A comparison of characteristic European works such as *The Red
and the Black*, the lyrics of Blake, and the *Prelude* with "Song of
Myself" leads us to an important distinction. In their presentation
of a natural history of the self, Stendhal, Blake, and Wordsworth
trace the passage of the individual from innocence to experience, from
solitude to society. They tell us that the inevitable and proper task of
the individual is to transcend, although not to abandon, his innocence through *social* experience. Temperamental anarchists though
these authors may sometimes be, and corrupt as they may think
society is, they nevertheless believe that society is a redemptive agent,
without which innocence is helpless or even culpable.

Our American literary tradition has differed radically from the
European on this point. At the heart of the fiction of such writers as
Cooper, Melville, Mark Twain, and Faulkner, as modern criticism
has often pointed out, there is "a version of pastoral." It is a dream
of innocence and freedom which invites the young man to escape
society and to seek adventure as well as the fulfillment of his moral
being amid the influences and sanctions of wilderness, sea, or river.
This pastoral myth encourages the neophyte to regard women either
as seraphic creatures unsuited to the rigors of the free masculine life
or as threatening harpies who wish only to destroy the dream of
masculine freedom and subdue the male to the conventions of society.
Certainly from the point of view of Western culture the representation of women by some of the classic American authors is a striking
absurdity. Could Western culture, gazing at Cooper's Alice Munroe
and Judith Hutter, Melville's Yillah and Hautia, Hawthorne's Hilda
and Miriam, these innocent fair and sinister dark "women," believe
them to be a compensation for the pang of America's birth? The
myth has, however, its own sort of love, first codified perhaps in
Cooper's *Deerslayer*. Natty Bumppo's love takes two forms, a nature
mysticism (my love, says Cooper's hero in rejecting Judith Hutter
because she is sexually tainted, is in the green foliage of the forest
and the clear waters of the lake) or the tranquil idyl of masculine
companionship (Natty and Chingachgook). Natty Bumppo, according

to Balzac "a magnificent moral hermaphrodite, born between the savage and the civilized states of man," was a spiritual father of Walt Whitman; he was also, as we learn from the conversations with Traubel, one of Whitman's favorite fictional characters.

Urbanite though he was, everything in Whitman's upbringing and native temperament fitted him to be the devotee of this pastoral myth. So powerfully did he feel its demands, in fact, that in "Song of Myself" he not only celebrated his acceptance of the myth; he burst through its usual limits and transcended its usual meaning. In most of the classic American authors, society is not ultimately denied. It is merely deplored and temporarily abandoned, for in the minds of each there lurks somewhere over the horizon of the pastoral idyl a social convention. Even in treating what they take to be their most important theme, the initiation of the neophyte, Cooper, Melville, and Faulkner, intimate, despite their genuine democratic feelings, that it must occur in a context of spiritual or moral hierarchy. Cooper's *Satanstoe,* Hawthorne's *House of the Seven Gables,* Melville's *Pierre,* Faulkner's *Sound and the Fury* are firmly enough conscious of social and historical values to make them excellent dramas of the decline of families. Hawthorne and James are intensely conscious of moral obligations and moral differences. Emily Dickinson and Melville are struck by the definitive disjunctions which may exist between man and nature, or man and god, or man and fellow-man. In short, the preponderant tendency of the classic American writers —despite their broad areas of commonalty with Whitman (and Emerson)—has been toward an insistence on placing the individual in a world in which inequities, distinctions, and limitations are radically present. This has implied at least a fluctuating sense of society, and if Whitman's literary peers did not make so much of society as, by and large, their European contemporaries did, they nevertheless had enough moral skepticism to keep them from supposing they could get along without it. But in "Song of Myself" Whitman does not content himself with deploring society and taking to the woods with his bachelor companions. He entirely destroys society by imaginatively transfiguring it so that it becomes, as it were, merely the particular locus of the innocent pastoral world. Society is first denounced and then poetically transfigured in such a way that it can be absorbed into the native sensations, desires, and aspirations of the nonsocial man. Whitman's mind—as exemplified in "Song of Myself"—was perfectly utopian and this is, of course, one reason why we do not freely read and enjoy his greatest poem. The modern mind has been made so fully aware of the historical tragedies implied by utopian politics that it has forgotten the distinctive human virtues of the radical utopian vision. One may add that only in his early poems is Whitman the free spirit. Although there is still some radical utopian feeling in such a later work as *Democratic Vistas,* the same impulses which find poetic expression in "Song of Myself" take on in the prose polemics of *Democratic Vistas* a conservative, prudential tone.

This transfiguration of society has several advantages for the poet, and Whitman has made resplendent use of them in "Song of Myself." It gives the poet an enormous and brilliant egotism. The unfolding discoveries about himself and about what can be done poetically with his ideas about himself provide a refreshing current of exhilaration and a scene of action which we can believe to be free of man-made limitations and proscriptions. The idea of perfect freedom, of the "eligibility" of the self to everything else—the nation, the cosmos, all other selves—this is the valuable illusion created by Whitman's first great poem: The insouciance, the continuous upwelling sense of novelty, the brash self-assurance which alternates so charmingly with grave humor and tender concern for the suffering of others and of the self—these qualities and many more save Whitman's egotism from being merely repellent and "rhetorical."

Granted, these are not qualities which excite our age, which is very much an age of moral gloom. Granted, too, that Whitman's moral vision is dubious and contradictory. One must admit, furthermore, that although it has its own virtues, Whitman's utopian version of the American pastoral myth has so far proved less artistically dependable, less suggestive of imaginative possibility than the myth as conceived by the other classic authors. And despite Whitman's much asserted Americanism, theirs seems just at present to be historically the more influential myth. As I have suggested before, Whitman achieved the remarkable feat of being an eccentric by taking more literally and mythicizing more simply and directly than anyone else the expressed intentions and ideals of our democracy. He is, in "Song of Myself," the only really "free" American. He is, or seems to be, beyond good and evil, beyond the compulsion to pit his ideals against history and social reality. Cooper, Melville, Mark Twain are never so transcendently free; their dreams are troubled and their having dreams makes them sad and guilty; they impose upon us the weary task of moral judgment and upon themselves a willed and rhetorical self-justification. And if Whitman affords a welcome contrast to our American moralists, he also floods the ego with a vital gaiety of a special quality unknown to Europe—unless, indeed, the note was struck by Nietzsche, who complains of the thinkers and scholars of his time because "thinking itself is regarded by them as something slow and hesitating, almost as a trouble, and often enough as 'worthy of the sweat of the noble'—not at all as something easy and divine, closely related to dancing and exuberance!" In "Song of Myself" there is none of that straining desperation, that gloomy, willful, grammatical Romanticism which always threatens to take the joy out of the egotism of Byron, Carlyle, and sometimes of Nietzsche himself, no sense of the fated will of the European nineteenth century urging itself toward its melodramatic suicide. And so it is possible sometimes to prefer Whitman's comic vision to the social melodrama of the European writers and the moral idyls of Whitman's compatriots, to value it separately and for what it is—a great releasing and regenerative force.

One may even suppose that future readers may find Whitman more relevant to their vital concerns than the tragic moralists among our American writers. Of these tragic moralists, with their pastoral legend, Cooper may seem the first and Hemingway the last. Yet Whitman may be regarded as more modern than Hemingway. For was it not Whitman who first sought out the grounds on which in the midst of our urban modernization the individual with all his dilemmas and aspirations can exist, whereas Hemingway still clings to a version of nineteenth-century Romanticism which in Melville and Mark Twain was already nostalgic? The future reader may not think it an extreme case if someone should remark to him that Whitman's utopian rejection of society is under modern conditions the necessary first step toward the preservation of what is vital in society and the revitalization of what is not, and, furthermore, that despite his intellectual shortcomings, despite even the final disappearance of his idealism into the All, Whitman knew more of the homely root facts of the life of modern society than did Melville or Mark Twain, and that at his best his vision stubbornly began and ended with these root facts. . . .

18

Newton Arvin: THE WHALE [1950]

. . . There is a passage in *Moby Dick* in which Melville deprecates
the possibility that some ignorant landsmen will scout at the White
Whale as "a monstrous fable, or still worse and more detestable, a
hideous and intolerable allegory." It is quite plain that the remark
has two edges and is meant to be ironical; it is plain, too, however,
that Melville was in fact earnestly avoiding what we should now call
allegory, in the sense in which we would use it of *Mardi.* The word
"symbolism," in its literary bearing, had not come into use at the
time *Moby Dick* was written; it was nearly twenty years before it did
so, although Emerson had already dwelt with extraordinary eloquence and subtlety, in the essay on "The Poet," on the role of symbols both in experience and in art. If Melville had had the word, no
doubt he would have used it in his own thinking about the books; as
it was, he was limited to the older and less suitable one. As almost
always happens in literary history, the *thing* had come before the
term for it; and so, when Melville answered an appreciative letter of
Sophia Hawthorne's, a month or two after *Moby Dick* had appeared,
he expressed himself in this manner: "I had some vague idea while
writing it, that the whole book was susceptible of an allegorical construction, and also that *parts* of it were—but the speciality of many
of the particular subordinate allegories, were first revealed to me,

after reading Mr. Hawthorne's letter which, without citing any particular examples, yet intimated the part-and-parcel allegoricalness of the whole."

There is a little touch here of the serious artists' particular sort of frivolity and disingenuousness, as one is pleased to find; it was the right tone for Melville to take, now that his book was well behind him. But of course he had had much more than a "vague idea" while writing *Moby Dick* that his fable, his images, his personages were the bearers of complex and unstatable meanings that no prosaic apprehension of them, even one that would be appropriate to other literary forms, could account for. Emerson's remarks had been highly symptomatic, as some of Carlyle's had also been, and the poetic mind in America was already symbolist in everything but the program, as Poe's and Hawthorne's work had shown and as Whitman's was soon to show. Unlike these others as he was in the special grain of his mind, Melville was at one with them in the conviction they all shared, the conviction that "objects gross" are only provisionally real, and that the eventual reality is the "unseen soul" they embody. In that familiar sense they were all "transcendentalists": their assumptions were those of romantic idealism, and their literary practice was in entire keeping with these. Ahab of course is only putting it all in his own manner when he speaks to Starbuck in a familiar passage thus: "All visible objects, man, are but as pasteboard masks. But in each event—in the living act, the undoubted deed—there, some unknown but still reasoning thing puts forth the mouldings of its features from behind the unreasoning mask." Or later, apostrophically: "O Nature, and O soul of man! how far beyond all utterance are your linked analogies! not the smallest atom stirs or lives on matter, but has its cunning duplicate in mind."

Such is Melville's personal version of the doctrine of Correspondences that lay below so much romantic and symbolist writing, as a similar doctrine of analogies lay below medieval allegory. That he entertained some such view has long been a familiar fact, and there is nothing remarkable now in saying that *Moby Dick,* in a sense that does not quite hold for any other American book, is a symbolist prose romance. Its leading images are symbols in the strict sense, not allegorical devices or emblems; symbols in the sense that their primal origins are in the unconscious, however consciously they have been organized and controlled; that on this account they transcend the personal and local and become archetypal in their range and depth; that they are inexplicit, polysemantic, and never quite exhaustible in their meanings. "The profounder emanations of the human mind," said Melville himself a little later in *Pierre,* "never unravel their own intricacies"; and he cannot have been unaware that his own book would present difficulties to the unraveler. Many of these have long since been disentangled, yet something always remains to be added, however slight, to any cluster of interpretations, however rich. It may be useful here to speak of *Moby Dick* and its meanings by adopting our own version of Dante's "fourfold interpretation" (which is of course inapplicable) and suggesting that the intricacies of the book may be reduced to four planes of significance; that these may be called the literal, the oneiric or psychological, the moral, and the mythic.

Of the first of these, the literal, not much (by definition) demands saying. What is chiefly important is not to allow ourselves to forget that it is there, just as it is in Dante's poem, and that the literary critic, like the Biblical exegete, must remember Pascal's salutary warning against two errors: "1. To take everything literally. 2. To take everything spiritually." Taking everything in *Moby Dick* "spiritually" means not taking it spiritually enough; the intangible meanings of the romance would not be so wide-reaching and deep-plunging as they are if they were not embodied in a fable of which virtually every detail has a hard, concrete, prosaic, and even naturalistic substantiality. There are some exceptions to this, as the principle of contrast demands; the Spirit-Spout is one of them, and the actual make-up of the crew is another. Miscellaneous as the real crews of the whalers were, we are not intended to suppose literal-mindedly that any one of them ever included as harpooneers a Gayhead Indian, a Negro, and a Polynesian, as well as a boat's crew of Parsees, and along with them a Maltese sailor, a Tahitian sailor, an Icelandic, a Chinese, a Danish sailor, and so on. Yet all these freedoms with realism are dilatations of fact, not pure fantasies; even the Spirit-Spout doubtless had its origin in the surely quite breath-taking sight, at sea, of a Sperm Whale's jetting spout beheld at some distance on a moonlight night. The mere *scaffolding* of *Moby Dick,* as hundreds of readers have felt, would remain firm and stable if there were no question of symbols whatever.

The literalness of the book has another facet, however, to which justice has not been done. It is the facet provided largely by the factual chapters about whales and whaling. The true purpose of these chapters is to provide the book with an even intenser literalness than it otherwise has, and this on a serious intellectual level. This literalness, not of course stylistically but in substance, is that of systematic and exact knowledge; it is the literalness of the natural and especially the biological sciences. It is all, or much of it, translated into imaginative or humorous terms, and Melville insists on having his joke by arguing that the whale is not a mammal but *"a spouting fish with a horizontal tail."* Yet the motive behind these chapters remains a serious one. Transcendentalist though he was at the center of his mentality, Melville had too tough and too capacious a mind to fall willingly into mere vaporous and subjective idealism. He was a romantic idealist with a passion for actuality, for precise knowledge, for facts; he was an intuitionalist who wished, in his essential reliance on the nonrational and the superrational, not to fall a victim to mindlessness; not to foreswear the sanctions of the intellect. "Undeniably," says Bardianna in *Mardi,* "reason was the first revelation; and so far as it tests all others, it has precedence over them . . . so far as it goes, for us, it is reliable."

A passage like this, one hurriedly notes, must be seen in the context of Melville's whole work; taken by itself it is misleading: the fact is of course that Melville was no simple-minded idolater of what Wordsworth had called "our meddling intellect." There was a painful division in his mind, as in the minds of many of his contemporaries, between his distrust of the discursive reason and his respect for it; he suffered deeply from the inner dissociations of his age. Yet his aspiration, like Thoreau's for example, was to triumph over them; to do justice both to "visible objects," masks as they are, and to the immaterial reality that, as he believed, lies behind them. It was an impossible task, so profoundly split, so dualized was the mind of his time, and his own as representative of it. But it was a task of which Melville intuitively felt the momentousness, and as a result *Moby Dick,* symbolist romance that it is, draws close at one pole to the bias of naturalism. The White Whale is a symbol, certainly, and even some of the details of his anatomy contribute to what he symbolizes; but their literal value is there all the while, and we must know how to give the proper, prosaic attention even to a half-humorous classification (the Folio Whale, the Octavo Whale, and so on), to the measurement of the whale's skeleton, to the facts about his blubber, his sense-organs, his spermaceti, and his flukes. We are in the company, and should recognize it, not only of Coleridge and Carlyle and Emerson but of Linnaeus and Cuvier.

We leave their company abruptly, however, when we move beyond the reading of *Moby Dick* as literal narrative and exposition, and begin to read it as what, on one plane, it is, an oneiric or dreamlike projection of Melville's unconscious wishes and obscure inward contests. *On one plane* the book is this, and on that plane only; for of course *Moby Dick* is not a dream but a work of imaginative art, and this means that it is the product of a complex creative process of which a great part has been conscious, deliberate, reflective: the formless spontaneity of an actual dream, along with much else, has been transcended. It shares with a dream, however, its sources in the unconscious, its dependence on irrational symbols, and its power to give expression to deep, instinctive, irrational fears and desires. How much of the sway it exercises over us depends on this!

When we read *Moby Dick* in this manner we are conscious of being presented at the very outset with one dominating oneiric image, the image of self-destruction; and then, as the action unrolls itself, and Ahab advances slowly to the forescene, we are given its counterpart and equivalent, the image of murderous destructiveness directed outward against the Other. From one point of view, what is dreamlike in the book may be said to move back and forth between these two poles, the suicidal wish, the longing for self-extinction, and its necessary antithesis, so deeply dependent upon it emotionally, the desire to inflict death upon what is, or what one imagines to be, the source of one's suffering. To undergo a kind of suicide is the motive that, along with the idea of the Whale (so closely bound up with it), impels Ishmael in the first place to go off to sea. Whenever, he says, he finds himself involuntarily pausing before coffin warehouses, and bringing up the rear of every funeral he meets, then he accounts it high time to get to sea as soon as he can: "With a philosophical flourish Cato throws himself upon his sword; I quietly take to the ship." There follows a series of hypnotic meditations on the allurements of the sea, of water generally, in which that element figures, though in a complex and iridescent way, as a symbol of death; of a return to the primal liquidity, oblivion, nonbeing. The sailing of the *Pequod* is to be for Ishmael a temporary passage out of existence.

Meanwhile, however, the death-wish has met with a check and a corrective; Thanatos has entered into a contest with Eros, and Ishmael, in his deathful loneliness encountering the savage Queequeg, has formed a solemn friendship with him, formed what he calls a marriage; the longing to love and to be loved has evoked its own oneiric symbol, and from this point forward Ishmael gradually ceases to be the man committed wholly to death. A dreamlike "displacement" occurs, and the accent shifts to Ahab, another embodiment of the self, and to Ahab's will to death, which expresses itself not directly as the conscious purpose of suicide, but indirectly as the purpose to wreak destruction on Moby Dick. It is true that Ishmael succumbs with part of his being to Ahab's ferocious hate: "A wild, mystical, sympathetical feeling was in me," he says; "Ahab's quenchless feud seemed mine." But the verb is "seemed" not "was," and already there is the possibility of Ishmael's recovering the will to live.

From this point on we are only intermittently and in flashes aware of him. It is Ahab in whom the most intense emotions of the dream are now concentrated. He is what our wildest, most egoistic, most purely destructive malevolence could wish to be, this old Quaker skipper from Nantucket; obsessed to the point of monomania with the will to destroy the hated thing, yet free from all mere smallnesses, "a grand, ungodly, godlike man." He is our hatred ennobled, as we would wish to have it, up to heroism. Moreover, he has in fact been terribly and vitally injured by Moby Dick. The Whale, in what looks like conscious malice, has reaped Ahab's leg away with his frightful, sickle-shaped jaw, and Ahab must now rely on a dead, artificial leg made of a Sperm Whale's jawbone. A kind of castration, in short, has been not only imagined and dreaded but inflicted, and the phallic source of vital potency has been replaced by an image of impotence and lifelessness, constructed from the skeleton of the injurer himself. Not only so, but in a kind of redoubled, repetitive, dreamlike manner, we hear that this apparently impotent limb has itself turned upon Ahab, and that before the sailing of the *Pequod* he had been found one night fallen in the streets of Nantucket with his artificial leg so twisted about that it had smitten his groin like a stake and almost pierced it.

A profound sexual injury is transparently symbolized here, and Ahab's "ivory" leg is an equivocal symbol both of his own impotence and of the independent male principle directed cripplingly against him. It had been fashioned from the polished bone of a Sperm Whale's jaw, though not of course from Moby Dick's own: what, then, does Moby Dick himself, on this deep instinctive plane, shadow forth? It would be easiest to say simply the father, the father who imposes constraint upon the most powerful instincts, both egoistic and sexual; the father also who threatens even to destroy the latter by castration and may indeed, in all but the literal sense, carry out the threat. On the deepest level, this is the oneiric truth about Moby Dick, but it is Melville with whom we have to reckon throughout, and for whom we have to remember how soon, and how overbearingly, the paternal role was played by Maria Melville. On every ground we are forced to confront a profound ambiguity in Moby Dick and to end by confessing that he embodies neither the father merely nor the mother but, by a process of condensation, the *parental* principle inclusively. Of his basic maleness there can be no question, not only because we are everywhere reminded of his preternatural power and masculine strength but because, in detail, we are required to contemplate the "battering-ram" of his head, the highly prized spermaceti with which it is so richly stored, his phallus ("The Cassock"), and his tail (with its "Titanism of power"); there is even a suggested association with the phallic serpent-god of the Ophites. Yet along with all this we cannot ignore a certain bisexuality in the image, if not literally of Moby Dick, then of the Sperm Whale generally; a bisexuality that is conveyed to us partly by the glimpses we have into his "beautiful" mouth and "the great Kentucky Mammoth Cave of his stomach"—that stomach in which, as Father Mapple's sermon reminds us, Jonah was swallowed up as in a womb—but also, and chiefly, by the obstetric imagery of the chapter (LXXVIII) in which Tashtego falls into the liquid depths of a Sperm Whale's severed head and is rescued or "delivered," like a baby, by Queequeg.

Moby Dick is thus the archetypal Parent; the father, yes, but the mother also, so far as she becomes a substitute for the father. And the emotions Moby Dick evokes in us are the violently contradictory emotions that prevail between parent and child. Too little, curiously, has been made of this; what dominates most accounts of the White Whale is the simple vindictive emotion that Ahab is alleged to feel toward him, and of course there can be no question of his Oedipal bitterness toward Moby Dick: his conviction that the Whale is the embodiment of "all the subtle demonisms of life and thought"; in short, "all evil." Yet hatred of this obsessive and even paranoid sort is but the deformation of a still more deep-seated love, and Ahab is tightly bound to Moby Dick as an unhappy child to a parent too passionately loved. The emotion, however, that the Sperm Whale inspires is not restricted to Ahab's monomaniac vengefulness: from the very outset we are conscious also of Ishmael's feelings, and though at one pole these are identified with Ahab's, at the other they are by no means the same. They are, at any rate, more openly and obviously contradictory: the "grand hooded phantom," as it swims before Ishmael's fancy, may inspire a kind of fear but it inspires also an intensity of mystical longing that is something like love. It is a sort of love that lies behind that passionate preoccupation with every detail, however trifling, that characterizes the regarded object, and it is a sort of love, though an imperfectly fulfilled one, that brings Moby Dick before our imaginations as a creature of "majestic bulk," "pervading dignity," and "appalling beauty."

In his role of archetypal parent, in fact, Moby Dick is the object of an excessive and an eventually crippling love, as Maria Melville was for her son; and the consequence is the vital injury symbolized by the loss of Ahab's leg, an injury to the capacity for heterosexual love. Both Ahab and Ishmael suffer in this way, but Ahab far the more terribly of the two. Ishmael, by somehow preserving a complexity of feeling toward the White Whale, has preserved also his capacity for selfless love even though this is directed toward his own sex and even toward a member of his own sex, Queequeg, who embodies both the grandeur and the limitations of the primitive, the prerational, the instinctive. Nevertheless it is love that Ishmael deeply feels toward Queequeg, and it is the imagination of an even more comprehensive love that comes to him as he sits before a tub of cooling spermaceti, squeezing its congregated globules back into fragrant fluid, and washing his hands and his heart, as he does so, of "our horrible oath." The capacity to imagine an all-embracing love, which proves to be Ishmael's salvation, Ahab has fatally lost. He has lost it so far that he has succeeded in hardening his heart even toward his young wife and their child, whom he has frankly deserted; what wretched vestiges of pure human feeling are left in him go out to the small black boy Pip, and to him reluctantly. Ahab is dedicated now to mere destruction, and he ends by attaining his suicidal wish and meeting his death by water. Ishmael, thanks to his rejection of mere hatred, survives the wreck; is picked up before he drowns by "the devious-cruising *Rachel*," the vessel that is itself a symbol of bereaved motherhood. In the end, the dream embodies a will to live triumphing over the will to die.

Meanwhile the unconscious and instinctive sources of the fable have expressed themselves in still other onciric symbols. The very setting of the whole narrative, on board a ship from which of necessity everything female has been excluded, is itself dreamlike and wishful. Of all the countersailing vessels the *Pequod* meets, only one is an image of prosperity and jolliness, and this vessel is revealingly named the *Bachelor*—that "glad ship of good luck" which is heading back to Nantucket laden to its very bulwarks and mastheads with abounding spermaceti. The weapons with which the Sperm Whale is attacked and slaughtered are appropriately phallic symbols—harpoons, lances, cutting-spades, and the like—and if there were any uncertainty about the nature of Ahab's injury, on this instinctive plane, it would not survive a careful scrutiny of the doubloon he nails to the mainmast as a promised reward for the man who first sights Moby Dick. This golden coin from Ecuador bears on its exposed side three unmistakable symbols in the form of three Andean mountain-peaks, one of them flaming like a volcano, one bearing a tower on its top, and the third a crowing cock. Queequeg, gazing at it, as Stubb watches him from a little distance, glances from the coin to his thighbone, "comparing notes," and seems, as Stubb fancies, to find something in that vicinity: "I guess it's Sagittarius, or the Archer." The coin that is to reward the sailor who first glimpses the White Whale, and who proves to be Ahab himself, is one that symbolizes, among other things, the virility that Moby Dick has destroyed.

The moral meanings of *Moby Dick,* though of course they transcend its oneiric meanings and exist in a sense on another plane, are by no means independent of them: on the contrary, the unity of the book is so masterly that only by artifice can we disentangle its various strands of significance. From the oneiric point of view Ahab is the suffering and neurotic self, lamed by early experience so vitally that it can devote itself only to destructive ends and find rest only in self-annihilation. No reader of the book, to be sure, could fail to feel how imperfectly this clinical description fits the grandiose captain of the *Pequod*: he embodies a form of sickness, certainly, but in doing so he embodies also, and on a higher imaginative plane, a form of tragedy. The two, however, originate and eventuate together.

Ahab is not only the sick self; he is, for his time and place, the noblest and most complete embodiment of the tragic hero. He is modern man, and particularly American man, in his role as "free" and "independent" Individual, as self-sustaining and self-assertive Ego, of forcible will and unbending purpose all compact, inflexible, unpitying, and fell, but enlarged by both his vices and his strength to dimensions of legendary grandeur. About Ahab's moral largeness there can be no uncertainty: the cleansing effect of *Moby Dick* depends vitally upon that. He is described as not only "grand" but even "godlike," and godlike—in a sense that is at once Greek and Yankee, at once classical and contemporary—everyone feels him to be. He has such Areté, says Melville in effect, as a grim and shaggy old whale-hunter from Nantucket can have, and that is much; his very appearance suggests a demigod: "His whole high, broad form seemed made of solid bronze, and shaped in an unalterable mould, like Cellini's cast Perseus." He calls himself "proud as a Greek god," and indeed his pride is noble enough to endure the comparison. In its highest expression it is the heroic self-trust and self-regard of the modern Western man asserted in the teeth of all that would overbear and diminish him, whether natural or beyond nature. This is what Ahab affirms in the Aeschylean scene in which he defies the flaming corposants: "I own thy speechless, placeless power; but to the last gasp of my earthquake life will dispute its unconditional, unintegral mastery in me. In the midst of the personified impersonal, a personality stands here."

This is the very rapture of ideal individualism: neither Carlyle nor Emerson nor Nietzsche ever uttered it more loftily. Yet even as he pronounces his great tirade Ahab is dimly and bitterly aware that what he says is not true: what stands there is not, in the high sense, a personality, but only a proud and defiant will. Ahab has long since ceased to be a personality, if that word is to be understood as signifying a human being in all his wholeness and roundness. He has ceased to be anything but an Ego; a noble Ego, to be sure; a heroic one; but *that* rather than a Self. He is no longer a free mind: his thought has become the slave of his insane purpose. He is no longer emotionally free: his heart has become the slave of his consuming hate. Nor is he any longer morally free: his conscience too has allowed itself to be deadened and stupefied by the compulsive quest for Moby Dick. Just how empty, in this sense, is his claim to be a "queenly personality," he himself betrays when he exhibits what his monomania has done to his very conception of humanity, of "a complete man after a desirable pattern." In the scene with the old carpenter, who is making a new leg for him, Ahab, half soliloquizing, half addressing the carpenter, imagines such a man as, first, physically gigantic, and then as having "no heart at all, brass forehead, and about a quarter of an acre of fine brains."

Fine "brains," yes, as who should say "fine nerves"; not a fine and free intelligence, disinterestedly committed to the search for impersonal truth; what Ahab wants is hardly more than an anatomical organ that will act efficiently and mechanically in the service of his overbearing will. How much he cares for the intellect, in any serious sense, he demonstrates vividly enough in his destruction of the quadrant and his imprecation against science: "Science! Curse thee, thou vain toy. . . ." The capacity for pure thought had once been in him, and even in his ruin, as he leans over the bulwarks of the predestined ship, on the day before they encounter the White Whale, Ahab has a moment of something like speculative freedom: he allows himself, in his transitory and final weakness, to wonder what unearthly thing it is that, "against all natural lovings and longings," is impelling him forward to what he knows is disaster. Even now, however, he does not sincerely wish to find the answer: what he wishes is to judge himself ultimately blameless and irresponsible, and in the next breath he gives his evasive reply: "By heaven, man, we are turned round and round in this world, like yonder windlass, and Fate is the handspike." No wonder that, a minute later, he sees the satanic Fedallah's eyes leering up at him from their watery reflection.

It is partly his momentary gleams of insight, nevertheless, that preserve Ahab's tragic stature even in his perdition. He has penetrated to one of the fatal truths about himself when he uses the phrase, "against all natural lovings and longings." His ideal man would have "no heart at all," and he himself has striven with terrible success to destroy his own great native capacity for love. To have yielded to it—to have yielded to what is clearly his ardor of affection for his wife and child, to his love for little Pip, to his spontaneous movement of compassion for the bereaved Captain Gardiner—this would have been to open a breach in the massive wall of his self-sufficiency; and so rigid is his egoistic fixity that he cannot afford or admit the slightest concession to a self-forgetful thought. The idea of pure independence has become an insanity with him: the thought of dependence in any form is a torment. It enrages him that he must be a debtor to "this blockhead" of a carpenter for a bone to stand on: "Cursed be that mortal interindebtedness which will not do away with ledgers. I would be free as air; and I'm down in the whole world's books." Again, with his wonderful, intermittent self-knowledge, Ahab is right: he is not genuinely independent, but on the contrary peculiarly dependent, and on the whole world. It is a sterile dependence, however, not a creative one, because it is imposed from without by circumstance, not accepted from within by the ethical imagination; and Ahab has his reward. He gets not independence but isolation; and, since he is after all human, it is unendurable. He has lived, as he himself says, "in a desolation of solitude," and it destroys him. He has refused to accept the interdependence that is the condition of genuinely human existence, and we can at least imagine that, like Jonah in Father Mapple's sermon, "he feels that the dreadful punishment is just." Objectively it is so.

The wild joy of self-assertion was never more contagiously rendered than in the great scene on the quarter-deck. The misery of self-assertion was never more terribly conveyed than in the stern and solemn chapters with which *Moby Dick* approaches its catastrophe. It is the succession of the one emotion by the other that imparts to the book its primordially tragic quality. In our identification with Ahab we have undergone the double movement of aggression and submission, of self-assertion and self-surrender, that is the secret of the tragic release, and we are freed by it. That is what Melville himself meant by the familiar remark in a letter to Hawthorne: "I have written a wicked book, and feel spotless as the lamb." In the person of Ahab he had accepted the ultimate penalty, which he knew to be a just one, for his egoistic strivings.

The tragic error for which Ahab suffers is an archetypal one; it has both its general and its particular aspects, both its placeless and its local application. The raging egoism Ahab embodies has something in common with the Hubris of Greek tragedy, as it has also something, and still more, in common with the Christian sin of pride;

but it is neither quite the one nor quite the other. There is something of Prometheus, of Agamemnon, of Oedipus in Ahab: he is guilty of an inflated arrogance similar to theirs, a similar conviction of his superiority to the mass of ordinary men. The true antithesis of Hubris, however, is moderation, and moderation is no cardinal virtue in Melville's calendar; Starbuck embodies that, and Starbuck hovers between a golden *mediocritas* and plain mediocrity. So with the sin of pride: we are far closer to Ahab's error here, as with Melville's deep spiritual derivation from Calvinist Christianity we are bound to be. Father Mapple's sermon is intended to make us understand that Ahab, like Jonah, has in a certain sense sinned through his proud refusal to obey God's will, or its equivalent; pride and disobedience, in at any rate some dimly Christian senses, are at the root of Ahab's wickedness. The true antithesis of spiritual pride, however, is Christian humility; and this is only somewhat closer to Melville's positive thought than moderation is. A purely Christian submission and endurance, indeed, he describes in the chapter on "The Tail" as merely negative and feminine virtues, though they are, he adds, the peculiar practical virtues of Christ's teachings.

No, neither moderation nor humility is the true alternative to Ahab's error, and this because his error itself is not really Hubris and not really, in the strictest sense, spiritual pride. It is something closer to Ahab's actual world than either. Without an awareness of the gods' displeasure and jealousy in the offing, there is little intensity left in the idea of Hubris, and the conviction of the sinfulness of spiritual pride is at any rate transformed when the dogma of Original Sin is discarded. There was a level of Melville's complex mind on which the jealousy of the pagan gods could seem terribly real to him; there was certainly a level on which he was capable of darkly "believing" in Original Sin. In the fullest conscious sense, however, he believed in neither. What he felt as a menace in himself, and what he saw at work in the scene about him, was very like what Hawthorne felt and saw: a complex moral reality of which one pole was a pure and strong affirmation of the grandeur of the individual, and the other pole a wild egoism, anarchic, irresponsible, and destructive, that masqueraded in the kingly weeds of self-reliance. It is no accident that Ahab, as a whale-hunter, represents one of the great exploitative, wasteful, predatory industries of the nineteenth century; from this point of view the Whale embodies nothing so much as the normally innocent and indifferent forces of wild nature—the forests, the soil, the animal life of land and sea—that nineteenth-century man was bent on raping to his own egoistic ends. On the last day of the chase, in spite of what he has suffered at their hands, Moby Dick seems intent only on

swimming as swiftly and as straight as possible away from the *Pequod*.
"See!" cries the good Starbuck to Ahab. "Moby Dick seeks thee not!
It is thou, thou, that madly seekest him!"

The alternative to Ahab's egoism is not, then, the ideal of "Nothing
too much," nor is it a broken and a contrite heart. On one level it is
an intuition that carries us beyond morality, in the usual sense, into
the realm of cosmic piety; on the usual ethical level, however, it is a
strong intuition of human solidarity as a priceless good. Behind Melville's expression of this, one is conscious of the gravity and the tenderness of religious feeling, if not of religious belief; it came to him
in part from the Christian tradition in which he had been nurtured.
The form it took in him, however, is no longer specifically Christian;
as with Hawthorne and Whitman, it was the natural recoil of a sensitive imagination, enriched by the humanities of romantic idealism,
against the ruinous individualism of the age. It is Melville's version
of Hawthorne's "magnetic chain of humanity," of Whitman's "manly
attachment": so far, it is an essentially humanistic and secular principle.

Ishmael, again, whose very name suggests a desperate estrange-
ment, becomes nevertheless the narrative agent of these affirmations.
Solitary and embittered as he first appears to us, Ishmael seems
scarcely to have hardened the outermost surface of his heart: even
before he has departed from New Bedford, his distrusts and his re-
sentments have yielded to the outgoing affectionateness of "this
soothing savage," Queequeg; and on the passage over to Nantucket
he responds at once to the meaning of one of Queequeg's acts. A
silly bumpkin, who has jeered at the outlandish appearance of
Ishmael's new friend, is flung overboard by a sweep of the boom,
and in spite of the fellow's behavior Queequeg risks his life in order
to rescue him. When it is all over he leans back against the bulwarks
of the little schooner as if to say: "It's a mutual, joint-stock world,
in all meridians. We cannibals must help these Christians."

Ishmael is soon bound to Queequeg, and rejoices to be bound, in
a relation of tenderest fraternity; this involves risks, appalling risks,
as he learns, but these risks he is glad to take. As an oarsman under
Queequeg, it becomes Ishmael's scary duty, when the body of a
whale is lashed to the side of the ship, to bind himself to one end
of a monkey-rope at the other end of which Queequeg is bound;
secured by this, Queequeg stumbles back and forth on the whale's
slippery back attempting to cut a hole in it for the insertion of the
blubber-hook. As Ishmael leans over the bulwarks holding on to his
end of the rope, it comes over him that he and Queequeg are now
wedded indeed, and that if poor Queequeg should sink to rise no

more, both honor and usage demand that Ishmael should descend with him into the depths: "My own individuality was now merged in a joint-stock company of two"—a sobering but also a softening thought. "Well, well, my dear comrade and twin-brother, thought I as I drew in and then slacked off the rope to every swell of the sea—what matters it, after all? Are you not the precious image of each and all of us men in this whaling world?"

It is true that, in feeling this, Ishmael feels also how far he is from having a perfectly free will, how dependent he is on the mistakes and the misfortuncs of other men. Yet the two kinds of dependency are here merged into one, and it is the creative dependency of fraternal emotion that prevails.

Deep as are the psychological meanings, and serious as are the moral meanings, of *Moby Dick,* they by no means exhaust between them the richness of its interest or the scope of its significance. In the end, as one reflects on the book, one is aware that one must reckon with the most comprehensive of all qualities, the quality that can only be called mythic. Few words even in our time have been used more glibly than the word "myth"; it has ended by taking on some of the hollow sanctity of the mystic syllable Ôm in the mouths of the unenlightened. When one uses it, however, in association with *Moby Dick,* it means something precise and indispensable; and it is used here in the sense of an imagined narrative in which the leading roles are played by divine or godlike personages, engaged in symbolic actions amid symbolic objects; which embodies some form of the conflict between human wishes and nonhuman forces, and which has its roots in a philosophically serious desire to comprehend the meaning of nature and the destiny of man. The literary expression toward which myth in this sense typically moves is the epic or some closely comparable form.

If *Moby Dick* has a strongly mythic character, it is partly because the human setting out of which it emerged, as we have repeatedly seen, reproduced many of the conditions of a myth-making phase of culture. There was much in Melville's own experience too—his life among the Taipis and Tahitians, as well as much else—that, along with the bias of his own creative faculty, led straight in the mythic direction. There was a mingling in his nature, as in that of every greatly endowed poet, of the primitive and the highly civilized; of the naive and the literate, even the bookish; of the primitive capacity to "think" in symbols and the cultivated capacity to deal in abstractions. He was unique, moreover, among American writers of his time in the particular quality of his intellectual and moral seriousness; unique in his troubled preoccupation with problems that Emerson and Thoreau simply passed by, and that Hawthorne was intellectually too incurious to consider deeply. Like a truly myth-making poet's, Melville's imagination was obsessed by the spectacle of a natural and human scene in which the instinctive need for order and meaning seems mainly to be confronted by meaninglessness and disorder; in which the human will seems sometimes to be sustained but oftener to be thwarted by the forces of physical nature, and even by agencies that lie behind it; in which goodness and evil, beneficence and destructiveness, light and darkness, seem bafflingly intermixed. In none of the great formulations that were available to him, neither in Calvinist Christianity nor in romantic optimism, could Melville discover a myth that for him was adequate to the lighting up of these obscurities.

Moby Dick is his endeavor to construct his own myth. The personages of the fable, ordinary as they begin by seeming, very soon take on the large outlines and the poetic typicality of figures in legend or edda. They are engaged, moreover, in an action that is profoundly archetypal—that is, in a voyage by sea that is also a hunt or a quest, and that reaches its culmination in an all but complete catastrophe. As they do so they move among primordial forces in which their destinies seem involved almost as if they were Greek or Norse or Polynesian demigods or heroes—forces such as the sea that is both the source of life and the extinction of it, the solid land that is both safety and peril, the spires of flame that must be defied but also worshipped, the wind that is sometimes "glorious and gracious" and sometimes tainted and cowardly, the sun "like a royal czar and king," and the moonlight or starlight that serves to irradiate the mystic Spirit Spout. So intense is the animation, so nearly personal is the vitality, of these elemental forces that hardly a step would be needed to transform them into actual deities. Melville himself indeed remarks that the Greeks gave the sea a deity of its own; he calls the northeast wind by its Greek name, Euroclydon, and Ahab defies the fire of the corposants in language that leaves no doubt of its mythic deification. Nowhere, however, is Melville's myth-making power at work in a more truly primordial sense than in the creation of the White Whale himself.

Here chiefly, in the aggrandizement of a huge and fearsome animal to deiform proportions, does Melville surpass all other poets of his century in the rejuvenation of myth. On this ground he is quite incomparable; no other writer of the century can be set beside him. He himself could not wholly have realized how deep a descent he was making into the quarry of the past by penetrating so far as he did into the region of animal existence. He had some sense of this, but it was a flickering one: unavailable to him in his generation was the knowledge of primitive thought and belief that enables us now to see Moby Dick for the deeply primordial symbol he is. Only a man who had himself been a hunter of wild beasts—only a man who had been in at the kill of a tormented Sperm Whale—could have re-entered so far into the intense and complex feelings with which the primitive hunter regards the animals about him and especially his chief prey; into that lost, archaic mingling of fear and gratitude, of resentment and veneration, in which all the savage's emotions toward the animal are steeped, and which leads him again and again to endow it with an awful divinity. Of all this Melville had little or no "knowledge" but a penetrating intuition. The three pagan harpooneers on the *Pequod,* Queequeg, Tashtego, and Daggoo, have all seen Moby Dick before; when Ahab speaks for the first time of the White Whale to his crew, they and they alone are at once aware what creature it is that he means.

"Your true whale-hunter is as much a savage as an Iroquois," Melville himself says, and he adds: "I myself am a savage." Certainly in his half-fearful, half-worshipful attitude toward the Sperm Whale he was closer to the primitive than to the civilized mind; and he gives us his own clues to this when he identifies the Whale with the dragons of Perseus and St. George, or recalls that the Hindu god Vishnu was incarnate in a whale. Yet he probably did not know, literally, that for many primitive peoples—for peoples as remote from one another as the Annamese, the Tongans, and the Unalit Eskimos—the whale is, or once was, the object of a solemn cult, a sacred animal as truly as the cow or the bear was elsewhere. He probably had not heard that some of these peoples prepared themselves for a whale-hunt by fasting for days beforehand, by bathing themselves repeatedly, and by other rites; that some of them, after a whale's life had been taken, propitiated his ghost by holding a communal festival; and that others, when a dead whale was washed ashore, accorded it solemn burial and preserved its bones in a small pagoda near the sea.

Melville knew that whiteness in animals had often been a mark of special sanctity; he alludes to the sacred White Dog of the Iroquois and the White Elephant of Pegu; did he know, however, that the White Whale itself was so superstitiously regarded by the Eskimos of Bering Strait that a hunter who had helped to kill one was forbidden to do any work for four days thereafter, and that the shore where a dead White Whale had been beached was thenceforth tabu? It is of no real importance whether he knew of these things or not; in the contemplation of the great white monster and its mystic ways, he could rely upon a deeper and more primeval knowledge than any he could have acquired from Tylor or Frazer. His imagination ran before the anthropologists; he forefelt, as other poets have done, what the savants would later confirm.

He could rely, in all this, upon the aboriginal myth-making fancy, still strong in his own nature, for which birds and beasts were not simply "lower animals" but creatures somehow identifiable with the beneficent or the malignant potencies of all nature; the fancy that again and again transformed these creatures into gods—eagle-gods, bear-gods, fish-gods, and the like. Even among nineteenth-century whalers generally there may have survived, obscurely and dumbly, much more of this fearful and worshipful emotion than has ever been supposed, and Melville may be pointing to this when he makes Starbuck say of the heathen crew of the *Pequod* that the White Whale is their "demigorgon"—Demogorgon, as he should have said if he meant the mysterious infernal deity to whom Milton and Shelley allude, but he may well have been confusing Demogorgon with the creative Demiurgos of Platonic or Gnostic thought. In any case, there can be no doubt about Moby Dick's deific attributes. There is something godlike in the mere crude fact of his physical magnitude, his "majestic bulk." Physically he is the greatest of all animals that have ever existed, and in proportion to his vast magnitude is his potency, the potency that exhibits itself in his terrific speed, in the dreadful strength of his great jaw, and in the "Titanism of power" with which he wields his massive tail. He is not only physically huge and appallingly powerful, but—as one realizes when one reflects on the problem of his spout—there is in his whole being a "great inherent dignity and sublimity." Moby Dick is godlike in his beauty too, and when, after so many months of search, we at last sight him, gliding swiftly and mildly through the sea, he seems more beautiful even than Zeus himself swimming in the shape of a white bull, with Europa, toward his nuptial bower in Crete: "not Jove, not that great majesty Supreme! did surpass the glorified White Whale as he so divinely swam."

Beautiful he may be, yet to the whalemen who have encountered him, or even to those who have only heard of such encounters, there is something so terrible, so mysterious, in the ferocity and the apparently intelligent malignity with which Moby Dick has rounded upon his attackers, that they have ended by refusing to believe that such a creature is fit prey for mortal man. Some of them have persuaded themselves that he is actually ubiquitous; that he has been sighted in opposite latitudes at the same instant of time; and not only so, but that he is immortal, and that no lance forged of earthly iron can ever destroy him.

Certainly the penalty for attacking him seems always to have been death and destruction in some frightful form, yet Moby Dick appears never to have sought these encounters himself, and to have dealt out ruin only when provoked by his pursuers. Demoniac as he can be when hunted and harpooned, he himself seems rather to evade than to seek these meetings, and perhaps, as the common-sensical English ship-surgeon, Dr. Bunger, suggests, what Ahab takes for the White Whale's malice is only his awkwardness. In any case, if we regard Moby Dick not as an individual but as representative of a species, as an archetypal Sperm Whale, it is not mainly of his malice that we are reminded but of his unintentional beneficence. On occasion he may have been the apparently conscious cause of much evil and suffering, but certainly he is also the source of great and even priceless goods. For many men, both primitive and civilized, his flesh and his spermaceti have served as food. When ambergris is found in his bowels, ignoble as that derivation is, the Sperm Whale becomes the bestower upon mankind of the precious sweetness of perfume. His chief gift to them, however, has not been sweetness but light: it is of spermaceti that the best candles are made, and with sperm-oil that the best lamps are lighted. Illumination, not darkness and terror, is Moby Dick's great boon to humanity. And when we meditate on this fact, we are less sure than we would otherwise be that the mad Gabriel of the *Jeroboam* is as mad as he seems when he warns Captain Mayhew that Moby Dick is the Shaker God incarnated.

However this may be, he is certainly not the God of orthodox or even of modernist Christianity. That is the meaning of his whiteness, of that "visible absence of color" which is at the same time "the concrete of all colors," and hence is the symbol of "a colorless, all-color of atheism from which we shrink." That beautiful and frightful whiteness appeals to our souls so powerfully because it may symbolize both the most spiritual of things, even the Christian Deity, and also the things most appalling to mankind. It cannot, and in Moby Dick it does not, reassuringly and finally symbolize the Christian God, transcendent and absolute, and, however mysterious in His workings, a God of absolute love and justice and truth. A cosmic scene lorded over by the White Whale is one from which the soul-freezing possibility of an ultimate atheism is never wholly absent, and of course it was terribly present to Melville's spirit when he wrote the book. Moby Dick's whiteness, however, may and does symbolize not only negation and denial but "all colors"; all positive goods, fulfillments, benefits. It is a symbol of profound and irreducible ambiguity, but that ambiguity has a pole of lightness as well as a pole of darkness.

The White Whale is a grandiose mythic presentation of what is godlike in the cosmos as this could be intuited by a painfuly meditative and passionately honest poetic mind in the heart of the American nineteenth century. Moby Dick is an Animal God such as only the imagination of that century in the Western world could have conceived and projected; a god in Nature, not beyond it; an emergent deity, not an Absolute; a deity that embodies the physical vastness of the cosmos in space and time as astronomy and geology have exhibited it; a deity that represents not transcendent purpose and conscious design but *mana;* energy; power—the half-conscious, half-unconscious power of blind, restless, perhaps purposeless, but always overbearing and unconquerable force. There is terror in such a conception, as indeed there is, on one side, in the Calvinist conception of a transcendently powerful and justly wrathful God; and Moby Dick owes something to the deity of Calvin and Edwards. He is not that deity, however, if only because nothing assures us that he is capable of loving man as Calvin's God loved him despite his sinfulness; we cannot imagine Moby Dick as conferring upon mankind the ultimate gift of free and unmerited grace. Yet terrible though Moby Dick is in his apparent and perhaps real indifference to men, he is also sublime, sublime as the cosmos itself is, in its unimaginable magnitude, its appalling beauty, and the demiurgic creativity of power that seems everywhere to be at work and alive within it.

This is a nature myth such as only a nineteenth-century imagination, obsessed with the spectacle of impersonal force and ceaseless physical change, could have created, though Melville had unconsciously drawn, in creating it, on a whole complex of thoughts that had come to him from reading, or reading about, Job, the Stoics, the Gnostics and Manicheans, Spinoza, and the men of science. It is a myth such as other minds of the nineteenth century were groping toward, and one can see dim analogies to Moby Dick in Schopenhauer's blind irrational Will, in Herbert Spencer's Unknowable, and still more truly in Hardy's Immanent Will or Urging Immanence. In the traditional Christian God, the omniscient and loving Father, Melville had now lost all confident belief; *that* God survived in his mind, when he wrote *Moby Dick,* only as a symbol of human fraternity and the quasi-religious sense of equality: "The great God absolute! The centre and circumference of all democracy! His omnipresence, our divine equality!" The language here seems traditional enough, but it is unsupported by anything else in the action or the imagery of the book, and the truth is that the God of Melville's fathers has yielded place, at every other point, to the godlike and portentous White Whale.

The mating of romantic idealism with the masculine sense of reality in Melville's mind has begotten here a myth that approaches, if it does not quite overtake, a naturalistic theism. The question remains: If Moby Dick embodies the deific principle in nature, what spiritual meaning can he have for mankind as an object of worship?

The answer would have to be that, in the fullest sense of worship, he could have a very uncertain one, if he could have one at all. It is evident that, like Spinoza's God, Moby Dick cannot be imagined as, strictly speaking, either loving man or hating him; and, conversely, he is hardly conceived as sustainedly and satisfyingly inspiring that "intellectual love" which, according to Spinoza, the free man himself can feel toward God. A positive attitude he does nevertheless inspire, though certainly it is in the end a more austere and far less solacing attitude than that of happy and confident worship. The great clue to this, again, is the symbolism of the doubloon that Ahab nails to the mainmast. This coin was minted in the republic of Ecuador, "a country planted in the middle of the world, and beneath the great equator, and named after it; and it had been cast midway up the Andes, in the unwaning clime that knows no autumn." Arching over the mountain peaks stamped on it, one sees a segment of the zodiac and "the keystone sun entering the equinoctial point at Libra."

Obsessed with his proud and impious interpretation of the symbols on the coin, Ahab quite fails to understand its still deeper significance, quite fails to see that the coin he himself has nailed up is an emblem, not, to be sure, of ethical moderation in the Greek sense, but of the Double Vision; the vision, so to say, of the equatorial line from which one may look out on both North and South with equal comprehensiveness; the balanced vision of the sun itself as it enters the constellation of Libra, or the Scales. This is the vision, surely, with which a wise man would contemplate Moby Dick, stoically accepting the fact that the White Whale, the cosmic force, has again and again unconsciously wrought havoc and destruction, and will doubtless continue to do so; but recognizing too that Moby Dick is, or may be made to be, the source of much genuine good—of nourishment, of fragrance, of light—and that, though "I know him not, and never will," one can glory in the spectacle of his sublimity.

That is what Ishmael has revealed a capacity to do, and it is the deepest reason for his rebirth from the sea. Ahab, on the other hand, has shown no such capacity; on the contrary, he has persisted in identifying Moby Dick with "all evil," and piling upon the whale's white hump "all the general rage and hate felt by his whole race from Adam down." But this is both madness and wickedness. Evil exists, it is true; essential Evil; it is no illusion, as Emerson would have it, but a dense and unexorcisable reality. So far as the reality of Evil is that of suffering, Moby Dick is indeed the source of much of it; but that is only one aspect of his dual nature, and moreover, so far as the reality of Evil is moral, so far as Evil connotes an evil will, then Moby Dick does not embody this at all: the one who does embody it is Ahab's own harpooner, the diabolic Fedallah, to whom

Ahab has surrendered his moral freedom, and whom Stubb quite properly identifies as the devil in disguise. "One cannot sustain an indifferent air concerning Fedallah." One cannot, indeed, for he is a principle of pure negation, of hatred instead of love, vindictiveness instead of charity, destruction instead of creativeness. Ahab has sold his soul to the fire-worshipping Parsee, the Parsee who, in this case, worships fire not as a symbol of light and truth but as a symbol of raging and destructive Evil. Moby Dick, however, is indestructible, and the upshot of their impious onslaught upon him is not his but their destruction.

There would be a religious solace in this thought if one could believe that Moby Dick, with his immunity and immortality, were in conscious, benevolent collaboration with the forces of love in their struggle against the forces of hate. As it is, one must be content with the consolations of philosophy in *Moby Dick,* or rather with those of a philosophical mythology; one cannot avert one's eyes from the fact that good and innocent men—Starbuck, Queequeg, and others—are involved in Ahab's doom. One can tell oneself that mad and wicked men inevitably wreak their own destruction in attempting to thwart the workings of "nature"; one cannot tell oneself that wise and virtuous men are preserved from suffering and fatality. They only *may* be, as Ishmael is.

Something else, however, is suggested in the book, though only obscurely, and this is something that takes us closer, if not to religion in the fullest sense, at any rate to a certain form of natural piety. Some years after he had written *Moby Dick,* Melville was sufficiently struck by a sentence of Spinoza's, quoted by Matthew Arnold, to mark the passage in his copy of Arnold's essays. The sentence is this: "Our desire is not that nature may obey us, but, on the contrary, that we may obey nature." Already in *Moby Dick* there had been an intimation of this cosmic submissiveness. The desire to understand, to fathom, the whole truth about the White Whale—the desire that is manifest at every turn in the explanatory and meditative passages —this is at least the true beginning of wisdom. The willingness to submit, to accept, to "obey," in that sense, would naturally follow. Father Mapple, indeed, in his sermon—employing, of course, the familiar language of faith—makes provision for this when he says that "all the things that God would have us do are hard for us to do. . . . And if we obey God, we must disobey ourselves; and it is in this disobeying ourselves, wherein the hardness of obeying God consists." The "will" of nature, even if there is something godlike in it, is hardly synonymous with God's will in the Christian sense. Yet *Moby Dick* seems to say that one might arrive at a kind of peace by obeying it.

19

Allen Tate: EMILY DICKINSON [1932]

Great poetry needs no special features of difficulty to make it mysterious. When it has them, the reputation of the poet is likely to remain uncertain. This is still true of Donne, and it is true of Emily Dickinson, whose verse appeared in an age unfavorable to the use of intelligence in poetry. Her poetry is not like any other poetry of her time; it is not like any of the innumerable kinds of verse written today. In still another respect it is far removed from us. It is a poetry of ideas, and it demands of the reader a point of view—not an opinion of the New Deal or of the League of Nations, but an ingrained philosophy that is fundamental, a settled attitude that is almost extinct in this eclectic age. Yet it is not the sort of poetry of ideas which, like Pope's, requires a point of view only. It requires also, for the deepest understanding, which must go beneath the verbal excitement of the style, a highly developed sense of the specific quality of poetry—a quality that most persons accept as the accidental feature of something else that the poet thinks he has to say. This is one reason why Miss Dickinson's poetry has not been widely read.

There is another reason, and it is a part of the problem peculiar to a poetry that comes out of fundamental ideas. We lack a tradition of criticism. There were no points of critical reference passed on to us from a preceding generation. I am not upholding here the so-called dead hand of tradition, but rather a rational insight into the meaning of the present in terms of some imaginable past implicit in our own lives: we need a body of ideas that can bear upon the course of the spirit and yet remain coherent as a rational instrument. We ignore the present, which is momentarily translated into the past, and derive our standards from imaginative constructions of the future. The hard contingency of fact invariably breaks these standards down, leaving us the intellectual chaos which is the sore distress of American criticism. Marxian criticism has become the latest disguise of this heresy.

Still another difficulty stands between us and Miss Dickinson. It is the failure of the scholars to feel more than biographical curiosity about her. We have scholarship, but that is no substitute for a critical tradition. Miss Dickinson's value to the research scholar, who likes historical difficulty for its own sake, is slight; she is too near to possess the remoteness of literature. Perhaps her appropriate setting would be the age of Cowley or of Donne. Yet in her own historical setting she is, nevertheless, remarkable and special.

Although the intellectual climate into which she was born, in 1830, had, as all times have, the features of a transition, the period was also a major crisis culminating in the war between the States. After that war, in New England as well as in the South, spiritual crises were definitely minor until the First World War.

Yet, a generation before the war of 1861-65, the transformation of New England had begun. When Samuel Slater in 1790 thwarted the British embargo on mill machinery by committing to memory the whole design of a cotton spinner and bringing it to Massachusetts, he planted the seed of the "Western spirit." By 1825 its growth in the East was rank enough to begin choking out the ideas and habits of living that New England along with Virginia had kept in unconscious allegiance to Europe. To the casual observer, perhaps, the New England character of 1830 was largely an eighteenth-century character. But theocracy was on the decline, and industrialism was rising—as Emerson, in an unusually lucid moment, put it, "Things are in the saddle." The energy that had built the meeting-house ran the factory.

Now the idea that moved the theocratic state is the most interesting historically of all American ideas. It was, of course, powerful in seventeenth-century England, but in America, where the long arm of Laud could not reach, it acquired an unchecked social and political influence. The important thing to remember about the puritan theocracy is that it permeated, as it could never have done in England, a whole society. It gave final, definite meaning to life, the life of pious and impious, of learned and vulgar alike. It gave—and this is its significance for Emily Dickinson, and in only slightly lesser degree for Melville and Hawthorne—it gave an heroic proportion and a tragic mode to the experience of the individual. The history of the New England theocracy, from Apostle Eliot to Cotton Mather, is rich in gigantic intellects that broke down—or so it must appear to an outsider—in a kind of moral decadence and depravity. Socially we may not like the New England idea. Yet it had an immense, incalculable value for literature: it dramatized the human soul.

But by 1850 the great fortunes had been made (in the rum, slave, and milling industries), and New England became a museum. The whatnots groaned under the load of knickknacks, the fine china dogs and cats, the pieces of Oriental jade, the chips off the leaning tower of Pisa. There were the rare books and the cosmopolitan learning. It was all equally displayed as the evidence of a superior culture. The Gilded Age had already begun. But culture, in the true sense, was disappearing. Where the old order, formidable as it was, had held all this personal experience, this eclectic excitement, in a comprehensible whole, the new order tended to flatten it out in a common experience that was not quite in common; it exalted more and more the personal and the unique in the interior sense. Where the old-fashioned puritans got together on a rigid doctrine, and could thus be individualists in manners, the nineteenth-century New Englander, lacking a genuine religious center, began to be a social conformist. The common idea of the Redemption, for example, was replaced by the conformist idea of respectability among neighbors whose spiritual disorder, not very evident at the surface, was becoming acute. A great idea was breaking up, and society was moving towards external uniformity, which is usually the measure of the spiritual sterility inside.

At this juncture Emerson came upon the scene: the Lucifer of Concord, he had better be called hereafter, for he was the light-bearer who could see nothing but light, and was fearfully blind. He looked around and saw the uniformity of life, and called it the routine of tradition, the tyranny of the theological idea. The death of Priam put an end to the hope of Troy, but it was a slight feat of arms for the doughty Pyrrhus; Priam was an old gentleman and almost dead. So was theocracy; and Emerson killed it. In this way he accelerated a tendency that he disliked. It was a great intellectual mistake. By it Emerson unwittingly became the prophet of a piratical industrialism, a consequence of his own transcendental individualism that he could not foresee. He was hoist with his own petard.

He discredited more than any other man the puritan drama of the soul. The age that followed, from 1865 on, expired in a genteel secularism, a mildly didactic order of feeling whose ornaments were

Lowell, Longfellow, and Holmes. "After Emerson had done his work," says Mr. Robert Penn Warren, "any tragic possibilities in that culture were dissipated." Hawthorne alone in his time kept pure, in the primitive terms, the primitive vision; he brings the puritan tragedy to its climax. Man, measured by a great idea outside himself, is found wanting. But for Emerson man is greater than any idea and, being himself the Over-Soul, is innately perfect; there is no struggle because—I state the Emersonian doctrine, which is very slippery, in its extreme terms—because there is no possibility of error. There is no drama in human character because there is no tragic fault. It is not surprising, then, that after Emerson New England literature tastes like a sip of cambric tea. Its center of vision has disappeared. There is Hawthorne looking back, there is Emerson looking not too clearly at anything ahead: Emily Dickinson, who has in her something of both, comes in somewhere between.

With the exception of Poe there is no other American poet whose work so steadily emerges, under pressure of certain disintegrating obsessions, from the framework of moral character. There is none of whom it is truer to say that the poet *is* the poetry. Perhaps this explains the zeal of her admirers for her biography; it explains, in part at least, the gratuitous mystery that Mrs. Bianchi, a niece of the poet and her official biographer, has made of her life. The devoted controversy that Miss Josephine Pollitt and Miss Genevieve Taggard started a few years ago with their excellent books shows the extent to which the critics feel the intimate connection of her life and work. Admiration and affection are pleased to linger over the tokens of a great life; but the solution to the Dickinson enigma is peculiarly superior to fact.

The meaning of the identity—which we merely feel—of character and poetry would be exceedingly obscure, even if we could draw up a kind of Binet correlation between the two sets of "facts." Miss Dickinson was a recluse; but her poetry is rich with a profound and varied experience. Where did she get it? Now some of the biographers, nervous in the presence of this discrepancy, are eager to find her a love affair, and I think this search is due to a modern prejudice: we believe that no virgin can know enough to write poetry. We shall never learn where she got the rich quality of her mind. The moral image that we have of Miss Dickinson stands out in every poem; it is that of a dominating spinster whose very sweetness must have been formidable. Yet her poetry constantly moves within an absolute order of truths that overwhelmed her simply because to her they were unalterably fixed. It is dangerous to assume that her "life," which to the biographers means the thwarted love affair she is supposed to have had, gave to her poetry a decisive direction. It is even more dangerous to suppose that it made her a poet.

Poets are mysterious, but a poet, when all is said, is not much more mysterious than a banker. The critics remain spellbound by the technical license of her verse and by the puzzle of her personal life. Personality is a legitimate interest because it is an incurable interest, but legitimate as a personal interest only; it will never give up the key to anyone's verse. Used to that end, the interest is false. "It is apparent," writes Mr. Conrad Aiken, "that Miss Dickinson became a hermit by deliberate and conscious choice"—a sensible remark that we cannot repeat too often. If it were necessary to explain her seclusion with disappointment in love, there would remain the discrepancy between what the seclusion produced and the seclusion looked at as a cause. The effect, which is her poetry, would imply the whole complex of anterior fact, which was the social and religious structure of New England.

The problem to be kept in mind is thus the meaning of her "deliberate and conscious" decision to withdraw from life to her upstairs room. This simple fact is not very important. But that it must have been her sole way of acting out her part in the history of her culture, which made, with the variations of circumstance, a single demand upon all its representatives—this is of the greatest consequence. All pity for Miss Dickinson's "starved life" is misdirected. Her life was one of the richest and deepest ever lived on this continent.

When she went upstairs and closed the door, she mastered life by rejecting it. Others in their way had done it before; still others did it later. If we suppose—which is to suppose the improbable—that the love affair precipitated the seclusion, it was only a pretext; she would have found another. Mastery of the world by rejecting the world was the doctrine, even if it was not always the practice, of Jonathan Edwards and Cotton Mather. It is the meaning of fate in Hawthorne: his people are fated to withdraw from the world and to be destroyed. And it is one of the great themes of Henry James.

There is a moral emphasis that connects Hawthorne, James, and Miss Dickinson, and I think it is instructive. Between Hawthorne and James lies an epoch. The temptation to sin, in Hawthorne, is, in James, transformed into the temptation not to do the "decent thing." A whole world-scheme, a complete cosmic background, has shrunk to the dimensions of the individual conscience. This epoch between Hawthorne and James lies in Emerson. James found himself in the post-Emersonian world, and he could not, without violating the detachment proper to an artist, undo Emerson's work; he had that kind of intelligence which refuses to break its head against history. There was left to him only the value, the historic role, of rejection. He could merely escape from the physical presence of that world which, for convenience, we may call Emerson's world: he could only take his Americans to Europe upon the vain quest of something that they had lost at home. His characters, fleeing the wreckage of the puritan culture, preserved only their honor. Honor became a sort of forlorn hope struggling against the forces of "pure fact" that had got loose in the middle of the century. Honor alone is a poor weapon against nature, being too personal, finical, and proud, and James achieved a victory by refusing to engage the whole force of the enemy.

In Emily Dickinson the conflict takes place on a vaster field. The enemy to all those New Englanders was Nature, and Miss Dickinson saw into the character of this enemy more deeply than any of the others. The general symbol of Nature, for her, is Death, and her weapon against Death is the entire powerful dumb-show of the puritan theology led by Redemption and Immortality. Morally speaking, the problem for James and Miss Dickinson is similar. But her advantages were greater than his. The advantages lay in the availability to her of the puritan ideas on the theological plane.

These ideas, in her poetry, are momently assailed by the disintegrating force of Nature (appearing as Death) which, while constantly breaking them down, constantly redefines and strengthens them. The values are purified by the triumphant withdrawal from Nature, by their power to recover from Nature. The poet attains to a mastery over experience by facing its utmost implications. There is the clash of powerful opposites, and in all great poetry—for Emily Dickinson is a great poet—it issues in a tension between abstraction and sensation in which the two elements may be, of course, distinguished logically, but not really. We are shown our roots in Nature by examining our differences with Nature; we are renewed by Nature without being delivered into her hands. When it is possible for a poet to do this for us with the greatest imaginative comprehension, a possibility that the poet cannot himself create, we have the perfect literary situation. Only a few times in the history of English poetry has this situation come about: notably, the period between about 1580 and the Restoration. There was a similar age in New England from which emerged two talents of the first order—Hawthorne and Emily Dickinson.

There is an epoch between James and Miss Dickinson. But between her and Hawthorne there exists a difference of intellectual quality. She lacks almost radically the power to seize upon and understand abstractions for their own sake; she does not separate them from the sensuous illuminations that she is so marvelously adept at; like Donne, she *perceives abstraction* and *thinks sensation*.

But Hawthorne was a master of ideas, within a limited range; this narrowness confined him to his own kind of life, his own society, and out of it grew his typical forms of experience, his steady, almost obsessed vision of man; it explains his depth and intensity. Yet he is always conscious of the abstract, doctrinal aspect of his mind, and when his vision of action and emotion is weak, his work becomes didactic. Now Miss Dickinson's poetry often runs into quasi-homiletic forms, but it is never didactic. Her very ignorance, her lack of formal intellectual training, preserved her from the risk that imperiled Hawthorne. She cannot reason at all. She can only *see*. It is impossible to imagine what she might have done with drama or fiction; for, not approaching the puritan temper and through it the puritan myth, through human action, she is able to grasp the terms of the myth directly and by a feat that amounts almost to anthropomorphism, to give them a luminous tension, a kind of drama, among themselves.

One of the perfect poems in English is "The Chariot," and it illustrates better than anything else she wrote the special quality of her mind. I think it will illuminate the tendency of this discussion:

> Because I could not stop for death,
> He kindly stopped for me;
> The carriage held but just ourselves
> And immortality.
>
> We slowly drove, he knew no haste,
> And I had put away
> My labor, and my leisure too,
> For his civility.
>
> We passed the school where children played,
> Their lessons scarcely done;
> We passed the fields of gazing grain,
> We passed the setting sun.
>
> We paused before a house that seemed
> A swelling of the ground;
> The roof was scarcely visible,
> The cornice but a mound.
>
> Since then 'tis centuries; but each
> Feels shorter than the day
> I first surmised the horses' heads
> Were toward eternity.

If the word "great" means anything in poetry, this poem is one of the greatest in the English language. The rhythm charges with movement the pattern of suspended action back of the poem. Every image is precise and, moreover, not merely beautiful, but fused with the central idea. Every image extends and intensifies every other. The third stanza especially shows Miss Dickinson's power to fuse, into a single order of preception, a heterogeneous series: the children, the grain, and the setting sun (time) have the same degree of credibility; the first subtly preparing for the last. The sharp *gazing* before *grain* instills into nature a cold vitality of which the qualitative richness has infinite depth. The content of death in the poem eludes explicit definition. He is a gentleman taking a lady out for a drive. But note the restraint that keeps the poet from carrying this so far that it becomes ludicrous and incredible; and note the subtly interfused erotic motive, which the idea of death has presented to most romantic poets, love being a symbol interchangeable with death. The terror of death is objectified through this figure of the genteel driver, who is made ironically to serve the end of Immortality. This is the heart of the poem: she has presented a typical Christian theme in its final irresolution, without making any final statements about it. There is no solution to the problem; there can be only a presentation of it in the full context of intellect and feeling. A construction of the human will, elaborated with all the abstracting powers of the mind, is put to the concrete test of experience: the idea of immortality is confronted with the fact of physical disintegration. We are not told what to think; we are told to look at the situation.

The framework of the poem is, in fact, the two abstractions, mortality and eternity, which are made to associate in equality with the images: she sees the ideas, and thinks the perceptions. She did, of course, nothing of the sort; but we must use the logical distinctions, even to the extent of paradox, if we are to form any notion of this rare quality of mind. She could not in the proper sense think at all, and unless we prefer the feeble poetry of moral ideas that flourished in New England in the eighties, we must conclude that her intellectual deficiency contributed at least negatively to her great distinction. Miss Dickinson is probably the only Anglo-American poet of her century whose work exhibits the perfect literary situation—in which is possible the fusion of sensibility and thought. Unlike her contemporaries, she never succumbed to her ideas, to easy solutions, to her private desires.

Philosophers must deal with ideas, but the trouble with most nineteenth-century poets is too much philosophy; they are nearer to being philosophers than poets, without being in the true sense either. Tennyson is a good example of this; so is Arnold in his weak moments. There have been poets like Milton and Donne, who were not spoiled for their true business by leaning on a rational system of ideas, who understood the poetic use of ideas. Tennyson tried to mix a little Huxley and a little Broad Church, without understanding either Broad Church or Huxley; the result was fatal, and what is worse, it was shallow. Miss Dickinson's ideas were deeply imbedded in her character, not taken from the latest tract. A conscious cultivation of ideas in poetry is always dangerous, and even Milton escaped ruin only by having an instinct for what in the deepest sense he understood. Even at that there is a remote quality in Milton's approach to his material, in his treatment of it; in the nineteenth century, in an imperfect literary situation where literature was confused with documentation, he might have been a pseudo-philosopher-poet. It is difficult to conceive Emily Dickinson and John Donne succumbing to rumination about "problems"; they would not have written at all.

Neither the feeling nor the style of Miss Dickinson belongs to the seventeenth century; yet between her and Donne there are remarkable ties. Their religious ideas, their abstractions, are momently toppling from the rational plane to the level of perception. The ideas, in fact, are no longer the impersonal religious symbols created anew in the heat of emotion, that we find in poets like Herbert and Vaughan. They have become, for Donne, the terms of personality; they are mingled with the miscellany of sensation. In Miss Dickinson, as in Donne, we may detect a singularly morbid concern, not for religious truth, but for personal revelation. The modern word is self-exploitation. It is egoism grown irresponsible in religion and decadent in morals. In religion it is blasphemy; in society it means usually that culture is not self-contained and sufficient, that the spiritual community is breaking up. This is, along with some other features that do not concern us here, the perfect literary situation.

II

Personal revelation of the kind that Donne and Miss Dickinson strove for, in the effort to understand their relation to the world, is a feature of all great poetry; it is probably the hidden motive for writing. It is the effort of the individual to live apart from a cultural tradition that no longer sustains him. But this culture, which I now wish to discuss a little, is indispensable: there is a great deal of shallow nonsense in modern criticism which holds that poetry—and this is a half-truth that is worse than false—is essentially revolutionary. It is only indirectly revolutionary: the intellectual and religious background of an age no longer contains the whole spirit, and the poet proceeds to examine that background in terms of immediate experience. But the background is necessary; otherwise all the arts (not only poetry) would have to rise in a vacuum. Poetry does not dispense with tradition; it probes the deficiencies of a tradition. But it must have a tradition to probe. It is too bad that Arnold did not explain his doctrine, that poetry is a criticism of life, from the viewpoint of its background: we should have been spared an era of academic misconception, in which criticism of life meant a diluted pragmatism, the criterion of which was respectability. The poet in the true sense "criticizes" his tradition, either as such, or indirectly by comparing it with something that is about to replace it; he does what the root-meaning of the verb implies—he *discerns* its real elements and thus establishes its value, by putting it to the test of experience.

What is the nature of a poet's culture? Or, to put the question properly, what is the meaning of culture for poetry? All the great poets become the material of what we popularly call culture; we study them to acquire it. It is clear that Addison was more cultivated than Shakespeare; nevertheless Shakespeare is a finer source of culture than Addison. What is the meaning of this? Plainly it is that learning has never had anything to do with culture except instrumentally: the poet must be exactly literate enough to write down fully and precisely what he has to say, but no more. The source of a poet's true culture lies back of the paraphernalia of culture, and not all the historical activity of an enlightened age can create it.

A culture cannot be consciously created. It is an available source of ideas that are imbedded in a complete and homogeneous society. The poet finds himself balanced upon the moment when such a world is about to fall, when it threatens to run out into looser and less self-sufficient impulses. This world order is assimilated, in Miss Dickinson, as medievalism was in Shakespeare, to the poetic vision; it is brought down from abstraction to personal sensibility.

In this connection it may be said that the prior conditions for great poetry, given a great talent, may be reduced to two: the thoroughness of the poet's discipline in an objective system of truth, and his lack of consciousness of such a discipline. For this discipline is a number of fundamental ideas the origin of which the poet does not know; they give form and stability to his fresh perceptions of the world; and he cannot shake them off. This is his culture, and, like Tennyson's God, it is nearer than hands and feet. With reasonable certainty we unearth the elements of Shakespeare's culture, and yet it is equally certain—so innocent was he of his own resources—that he would not know what our discussion is about. He appeared at the collapse of the medieval system as a rigid pattern of life, but that pattern remained in Shakespeare what Shelley called a "fixed point of reference" for his sensibility. Miss Dickinson, as we have seen, was born into the equilibrium of an old and a new order. Puritanism could not be to her what it had been to the generation of Cotton Mather—a body of absolute truths; it was an unconscious discipline timed to the pulse of her life.

The perfect literary situation: it produces, because it is rare, a special and perhaps the most distinguished kind of poet. I am not trying to invent a new critical category. Such poets are never very much alike on the surface; they show us all the varieties of poetic feeling; and, like other poets, they resist all classification but that of temporary convenience. But, I believe, Miss Dickinson and John Donne would have this in common: their sense of the natural world is not blunted by a too-rigid system of ideas; yet the ideas, the abstractions, their education or their intellectual heritage, are not so weak as to let their immersion in nature, or their purely personal quality, get out of control. The two poles of the mind are not separately visible; we infer them from the lucid tension that may be most readily illustrated by polar activity. There is no thought as such at all; nor is there feeling; there is that unique focus of experience which is at once neither and both.

Like Miss Dickinson, Shakespeare is without opinions; his peculiar merit is also deeply involved in his failure to think about anything; his meaning is not in the content of his expression; it is in the tension of the dramatic relations of his characters. This kind of poetry is at the opposite of intellectualism. (Miss Dickinson is obscure and difficult, but that is not intellectualism.) To T. W. Higginson, the editor of *The Atlantic Monthly,* who tried to advise her, she wrote that she had no education. In any sense that Higginson could understand, it was quite true. His kind of education was the conscious cultivation of abstractions. She did not reason about the world she saw; she merely saw it. The "ideas" implicit in the world within her rose up, concentrated in her immediate perception.

That kind of world at present has for us something of the fascination of a buried city. There is none like it. When such worlds exist, when such cultures flourish, they support not only the poet but all members of society. For, from these, the poet differs only in his gift for exhibiting the structure, the internal lineaments, of his culture by threatening to tear them apart: a process that concentrates the symbolic emotions of society while it seems to attack them. The poet may hate his age; he may be an outcast like Villon; but this world is always there as the background to what he has to say. It is the lens through which he brings nature to focus and control—the clarifying medium that concentrates his personal feeling. It is ready-made; he cannot make it; with it, his poetry has a spontaneity and a certainty of direction that, without it, it would lack. No poet could have invented the ideas of "The Chariot"; only a great poet could have found their imaginative equivalents. Miss Dickinson was a deep mind writing from a deep culture, and when she came to poetry, she came infallibly.

Infallibly, at her best; for no poet has ever been perfect, nor is Emily Dickinson. Her precision of statement is due to the directness with which the abstract framework of her thought acts upon its unorganized material. The two elements of her style, considered as point of view, are immortality, or the idea of permanence and the physical process of death or decay. Her diction has two corresponding features: words of Latin or Greek origin and, sharply opposed to these, the concrete Saxon element. It is this verbal conflict that gives her verse its high tension; it is not a device deliberately seized upon, but a feeling for language that senses out the two fundamental components of English and their metaphysical relation: the Latin for ideas and the Saxon for perceptions—the peculiar virtue of English as a poetic language.

Like most poets Miss Dickinson often writes out of habit; the style that emerged from some deep exploration of an idea she carried on as verbal habit when she has nothing to say. She indulges herself:

> There's something quieter than sleep
> Within this inner room!
> It wears a sprig upon its breast,
> And will not tell its name.
>
> Some touch it and some kiss it,
> Some chafe its idle hand;
> It has a simple gravity
> I do not understand!
>
> While simple hearted neighbors
> Chat of the "early dead,"
> We, prone to periphrasis,
> Remark that birds have fled!

It is only a pert remark; at best a superior kind of punning—one of the worst specimens of her occasional interest in herself. But she never had the slightest interest in the public. Were four poems or five published in her lifetime? She never felt the temptation to round off a poem for public exhibition. Higginson's kindly offer to make her verse "correct" was an invitation to throw her work into the public ring—the ring of Lowell and Longfellow. He could not see that he was tampering with one of the rarest literary integrities of all time. Here was a poet who had no use for the supports of authorship— flattery and fame; she never needed money.

She had all the elements of a culture that has broken up, a culture that on the religious side takes its place in the museum of spiritual antiquities. Puritanism, as a unified version of the world, is dead; only a remnant of it in trade may be said to survive. In the history of puritanism she comes between Hawthorne and Emerson. She has Hawthorne's matter, which a too irresponsible personality tends to dilute into a form like Emerson's; she is often betrayed by words. But she is not the poet of personal sentiment; she has more to say than she can put down in any one poem. Like Hardy and Whitman, she must be read entire; like Shakespeare, she never gives up her meaning in a single line.

She is therefore a perfect subject for the kind of criticism which is chiefly concerned with general ideas. She exhibits one of the permanent relations between personality and objective truth, and she deserves the special attention of our time, which lacks that kind of truth.

She has Hawthorne's intellectual toughness, a hard, definite sense of the physical world. The highest flights to God, the most extravagant metaphors of the strange and the remote, come back to a point of casuistry, to a moral dilemma of the experienced world. There is, in spite of the homiletic vein of utterance, no abstract speculation, nor is there a message to society; she speaks wholly to the individual experience. She offers to the unimaginative no riot of vicarious sensation; she has no useful maxims for men of action. Up to this point her resemblance to Emerson is slight: poetry is a sufficient form of utterance, and her devotion to it is pure. But in Emily Dickinson the puritan world is no longer self-contained; it is no longer complete; her sensibility exceeds its dimensions. She has trimmed down its supernatural proportions; it has become a morality; instead of the tragedy of the spirit there is a commentary upon it. Her poetry is a magnificent personal confession, blasphemous and, in its self-revelation, its honesty, almost obscene. It comes out of an intellectual life towards which it feels no moral responsibility. Cotton Mather would have burnt her for a witch.

20

Bernard DeVoto: INTRODUCTION TO
MARK TWAIN [1946]

The first truly American literature grew out of the tidewater culture
of the early republic. It was the culture of a people who, whatever
their diversity, were more homogeneous in feeling and belief than
Americans as a people have ever been since them. We have come to
think of the literature whose greatest names are Emerson and Poe,
Thoreau and Melville, Hawthorne and Whitman, as our classic period, and in a very real sense the republic that shaped their mind was
classical. It felt a strong affinity for the Roman Republic, it believed
that Roman virtues and ideas had been expressed in the Constitution,
it gave us a great architectural style because it identified its own emotions in the classic style. When Horatio Greenough let a toga fall
from Washington's naked shoulders he was not out of tune with contemporary taste: Washington seemed a kind of consul, so did Jefferson, and in the portaits of them which our stamps and coins preserve
they have a Roman look. This classical republican culture was at its
most vigorous when our classic writers were growing up. But there
is an element of anachronism in all literature, and while these men
were themselves in full vigor American culture entered a new phase.

The culture of the early republic crossed the Alleghenies in two streams, one Southern, the other mainly New England; but they were more like each other than either was like the one which their mingling presently helped to produce. For beyond the mountains people found different landscapes, different river courses, different relationships of sky and wind and water, different conceptions of space and distance, different soils and climates—different conditions of life. Beyond still farther mountains lay Oregon and California— and they were implicit in the expanding nation as soon as the treaty that gave us Louisiana was signed—but first the United States had to incorporate the vast expanse between the eastern and the western heights of land. That area is the American heartland. Its greatest son was to call it the Egypt of the West because nature had organized it round a central river and it touched no ocean, but it came into the American consciousness as the Great Valley. When the tidewater culture came to the Great Valley it necessarily broke down: new conditions demanded adaptations, innovations, new combinations and amplifications. The new way of life that began to develop there had a different organization of feeling, a different metabolism of thought. It was no more native , no more "American," than that of the first republic, but it was different and it began to react on it.

The heartland was midcontinental and its energies were oriented toward the river at its center—and were therefore turned away from Europe, which had been a frontier of the early republic. And life in the heartland, with its mingling of stocks, its constant shifting of population, and its tremendous distances, led people in always increasing numbers to think continentally. Both facts were fundamental in the thought and feeling of the new culture.

The American littoral came only slowly, with greater slowness than the fact demanded, to realize that the nation's center of gravity was shifting westward. It tragically failed to understand one consequence of that shift, thirty years of contention between the Northeast and the South to dominate the Great Valley or at least achieve a preferential linkage with it. The failure to understand was in great part a failure to think continentally—as was made clear at last when the Civil War demonstrated that no peaceful way of resolving the contention had been found. Even now too many Americans fail to understand that the war, the resolution by force, only made explicit the organization of our national life that is implicit in the geography which the Great Valley binds together. Abraham Lincoln understood our continental unity; he argued it persistently down to the outbreak of the war and from then on. And Lincoln was a distillation of the heartland culture.

Lincoln's feeling for the continentalism of the American nation was so intense that it almost transcended the transcendent facts. It was a deposit in the very cells of his bones from the soil of the Great Valley. He was, Herndon rightly says, one of the limestone men, the tall, gaunt, powerful, sallow, saturnine men who appear in quantity enough to constitute a type when the wilderness on both sides of the Ohio comes under the plow. His radical democracy was wrought from the experience of the Great Valley. In his ideas and beliefs as in the shadowed depths of his personality there is apparent a new articulation of American life. His very lineaments show it. When you turn from the Jefferson nickel to the Lincoln penny as when you turn from Jefferson's first inaugural address to any of Lincoln's state papers, in the flash of a total and immediate response you understand that you have turned from one era to a later one. You have turned from the tidewater republic to the continental empire.

Lincoln expressed a culture and brought a type to climax. Similarly, when that culture found major literary expression it did so from a rich and various, if humble, literary tradition. As always, the literary expression was the later one; the economic, social, and political impact was felt much earlier. The lag, however, was not so great as Walt Whitman thought. Whitman was sixty when in 1879 he traveled across the Great Valley to its western limit, where the Front Range walls it off. He traversed it with a steadily growing conviction that here in the flesh were the people whose society he had envisioned in so many rhapsodies, Americans who had been fused, annealed, compacted (those are his words) into a new identity. He felt that literature had not yet spoken to these prairie people, "this continental inland West," that it had not yet spoken for them, that it had not made images for their spirit.

The poet supposed that he was speaking of things still to come but he was already wrong by a full ten years. The thing had happened. And the first notification that it had happened can be dated with an exactness not often possible in the history of literature. That notification came in 1869 with the appearance of a book of humorous travel sketches by Samuel Langhorne Clemens, who, faithful to the established tradition, signed it with a pen name, Mark Twain.

Innocents Abroad was greeted with an enthusiasm that made Mark Twain a celebrity overnight, and with too much misunderstanding of a kind that was to persist throughout his career. It was a funny book and a cardinal part of its fun was its disdain of European culture. This disdain, the mere fact of making humor of such disdain, and its frequent exaggeration into burlesque all produced an effect of shock—in most ways a delightful shock but in some ways an uneasy one. Yet the point was not the provinciality of such humor, though it was frequently provincial, and not its uncouthness, though it was sometimes uncouth, but the kind of consciousness it implied. Again it is absurd to speak of this as the first American literature that was independent of European influences, for our literature had obediently divorced itself from Europe as soon as Emerson ordered it to. The humorous core of *Innocents Abroad* was not independence of Europe, but indifference to it. Thoreau and Emerson and Poe were detached from Europe but completely aware of being heirs to it, but here was a literature which had grown up in disregard of Europe—which had looked inward toward the Mississippi and not outward beyond the Atlantic. Failure to appreciate the implications of this difference was one reason, no doubt the weightiest one, why for two full generations literary critics thought of Mark Twain as no more than a clown. But the same identity, the same organization of personality, that made Lincoln the artificer of our continental unity was what made Mark Twain a great writer.

There are striking affinities between Lincoln and Mark Twain. Both spent their boyhoods in a society that was still essentially frontier; both were rivermen. Both absorbed the midcontinental heritage: fiercely equalitarian democracy, hatred of injustice and oppression, the man-to-man individualism of an expanding society. Both were deeply acquainted with melancholy and despair; both were fatalists. On the other hand, both were instinct with the humor of the common life and from their earliest years made fables of it. As humorists, both felt the basic gravity of humor; with both it was an adaptation of the mind, a reflex of the struggle to be sane; both knew, and Mark Twain said, that there is no humor in heaven. It was of such resemblances that William Dean Howells was thinking when he called Mark Twain "the Lincoln of our literature."

II

Samuel Clemens was born at Florida, Monroe County, Missouri, on November 30, 1835, a few months after his parents reached the village from Tennessee. His father was a Virginian, his mother a Kentuckian, and as a family they had made three moves before this one. Florida was a handful of log cabins only two hundred miles east of the Indian Country and in the earliest stage of frontier economy. Though he could have only a generalized memory of it, Sam's earliest years were thus spent in the "Sweet Betsy from Pike" society which has contributed a color and a flavor of its own to American legendry. More: the town was located at the forks of that Salt Creek which figures in the folk proverbs. He could retain little conscious memory of the chinked-log, open-fireplace hamlet with its woods-runners and movers; mostly it would mean the immediacy of nature, the infinity of the forest, the ease of escape into solitude and an all-encompassing freedom. He was still short of four when the Clemenses made their last move, this time eastward. They seem to have been movers by force of circumstance, not instinct; it was always the pressure of poverty and the hope of betterment that impelled them on. But they bequeathed restlessness to their son.

The final move brought them to Hannibal, an older settlement than Florida and perhaps four times as large but still short of five hundred inhabitants. Hannibal is the most important single fact in the life of Samuel Clemens the person and Mark Twain the writer. It too was lapped round by forest; it maintained the romantic mystery, the subliminal dread, and the intimacy with nature that he had been born to; but it had passed the pioneering stage. It must be seen as a later stage that characterized all our frontier east of the great plains, after the actual frontier of settlement had pushed westward, after the farms had been brought in and functional communities had been established, but while the frontier crafts and values and ways of thinking lingered on, a little mannered perhaps, a little nostalgic, but still vital. The frontier thugs had passed to other fields or degenerated to village loafers and bullies. There were a few Indians near by and sizable numbers not too far away but they were a spectacle, not a threat. A few hunters and trappers ranged the woods but they were relics, brush folk, not of the great race. There were as many frame houses as log cabins; if the schoolhouse had a puncheon floor, the squire's wife had a silk dress from St. Louis. Caste lines were almost nonexistent. Hannibal was a farmers' market village. More than half of its inhabitants were Southerners, but Southerners modified by the Great Valley. Its slaves were servants, not gang laborers.

But also Hannibal was on the Mississippi. Here enters the thread of cosmopolitanism that is so paradoxically interwoven with the extreme provincialism of this society. Steamboats bore the travelers and commerce of half a continent past the town wharf. Great rafts of logs and lumber—it was the latter kind that Huck and Jim traveled on—came down from Wisconsin. A population of freighters, movers, and mere drifters in shanty boats, keelboats, broadhorns, mackinaws, and scows added pageantry. Other types and other costumery came down from the lakes and northern rivers: voyageurs, trappers, winterers, Indians of the wilderness tribes always seen in ceremonial garments on their way to make treaties or collect annuities. All these belonged to the rapidly widening movement of the expanding nation. Moreover, Hannibal was within the aura of St. Louis, eighty miles away, and St. Louis was the port through which the energies of a truly imperial expansion were moving toward Santa Fe, Oregon, and California. Perhaps dimly but quite permanently any river town so near St. Louis would give even the most local mind an awareness of the continental divide, the Columbia, the Pacific, the Southwest. A town that may have never heard of Zebulon Pike or John Ledyard or Jonathan Carver nevertheless felt the national will that had turned them westward. The year of Mark's birth, 1835, may properly be taken as the year when the final phase of our continental expansion began. And the fruitfulness of Hannibal for Mark's imagination may reasonably be said to have stopped with his tenth year, just before that final phase raised up the irrepressible conflict.

For two things remain to be said of the society that shaped Sam Clemens's mind and feelings: that its post-pioneer, frontier stage stops short of the industrial revolution, and that the sectional conflict which produced the Civil War has not yet shown itself. The life which is always most desirable in Mark's thinking is the pre-industrial society of a little river town; it is a specific identification of Hannibal. Whereas the evils of life are the eternal cruelties, hypocrisies, and stupidities of mankind which have nothing to do with time or place but result from Our Heavenly Father's haste in experimenting when He grew dissatisfied with the monkey.

As the St. Petersburg of *Tom Sawyer,* Hannibal is one of the superb idyls of American literature, perhaps the supreme one. A town of sun, forest shade, drowsy peace, limpid emotions, simple humanity—and eternity going by on the majestic river. Even here, however, a mood of melancholy is seldom far away: a melancholy of the river itself, of our westering people who had always known solitude, and of a child's feeling, which was to grow through the years, that he was a stranger and a mysterious one under the stars. And below the melancholy there is a deeper stratum, a terror or disgust that may break through in a graveyard at midnight or at the sound of unidentified voices whispering above the water. This is in part fantasy, but in part also it is the weary knowledge of evil that paints Hannibal in far different colors in *Pudd'nhead Wilson* or *Huckleberry Finn.*

Almost as soon as he begins to write, Mark Twain is a citizen of the world, but he is always a citizen of Hannibal too. He frequently misunderstood himself, but he knew that quite clearly. In a postscript to a letter . . . he says: "And yet I can't go away from the boyhood period & write novels because *capital* [that is, personal experience] is not sufficient by itself & I lack the other essential: interest in handling the men & experiences of later times."

While still a boy, he was apprenticed to a printer and so got the education that served more nineteenth-century American writers than any other. (It was a surprisingly extensive education. By twenty he knew the English classics thoroughly, was an inveterate reader of history, and had begun to cultivate his linguistic bent.) The trade eventually led him to newspaper reporting but first it took him on a series of Wanderjahre toward which heredity may have impelled him. At eighteen he went to St. Louis and on to New York. Philadelphia followed, Muscatine, St. Louis again, Keokuk (where he began to write humorous newspaper sketches), and Cincinnati, always setting type on a newspaper or in a job shop. He was twenty-two years old (and, if his memory can be trusted, ripe with a characteristic fantasy of South American adventure) when the American spectacle caught him up. In 1857 he began his apprenticeship to a Mississippi pilot.

Little need be said about his piloting in a book that includes "Old Times on the Mississippi," a study in pure ecstasy. The book is of course stamped from his memory, which was always nostalgic, and from the romancing half of his twinned talent. It records a supreme experience about whose delight there can be no doubt whatever, and it testifies to Mark's admiration of all skills and his mastery of one of the most difficult. But piloting gave him more than ever got into "Old Times" or its enlargement, *Life on the Mississippi.* "Flush Times" would have done as well as "Old Times" to describe the climactic years of the prewar Mississippi Valley, with the rush and fever of the expanding nation. Those years vastly widened Mark's knowledge of America and fed his insatiable enjoyment of men, his absorbed observation of man's depravity, and his delight in spectacle.

The Civil War put an end to piloting. Mark has described his experience and that of many others in that war, in all wars, in a sketch which is one of the best things he ever wrote. "The Private History of a Campaign That Failed" could not be spared from the mosaic of our national catastrophe; it is one of the contexts in which Mark Twain has perfectly refracted a national experience through a personal one. When his military career petered out in absurdity, he joined the great national movement which even civil war could not halt. His older brother, the gentle zany Orion, was made Secretary of the Territory of Nevada and, paying the Secretary's passage west, Mark went along. In Nevada he found another national retort, another mixed and violent society, another speculative flush times. He became a drunkard of speculation, a prospector, a hunter of phantasmal mines, a silver miner, a laborer in a stamp mill, and at last a newspaperman. He went to work for that fabulous paper *The Territorial Enterprise* of Virginia City as an "editor," that is to say a reporter. And it was here that he took his immortal *non de plume,* a phrase from the pilot's mystery. "Mark Twain" was signed to a species of humor in which Sam Clemens had been immersed ever since his apprenticeship, the newspaper humor of the Great Valley, which was in turn a development of the pungent oral humor he had heard from childhood on. Far from establishing a literary tradition, Mark Twain brought one to culmination.

After less than two years on the *Enterprise* he went to California, in 1864. He had met Artemus Ward in Nevada; now he joined the transient, bright Bohemia of the Golden Gate: Bret Harte, Prentice Mulford, Charles Warren Stoddard, Charles H. Webb, Ada Clare, Ina Coolbrith, still slighter and more forgotten names. He got a new kind of companionship and his first experience of literary sophistication. After a short time as a reporter he began to write humor for the Coast's literary papers, the *Californian* and the *Golden Era.* Promptly his work developed a strain of political and ethical satire which it never lost: the humorist was seldom separable from the satirist from this year on. That is to say, the individual humor of Mark Twain with its overtones of extravaganza and its undercurrent of misanthropy was, however crude and elliptical, fully formed by the end of 1864. He had not yet revealed the novelist's power to endow character with life, but it—together with a memorable talent for the vernacular—was made clear to anyone with eyes on December 16, 1865, when the New York *Saturday Press* published "Jim Smiley and His Jumping Frog."

The immortal story derived from still another Western experience, one which had made Mark, however lackadaisically, a pocket miner. He had sent it east at Artemus Ward's suggestion, but only an accident got it into type. It was a momentary smash hit, and so Mark was not altogether an unknown when he went to New York in 1867. Before he went there, however, he had reached the farthest limit of the expansionist dream, having gone to the Sandwich Islands as a newspaper correspondent. That voyage in turn had initiated his career as a lecturer. He had a marked histrionic talent; for years he barnstormed or made occasional appearances as a public "reader" and storyteller; all his life was making the after-dinner appearances of that vanished age, which pleased his vanity and gratified the longings of an actor *manqué.* But he went to New York as a correspondent: he had arranged to travel to Europe and the Holy Land with a conducted tour. In 1867 he published his first book, a collections of sketches called *The Celebrated Jumping Frog of Calaveras County* after the best of them, but the year is more notable for the travel letters he wrote for the *Alta California* and the New York

Tribune. He made a book of them after his return, meanwhile writing free-lance humor and Washington correspondence. The book, *Innocents Abroad,* was published in 1869.

All this has been detailed to show how deep and various an experience of American life Mark Twain had had when he began to write. The rest of his biography is also strikingly typical of nineteenth-century America, but the seed-time has now been accounted for. It is not too much to say that he had seen more of the United States, met more kinds and castes and conditions of Americans, observed the American in more occupations and moods and tempers—in a word had intimately shared a greater variety of the characteristic experiences of his countrymen—than any other major American writer. . . .

III

Mark Twain was a man of moods, of the extreme of moods. He had a buoyancy which, twinned as it was with gentleness and intuition and wit, gave him a personal magnetism which his friends did not hesitate to call enchantment. Yet it alternated with an anger that readily became fury and was rooted in a revulsion between disgust and despair. The alternation suggests a basic split; it is clearly marked in his personality and equally evident in his books. The splendor his friends felt, his kindness to the unfortunate and the lowly and the oppressed, his generosity, his sensitiveness unite in a singular luminosity of spirit. Yet he was capable of savage vindictiveness, he exaggerated small or imaginary grievances out of all reason, and on little or no provocation he repeatedly believed himself misrepresented or betrayed. One doubts if any other American writer was ever so publicly beloved or privately adored; one is certain that no other was involved in so many lawsuits. "I am full of malice, saturated with malignity," he wrote eight months before his death. His malice and malignity of that moment were for the damned human race, but he could feel them in his private life whenever he thought he had been wronged. When *A Connecticut Yankee* was finished he wrote Howells that if he could write it over again "there wouldn't be so many things left out. They burn in me and they keep multiplying and multiplying, but now they can't even be said. And besides they would require a library—and a pen warmed up in hell." With a pen warmed up in hell he did fill a library and an extraordinary bulk of letters too. If it was sometimes avenging personal, usually imaginary wrongs, that private activity was only a reflex of the public function. For what burned in him was hatred of cruelty and injustice, a deep sense of human evil, and a recurrent accusation of himself. Like Swift he found himself despising man while loving Tom, Dick, and Harry so warmly that he had no proper defense against the anguish of human relationships. The trouble was that in terms of either earth or heaven he was never sure what to make of Samuel L. Clemens and so is recorded on both sides.

He is usually to be found on both sides of any question he argues. His intelligence was intuitive, not analytical. He reasoned fluently, with an avidity that touched most of the surface flow of his time, but superficially and with habitual contradictions. He had little capacity for sustained thought and to get to the heart of a question had to abandon analysis and rely on feeling. The philosophy which he spent years refining and supposed he had perfected is a sophomoric determinism. Even so, it is less a philosophy than a symbol or a rationalization; the perceptions it stood for are expressed at the level of genius in his fiction—not as idea but in terms of human life. Most of the nineteenth century's optimisms were his also. He fiercely championed the democratic axioms; they are the ether of his fiction and the fulcrum of his satire. He thought too that the nineteenth century, especially as Progress, and more especially as Progress in the United States, was the happiest estate of man; he believed that it was bringing on a future of greater freedom and greater happiness. This was basic and spontaneous in his mind, but at the same time he felt something profoundly wrong. There seemed to be some limitation to freedom, some frustration of happiness. He never really came to grips with the conflict. Only in the last fifteen years of his life did he ascribe any part of what might be wrong to any but superficial injustices in American life or any but slight dislocations in our system. By the time he became aware of serious threats to freedom they did not seem to matter much: he was so absorbed in the natural depravity of man that the collapse or frustration of democracy, which he was by then taking for granted, seemed only an unimportant detail. Ideally, his last years would have been spent in more rigorous analysis—if not of the objective data, then of his intuitive awareness of them. They were not and so his judgments remained confused—and his principal importance in our literature belongs to his middle years, the period when his mind and feelings are in healthy equilibrium. It is an importance of his perceptions, not his thinking, and it exists primarily in his fiction, most purely in *Huckleberry Finn*. The best of Mark Twain's fiction is, historically, the first mature realization in our literature of a conflict between the assumptions of democracy and the limitations on democracy. Between the ideal of freedom and the nature of man.

Not less important is the fact that there is a reconciliation, even an affirmation. Detachment could be no greater but it is still some-how compassionate; condemnation could be no more complete, but it is somehow magnanimous. The damned human race is displayed with derision and abhorrence, yet this is on the ground that it has fallen short of its own decencies. Moreover at least *Huckleberry Finn* has a hero, the only heroic character (apart from Joan of Arc, a de-bauch of gyneolatry) he ever drew, and it is the essence of what Mark Twain had to say that the hero is a Negro slave. It has also a vindica-tion not only of freedom, but of loyalty and decency, kindness and courage; and it is the essence of Mark Twain that this vindication is made by means of a boy who is a spokesman of the folk mind and whom experience has taught wariness and skepticism. Like all great novels *Huckleberry Finn* moves on many levels of significance, but it describes a flight and a struggle for freedom and the question it turns on is a moral question.

Mark found zest and gusto—nouns that do not describe very much American literature of the first rank—in whatsoever was alive. He liked few novels except those of his intimate friends. What he praised in the ones he did like was reality of behavior, speech, or motive; his notebooks are sulphurous with comments on merely lit-erary, that is false, characters. His taste was for biography, auto-biography, history—life direct, men revealing themselves. No doubt the race was damned but it was fascinating. And that was proper for if his fiction is the best of his work, his most salient talent as a novel-ist is the life-giving power. It is a careless and prodigal fecundity, but nevertheless remarkably concentrated. Old Man Finn, for in-stance, is greatly imagined and he seems to fill the first half of the book, yet he appears in only a few pages. Mrs. Judith Loftus lives completely in a single chapter. A mere passer-by, a casual of the river or a thug heard talking in a frowzy town, may reveal a whole personality in a few paragraphs. Nor is this fecundity confined to Mark's fiction, for the framework of all his books is anecdotal and all the people in them are dramatized. The whole population of his principal books, nine-tenths of the population of all his books, has the same vividness. Boys, villagers, the rivermen, the Negroes, Col-onel Sellers, the two great vagabonds—there is nothing quite like the Mark Twain gallery elsewhere in American literature.

But there is a striking limitation: nowhere in that gallery are there women of marriageable age. No white women, that is, for the slave Roxana in *Pudd'nhead Wilson* lives as vividly as Old Man Finn himself. It must be significant that the only credible woman of an age that might sanction desire is withdrawn from desire behind the barrier of race. None of Mark Twain's nubile girls, young women, or young matrons are believable; they are all bisque, saccharine, or tears. He will do girl children in the romantic convention of boys' books and he is magnificent with the sisterhood of worn frontier wives whom Aunt Polly climaxes, but something like a taboo drains reality from any woman who might trouble the heart or the flesh. There is no love story in Mark Twain, there is no love at all beyond an occasional admission, for purposes of plot only, that someone is married or is going to be. Women seldom have husbands and men seldom have wives unless they are beyond middle age. Mark's endless absorption in human motives did not, for literary purposes at least, extend to sexual motives. Sex seems to be forbidden unless it can be treated mawkishly, and this writer of great prose who habitually flouted the genteel proprieties of language was more prudish than the most tremulous of his friends in regard to language that might suggest either desire or its gratification. So there is a sizable gap in the world he created. That gap has never been accounted for. Certainly there was nothing bloodless about Mark Twain; and his marriage, one of the happiest of literary marriages, was clearly passionate. Yet he did not marry till he was thirty-five (1870), and there may have been something permissive—to a man whose characters have usually lost a father if not both parents—in the fact that he married an invalid.

Few Americans have written as much as Mark Twain. His published works are not much greater in bulk than his unpublished manuscripts, the books he finished fewer than the ones he broke off and abandoned. He wrote on impulse and enthusiasm and while they lasted he wrote easily, but he wrote as needs must, for he had little faculty of self-criticism and but small ability to sustain or elaborate an idea. He was best at the short haul. Not only his fiction but the personalized narrative that is the vehicle of *Innocents Abroad, A Tramp Abroad, Life on the Mississippi,* and much else is episodic. When what he was writing was in circuit with his deepest perceptions he was superb. The breaking of the circuit always threw him into extemporization, which meant that fiction fell away into extravaganza and satire into burlesque. At such times he did not know that he was flatting; the serious artist could become a vaudeville monologuist in a single page without being aware that the tone had changed. That such a well-imagined novel as *Pudd'nhead Wilson* was written round the grotesque joke called "Those Extraordinary Twins" would be incredible if the same tone-deafness were not plentifully evident elsewhere. He thought the mawkish *Joan of Arc* and the second-rate *The Prince and the Pauper* his best work. He interrupted his masterpiece before it was half-finished, liking it so little that he threatened to burn it, and ignored it for six years during which, though he wrote constantly, he wrote nothing of importance. Then he finished it almost as casually as he had begun it. There is no greater book in American literature, but critics agree that the last quarter of it is impaired by the extravaganza that begins when Huck gets to Uncle Silas's farm. It is typical of Mark Twain that he felt no difference in kind or key between this admittedly superb extravaganza and the searching of American society and human experience that precedes it. In fact, the delivery of Jim from the dungeon was one of Mark's favorite platform readings.

Furthermore, he lacked the attribute of the artist—whatever it may be—that enables him to think a novel through till its content has found its own inherent form. Of his novels only *Joan of Arc, The Prince and the Pauper,* and *Tom Sawyer* have structures that have developed from within; significantly, all are simple and only one is first-rate. Mark lived with his material for a long time, sometimes for many years, but not consciously, not with critical or searching dissatisfaction. A book must come of its own momentum from the unconscious impulse, be it as a whole, as a fragment, or as something that hardly got started before it broke off. This is to say that he had no conscious aesthetic. He stood at the opposite pole from Henry James, with the other great contemporary of both, Howells, in between but nearer to James. Yet he had as large a share as either of them in creating the modern American novel.

The explanation for his lack of self-criticism and for his innocence of aesthetics is not to be found in the supposed naiveté of the society that bore him. In the first place, that society was far from naive; in the second place, not only did the fine artist Howells come from it, but Mark himself raised its native tale-telling to a fine art, which surely establishes a discipline. He had, besides, two other disciplines: that of the daily job, which he observed as faithfully as any writer who ever lived, and the taskmastership of a great style. Nor can Mark's own explanation, which he pleads so earnestly in the letter to Andrew Lang, be supported: that he wrote for the belly and members only. *Huckleberry Finn* is no more written for the belly and members only than *War and Peace* is or *Recherche du Temps Perdu.* But it is written at the behest of an instinctive drive, and explanation need go no further if it could, for this time at least Mark's whole personality was behind it. In short, he wrote trivially or splendidly or magnificently as what appears to have been little more than chance might determine: he was not a fully self-conscious artist. But when he wrote greatly he was writing from an inner harmony of desire and will. Or call it a harmony of his deepest self and his inheritance from the Great Valley.

Only that harmony, seen in relation to time and history, can explain him. For no man ever became a great writer more inadvertently than Mark Twain. He first became famous as a superior Artemus Ward, and that corresponded to his idea of himself. A long time passed before he had any desire to be more. He exploited a jokemakers talent as systematically as a production manager could have done it for him, delighted by the discovery that he could raise his status, prestige, and income beyond Tom Sawyer's dreams. Nevertheless there is the paradox that almost from the beginning the attack of the funny man had been supported by that of a serious artist. Already in "The Jumping Frog" mastery of fictional character is clearly presaged, and the prophecy is fulfilled as early as *The Gilded Age* (1874). By *The Gilded Age* also a satirist is dealing maturely with a wide expanse of American life. From this composite the funny man cannot be separated out for a long time, and during that time there are only sporadic indications that Mark saw either the novelist or the satirist as more than instrumentalities of the humorist. The paradox resists criticism. One can only repeat that Mark Twain's greatness developed because the time and the continent had shaped him at their core.

This representative centrality goes on undiminished after the establishment of his fame. Following his marriage he was briefly a newspaper owner in Buffalo but abandoned that career to move to a provincial New England city, Hartford, and set up as a professional writer. His periodic restlessness continued; he never spent the full year in Hartford, he made at least twelve trips abroad, and he once expatriated himself for nine years. The Hartford period, 1874-1891, covered his greatest happiness and the beginning of his catastrophe. His was an unusually happy family life, and he was the center of an always widening circle. Howells and the Rev. Joseph Twichell were his closest friends; Cable, Aldrich, most of the leading writers of his generation were of the circle, and it widened to include the rich, the famous, and the great. Mark ruled it by divine right: there have always been conflicting opinions about his books, but only one has ever been possible about his dominion over men's affections. He seemed alien to mortality. A fantasy of his childhood is frequently set down in notes and fragments of manuscript: the child had identified himself with a romantic stranger in Hannibal, a mysterious, perhaps supernatural visitor from Elsewhere. As the one-gallus village boy came to be a world figure, that fantasy seemed on the way to being confirmed. There was further confirmation as the author of *The Gilded Age* entered with a blithe and innocent heart on another career, as a speculator, and the stamp-mill operator and tramp printer, who sincerely believed all his life that he was a member of the laboring class, undertook with the same innocence to be an industrial promoter.

Always convinced that his publishers were defrauding him, Mark had established his own firm to publish his books. The expansion it underwent in order to handle the bestseller of the generation, *Personal Memoirs of U. S. Grant,* could not be sustained. The firm sank into insolvency and finally went bankrupt. It could probably have been saved except that the most fantastic of Mark's promotions failed at the same time and left him bankrupt. For years he had been pouring his earnings and his wife's fortune into a mechanical typesetter which would indeed have made him a multimillionaire if it had succeeded. Its failure and that of the publishing firm were only the beginning of a series of disasters on the same scale as his fantastic rise. He paid off his indebtedness by a heroic lecture tour that took him round the world but his health broke. The oldest of his three daughters, the one who seemed most like him in temperament and talent, died during his absence. An agonizing personality change in his youngest daughter was finally diagnosed as epilepsy. Mrs. Clemens declined into permanent invalidism and in 1904 died.

This prolonged catastrophe brought Mark's misanthropy out of equilibrium; it dominated the rest of his life. The disasters were, of course, personal and yet it is hardly straining the facts to find him here also representative of the nineteenth-century America that had already found so much expression in him. As the century neared its end there was a good deal of pessimism and disenchantment in the United States. A wave of doubt and questioning swept many minds. The people who began an imperialistic adventure in the Pacific with the same naive enthusiasm that had taken Mark Twain into the industrial life were widely, at the very time they stepped out on the world stage, beginning to be troubled about themselves. The nineteenth century, looking back on its course, found cause to be dismayed. Was the democratic dream being served as well as the nation had assumed? Had the United States gone wrong somewhere during the avalanche of expansion? Were there, then, limits to what democracy could do, or flaws or contradictions in its theses, or impassable barriers in its path? Was the good time ending, were the vigorous years running out under a gathering shadow?

However deep or shallow this *fin de siècle* weariness may have been in the United States at large, Mark Twain's last fifteen years must be seen as related to it, if only distantly. During this period he wrote as much as in any similar length of time in his life, perhaps more, but most of it is fragmentary, unfinished. Almost all of it deals with the nature of man, man's fate, and man's conception of honor and morality. There are fables, dialogues, diatribes—sometimes cold, sometimes passionate, derisive, withering, savage. Mark sees the American republic perishing, like republics before it, through the ineradicable cowardice, corruption, and mere baseness of mankind. He elaborates theories, which he embodies in imaginary histories of the world (and sometimes of extra-mundane societies) to support his prophecy, and yet he cannot be much troubled by the going-down of this western land, for year by year he is writing a general apocalypse. The Old Testament fables had always served him for humorous derision of man's gullibility, but now he uses them as missiles in a ferocious attack on human stupidity and cruelty. Man is compact of malignity, cowardice, weakness, and absurdity, a diseased organism, a parasite on nature, a foolish but murderous animal much lower than the swine.

Yet *What Is Man?* (published anonymously in 1906 but written before the turn of the century), the fullest of many developments of these themes, cannot be seen solely as a document in anthropophobia. It is also in complex ways a justification, even a self-justification. Its fixed universe, with an endless chain of cause and effect from the beginning of time, permits Mark to compose many variations on the theme of human pettiness, but also it serves to free man of blame —and thus satisfies a need deeply buried in Mark's personal remorse. To this period also belongs *Mark Twain's Autobiography,* which serves him as an escape into the security of the boyhood idyl he had made immortal in *Tom Sawyer.* The need to escape is significant, but the release is even more so, for it breaks the obsession signified by *What Is Man?* But a much truer release and a fulfillment as well came, as always, when Mark turned from reasoning to the instinctual portions of his mind. The highest reach of his last period is *The Mysterious Stranger.* It is an almost perfect book—perfect in expression of his final drive, in imaginative projection of himself, in tone and tune, in final judgment on the nature of man and the experience of Mark Twain. It is on a humbler level than his great books. More than any of them it is Mark Twain somewhat in disregard of America. It is not, finally, a major work; but in its small way it is a masterpiece. Those who know and love Mark Twain will always find it is as revealing as *Huckleberry Finn.*

IV

Mark Twain died in 1910 with, as he had foretold, the return of the mysterious visitor from beyond the solar system under whose sign he had been born, Halley's comet. His last years had been as full of honors as his middle years had been of fame. Even so, in 1910 it was hardly possible to define his importance in American literature as clearly as we can after another generation.

No doubt his first importance in that literature is the democratizing effect of his work. It is a concretely liberating effect, and therefore different in kind from Whitman's vision of democracy, which can hardly be said to have been understood by or to have found a response among any considerable number of Americans. Mark Twain was the first great American writer who was also a popular writer, and that in itself is important. Much more important is the implicit and explicit democracy of his books. They are the first American literature of the highest rank which portrays the ordinary bulk of Americans, expresses them, accepts their values, and delineates their hopes, fears, decencies, and indecencies as from within. The area proper to serious literature in the United States was enormously widened by them, in fact widened to the boundaries it still observes today. There have been no acknowledged priorities of caste in American writing since Mark Twain. Moreover, in his native equal-itarian point of view, in his assertion of the basic democratic axioms, in his onslaught on privilege, injustice, vested power, political pre-tense, and economic exploitation (much of it admittedly superficial or confused, though much else is the most vigorous satire we have), in his transmutation of the town-meeting or country-store sharpness of judgment into a fine art—he is midnineteenth-century American democracy finding its first major voice in literature, ultimately its strongest voice. In him the literature of democracy becomes more robust than it had been before, such part of that literature, at least, as may be said to contain multitudes and speak to them. And this, to return to our starting point, embodies the transforming experience of the American people as they occupied the Great Valley and pushed beyond it, on the way forging the continental mind.

The nature of his writing is hardly less important. Mark Twain wrote one of the great styles of American literature, he helped de-velop the modern American style, he was the first writer who ever used the American vernacular at the level of art. There has been some failure to understand this achievement. Shortly before this Introduction was written, the most pontifical American critic guessed that Mark must have turned to the vernacular of *Huckleberry Finn* because he lacked education, was unacquainted with literary tradi-tions, and therefore wrote thin or awkward prose. That absurdity disregards Mark's life and his books as well. The reader may deter-mine herein whether the style of *The Mysterious Stranger* lacks strength or subtlety, lacks any quality whatever for the effects re-quired of it, or if that represents too late a period, may turn to

"Old Times on the Mississippi," which was written before *Huckleberry Finn,* or "The Private History of a Campaign That Failed," which was written while *Huck* was still half finished. Mark Twain wrote English of a remarkable simplicity and clarity, and of singular sensitiveness, flexibility, and beauty as well. Its simplicity might deceive a patronizing reader for the sentence structure is not involved, usually consisting of short elements in natural sequence, and in order to understand without analysis how much art has gone into it one must have an ear for the tones and accents of speech as well as some feeling for the vigor of words. It is so lucid that it seems effortless—but just what is style?

Now, it is important that Mark made the American vernacular the medium of a great novel. Even before that he had used local, class, and racial dialects with immeasurably greater skill than anyone before him in our literature. "The Jumping Frog" raised dialects above the merely humorous use which was the only one they had previously had and gave them a function in the writing of fiction. And the first two chapters of *The Gilded Age* bring to American literature genuine Negro speech and a rural dialect that are both genuine and an instrument of art—literally for the first time. In the rendition of Negro speech he may have had one equal, though there are those who will not grant that Harris is an equal; but it is doubtful if anyone has used the dialects of the middle South, or for that matter any other American dialect, as well as he. This on the basis of *The Gilded Age* and its immediate successors: the achievement of *Huckleberry Finn* is greater still. Huck's style, which is the spoken language of the untutored American of his place and time, differentiates the most subtle meanings and emphases and proves capable of the most difficult psychological effects. In a single step it made a literary medium of the American language; the liberating effect on American writing could hardly be overstated. Since *Huckleberry Finn* the well of American undefiled has flowed confidently.

Nevertheless, Mark's principal service to the American language was not Huck's vernacular: it lay within the recognized limits of literary prose. Within those limits he was a radical innovator, a prime mover who changed the medium by incorporating in it the syntax, the idioms, and especially the vocabulary of the common life. The vigor of his prose comes directly from the speech of the Great Valley and the Far West. A superlative may be ventured: that Mark Twain had a greater effect than any other writer on the evolution of American prose.

His place in that evolution cannot be analyzed or even illustrated here. He is in the direct succession and he powerfully accelerates the movement. The evolution is of course older than our independence, even older than our nationality—which it helped to produce. Only an American could have said, "We must all hang together, or assuredly we shall all hang separately" in the traditional context. Only an American could have written, "It is not necessary that a man should earn his living by the sweat of his brow unless he sweats easier than I do." Only an American could have written, "the calm confidence of a Christian with four aces." The sequence is Franklin, Thoreau, Mark Twain; and the point here made lightly can be made with as profound a search into the fusion of thought, expression, and nationality as anyone may care to undertake. But before Mark Twain no American, no one writing in English, could have launched a novel into the movement of fiction with such a passage as:

At the end of an hour we saw a far-away town sleeping in a valley by a winding river, and beyond it on a hill, a vast gray fortress with towers and turrets, the first I had ever seen out of a picture.
"Bridgeport?" said I, pointing.
"Camelot," said he.

Such questions as these, however, interest the historian of literature more than the general reader. The general reader who, it may be worth reminding you, continues to read Mark Twain, here and in Europe, more often by far than any other of our great dead. It is not difficult to say why. . . .

21

T. S. Eliot: HENRY JAMES [1918]

I. In Memory

Henry James has been dead for some time. The current of English literature was not appreciably altered by his work during his lifetime; and James will probably continue to be regarded as the extraordinarily clever but negligible curiosity. The current hardly matters; it hardly matters that very few people will read James. The "influence" of James hardly matters: to be influenced by a writer is to have a chance inspiration from him; or to take what one wants; or to see things one has overlooked; there will always be a few intelligent people to understand James, and to be understood by a few intelligent people is all the influence a man requires. What matters least of all is his place in such a Lord Mayor's show as Mr. Chesterton's procession of Victorian Literature. The point to be made is that James has an importance which has nothing to do with what came before him or what may happen after him; an importance which has been overlooked on both sides of the Atlantic.

I do not suppose that anyone who is not an American can *properly* appreciate James. James's best American figures in the novels, in spite of their trim, definite outlines, the economy of strokes, have a fullness of existence and an external ramification of relationship which a European reader might not easily suspect. The Bellegarde family, for instance, are merely good outline sketches of an intelligent foreigner; when more is expected of them, in the latter part of the story, they jerk themselves into only melodramatic violence. In all appearance Tom Tristram is an even slighter sketch. Europeans can recognize him; they have seen him, known him, have even penetrated the Occidental Club; but no European has the Tom Tristram element in his composition, has anything of Tristram from his first visit to the Louvre to his final remark that Paris is the only place where a white man can live. It is the final perfection, the consummation of an American to become, not an Englishman, but a European—something which no born European, no person of any European nationality, can become. Tom is one of the failures, one of nature's misfortunes, in this process. Even General Packard, C. P. Hatch, and Miss Kitty Upjohn have a reality which Claire de Cintré misses. Noémie, of course, is perfect, but Noémie is a result of the intelligent eye, her existence is a triumph of the intelligence, and it does not extend beyond the frame of the picture.

For the English reader, much of James's criticism of America must merely be something taken for granted. English readers can appreciate it for what it has in common with criticism everywhere, with Flaubert in France and Turgenev in Russia. Still, it should have for the English an importance beyond the work of these writers. There is no English equivalent for James, and at least he writes in this language. As a critic, no novelist in our language can approach James; there is not even any large part of the reading public which knows what the word "critic" means. (The usual definition of a critic is a writer who cannot "create"—perhaps a reviewer of books.) James was emphatically not a successful *literary critic*. His criticism of books and writers is feeble. In writing of a novelist, he occasionally produces a valuable sentence out of his own experience rather than in judgment of the subject. The rest is charming talk, or gentle commendation. Even in handling men whom he could, one supposes, have carved joint from joint—Emerson, or Norton—his touch is uncertain; there is a desire to be generous, a political motive, an admission (in dealing with American writers) that under the circumstances this was the best possible, or that it has fine qualities. His father was here keener than he. Henry was not a literary critic.

He was a critic who preyed not upon ideas, but upon living beings. It is criticism which is in a very high sense creative. The characters, the best of them, are each a distinct success of creation: Daisy Miller's small brother is one of these. Done in a clean, flat drawing, each is extracted out of a reality of its own, substantial enough; everything given is true for that individual; but what is given is chosen with great art for its place in a general scheme. The general scheme is not one character, nor a group of characters in a plot or merely in a crowd. The focus is a situation, a relation, an atmosphere, to which the characters pay tribute, but being allowed to give only what the writer wants. The real hero, in any of James' stories, is a social entity of which men and women are constituents. It is, in *The Europeans,* that particular conjunction of people at the Wentworth house, a situation in which several memorable scenes are merely timeless parts, only occurring necessarily in succession. In this respect, you can say that James is dramatic; as what Pinero and Mr. Jones used to do for a large public, James does for the intelligent. It is in the chemistry of these subtle substances, these curious precipitates and explosive gases which are suddenly formed by the contact of mind with mind, that James is unequaled. Compared with James's, other novelists' characters seem to be only accidentally in the same book. Naturally, there is something terrible, as disconcerting as a quicksand, in this discovery, though it only becomes absolutely dominant in such stories as *The Turn of the Screw.* It is partly foretold in Hawthorne, but James carried it much further. And it makes the reader, as well as the personae, uneasily the victim of a merciless clairvoyance.

James's critical genius comes out most tellingly in his mastery over, his baffling escape from, Ideas; a mastery and an escape which are perhaps the last test of a superior intelligence. He had a mind so fine that no idea could violate it. Englishmen, with their uncritical admiration (in the present age) for France, like to refer to France as the Home of Ideas; a phrase which, if we could twist it into truth, or at least a compliment, ought to mean that in France ideas are very severely looked after; not allowed to stray, but preserved for the inspection of civic pride in a Jardin des Plantes, and frugally dispatched on occasions of public necessity. England, on the other hand, if it is not the Home of Ideas, has at least become infested with them in about the space of time within which Australia has been overrun by rabbits. In England ideas run wild and pasture on the emotions; instead of thinking with our feelings (a very different thing) we corrupt our feelings with ideas; we produce the political, the emotional idea, evading sensation and thought. George Meredith (the disciple of Carlyle) was fertile in ideas; his epigrams are a facile substitute for observation and inference. Mr. Chesterton's brain swarms with ideas; I see no evidence that it thinks. James in his novels is like the best French critics in maintaining a point of view, a viewpoint untouched by the parasite idea. He is the most intelligent man of his generation.

The fact of being everywhere a foreigner was probably an assistance to his native wit. Since Byron and Landor, no Englishman appears to have profited much from living abroad. We have had Birmingham seen from Chelsea, but not Chelsea seen (really *seen*) from Baden or Rome. There are advantages, indeed, in coming from a large flat country which no one wants to visit; advantages which both Turgenev and James enjoyed. These advantages have not won them recognition. Europeans have preferred to take their notion of the Russian from Dostoevsky and their notion of the American from, let us say, Frank Norris if not O. Henry. Thus, they fail to note that there are many kinds of their fellow-countrymen, and that most of these kinds, similarly to the kinds of *their* fellow-countrymen, are stupid; likewise with Americans. Americans also have encouraged this fiction of a general type, a formula or idea, usually the predaceous square-jawed or thin-lipped. They like to be told that they are a race of commercial buccaneers. It gives them something easily escaped from, moreover, when they wish to reject America. Thus the novels of Frank Norris have succeeded in both countries; though it is curious that the most valuable part of *The Pit* is its satire (quite unconscious, I believe; Norris was simply representing faithfully the life he knew) of Chicago society after business hours. All this show of commercialism which Americans like to present to the foreign eye James quietly waves aside; and in pouncing upon his fellow-countryman after the stock exchange has closed, in tracking down his vices and absurdities across the Atlantic, and exposing them in their highest flights of dignity or culture, James may be guilty of what will seem to most Americans scandalously improper behavior. It is too much to expect them to be grateful. And the British public, had it been more aware, would hardly have been more comfortable confronted with a smile which was so far from breaking into the British laugh. Henry James's death, if it had been more taken note of, should have given considerable relief "on both sides of the Atlantic," and cemented the Anglo-American Entente.

II. The Hawthorne Aspect

My object is not to discuss critically even one phase or period of James, but merely to provide a note, *Beiträge,* toward any attempt to determine his antecedents, affinities, and "place." Presumed that James's relation to Balzac, to Turgenev, to anyone else on the continent is known and measured—I refer to Mr. Hueffer's book and to Mr. Pound's article—and presumed that his relation to the Victorian novel is negligible, it is not concluded that James was simply a clever young man who came to Europe and improved himself, but that the soil of his origin contributed a flavor discriminable after transplantation in his latest fruit. We may even draw the instructive conclusion that this flavor was precisely improved and given its chance, not worked off, by transplantation. If there is this strong native taste, there will probably be some relation to Hawthorne; and if there is any relation to Hawthorne, it will probably help us to analyze the flavor of which I speak.

When we say that James is "American," we must mean that this "flavor" of his, and also more exactly definable qualities, are more or less diffused throughout the vast continent rather than anywhere else; but we cannot mean that this flavor and these qualities have found literary expression throughout the nation, or that they permeate the work of Mr. Frank Norris or Mr. Booth Tarkington. The point is that James is positively a continuator of the New England genius; that there is a New England genius, which has discovered itself only in a very small number of people in the middle of the nineteenth century—and which is not significantly present in the writings of Miss Sara Orne Jewett, Miss Eliza White, or the Bard of Appledore, whose name I forget. I mean whatever we associate with certain purlieus of Boston, with Concord, Salem, and Cambridge, Mass.: notably Emerson, Thoreau, Hawthorne, and Lowell. None of these men, with the exception of Hawthorne, is individually very important; they all can, and perhaps ought to be made to look very foolish; but there is a "something" there, a dignity, about Emerson, for example, which persists after we have perceived the taint of commonness about some English contemporary, as, for instance, the more intelligent, better-educated, more alert Matthew Arnold. Omitting such men as Bryant and Whittier as absolutely plebeian, we can still perceive this halo of dignity around the men I have named, and also Longfellow, Margaret Fuller and her crew, Bancroft and Motley, the faces of (later) Norton and Child pleasantly shaded by the Harvard elms. One distinguishing mark of this distinguished world was very certainly leisure; and importantly not in all cases a leisure given by money, but insisted upon. There seems no easy reason why Emerson or Thoreau or Hawthorne should have been men of leisure; it seems odd that the New England conscience should have allowed them leisure; yet they would have it, sooner or later. That is really one of the finest things about them, and sets a bold frontier between them and a world which will at any price avoid leisure, a world in which Theodore Roosevelt is a patron of the arts. An interesting document of this latter world is *Letters* of a nimbly dull poet of a younger generation, of Henry James's generation, Richard Watson Gilder, Civil Service Reform, Tenement House Commissioner, Municipal Politics.

Of course leisure in a metropolis, with a civilized society (the society of Boston was and is quite uncivilized but refined beyond the point of civilization), with exchange of ideas and critical standards, would have been better; but these men could not provide the metropolis, and were right in taking the leisure under possible conditions.

Precisely this leisure, this dignity, this literary aristocracy, this unique character of a society in which the men of letters were also of the best people, clings to Henry James. It is some consciousness of this kinship which makes him so tender and gentle in his appreciation of Emerson, Norton, and the beloved Ambassador. With Hawthorne, as much the most important of these people in any question of literary art, his relation is more personal; but no more in the case of Hawthorne than with any of the other figures of the background is there any consideration of influence. James owes little, very little, to anyone; there are certain writers whom he consciously studied, of whom Hawthorne was not one; but in any case his relation to Hawthorne is on another plane from his relation to Balzac, for example. The influence of Balzac, not on the whole a good influence, is perfectly evident in some of the earlier novels; the influence of Turgenev is vaguer, but more useful. That James was, at a certain period, more moved by Balzac, that he followed him with more concentrated admiration, is clear from the tone of his criticism of that writer compared with the tone of his criticism of either Turgenev or Hawthorne. In *French Poets and Novelists,* though an early work, James's attitude toward Balzac is exactly that of having been very much attracted from his orbit, perhaps very wholesomely stimulated at an age when almost any foreign stimulus may be good, and having afterwards reacted from Balzac, though not to the point of injustice. He handles Balzac shrewdly and fairly. From the essay on Turgenev there is on the other hand very little to be got but a touching sense of appreciation; from the essay on Flaubert even less. The charming study of Hawthorne is quite different from any of these. The first conspicuous quality in it is tenderness, the tenderness of a man who had escaped too early from an environment to be warped or thwarted by it, who had escaped so effectually that he could afford the gift of affection. At the same time he places his finger, now and then, very gently on some of Hawthorne's more serious defects as well as his limitations.

"The best things come, as a general thing, from the talents that are members of a group; every man works better when he has companions working in the same line, and yielding the stimulus of suggestion, comparison, emulation." Though when he says that "there was manifestly a strain of generous indolence in his [Hawthorne's] composition" he is understating the fault of laziness for which Hawthorne can chiefly be blamed. But gentleness is needed in criticizing Hawthorne, a necessary thing to remember about whom is precisely the difficult fact that the soil which produced him with his essential flavor is the soil which produced, just as inevitably, the environment which stunted him.

In one thing alone Hawthorne is more solid than James: he had a very acute historical sense. His erudition in the small field of American colonial history was extensive, and he made most fortunate use of it. Both men had that sense of the past which is peculiarly American, but in Hawthorne this sense exercised itself in a grip on the past itself; in James it is a sense of the sense. This, however, need not be dwelt upon here. The really vital thing, in finding any personal kinship between Hawthorne and James, is what James touches lightly when he says that "the fine thing in Hawthorne is that he cared for the deeper psychology, and that, in his way, he tried to become familiar with it." There are other points of resemblance, not directly included under this, but this one is of the first importance. It is, in fact, almost enough to ally the two novelists, in comparison with whom almost all others may be accused of either superficiality or aridity. I am not saying that this "deeper psychology" is essential, or that it can always be had without loss of other qualities, or that a novel need be any the less a work of art without it. It is a definition; and it separates the two novelists at once from the English contemporaries of either. Neither Dickens nor Thackeray, certainly, had the smallest notion of the "deeper psychology"; George Eliot had a kind of heavy intellect for it (Tito) but all her genuine feeling went into the visual realism of *Amos Barton*. On the continent it is known; but the method of Stendhal or of Flaubert is quite other. A situation is for Stendhal something deliberately constructed, often an illustration. There is a bleakness about it, vitalized by force rather than feeling, and its presentation is definitely visual. Hawthorne and James have a kind of sense, a receptive medium, which is not of sight. Not that they fail to make you *see*, so far as necessary, but sight is not the essential sense. They perceive by antennae; and the "deeper psychology" is here. The deeper psychology indeed led Hawthorne to some of his absurdest and most characteristic excesses; it was forever tailing off into the fanciful, even the allegorical, which is a lazy substitute for profundity. The fancifulness is the "strain of generous indolence," the attempt to get the artistic effect by meretricious means. On this side a critic might seize hold of *The Turn of the Screw,* a tale about which I have many doubts; but the actual working out of this is different from Hawthorne's, and we are not interested in approximation of the two men on the side of their weakness. The point is that Hawthorne was acutely sensitive to the situation; that he did grasp character through the relation of two or more persons to each other; and this is what no one else, except James, has done. Furthermore, he does establish, as James establishes, a solid atmosphere, and he does, in his quaint way, get New England, as James gets a larger part of America, and as none of their respective contemporaries get anything above a village or two, or a jungle. Compare, with anything that any English contemporary could do, the situation which Hawthorne sets up in the relation of Dimmesdale and Chillingworth. Judge Pyncheon and Clifford, Hepzibah and Phoebe, are similarly achieved by their relation to each other; Clifford, for one, being simply the intersection of a relation to three other characters. The only dimension in which Hawthorne could expand was the past, his present being so narrowly barren. It is a great pity, with his remarkable gift of observation, that the present did not offer him more to observe. But he is the one English-writing predecessor of James whose characters are *aware* of each other, the one whose novels were in any deep sense a criticism of even a slight civilization; and here is something more definite and closer than any derivation we can trace from Richardson or Marivaux.

The fact that the sympathy with Hawthorne is most felt in the last of James's novels, *The Sense of the Past,* makes me the more certain of its genuineness. In the meantime, James has been through a much more elaborate development than poor Hawthorne ever knew. Hawthorne, with his very limited culture, was not exposed to any bewildering variety of influences. James, in his astonishing career of self-improvement, touches Hawthorne most evidently at the beginning and end of his course; at the beginning, simply as a young New Englander of letters; at the end, with almost a gesture of approach. *Roderick Hudson* is the novel of a clever and expanding young New Englander; immature, but just coming out to a self-consciousness where Hawthorne never arrived at all. Compared with *Daisy Miller* or *The Europeans* or *The American* its critical spirit is very crude. But *The Marble Faun,* the only European novel of Hawthorne, is of Cimmerian opacity; the mind of its author was closed to new impressions though with all its Walter Scott—*Mysteries of Udolpho* upholstery the old man does establish a kind of solid moral atmosphere which the young James does not get. James in *Roderick Hudson* does very little better with Rome than Hawthorne, and as he confesses in the later preface, rather fails with Northampton.•

He does in the later edition tone down the absurdities of Roderick's sculpture a little, the pathetic Thirst and the gigantic Adam; Mr. Striker remains a failure, the judgment of a young man consciously humorizing, too suggestive of *Martin Chuzzlewit.* The generic resemblance to Hawthorne is in the occasional heavy facetiousness of the style, the tedious whimsicality how different from the exactitude of *The American Scene,* the verbalism. He too much identifies himself with Rowland, does not see through the solemnity he has created in that character, commits the cardinal sin of failing to "detect" one of his own characters. The failure to create a situation is evident: with Christina and Mary, each nicely adjusted, but never quite set in relation to each other. The interest of the book for our present purpose is what he does *not* do in the Hawthorne way, in the instinctive attempt to get at something larger, which will bring him to the same success with much besides.

The interest in the "deeper psychology," the observation, and the sense for situation, developed from book to book, culminate in *The Sense of the Past* (by no means saying that this is his best), uniting with other qualities both personal and racial. James's greatness is apparent both in his capacity for development as an artist and his capacity for keeping his mind alive to the changes in the world during twenty-five years. It is remarkable (for the mastery of a span of American history) that the man who did the Wentworth family in the eighties could do the Bradhams in the hundreds. In *The Sense of the Past* the Midmores belong to the same race as the Wentworths, indeed as the Pyncheons. Compare the book with *The House of the Seven Gables* (Hawthorne's best novel after all); the situation, the "shrinkage and extinction of a family" is rather more complex, on the surface, than James's with (so far as the book was done) fewer character relations. But James's real situation here, to which Ralph's mounting the step is the key, as Hepzibah's opening of her shop, is a situation of different states of mind. James's situation is the shrink-

---

• *Was Hawthorne at all in James's mind here? In criticizing the* House of the Seven Gables *he says* "it renders, to an initiated reader, the impression of a summer afternoon in an elm-shaded New England town," *and in the preface to* Roderick Hudson *he says* "what the early chapters of the book most 'render' to me today is not the umbrageous air of their New England town."

age and extinction of an idea. The Pyncheon tragedy is simple; the "curse" upon the family a matter of the simplest fairy mechanics. James has taken Hawthorne's ghost-sense and given it substance. At the same time making the tragedy much more ethereal: the tragedy of that "Sense," the hypertrophy, in Ralph, of a partial civilization; the vulgar vitality of the Midmores, in their financial decay contrasted with the decay of Ralph in his financial prosperity, when they precisely should have been the civilization he had come to seek. All this watched over by the absent but conscious Aurora. I do not want to insist upon the Hawthorneness of the confrontation of the portrait, the importance of the opening of a door. We need surely not insist that this book is the most important, most substantial sort of thing that James did; perhaps there is more solid wear even in that other unfinished *Ivory Tower*. But I consider that it was an excursion which we could well permit him, after a lifetime in which he had taken talents similar to Hawthorne's and made them yield far greater returns than poor Hawthorne could harvest from his granite soil; a permissible exercise, in which we may by a legitimately cognate fancy seem to detect Hawthorne coming to a mediumistic existence again, to remind a younger and incredulous generation of what he really was, had he had the opportunity and to attest his satisfaction that that opportunity had been given to James.

22

Ezra Pound: HENRY JAMES [1918]

This essay on James is a dull grind of an affair, a Baedecker to a continent.

I set out to explain, not why Henry James is less read than formerly—I do not know that he is. I tried to set down a few reasons why he ought to be, or at least might be, more read.

Some say that his work was over, well over, finely completed; there is mass of that work, heavy for one man's shoulders to have borne up, labor enough for two lifetimes; still we would have had a few more years of his writing. Perhaps the grasp was relaxing, perhaps we should have had no strongly planned book; but we should have had paragraphs here and there, and we should have had, at least, conversation, wonderful conversation; even if we did not hear it ourselves, we should have known that it was going on somewhere. The massive head, the slow uplift of the hand, *gli occhi onesti e tardi,* the long sentences piling themselves up in elaborate phrase after phrase, the lightning incision, the pauses, the slightly shaking admonitory gesture with its "wu-a-wait a little, wait a little, something will come"; blague and benignity and the weight of so many years' careful, incessant labor of minute observation always there to enrich the talk. I had heard it but seldom, yet it is all unforgettable.

The man had this curious power of founding affection in those who had scarcely seen him and even in many who had not, who but knew him at second hand.

No man who has not lived on both sides of the Atlantic can well appraise Henry James; his death marks the end of a period. *The Times* says: "The Americans will understand his changing his nationality," or something of that sort. The "Americans" will understand nothing whatsoever about it. They have understood nothing about it. They do not even know what they lost. They have not stopped for eight minutes to consider the meaning of his last public act. After a year of ceaseless labor, of letter writing, of argument, of striving in every way to bring in America on the side of civilization, he died of apoplexy. On the side of civilization—civilization● against barbarism, civilization, not Utopia, not a country or countries where the right always prevails in six weeks! After a lifetime spent in trying to make two continents understand each other, in trying, and only his thoughtful readers can have any conception of how he had tried, to make three nations intelligible one to another. I am tired of hearing pettiness talked about Henry James's style. The subject has been discussed enough in all conscience, along with the minor James. Yet I have heard no word of the major James, of the hater of tyranny; book after early book against oppression, against all the sordid petty personal crushing oppression, the domination of modern life; not worked out in the diagrams of Greek tragedy, not labeled "epos" or "Aeschylus." The outbursts in *The Tragic Muse,* the whole of *The Turn of the Screw,* human liberty, personal liberty, the rights of the individual against all sorts of intangible bondage!● the passion of it, the continual passion of it in this man who, fools said, didn't

---

● *1929. I should probably be incapable of writing this paragraph now. But that is how things looked in 1918 and I see no reason to pretend that I saw them otherwise. I still believe that a Hohenzollern victory would have meant an intolerable postwar world. I think I write this without animus, and that I am quite aware of the German component indispensable to a complete civilization.*

● *This holds, despite anything that may be said of his fuss about social order, social tone. I naturally do not drag in political connotations, from which H. J. was, we believe, wholly exempt. What he fights is "influence," the impinging of family pressure, the impinging of one personality on another; all of them in highest degree damn'd, loathsome and detestable. Respect for the peripheries of the individual may be, however, a discovery of our generation; I doubt it, but it seems to have been at low ebb in some districts (not rural) for some time.*

"feel." I have never yet found a man of emotion against whom idiots didn't raise this cry.

And the great labor, this labor of translation, of making America intelligible, of making it possible for individuals to meet across national borders. I think half the American idiom is recorded in Henry James's writing, and whole decades of American life that otherwise would have been utterly lost, wasted, rotting in the unhermetic jars of bad writing, of inaccurate writing. No English reader will ever know how good are his New York and his New England; no one who does not see his grandmother's friends in the pages of the American books. The whole great assaying and weighing, the research for the significance of nationality, French, English, American.

"An extraordinary old woman, one of the few people who are really doing anything good." There were the cobwebs about connoisseurship, etc., but what do they matter? Some yokel writes in the village paper, as Henley had written before, "James's stuff was not worth doing." Henley has gone pretty completely. America has not yet realized that never in history had one of her great men abandoned his citizenship out of shame. It was the last act—the last thing left. He had worked all his life for the nation and for a year he had labored for the national honor. No other American was of sufficient importance for his change of allegiance to have constituted an international act; no other American would have been welcome in the same public manner. America passes over these things, but the thoughtful cannot pass over them.

Armageddon, the conflict? I turn to James's *A Bundle of Letters;* a letter from "Dr. Rudolph Staub" in Paris, ending:

"You will, I think, hold me warranted in believing that between precipitate decay and internecine enmities, the English-speaking family is destined to consume itself and that with its decline the prospect of general pervasiveness to which I allude above, will brighten for the deep-lunged children of the fatherland!"

We have heard a great deal of this sort of thing since; it sounds very natural. My edition of the volume containing these letters was printed in 1883, and the imaginary letters were written somewhat before that. I do not know that this calls for comment. Henry James's perception came thirty years before Armageddon. That is all I wish to point out. Flaubert said of the War of 1870: "If they had read my *Education Sentimentale,* this sort of thing wouldn't have happened." Artists are the antennae of the race, but the bullet-headed many will never learn to trust their great artists. If it is the business of the artist to make humanity aware of itself; here the thing was done, the pages of diagnosis. The multitude of wearisome fools will not learn their right hand from their left or seek out a meaning.

It is always easy for people to object to what they have not tried to understand.

I am not here to write a full volume of detailed criticism, but two things I do claim which I have not seen in reviewers' essays. First, that there was emotional greatness in Henry James's hatred of tyrrany; secondly, that there was titanic volume, weight, in the masses he sets in opposition within his work. He uses forces no whit less specifically powerful than the proverbial "doom of the house"— Destiny, *Deus ex machina*—of great traditional art. His art was great art as opposed to overelaborate or overrefined art by virtue of the major conflicts which he portrays. In his books he showed race against race, immutable; the essential Americanness, or Englishness or Frenchness—in *The American,* the difference between one nation and another; not flag-waving and treaties, not the machinery of government, but "why" there is always misunderstanding, why men of different race are not the same.

We have ceased to believe that we conquer anything by having Alexander the Great make a gigantic "joy-ride" through India. We know that conquests are made in the laboratory, that Curie with his minute fragments of things seen clearly in test tubes, in curious apparatus, makes conquests. So, too, in these novels, the essential qualities which make up the national qualities, are found and set working, the fundamental oppositions made clear. This is no contemptible labor. No other writer had so assayed three great nations or even thought of attempting it.

Peace comes of communication. No man of our time has so labored to create means of communication as did the late Henry James. The whole of great art is a struggle for communication. All things that oppose this are evil, whether they be silly scoffing or obstructive tariffs.

And this communication is not a leveling, it is not an elimination of differences. It is a recognition of differences, of the right of differences to exist, of interest in finding things different. Kultur is an abomination; philology is an abomination, all repressive uniforming education is an evil.

A SHAKE DOWN

I have forgotten the moment of lunar imbecility in which I conceived the idea of a "Henry James" number.• The pile of typescript

• Little Review, *Aug. 1918.*

on my floor can but annoyingly and too palpably testify that the madness has raged for some weeks.

Henry James was aware of the spherical form of the planet, and susceptible to a given situation, and to the tone and tonality of persons as perhaps no other author in all literature. The victim and the votary of the "scene," he had no very great narrative sense, or at least, he attained the narrative faculty but *per aspera,* through very great striving.

It is impossible to speak accurately of "his style," for he passed through several styles which differ greatly one from another; but in his last, his most complicated and elaborate, he is capable of great concision; and if, in it, the single sentence is apt to turn and perform evolutions for almost pages at a time, he nevertheless manages to say on one page more than many a more "direct" author would convey only in the course of a chapter.

His plots and incidents are often but adumbrations or symbols of the quality of his "people," illustrations invented, contrived, often factitiously and almost transparently, to show what acts, what situations, what contingencies would befit or display certain characters. We are hardly asked to accept them as happening. ●

He did not begin his career with any theory of art for art's sake, and a lack of this theory may have damaged his earlier work.

If we take *French Poets and Novelists* as indication of his then (1878) opinions, and novels of the nineties showing a later bias, we might contend that our subject began his career with a desire to square all things to the ethical standards of a Salem mid-week Unitarian prayer meeting, and that to almost the end of his course he greatly desired to fit the world into the social exigencies of Mrs. Humphry Ward's characters.

Out of these unfortunate cobwebs, he emerged into his greatness, I think, by two causes: first by reason of his hatred of personal intimate tyrannies working at close range; and secondly, in later life, because the actual mechanism of his scriptorial processes became so bulky, became so huge a contrivance for record and depiction, that the old man simply couldn't remember or keep his mind on or animadvert on anything but the authenticity of his impression.

I take it as the supreme reward for an artist; the supreme return that his artistic conscience can make him after years spent in its service, that the momentum of his art, the sheer bulk of his processes, the (*si licet*) size of his fly-wheel, should heave him out of himself,

---

● *Cf. Stendhal's rather unconvincing apology for the ultimate female in* Le Rouge et le Noir.

out of his personal limitations, out of the tangles of heredity and of environment, out of the bias of early training, of early predilections, whether of Florence, A.D. 1300, or of Back Bay of 1872, and leave him simply the great true recorder.

This reward came to Henry James in the ripeness of his talents; even further perhaps it entered his life and his conversation. The stages of his emergence are marked quite clearly in his work. He displays himself in *French Poets and Novelists,* constantly balancing over the question of whether or no the characters presented in their works are, or are not, fit persons to be received in the James family back-parlor.

In *The Tragic Muse* he is still didactic quite openly. The things he believes still leap out nakedly among the people and things he is portraying; the parable is not yet wholly incarnate in the narrative.

To lay all his faults on the table, we may begin with his self-confessed limitations, that "he never went down town." He displayed in fact a passion for high life comparable only to that supposed to inhere in the readers of a magazine called *Forget-me-not.*

Hardy, with his eye on the Greek tragedians, has produced an epic tonality, and *The Mayor of Casterbridge* is perhaps more easily comparable to the Grettir Saga than to the novels of Mr. Hardy's contemporaries. Hardy is, on the other side, a contemporary of Sir Walter Scott.

Balzac gains what force his crude writing permits him by representing his people under the ἀνάγκη of modernity, cash necessity; James, by leaving cash necessity nearly always out of the story, sacrifices, or rather fails to attain, certain intensities.

He never manages the classic, I mean as Flaubert gives us in each main character: *Everyman.* One may conceivably be bored by certain pages in Flaubert, but one takes from him a solid and concrete memory, a property. Emma Bovary and Frederic and M. Arnoux are respectively every woman and every man of their period. Maupassant's *Bel Ami* is not. Neither are Henry James's people. They are always, or nearly always, the bibelots.

But he does, nevertheless, treat of major forces, even of epic forces, and in a way all his own. If Balzac tried to give a whole civilization, a whole humanity, James was not content with a rough sketch of one country.

As Armageddon has only too clearly shown, national qualities are the great gods of the present and Henry James spent himself from the beginning in an analysis of these potent chemicals; trying to determine from the given microscopic slide the nature of the Frenchness, Englishness, Germanness, Americanness, which chemicals too little regarded, have in our time exploded for want of watching. They are the permanent and fundamental hostilities and incompatibles. We may rest our claim for his greatness in the magnitude of his protagonists, in the magnitude of the forces he analyzed and portrayed. This is not the bare matter of a number of titled people, a few duchesses and a few butlers.

Whatever Flaubert may have said about his *Education Sentimentale* as a potential preventive of the débâcle of 1870, *if people had* read it, and whatever Gautier's friend may have said about *Emaux et Camées* as the last resistance to the Prussians, from Dr. Rudolph Staub's paragraph in *The Bundle of Letters* to the last and almost only public act of his life, James displayed a steady perception and a steady consideration of the qualities of different Western races, whose consequences none of us can escape.

And these forces, in precisely that they are not political and executive and therefore transient, factitious, but in precisely that they are the forces of race temperaments, are major forces and are indeed as great protagonists as any author could have chosen. They are firmer ground than Flaubert's when he chooses public events as in the opening of the third part of *Education Sentimentale*.

The portrayal of these forces, to seize a term from philology, may be said to constitute "original research"—to be Henry James's own addendum; not that this greatly matters. He saw, analyzed, and presented them. He had most assuredly a greater awareness than was granted to Balzac or to Mr. Charles Dickens or to M. Victor Hugo who composed the *Légende des Siècles*.

His statement that he never went down town has been urged greatly against him. A butler is a servant, tempered with upper-class contacts. Mr. Newman, the American, has emerged from the making of washtubs; the family in *The Pupil* can scarcely be termed upper-class, however, and the factor of money, Balzac's ἀνάγκη, scarcely enters his stories.

We may leave Hardy writing Sagas. We may admit that there is a greater *robustezza* in Balzac's messiness, simply because he is perpetually concerned, inaccurately, with the factor of money, of earning one's exiguous living.

We may admit the shadowy nature of some of James's writing, and agree whimsically with "R.H.C."• (in the *New Age*) that James will be quite comfortable after death, as he had been dealing with ghosts all his life.

• *Pseudonym used by A. R. Orage.*

James's third donation is perhaps a less sweeping affair and of more concern to his compatriots than to any one who might conceivably translate him into an alien tongue, or even to those who publish his writings in England.

He has written history of a personal sort, social history well documented and incomplete, and he has put America on the map both in memoir and fiction, giving to her a reality such as is attained only by scenes recorded in the arts and in the writing of masters. Mr. Eliot has written, and I daresay most other American admirers have written or will write, that, whatever any one else thinks of Henry James, no one but an American can ever know, really know, how good he is at the bottom, how good his "America" is.

No Englishman can, and in less degree can any continental, or in fact any one whose family was not living on, say, West 23rd Street in the old set-back, two-story-porched red-brick vine-covered houses, etc., when Henry James was being a small boy on East 23rd Street; no one whose ancestors had not been presidents or professors or founders of Ha'vawd College or something of that sort, or had not heard of a time when people lived on 14th Street, or had known of some one living in Lexington or Newton "Old Place" or somewhere of that sort in New England, or had heard of the New York that produced "Fanny," New York the jocular and uncritical, or of people who danced with General Grant or something of that sort, would quite know *Washington Square* or *The Europeans* to be so autochthonous, so authentic to the conditions. They might believe the things to be "real," but they would not know how closely they corresponded to an external reality.

Perhaps only an exile from these things will get the range of the other half of James's presentations! Europe to the Transpontine New York of brown stone that he detested, the old and new New York in *Crapey Cornelia* and in *The American Scene,* which more than any other volumes give us our peculiar heritage, an America with an interest, with a tone of time not overstrained, not jejunely oversentimentalized, which is not a re-doing of school histories or the laying out of a fabulous period; and which is in relief, if you like, from Dickens or from Mark Twain's *Mississippi.* He was not without sympathy for his compatriots as is amply attested by Mr. and Mrs. B. D. Hayes of New York (*vide The Birthplace*) with whom he succeeds, I think, rather better than with most of his princely continentals. They are, at any rate, his bow to the Happy Genius of his country—as distinct from the gentleman who displayed the "back of a banker and a patriot," or the person whose aggregate features could be designated only as a "mug."

In his presentation of America he is greatly attentive, and, save for the people in *Coeur Simple,* I doubt if any writer has done more of "this sort of thing" for his country, this portrayal of the typical thing in timbre and quality—balanced, of course, by the array of spittoons in the Captiol (*The Point of View*).

Still if one is seeking a Spiritual Fatherland, if one feels the exposure of what he would not have scrupled to call, two clauses later, such a windshield, *The American Scene* greatly provides it. It has a mermaid note, almost to outvie the warning, the sort of nickel-plate warning which is hurled at one in the saloon of any great transatlantic boat; the awfulness that engulfs one when one comes, for the first time unexpectedly on a pile of all the *Murkhn* magazines laid, shingle-wise, on a brass-studded, screwed-into-place, baize-covered steamer table. The first glitter of the national weapons for driving off quiet and all closer signs of intelligence.•

Attempting to view the jungle of the work as a whole, one notes that, despite whatever cosmopolitan upbringing Henry James may have had, as witness *A Small Boy's Memoirs* and *Notes of a Son and Brother,* he nevertheless began in *French Poets and Novelists* with a provincial attitude from which it took him a long time to work free. Secondly, we see various phases of the "style" of his presentation or circumambience.

There is a small amount of prentice work. Let us say *Roderick Hudson, Casamassima.* There are lucky first steps in *The American* and *The Europeans,* as precocity of result, for certainly some of his early work is as permanent as some of the ripest, and more so than a deal of the intervening. We find (for in the case before us criticism must be in large part a weeding-out) that his first subject matter provides him with a number of good books and stories: *The American, The Europeans, Eugene Pickering, Daisy Miller, The Pupil, Brooksmith, A Bundle of Letters, Washington Square, The Portrait of a Lady,* before 1882 and, rather later, *Pandora, The Four Meetings,* perhaps *Louisa Pallant.* He ran out of his first material.

We next note a contact with the *Yellow Book,* a dip into "cleverness," into the epigrammatic genre, the bare epigrammatic style. It

---

• *I differ, beyond that point, with our author. I enjoy ascent as much as I loathe descent in an elevator. I do not mind the click of brass doors. I had indeed for my earliest toy, if I was not brought up in it, the rather slow and well-behaved elevator in a quiet and quietly bright huge sanatorium. The height of high buildings, the chasms of New York are delectable; but this is beside the point; one is not asked to share the views and tastes of a writer.*

was no better than other writers, not so successful as Wilde. We observe him to be not so hard and fine a satirist as is George S. Street.

We come then to the period of allegories (*The Real Thing, Dominick Ferrand, The Liar*). There ensues a growing discontent with the short sentence, epigram, etc., in which he does not at this time attain distinction; the clarity is not satisfactory, was not satisfactory to the author, his *donnée* being radically different from that of his contemporaries. The "story" not being really what he is after, he starts to build up his medium; a thickening, a chiaroscuro is needed, the long sentence; he wanders, seeks to add a needed opacity, he overdoes it, produces the cobwebby novel, emerges or justifies himself in *Maisie* and manages his long-sought form in *The Awkward Age*. He comes out the triumphant stylist in the *American Scene* and in all the items of *The Finer Grain●* collection and in the posthumous *Middle Years*.

This is not to damn incontinent all that intervenes, but I think the chief question addressed to me by people of good-will who do not, but are yet ready and willing to, read James, is: Where the deuce shall I begin? One cannot take even the twenty-four volumes, more or less selected volumes of the Macmillan edition all at once, and it is, alas, but too easy to get so started and entoiled as never to finish this author or even come to the best of him.

The laziness of an uncritical period can be nowhere more blatant than in the inherited habit of talking about authors as a whole. It is perhaps the sediment from an age daft over great figures, or a way of displaying social gush, the desire for a celebrity at all costs, rather than a care of letters.

To talk in any other way demands an acquaintance with the work of an author, a price few conversationalists care to pay, *ma chè*! It is the man with inherited opinions who talks about "Shelley," making no distinction between the author of the Fifth Act of *The Cenci* and of the *Sensitive Plant*. Not but what there may be a personal *virtù* in an author—appraised, however, from the best of his work when, that is, it is correctly appraised. People ask me what James to read. He is a very uneven author; not all of his collected edition has marks of permanence.

One can but make one's own suggestion:
The American, French Poets and Novelists, The Europeans, Daisy

---

● *Volume now labeled* Maud Evelyn *in the Macmillan collected edition. The titles in my essay are those of their "New York" edition.*

Miller, Eugene Pickering, Washington Square, A Bundle of Letters, Portrait of a Lady, Pandora, The Pupil, Brooksmith, What Maisie Knew and *The Awkward Age* (if one is "doing it all"), *Europe, Four Meetings, The Ambassadors, The American Scene, The Finer Grain* (all the volume, i.e. *The Velvet Glove, Mona Montravers, Round of Visits, Crapey Cornelia, Bench of Desolation*), *The Middle Years* (posthumous), *The Ivory Tower* (notes first) and *The Sacred Fount*.

I "go easy" on the more cobwebby volumes; the most Jamesian are indubitably *The Wings of a Dove* and *The Golden Bowl;* upon them devotees will fasten, but the potential devotee may as well find his aptitude in the stories of *The Finer Grain* volume where certain exquisite titillations will come to him as readily as anywhere else. If he is to bask in Jamesian tickle, nothing will restrain him and no other author will to any such extent afford him equal gratifications.

If, however, the reader does not find delectation in the list given above, I think it fairly useless for him to embark on the rest.

Part of James is a caviare, part I must reject according to my lights as bad writing; another part is a *spécialité,* a pleasure for certain temperaments only; the part I have set together above seems to me maintainable as literature. One can definitely say: "this is good"; hold the argumentative field, suffer comparison with other writers; with, say, the Goncourts, or Maupassant. I am not impertinently throwing books on the scrap heap; there are certain valid objections to James; there are certain standards which one may believe in, and having stated them, one is free to state that any author does not comply with them; always granting that there may be other standards with which he complies, or over which he charmingly or brilliantly triumphs.

James does not "feel" as solid as Flaubert; he does not give us *Everyman,* but, on the other hand, he was aware of things whereof Flaubert was not aware and in certain things supersedes the author of *Madame Bovary.* . . .

23

F. W. Dupee: APPROACHES TO HENRY JAMES [1951]

Pointing to some noisy girls in Venice, a friend once observed to James that those were the *real* Daisy Millers. It was a reproach: he had "idealized" his heroine. And he recorded the remark in his preface, in order to allow for the reproach but not to apologize. Newman (in *The American*) and Mr. Touchett and Isabel (in *The Portrait of a Lady*) are idealized even more, in their moral intelligence, which is shown to withstand all provocation, as well as to be consistent with great wealth, much ambition, and in Newman's case a rather rowdy past as a Western promoter. All this certainly represents an extreme refinement of life; and it is a wonder that James can persuade us that his people live and suffer, they who have so little body, so few nerves, with which to register their experience, who never seem to "forfeit" anything of their inward composure, and whose heads are not only unbowed but unbloody. They have, to be sure, as many ways of being moral as they have of being American. The conscience of a Rowland Mallett is anxious, didactic, given to judgment of self and others. But in all the greater figures conscience is a form of sensibility, a style of life, a state of mind to which judgment is alien and goodness for goodness's sake immaterial.

Intelligent without being intellectual, moral but not ethical, they reflect very little on conduct itself; and mainly they do what they have to do in order to be themselves. Their possession of a moral sense is for them a kind of fatality; it is also a kind of chivalry. It belongs among their patents of nobility; it adheres to them by reason of their assumption of membership in a natural aristocracy, which in Newman's case refers to his being an American but which in Isabel's is more nearly gratuitous. Nor do they, as we have said, acquire the moral sense in the usual school of suffering. In this respect their adversities are more symbolic than experiential. They are possessed of what Edmund Burke liked to call "the unbought grace of life."

"They are only winged busts," said André Gide about James's characters; "all the weight of the flesh is absent, all the shaggy, tangled undergrowth, all the wild darkness." And James himself seems to acknowledge the limitation, when, at the peril of retroactively compromising his portrait of Isabel, he shows her fleeing from Goodwood's kiss. With all his wider experience, James is more Puritan—if not simply less human—than Hawthorne, for whom, in *The Scarlet Letter,* the color of adultery is also the color of lifeblood and of roses. Again and again in James's novels the process of becoming one's self excludes physical intimacy with others.

> The *self's* a fine and private place
> But none, I think, do there embrace.

In *The Bostonians* and a dozen other stories, he is presently to give us acid accounts of too high-minded people; and sexual passion is to figure more and more prominently in his plots. But it will generally be associated with cruelty and corruption; it will nearly always constitute the extreme situation, a destructive element in which only the bad people immerse. In an age of insistent naturalism like ours, we tend thus to localize Jame's limitation in his suspicion of sex. Almost any age would be likely to see the same limitation, although in terms less specific. Presumably Gide's "wild darkness" is itself a more inclusive description, embracing all the passions. With so little knowledge of these, we may say, James's heroes are but imperfectly tempted. Their moral intelligence, for which he makes such claims in his prefaces, is something taken for granted.

Yet the wild darkness is notoriously the source of a false profundity in many writers. And in this respect as in others James knew how to make his limitations serve him. When things are absent from his work they are not furtively but conspicuously absent. It means something that they are not there. And Gide is surely mistaken when he goes on to say of the characters that "they are desperately mun-

dane" because "they never live except in relation to each other." It
is just in their relations that they live so bravely and are so little
mundane. That is their peculiar strength, their vital dimension.
Isabel's energy, if it is not that of sex, is that of sympathy, and
it is immense. But the interdependence of the characters is also a part
of James's economy of structure. Eliot's account of this is classic.
"Done in a clean, flat drawing each [character] is extracted out of
a reality of its own, substantial enough; everything given is true for
that individual; but what is given is chosen with great art for its
place in a general scheme. The general scheme is not one character,
nor a group of characters in a plot or merely in a crowd. The focus
is a situation, a relation, an atmosphere, to which the characters pay
tribute, but being allowed to give only what the writer wants. The
real hero, in any of James's stories, is a social entity of which men
and women are constituents."

Apart from his family, there was no such social entity in James's
own experience. It existed hardly more in modern Europe, as he
discovered, than in America, although the former was at least full
of the ghosts of it. He had therefore to invent his own social atmosphere. It is none the less persuasive; and if, in his early work, he
encourages his people to discover their limits, that is his tribute to
sociability rather than to any metaphysic of the human condition. In
his pioneering biography, *The Pilgrimage of Henry James,* Van Wyck
Brooks summed up the early work as presenting "the struggle for
the rights of personality—the central theme of all modern American
fiction." Such a view of James was natural to a man writing in the
prime of Sinclair Lewis and Sherwood Anderson, to a man intent
on praising the early as against the later work in support of his
contention that James's prolonged exile impaired his force. On one
of his sides James *was* such a critic of modern life as Lewis and
Anderson have been and as Brooks was; and this is as important a
side as any other. The pursuit of larger existences is a regular ritual
with his characters. He is one of the chief novelists of the present-day
mobility, the intrinsic restlessness. The oppression of dull years, the
dread of missed chances and lost identities, the horror of insignificance—these emotions are common to all the international stories;
they are especially powerful in some of the lesser ones which have
gone unmentioned here. There are people in them who dream and
dream of Europe and never get there; the poor schoolteacher of
"Four Meetings" gets no farther than Le Havre, where, cheated
of her travel money, she is obliged to take ship back to America.
The personal past, the past of family and home town, is nearly
always conceived by James as deadly, a kind of ache; and any rup-

ture with it is a good thing regardless of the consequences. That Roderick Hudson had better return to Northampton is suggested only by his unhappy and limited mother. Nor do Isabel's troubles or her conservatism ever turn her thoughts towards Albany and the ancestral house with the strange passageways and the papered-up door-lights—a kind of tomb—where she was first discovered by her aunt, whiling away a rainy afternoon over a history of German thought. Between herself and Albany stands the greatness of Gardencourt, the Touchetts' English estate, with its myriad rooms and illimitable lawns and vistas, the scene of her first entry into a larger world. For if the stories are full of the stress of penury and constraint, they are far richer in the related imagery of abundance: the summer season, the garden, the holiday, the party, the museum, the great house. James, moreover, was beforehand in the use of the transplantation plot, that device of modern novelists for unsettling the mind of a character—"transvaluing" his values—by removing him to an exotic place. *Daisy Miller* might easily have been called *Passage to Italy or Death in Rome.*

He was a "hater of tyranny," said Ezra Pound in 1918; and surely Pound, like Brooks, was right, even though both spoke too exclusively in the spirit of their generation. James anticipated that generation in many ways; and its spokesmen were sensitive to things in him which we, more enamored of his later work, and seeking in all fiction a similar mythic resonance, have allowed to become obscured. They recalled his contention that the novel as he practiced it was equally the child of myth (he would have said romance) and of history; they were more familiar with his claim to have been an historian of manners. What they (including Eliot as well) admired in him was the vivid economy of his American portraits, his devoted rendering of native speech. And Pound, praising his skill in the vignette, liked to quote such lines as the following, descriptive of an ambitious girl's attentions to her superseded parents: "These little offices were usually performed deftly, rapidly, with a minimum of words, and when their daughter drew near them, Mr. and Mrs. Day closed their eyes after the fashion of a pair of household dogs who expect to be scratched." His image-making was a large part of James's interest for the two poets in particular; and, in their determination to make poetry as well written as prose and as real as the novel, they paid him the compliment of being influenced by him. But he was also, as they maintained, a cultural historian of more than native importance. There was, as Pound expressed it, "the whole great assaying and weighing, the research for the significance of nationality, French, English, American." And Pound observed that "his art was great art as opposed to overelaborate or overrefined art by virtue of the major conflicts which he portrays."

Yet the critics of that age, Pound and Brooks in particular, ignored a whole side of James; or if they did not ignore it they dismissed it as inconsequential "fuss" or relegated it to the years of his supposed decline. This was his profound *skepticism* concerning "the rights of personality," his doubt whether anything so abstract might be said to be interesting, his entire dialectic of freedom. That skepticism is as firmly present in such a novel as *The Europeans* as it is in any performance of his later maturity. If a Daisy Miller or a Gertrude Wentworth seems to assert the rights of personality, this is not to say that the author himself does so. And that he does not may be seen from the more or less affectionate irony with which he normally envelops such figures. ("You are quite right to hate Gertrude, whom I also personally dislike," he wrote to a friend.) He is skeptical of rights and even more of personality, a word he could never use without enclosing it in quotation marks. Personality is what Gertrude admires so much in the Baroness, and Isabel at first in Osmond and Mme. Merle. Henrietta Stackpole and the Countess Gemini have it, but not Warburton, whose appeal is of another sort. As distinguished from the individuality of a Newman, an Isabel, or a Ralph Touchett, personality is aggressive, self-seeking in the cruder sense; it is perverse in Mme. Merle, touching in the Countess Gemini, funny in Henrietta. It is the too easy resource of those suffering from the dread of insignificance.

Freedom and individuality were such immense things to James that he was at pains to distinguish between the appearance and the fact of them. So too with another quality much prized by his Americans, the quality of innocence. There are various degrees and kinds of it among the early characters. The natural probity of the Wentworths is winning if narrow; that of Daisy Miller is winning but fatal. Only in the more heroic Americans are innocence, freedom, and individuality fully and positively present. In them the native zest for life is qualified by a feeling for life's limitations, a feeling James associates with the European mind. And what he seems to be saying is that one's consciousness of belonging to a given race or political group, or of contributing to some utopian future, is insufficient reason for one's asserting a primal innocence and freedom. These, James would maintain, are qualities of the individual, to be earned and enjoyed by him in that capacity. On the nature of man, however, he seems to have had no dogmatic convictions. Any faith he had in individuals was experimental, and so was any skepticism he felt towards men in the mass.

24

Ferner Nuhn: HENRY ADAMS AND
THE HAND OF THE FATHERS [1942]

A few months before the outbreak of the war in 1914, Henry James
in England received a letter from his friend Henry Adams in America.
James wrote in reply:

I have your melancholy outpouring of the 7th, and I know not how
better to acknowledge it than by the full recognition of its unmitigated
blackness. *Of course* we are lone survivors, of course the past is at the
bottom of an abyss—if the abyss *has* any bottom; of course, too, there's
no use talking unless one particularly *wants* to. But the purpose, almost,
of my printed divagations (*Notes of a Son and Brother*) was to show
you that one *can,* strange to say, still want to—or at least behave as if
one did; . . . I still find my consciousness interesting—under *cultivation*
of the interest. Cultivate it *with* me, dear Henry—that's what I hoped to
make you do—to cultivate yours for all that it has in common with mine.
. . . You see I still, in presence of life (or what you deny to be such)
have reactions—as many as possible. . . . It's, I suppose, because I am
that queer monster, the artist, an obstinate finality, an inexhaustible sensibility. . . .

Henry Adams, in March of 1914, was already referring, it seems,
to that "abyss" which Henry James was to see open a few months

later. The two men had much in common. Almost of the same years, they were both products of "the whole long age" before the war that James wrote of. They were world tourists, spiritually, each having left his simpler, more puritan home background to look for an education in "the great world." They were fastidious, self-conscious men, instinctively exclusive in taste, shrinking from everything "common" with about an equal aversion. Both had as little as possible to do with the general public, and the general public had in both cases reciprocated.

But there were important differences, as James's letter indicated. James was that "queer monster, the artist." Adams was not. He was not quite the artist, as he was not quite the scientist, the historian, the politician, or anything else specific. Adams had half-heartedly tried everything, but given himself to nothing. James had given himself absolutely to his mistress, Art.

That told the difference, and why James still "had reactions," and was "an obstinate finality." True, James had given himself aesthetically to what was partly an illusion—the glamour of the Golden Bowl of high European civilization. But this glamour, this enchantment, had led him on all these years, had kept him, in a sense, unscathed. It could do so as long as the "long age" held, and the enchantment was not broken either by James's personal participation in it, or by rude outside events.

Adams was no innocent, no glamourist, and no pure dedicated spirit. Unlike James, he was drawn himself to participate in the glittering life of power. We suspect that if a place in the sun had been offered him at the right time, on his own terms, he would quickly enough have taken it.

What were his terms? They were the terms of hereditary aristocracy, very much the same sort of terms of "high civilization" that James so admired in Europe. The trouble was that Adam's opportunity, like his heredity, lay in America. But America was a democracy, and alas would not meet Adams's aristocratic terms. They presupposed a privileged elite, an established social class, a political hereditary system, that simply did not exist in the United States. Adams could succeed in the hereditary political pattern only by joining in the democratic political melee. But this is what a fourth-generation Adams would not care to do.

Henry Adams is our outstanding case of the hereditary aristocrat in a democratic world. That was his dilemma, and that is his interest as a figure. Unlike James, Adams signifies more as a character than as an author. He may not be remembered much for anything original in the way of art or thought; he will be remembered for something distinctive in the way of a fate. Adams, who always felt that energy was hopelessly dissipating, never had a better idea for gathering his own than when he sat down to write his *Education*.

He is no simple figure, and *The Education* complicates as much as it explains. Adams showed various instincts, but the instinct he showed most strongly was the instinct for protection. He will not expose himself. Adams was always wrong, but no one else was right! Adams knew nothing, but no one else knew even that much! When he was a young man in the embassy at London, he had already got hold of this formula that was to become a lifetime defense. Writing his brother Charles, who was fighting with the Army of the Potomac, Henry was sure that "while my time *may* be wasted, I don't see but that your time *must* prove so."

Charles Francis, Junior, the most downright of the fourth-generation Adamses, made the only possible answer to such a dictum. "Now, my dear fellow," he wrote back from his field camp, where presumably he was well occupied saving the American Union, "speak for yourself."

It is what the reader would like to tell the author of *The Education* many times. Dear Henry, speak for yourself!

Henry would not speak for himself without also claiming to speak for everybody else. If energy seemed to him to be running downhill, then it was necessary to show that the universe was running downhill. At last he found a generation to listen to him, the disillusioned generation after the War. Henry Adams was dead, he could not hear himself being heard, but finally a weary world was ready to listen to Adams's story of futility.

Henry Adams was in a good position for disillusionment, this position of a hereditary aristocrat in a world that had outlived that pattern. He fits very well Thomas Mann's description of the Biblical Joseph, that he was "late . . . in time and in his soul, a very good specimen of a descendant, volatile, witty, difficult and interesting."

Such was Adams, and not only was he a "difficult descendant," but a descendant of a difficult tradition. His fathers were all a little like that. They had all fought in their way for American democracy, and all distrusted democracy except when run by an Adams. They had all found themselves opponents of European empire and class rule, and yet, as Henry wrote, they all owed much to Europe and the aristocratic idea. The truth is the Adamses were in a class by themselves—aristocrats in America, democrats in Europe. The home estate was just on the edge of the New World, and faced back toward the Old. The Adamses had never looked into the interior. Henry as a boy could watch the ships leaving Boston harbor for Europe, and they seemed to be asking him to go along. But he also expected to be sent to Washington.

The Adams world was an in-between world, in between the Old and the New, in between the eighteenth century and the twentieth, in between *vox Dei* and *vox populi,* in between religion and science, in between science and politics, in between politics and art. Only one thing seemed a certainty: the place and integrity of the Family itself, under God's will and instruction. But suppose even this certainty, during the nineteenth century, should begin to look doubtful? If the Adams line should feel this rock of faith in the family shake —or even worse, the rock of Faith itself—it would be truly tragic. And something of this sort seems to have happened about the fourth generation if not, as Brooks Adams insisted it already had happened, in the second.

The result in the fourth generation was the books on social decay written by Brooks and the books on the degradation of energy written by Henry.

This was why Henry, who had seen his own tradition fading away, was in an excellent position to speak for the traditional world that broke up in Europe in 1914. His disillusion had sharpened his eyes for disintegration anywhere. Long before 1914 he had foreseen the threat to Henry James's Golden Age of British Empire of the expansive force that lay in imperial Germany. He had no answer or remedy himself. Like T. S. Eliot, his eyes were open only to disaster. But after the war, he looked like the very spirit of postwar disillusion.

Young men who had seen meaningless sacrifice in Flanders hailed him as a brother. He would have understood Dadaism in Paris, and Noel Coward in London. Henry Adams's *Education,* that had got nowhere in an age of belief, got everywhere in an age of unbelief. It took its place with Proust and Hemingway and Joyce and Eliot as postwar literature, the literature of the Lost Generation of exiles and international wanderers, which had followed on Henry James's beglamoured generation of pilgrims and aesthetes.

Here was a postwar mind that had somehow developed in the prewar period. If Henry James expected to comfort such a mind with his own rapturous aesthetic creed, he was doomed to disappointment. An Adams, unable to comfort himself, would not be comforted by anyone else.

No woman, Henry Adams wrote in his *Education,* had ever driven him wrong; no man had ever driven him right. This I think is the clue to Adams's life and to the meaning of his books, especially the later works which often seem to disguise more than they reveal. His life was a struggle between the line of the Fathers in him, the Presidents and the public men who set the pattern for a career for which he was not fitted, and his own nature, which was sensitive, intuitive, artistic. Adams's writings break down into the books he wrote for men, and the books he wrote for women, and they are miles apart. Women urged him to follow his own nature, and Adams wrote *Esther* and *Mont-Saint Michel and Chartres* for them, and charming letters such as those from the South Seas. Men tried to draw him into public life, or told him to write history, and Adams broke himself in two again and again trying to live up to the dictates of the Fathers.

The conflict went on and on, to the last, a public man versus a private man, as Mabel La Farge, one of his favorite nieces, has written in her sensitive memoir. The public man still wrote for the world of men, wrote *The Rule of Phase,* for example, to satisfy the Fathers. It was all power and force and intellect, and described a universe without a spark of feeling in it. And it was a universe doomed, doomed to prove that a world that had allowed the Adams line of public men to run out must itself have run down. The rejected Fathers and their hard Law must be vindicated though the heavens fall.

Then there was *Chartres,* which turned against Law and the Fathers completely. It turned the universe over to the pity and caprice of lovely woman, who had always led Adams aright, and would forgive him where he had gone astray. It was as far on one side as *The Rule of Phase* was on the other, but at least it expressed the private man, the man of feeling, instead of the public manikin of irony and erudition. "No, sir, you can't do it, you can't impress God that way," William James had bluntly written Adams concerning *The Rule of Phase*—not by "wit and learning" in treating a tragic subject. Adams knew it at heart. *Chartres* admitted that God couldn't be mocked. It threw Adams's case upon the mercy of the Virgin.

As for *The Education* itself, it was on both sides at once; it answered everything double. One sentence confessed what the next denied. The inner and humbled Henry Adams begged to be understood for the tyranny worked upon his nature by the outer Henry Adams and the pattern of the Fathers. At the same time, the outer Henry Adams, with mockery and irony, defended himself against the world.

The preface to *The Education* came as close as Adams could publicly to asking for understanding. The preface said that it was only the manikin the book presented. Yet—and who can miss the whispered plea?—it just hinted that there was a suffering man behind the mask. "It must have the air of reality," he wrote of his puppet figure, "must be taken for real; must be treated as though it had life. Who knows? Possibly it had."

Naturally it had, and I think you can find the place in *The Education* that tells of the first serious break in Adams's life, which drove part of him inside a mask. It was when he was a young man in the years just after the Civil War and had put himself in a fair way to achieve a career that for once did not depend on the family position and the family inheritance—all that "nest of associations" signified by "the First Church, the Boston State House, Beacon Hill, John Hancock and John Adams, Mount Vernon Street and Quincy."

Young Henry had been his father's secretary in the embassy at London during the war years. After the war, Henry had perhaps hoped for an appointment in the incoming administration of General Grant, which he and his friends had somehow believed would be a "reform administration." The appointment, or whatever, did not come, and neither did "reform." Instead America's gaudiest period of high finance set in, and Henry with his brothers Brooks and Charles decided to take to their pens, and set up as critics of those public affairs which they had not been invited to help run themselves.

The result was the "Session" articles which appeared in magazines both in England and America. They were something new in American journalism: closely reasoned, factual articles exposing the inner workings of finance and railroads and government policy. They anticipated by many years the "muckraking" journalism of the twentieth century, and were in fact to be rediscovered as almost the first serious efforts at analyzing finance capitalism in the United States.

The important thing for our story is that they had a great success. Even Henry Adams, who could make anything look like failure, from Harvard College to God, had to admit that this venture looked like "a sufficient success." The articles were reprinted, pirated, and made political capital of by the thousands or hundreds of thousands of copies, all over the United States.

This venture was probably the nearest Henry Adams could come to reconciling his particular ambitions and divided genius. It was close to the world of action, which fascinated him, but away from contact with the public, which distressed him. If it was not actually literature, for which he had real feeling and talent, it was in that direction. Above all, it promised to give him a name of his own, an independent position, and a sense of confidence in his own powers, from which point a talented young man might go nearly anywhere.

It even showed that a fourth-generation Adams, with all his hereditary handicaps upon his head, might make a place for himself in a democracy.

But then what happened?

"No sooner had Adams" (wrote Adams in his *Education*) "made at Washington what he modestly hoped was a sufficient success, than his whole family set upon him to drag him away. For the first time since 1861 his father interposed; his mother entreated; and his brother Charles argued and urged him to go to Harvard College."

It was Henry Adams's little theory in *The Education* that his "failures" were all due either to lack of power in himself, or opportunity in the world. Either he lived in the wrong century, or else he lacked the right equipment; in any case, fate always stepped in to snatch victory from him.

Here is the instance that does not fit this theory. Neither Adams's powers nor his opportunity had failed; nor did fate step in, unless you call family opinion fate—which, in a deeper sense, it was. But this "failure" lay simply in Adams's own willingness to follow the family opinion instead of his own.

We happen to have evidence that Adams himself did have a different opinion from the family's in this case, and had already chosen differently on the question of Harvard. For it so happens that the offer from Harvard College first came to Henry when he was alone in England, about to return to America, and Henry without the family had decided against it. Henry with the family, however, was too much for Henry. When he arrived in America and was met by the solid family front, he decided against his decision. It is quite right as *The Education* puts it: to Harvard College went Henry, aged thirty-three, because, as Henry aged seventy wrote, his brother argued, his mother entreated, his father interposed.

It is not hard I think to find the family's reasons for the pressure put on Henry, and the point is that they were precisely reasons of family. Henry's "Session" articles, while they might be true, gave comfort to the wrong party, the non-Adams party. It is true, the Adams party was for the moment quite non-Adams, and full of improper people. But an Adams would do his reforming inside his party and not outside of it, in public. Henry's articles might be Henry's success—they might be Henry's salvation—but they were an Adams scandal, and they had to be stopped.

"So, at twenty-four hours' notice," says the autobiography in summary, "he broke his life in halves again in order to begin a new education on lines he had not chosen, in subjects for which he cared less than nothing; in a place he did not love, and before a future which repelled." You must allow here for Adams's usual exaggeration for the sake of neatness and symmetry. But I think the general sense is true. The incident seems crucial in Henry's life. This is where the sense of defeat begins. This is where the chapter heads in the autobiography becomes names of despair. Nor can you explain it on external grounds, for apparently this is just where Henry went on from success to success. He now became a brilliant teacher, a successful teacher, a celebrated historian—elected president of the American Historical Association. The defeat was an inner one, just as those chapter headings in *The Education* tell an inner and not an outer story. Only to the inner sense could these most successful years of Adams's life, after his removal to Harvard and before his wife's death, be called "Chaos" and "Failure."

The next chapter heading must tell an inner story too—"Twenty Years After"—since it fails to tell an outer story at all. Twenty years after what? Twenty years after the death of Mrs. Adams, of whose existence there is no hint in *The Education*. Yet in this same *Education* she was certainly the most important single character besides the author, as her death by her own hand was certainly, tragically, the most important single event. This was the greatest "breaking in halves" of Adams's life. No wonder we must read *The Education* by opposites! Disguising as it reveals, this is the place where it reveals most by telling nothing at all.

Nor can any outsider pretend to fill in this gap which Adams and his intimates have seen fit to leave blank. Adams had married Marian Hooper in 1872. He resigned from Harvard in 1878 and moved to Washington, where the Adamses became the center of a select and brilliant circle of Washington society. They were building a large house, designed by Richardson, just across the park from the White House itself—the hereditary focus of an Adams's ambition. Mrs. Adams' death occurred just as they were to move into the new home.

But Henry had long ago given up any real purpose to take part in national politics. The removal to Washington, the select dinner parties, the private intimacy with public men, the new house on Lafayette Square—all these were at best the simulacrum, not the substance, of a public career according to the way of the Fathers. No woman, Adams wrote, had ever led him astray, and we cannot believe he excepted his wife. Did Marian Adams instinctively distrust this life in the capital, to which they were now all the more committed by the house they had just built? She seemed discontented with her own lack of life direction. Did she perhaps feel that Adams's private indulgence of a passion for politics which he could no longer hope to exercise openly increased the indirection of both their lives? Did this enter into her dilemma?

I do not know. Other reasons are suggested for her act: that she had brooded over the death a year before of her father, of whom she had been very fond. There is the fact of childlessness, a matter of special importance, one might suppose, to Henry Adams himself, bound up as it would be with continuity of the hereditary line.

We do know that it was some years before Adams could face returning to the Washington home, and that the experience marked the turning of the private man toward a different element in his nature—the feminine element—and away from the pattern of the Fathers. It was at this time that Adams wanted to renounce his historical writings, and professed his regard for only one thing he had ever written, the novel *Esther.*

Esther is not a great novel, but it is about a woman's predicament; it involves among other things the death of her father, and the question of the heroine's faith in life; and it is written with sympathy for the woman's point of view. By all reports, the character of Esther was based specifically on Mrs. Adams, but the important thing is that it is a woman's book, and that Henry Adams in his bereavement liked to recall it. Adams had finally chosen, at least privately, between the Fathers and the Mothers. He had chosen the Mothers, and dethroned the Fathers from their rule over his soul.

Not that this happened all at once. Both Henry and Brooks Adams had long been interested in "feminism," and especially their theory (like the medieval one) of woman as the "fixed" element in society and man the roving one. As early as 1876 Henry had lectured on "The Primitive Rights of Women." Certain women among Adams's relatives and friends had been favorites, all the way from a grandmother down to a half-dozen real or nominal "nieces." These women saw and felt in him, apparently, what no man had seen or felt. In the South Seas, where Adams traveled during his years of exile, he had a chance to study matriarchy itself, as an actual surviving institution, and he left as a record the privately printed *Memoirs of Marau Taaroa, Last Queen of Tahiti.*

The death of Mrs. Adams touched this line of feeling with religious intensity. From this point (as Mr. Robert Spiller has also noted in his study of the book *Esther*), the road runs plainly to *Chartres* and the twelfth-century Virgin. This was the step from secular to sacred, from matriarchy to mariolatry, but it was a logical

step granting Adams's early and fundamental sense of conflict between the feminine elements in his nature and an overmasculine
world that he was supposed to master. It was perhaps too late to
straighten out what stood for law and what for love in the real
world of men and women, and so put together the broken halves of
his life. But it was possible to go back in fancy to a bygone world
in which he might reclaim the lost heritage of his nature—beauty and
feeling and woman's intuition.

The "Prayer of the Virgin of Chartres," as Mabel La Farge has
intimated, told the spiritual history that *The Education* disguised or
was silent upon. This was the enigmatic poem in manuscript, found
among Adams's papers at his death, and not published until Mrs.
La Farge printed it in her memoir. It cannot be called a success as
a work of art—*Mont-Saint Michel and Chartres* was much more
that—but more than any other writing it traced the intellectual
route by which Adams arrived at the altar he set up in private. It is
well worth examination, especially by those who have tended to take
Adams at his own public evaluation. It began:

> GRACIOUS LADY:—
> Simple as when I asked your aid before;
>   Humble as when I prayed for grace in vain
> Seven hundred years ago; weak, weary, sore
>   In heart and hope, I ask your help again.
>
> You, who remember all, remember me;
>   An English scholar of a Norman name.
> I was a thousand who then crossed the sea
>   To wrangle in the Paris school for fame.
>
> When your Byzantine portal was still young
>   I prayed there with my master Abelard;
> When Ave Maris Stella was first sung,
>   I helped to sing it there with St. Bernard.

And so the verses go on to sketch briefly what *Chartres* builds out
more fully—the time and place that Adams had now fled to in fancy
and where he conceived that the inner Adams might have had a
chance for expression. That was northern France in the day of the
building of the cathedrals, when the Virgin Mary ruled the Church
and the Church ruled much of the world, and both together in this
particular place inspired some of man's greatest and loveliest works.

To understand the salutation "Gracious Lady," however, we must
think not only of the twelfth-century Virgin, but of the medieval Lady
of Spiritual Love, whom we know most familiarly now in Dante's
Beatrice of the *Paradiso*. Lady Beatrice, we recall, had been a real

woman adored afar by Dante when she was alive. But after her death her role was even more important; she became the poet's spiritual mentor in divine philosophy and guide to the throne of the Virgin in heaven. Following once more a clue of Mrs. La Farge, we understand that the memory of Mrs. Adams figures in this invocation of "Gracious Lady." She has assumed a place somewhat like that of Dante's Beatrice, as an ideal mentor in spiritual matters. While it is the twelfth-century Virgin to whom the prayer is actually addressed, we know that this personal significance often lies just beneath the surface.

But it is the historical recapitulation of Adams's spiritual conflict that most interests us, and whose meaning we are trying to decipher. Significant in this connection is the character of the twelfth-century Henry Adams. He is an "English scholar of a Norman name," and do we not already foresee, for the imaginary Adams, the fate of the real one? Is not this the hand of the Fathers all over again? For what could be more socially correct for an Adams to have been in the twelfth century—out of all the million possible ancestors—than an Englishman of a Norman name; and if this were but the instinct for family correctness, would it not again be the death of the real man? Would it not mean that, even in the twelfth century, a Henry Adams could not be among the indistinguishable, even if to be so were to be one of the unknown architects of Chartres itself?

This choice may be a witting and sorry one, rather than for pure preference. Possibly Adams is telling himself that he *would* have been just that in the twelfth century, an English scholar of a Norman name. Even then, he may be saying, he would have had to turn back across the channel to reach the scene of the great flowering. Even then he would have been outside the common cause of faith. He would have come only "to wrangle in the Paris schools for fame."

Now, whether Adams saw that the wrangling for *fame* rather than for truth was also part of his twelfth-century doom, we cannot tell. From what follows, I rather think that he did not see this distinction even in his prayer to the Virgin—that this was part of the unconfessed rather than the confessed error. It is the "wit and learning" all over again, which William James said would never impress God. But in any case, it was to wrangle and not to believe that Adams saw himself as part of the great period of Catholic belief. And we see already that, though he had also prayed for grace to the Virgin, he had prayed in vain; and this thought is developed as we go on:

> For centuries I brought you all my cares,
>   And vexed you with the murmurs of a child;
> You heard the tedious burdens of my prayers;
>   You could not grant them, but at least you smiled.

Whatever this verse may mean in terms of Adams's problem, it must mean something different from the earlier verse about the "wrangling scholar." The petitioning child and the wrangling scholar must be different aspects of Adams's personality at least from his own view; though to the observer they might be closely related. The scholar is looking for truth and, if he merely wrangles, failing to find it; the petitioner is asking for mercy, for a boon, perhaps for an indulgence which not even the Virgin could grant. But the one character does not admit personal need while the other does—a most important distinction in the case of one hoping for help.

Just what these boons and murmurs might be, in terms of Adams's inner life, remains obscure, but we must believe they are closely related to the central conflict. Was it the boon of greater energy that Adams asked? He seemed always preoccupied by the question of energy. We know that his general energy was such that he could do the necessary research and writing to produce the eight or ten volumes of his *History* in a relatively short time for such a task, meanwhile carrying on other work such as teaching and editing. Yet his physical inheritance, or illness, as he half suggests in *The Education,* may have left him limited in some particular energy, perhaps emotional, which was the object of these murmurs against fate. On the other hand, psychological factors may have been the more important even with respect to such a matter; and the petition here may have been for the grace to overcome these difficulties in himself. There is the further possibility that the murmurs and tedious burden represented simply Adams's desire for success and fame according to the hereditary pattern, and were indulgences which heaven must deny because they could be got only by the genuine efforts of the man himself. In this last case we would find the scholar wrangling for fame and the child begging a boon identical.

But in any case, whether Adams asked for what fate absolutely had denied, or whether he asked insincerely for things which only his sincere faith and effort could have brought him, it is evident that the boons asked *were,* in a real sense, indulgences which could not be granted. What signifies is Adams's own description of them as the murmurs and tedious burdens of a child, who, unlike a mature man, asks for purely wishful things.

The prayer so far, in any case, gives us a Henry Adams with his conflict unsettled. Whatever kept the genuine nature from freeing itself is still present, and it is interesting to ask whether some way of emancipation had ever been possible. Surely we must allow within the range of possibility an actual triumph of the genuine man over the necessities that confronted him. Was the celebrated Adams name and heredity, in itself, such a handicap as to amount to "fate" for Henry Adams?

Charles Francis Adams, Junior, a fourth-generation Adams himself, made perhaps as true a comment on the subject of celebrated ancestors as can be made when, in the biography of his father, he described the latter's experience of five years of activity in the Massachusetts legislature. Charles Francis, Senior, too, was a marked man, "ticketed for life," as Henry wrote of himself, and he ventured only with misgivings upon his first attempt at public life. His son wrote, however, that the experience was happy and encouraging rather than not. "Gradually and insensibly he came to realize that no prejudice, either personal or because of family, really existed toward him; but, on the contrary, the great mass of the community actually felt an interest in him and a kindliness which, had he himself possessed only a little of the sympathetic quality, had he been only a degree less reserved in nature and repellent in manners, would have found expression, then and afterwards, in ways which could not have been otherwise than grateful to him."

I think the same comment might stand for Henry Adams's case. The "fate" of having celebrated ancestors was a matter of attitude inside Henry, rather than of circumstances outside him.

Nor can we take at face value the theory of Henry in his *Education* that he would have been "made" in John Adams's time by the same heredity which unmade him in his own time. John Adams was not a fourth-generation celebrated Adams. Henry Adams was not an unknown poor schoolteacher. Henry could start from where he started, with three generations of famous names behind him, or he could imagine himself in the situation of his great grandfather, starting with no name and from nowhere, like Abraham Lincoln or Ulysses Grant, but he could not argue they were the same situation.

No, I fear the fatal element was much closer to simple pride than to anything irreducible in Henry's situation. In this sense, the family's pattern became a handicap; in this sense it was "fate." The triumph of the personal Henry Adams would have meant the humility of the family Henry Adams, and that was not the sort of humility that Henry was prepared to cultivate.

There remains the further possibility, even in later life, of his recognizing fate for the insuperable fact that it appeared to have become. In other words, there would seem to have been possible a whole view of life providing it were now truly a tragic view.

Most of Adams's writings, as a matter of fact, had called logically for a tragic view—certainly *The Rule of Phase,* as William James insisted; just as certainly, in its different way, *Democracy,* as Mr.

Commager has implied in his essay on Adams. If the fate of humanity is what Adams said it must be, in *The Rule of Phase;* if the fate of America is such as Adams claimed its institutions inevitably determine it to be, in *Democracy,* then erudition and irony toward the one prospect and flippancy and derision toward the other were pitifully weak responses for any human being to make.

If one were to ask further why the tragic view of life was denied Adams, we can only return to our central point. We are dealing with the nemesis of a sense of born superiority. And if Adams felt himself above the common human lot to begin with, the same assumption insisted he was above the common lot even after his nemesis had treated him with uncommon severity.

This becomes a tragic fact to the observer, who realizes that fate had abused Adams's merit to about the extent that Adams had thought his merit above fate. It explains too why Adams is more important than his work. For we can see Adams as a tragic figure, while Adams in his writings could never see himself as other than an ironic or a pathetic, in a word, a futile one.

The case of Mr. T. S. Eliot, another son, or grandson, of New England troubled by the hand of the Fathers, shows how far the nemesis of a sense of superiority may drive a distinguished artist without making him a tragic poet. A truly tragic view of life brings unity; despair, like that expressed by *The Waste Land,* remains a matter of division. In Adams's case it should be plain that his irony, derision, self-mockery, parade of erudition, and occasional pathos (as in *Chartres*) showed in their various ways the divided man. Even the "Prayer to the Virgin" went on in alternations between Adams the wrangling scholar and Adams the erring child:

> If then I left you, it was not my crime,
>   Or if a crime, it was not mine alone.
> All children wander with the truant Time.
>   Pardon me too! You pardoned once your Son!
>
> For He said to you:—"Wist not that I
>   Must be about my Father's business?" So,
> Seeking his Father he pursued his way
>   Straight to the Cross towards which we all must go.
>
> So I too wandered off among the host
>   That racked the earth to find the father's clue.
> I did not find the Father, but I lost
>   What now I value more, the Mother—You!
>
> I thought the fault was yours that foiled my search;
>   I turned and broke your image on its throne,

Cast down my idol, and resumed my march
To claim the father's empire for my own.

Crossing the hostile sea, our greedy band
    Saw rising hills and forests in the blue;
Our father's kingdom in the promised land!
    —We seized it, and dethroned the father too.

And now we are the Father, with our brood,
    Ruling the Infinite, not Three but One;
We made our world and saw that it was good;
    Ourselves we worship, and we have no Son. . . .

Perhaps no further comment is needed on the more personal elements suggested in these lines. What concerns us is the historical analogy which the scholar Adams has built up to explain the erring child—and which we cannot help but feel is in part a defense even against his own impulse to confession.

Yet something may be said for the victim of a historic process. Descendants of a long line of Protestant patriarchs who tended to put the Law above the Prophets and the Old Testament above the New, Henry Adams had felt the harsher breath of his tradition, while a certain exclusiveness had kept him from knowing its more grateful side. (The Adamses never could stand an Emerson or a Channing.) It is not hard to make out the meanings in the verses. The Father stands for Law and Rule—the hereditary Adams pattern. The Mother stands for Love, and Henry Adams had got an overdose of law, while far too little scope had been allowed the principle of love.

The effort to trace this conflict back to the founder of Christianity himself is surely a dubious expedient. It is the witty scholar, we are sure, who here makes a play on words in order to try to make us believe that Jesus was seeking Rule more than Love—or some other kind of rule *than* love.

Nevertheless, we know that the Church, unfortunately, after the manner of institutions, tended to lean toward the Law, and perhaps because of the personality of its first great instituter, Paul, leaned away from love even when it stood for Love. And one half of the condition for any sort of human love, whether she stood in the relation of Wife, Mother, or Daughter, was allowed no such standing in the Church as had Father, Husband, Son. Yet the womanly, the motherly, the daughterly had to come into the Church somehow, and come in they did by way of the Virgin Mother (even, too, as the Daughter of St. Anne), who slowly and surely worked her way up to the very top, above the Trinity, as Adams delightedly insisted in *Chartres*.

Then came the break in the historic process which produced the actual Henry Adams—the Reformation—and there was a certain misfortune in the fact that the chief reason for the break, the need of the human mind to be sure it looks at the thing instead of merely the image of it, struck most hard at what had become most an image, the Virgin Mary. For with the removal of the image, much of what she had stood for was removed also, so that in this respect the Church was back to something like the barrenness as well as the purity of the primitive communion, except so far as it tried the even more doubtful expedient of bringing in the missing element by way of curling the hair and beard and softening the lips and eyes of its founder, the truly long-suffering Jesus.

What might be valid, then, in Adams's analogy is the dominance, especially in Calvinism, of the Father as all-powerful judge over the Mother as the agent of love and forgiveness. I need not dwell on the judicial-ecclesiastical-patriarchal type which actually did dominate so much of the life of early New England. Brooks Adams, in fact, wrote a book, *The Founding of Massachusetts,* to show the terror of a regime built on the identification of God's will with the edicts of a small group of self-righteous men. And even the ancestral mother, Abigail Adams, could collaborate in the harsher sort of Puritan rule with a firmness that would have pleased a Winthrop or Mather, as witness this admonition from a letter written to her eleven-year-old son, John Quincy Adams: ". . . for dear as you are to me, I would much rather you should have found your grave in the ocean you have crossed, or that an untimely death should crop you in your infant years, than see an immoral, profligate, or graceless child." In view of this background for the notion of "God, the judge," we can sympathize with the fourth-generation Henry Adams, the exception to the family rule for its men, not judicial and stern, but sensitive, shy, aesthetic, intuitive, in a sense, feminine, who yet found himself thrust perforce into a ready-made masculine mold which broke him rather than he it.

So much the historic analogy explains; yet we cannot press it to the length that the arguing scholar Adams here presses it without its once more becoming false. With regard to the question of woman's place, for instance, there is the other side to the medal of Puritan Protestantism. After all, the simple fact was—and it was a fact of simplicity—that wife and mother probably never before in the world had found truer places of respect than they did in Puritan New England. Respect was the key word, not chivalry or idealization, and before we are sure that women prefer chivalry to respect we ought to hear the testimony of the two other principals in Dante Alighieri's triangle of sacred and profane love: that is, of the honored but unused Lady, Beatrice herself, and of the used but unhonored woman, the nameless wife who bore Dante seven children in ten years and afterwards passed from life we know not how.

The very meaning of the Puritan movement had to do with the integration of truth—closing the gap between sacred and profane—and even when it looked as if the integer had been made needlessly narrow, it was in a real sense an effort to make a whole. Nothing became more characteristic of Puritan New England than that a worthy place was to be found for a thing or no place made for it at all. If it were in fact sin, it was to be cast out rather than accommodated, and this done withal in the world and not out of it.

True, this made for a strain, especially upon consciences sharpened to an exaggerated sense of sin, so that they saw it in areas of human life which Nature herself knew were good, for example in the natural rest and pleasure periods of living. It was just this unhappy tension, somehow prolonged into a more liberal day, which in fact produced such neo-New England Puritans as Henry Adams and T. S. Eliot, the conscience-stricken but not the conscience-cleared.

Yet we cannot take the testimony of the conscience-stricken that a new day of grace had not come to pass, that the same discrimination that had sought to leave out bad could not leave in good. There is no question what Henry Adams wanted to bring back: it was natural emotion, intuition, freedom, forgiveness, mutual pleasure—all that makes for the livability and flow of life as distinguished from (even when prospered by) its mere ordering. These he began to see, somewhat romantically, all centered in the nature of woman. It was she who refused to abide by masculine law, whether human or divine; it was she who worked according to another principle, inspiration, favor, desire, creative instinct—love. And so it was that the stricken widower returned to the past age that he felt had put woman at her highest: which had celebrated, adored, worshiped her. Yet we cannot take his word that the spirit he wanted, and which his inherited and legalistic conscience had frowned upon, could not have been found in his own world and time by anyone who cared to look for it where it actually was.

The rediscovery of most of what Adams meant by the Mother—Nature—had been the great intellectual movement of his family's time. Speaking broadly, it had transformed almost every sphere of life, from government to poetry, and affected almost every part of the Western world, except here and there an insulated spot like the Adams family estate itself. New England itself was in large part the child of this general movement, whose beginnings Adams had called a "wandering." But if it were a wandering away from the Virgin Mother of the Church (as it was only in a sense), surely it was a return to the mother of life, and on a plane, say in Emerson or Wordsworth, that did credit to the imagination of man. The sense of the wholeness of truth remained; and if something had temporarily been left out that was needed, now it was brought back as a good to be loved and not an evil to be feared.

All this the scholar Adams, in these verses, chose to ignore even while the penitent begged for the knowledge that would fill his ignorance. The knowledge, as I have suggested, could have been found by Adams almost any day a few miles from the Adams's Braintree, at Emerson's Concord; or if Concord were too rustic, it could have been got a little later at Camden, where Whitman lived, not far from Washington. Adams in his old age did in fact recall that Whitman had provided a place for Nature in a manner unmistakable, and unmistakably different from the way in which any New Englander would allow her a place, even when, like Emerson, he seemed to allow her every place. So far as the education of Henry Adams was concerned, the *Essays* of Emerson would have done just as well as Whitman's *Leaves of Grass*. Nothing could have been more instructive to a young Adams, in fact, than that Emerson as a young man had left the narrower way of the Law both on a point of conscience and a point of legalism. For Adams had been fated to do just the opposite: to stick by the legalism and deny his conscience. And in a hundred different forms Adams might have read the lesson that he was looking for: that reason and nature, love and law, meet at the point of man's conscience, to the greater and not the lesser freedom of both. Call it grace or virtue, freedom or control, it comes to the same thing. Man's conscience and his nature work best together, not at cross purposes; they do so according to man's nature.

Concord, in short, might have saved Adams a trip back to the twelfth century. But Adams no more than T. S. Eliot after him could see truth so close to home. Emerson and Concord looked "naïf" to young Adams. He had to grow much older and sadder before he learned that "naïf" meant native, and became a charming adjunct to truth in medieval France.

Much of the difficulty no doubt—and it was a difficulty—lay in the fact that a great deal of truth, like Emerson, had left off its ecclesiastical vestments. Its face did not shine with the same glory, or frown with the same authority, when reflected in the light of the open sky rather than an altar candle. Transition meant change;

change meant death and life; and the process always found some caught in between, with an old world dead and a new powerless to be born.

But the truth is that truth had long been making its way, much of it, into the world, and doing well on the whole. A good case might be made for this having been an object of most religious prophets: to drive truth back into the world. But if truth cannot be divided, one thing is certain: it is a most partial view which holds that ecclesiastical truth by itself is whole in a world that has secularized a good deal of it. The opposite view is equally partial: that truth itself is now profane and need not be abided by.

Henry Adams, one of the victims of the transitional process of his time, shifted characteristically between the two partial views. Sacred truth, to him, was alone respectable, but it was no longer true; secular truth was true enough, but it was not respectable. Poor Esther, in Adams's novel, fell into this predicament, and in fact practically all of Adams's books somehow dealt with it. As if to illustrate it once more, his "Prayer to the Virgin of Chartres" went on to include an absurd "Prayer to the Dynamo," which he asked the Virgin to listen to for a moment as "the last of the strange prayers humanity has wailed."

According to the theory that Adams was pleased to occupy himself with in his later years, the Dynamo in the twentieth century promised to take the place of the Virgin in the twelfth. That was where science was leading the world, he insisted, toward the worship of pure force. Science may well be left to speak for itself, in countries where it is allowed to speak for itself, but it is fairly clear that Adams was not speaking intelligibly for it. The Dynamo may symbolize anything one cares to make it symbolize: pure energy, or progress, or man's ingenuity, or power, or what, but it does not stand for a thing to be worshiped except to those who want to worship such things. In the twentieth century as in the twelfth there might be many who worshiped power or force. True scientists and philosophers, however, continued to be devoted to knowledge and truth, and not to power.

The twentieth century promised confusions enough, as Henry Adams clearly foresaw. Adams's own efforts at clarifying them, however, remain but one confusion the more. Concerning this "Prayer to the Dynamo" there is really no comment that improves upon the one Henry's brother Charles had made long before in a similar connection: let Henry, dear fellow, speak (or pray) for himself.

And so he went on to do, pray to the twelfth-century Virgin, in words not a little moving:

> Help me to see! not with my mimic sight—
>   With yours! which carried radiance, like the sun,
> Giving the rays you saw with—light in light—
>   Tying all sun and stars and worlds in one.
>
> Help me to know! not with my mocking art—
>   With you, who knew yourself unbound by laws;
> Gave God your strength, your life, your sight, your heart,
>   And took from him the Thought that Is—the Cause.
>
> Help me to feel! not with my insect sense—
>   With yours that felt all life alive in you;
> Infinite heart beating at your expense;
>   Infinite passion breathing the breath you drew!

And finally the prayer concludes upon a note that curiously mingles piety and mockery. The mockery is all for the Father, the piety all for the Mother. It sounds worse blasphemy than it really is, since Adams had simply turned over the attributes of divinity from a Father-God to a Mother-God, as the preceding three verses indicate. But there is little question what the verses tell. They tell the final drastic revolt of the son from the law of the Fathers, his partisan devotion now to the rule of the Mothers. I say partisan and drastic, for it is plain that the new faith is not an integration, but a displacement: of knowledge for instinct, reason for love. The Woman-God now reigns alone and supreme; the Man-God, a total failure, is banished to outer darkness:

> Help me to bear! not my baby load,
>   But yours; who bore the failure of the light,
> The strength, the knowledge and the thought of God—
>   The futile folly of the Infinite!

Yes, it is as one-sided and perverse as *The Rule of Phase,* this final private creed of Henry Adams. Where the public man had made the intellect a tyrant, the private man now set up the heart as a simpleton. *Chartres,* the book written for women, pays a dubious compliment to the sex by celebrating irrationality as woman's peculiar vitrue. She is not only compassionate, this Virgin Mother according to Adams, she is indulgent, and she is not only indulgent, she is stupid. Whole chapters in *Chartres* are written to show that the Queen of the Court of Heaven can be fooled. Adams had to have it all one way or all another. If the Fathers were reason without love, the Mothers had to be love without reason.

But we can understand the drastic reversal, for it is Henry Adams turning on Henry Adams, turning on the part of himself that had followed a false pattern, confessing the wrong that had been worked not only upon his own life but also, perhaps, upon his wife's. It was drastic, for it was a form of atonement.

This is an overturn and not a cure, and it is not to be recommended for general usage. The ills of the twentieth century would be helped as little by Adams's indulgent Virgin as they would by his tyrannous Dynamo. Yet as to the personal and private case, judgment is not for the outsider. Attitude is everything in such matters as Adams hinted at in his "Prayer to the Virgin"—for I question whether even here he exposed the really private man. We cannot know for certain the private attitude, and whether or not Adams had resolved in some part at least his conflict between Law and Love, and saw that Love, after all, is only a higher form of Law.

25

William Dean Howells: REALISM AND
THE AMERICAN NOVEL: *[Two Excerpts: 1891]*

. . . I would have our American novelists be as American as they
unconsciously can. Matthew Arnold complained that he found no
"distinction" in our life, and I would gladly persuade all artists in-
tending greatness of any kind among us that the recognition of the
fact pointed out by Mr. Arnold ought to be a source of inspiration
to them, and not discouragement. We have been now some hundred
years building up a state on the affirmation of the essential equality
of men in their rights and duties, and whether we have been right
or been wrong the gods have taken us at our word, and have responded to us with a civilization in which there is no "distinction"
perceptible to the eye that loves and values it. Such beauty and such
grandeur, or the beauty and grandeur in which the quality of solidarity so prevails that neither distinguishes itself to the disadvantage
of anything else. It seems to me that these conditions invite the artist
to the study and the appreciation of the common, and to the portrayal
in every art of those finer and higher aspects which unite rather than
sever humanity, if he would thrive in our new order of things. The
talent that is robust enough to front the everyday world and catch
the charm of its workworn, careworn, brave, kindly face, need not

fear the encounter, though it seems terrible to the sort nurtured in the superstition of the romantic, the bizarre, the heroic, the distinguished, as the things alone worthy of painting or carving or writing. The arts must become democratic, and then we shall have the expression of America in art; and the reproach which Mr. Arnold was half right in making us shall have no justice in it any longer; we shall be "distinguished". . . .

One of the great newspapers the other day invited the prominent American authors to speak their minds upon a point in the theory and practice of fiction which had already vexed some of them. It was the question of how much or how little the American novel ought to deal with certain facts of life which are not usually talked of before young people, and especially young ladies. Of course the question was not decided, and I forgot just how far the balance inclined in favor of a larger freedom in this matter. But it certainly inclined that way; one or two writers of the sex which is somehow supposed to have purity in its keeping (as if purity were a thing that did not practically concern the other sex, preoccupied with serious affairs) gave it a rather vigorous tilt to that side. In view of this fact it would not be the part of prudence to make an effort to dress the balance; and indeed I do not know that I was going to make any such effort. But there are some things to say, around and about the subject, which I should like to have some one else say, and which I may myself possibly be safe in suggesting.

One of the first of these is the fact, generally lost sight of by those who censure the Anglo-Saxon novel for its prudishness, that it is really not such a prude after all; and that if it is sometimes apparently anxious to avoid those experiences of life not spoken of before young people, this may be an appearance only. Sometimes a novel which has this shuffling air, this effect of truckling to propriety, might defend itself, if it could speak for itself, by saying that such experiences happened not to come within its scheme, and that, so far from maiming or mutilating itself in ignoring them, it was all the more faithfully representative of the tone of modern life in dealing with love that was chaste, and with passion so honest that it could be openly spoken of before the tenderest society bud at dinner. It might say that the guilty intrigue, the betrayal, the extreme flirtation even, was the exceptional thing in life, and unless the scheme of the story necessarily involved it, that it would be bad art to lug it in, and as bad taste as to introduce such topics in a mixed company. It could say very justly that the novel, in our civilization now always addresses a mixed company, and that the vast majority of the company are ladies, and that very many, if not most, of these ladies are young girls. If the novel were written for men and for married women alone, as in continental Europe, it might be altogether different. But the simple fact is that it is not written for them alone among us, and it is a question of writing, under cover of our universal acceptance, things for young girls to read which you would be put out-of-doors for saying to them, or frankly giving notice of your intention, and so cutting yourself off from the pleasure—and it is a very high and sweet one—of appealing to these vivid, responsive intelligences, which are none the less brilliant and admirable because they are innocent.

One day a novelist who liked, after the manner of other men, to repine at his hard fate, complained to his friend, a critic, that he was tired of the restriction he had put upon himself in this regard; for it is a mistake, as can be readily shown, to suppose that others impose it. "See how free those French fellows are!" he rebelled. "Shall we always be shut up to our tradition of decency?"

"Do you think it's much worse than being shut up to their tradition of indecency?" said his friend.

Then that novelist began to reflect, and he remembered how sick the invariable motive of the French novel made him. He perceived finally that, convention for convention, ours was not only more tolerable, but on the whole was truer to life, not only to its complexion, but also to its texture. No one will pretend that there is not vicious love beneath the surface of our society; if he did, the fetid explosions of the divorce trials would refute him; but if he pretended that it was in any just sense characteristic of our society, he could be still more easily refuted. Yet it exists, and it is unquestionably the material of tragedy, the stuff from which intense effects are wrought. The question, after owning this fact, is whether these intense effects are not rather cheap effects. I incline to think they are, and I will try to say why I think so, if I may do so without offence. The material itself, the mere mention of it, has an instant fascination; it arrests, it detains, till the last word is said, and while there is anything to be hinted. This is what makes a love intrigue of some sort all but essential to the popularity of any fiction. Without such an intrigue the intellectual equipment of the author must be of the highest, and then he will succeed only with the highest class of readers. But any author who will deal with a guilty love intrigue holds all readers in his hand, the highest with the lowest, as long as he hints the slightest hope of the smallest naughtiness. He need not at all be a great author; he may be a very shabby wretch, if he has but the courage or the trick of that sort of thing. The critics will call him "virile" and "passionate"; decent people will be ashamed to have been limed by him; but the low average will only ask another chance of flocking into his net. If he happens to be an able writer, his really fine and costly work will be unheeded, and the lure to the appetite will be chiefly remembered. There may be other qualities which make reputations for other men, but in his case they will count for nothing. He pays this penalty for his success in that kind; and every one pays some such penalty who deals with some such material. It attaches in like manner to the triumphs of the writers who now almost form a school among us, and who may be said to have established themselves in an easy popularity simply by the study of erotic shivers and fervors. They may find their account in the popularity, or they may not; there is no question of the popularity.

But I do not mean to imply that their case covers the whole ground. So far as it goes, though, it ought to stop the mouths of those who complain that fiction is enslaved to propriety among us. It appears that of a certain kind of impropriety it is free to give us all it will, and more. But this is not what serious men and women writing fiction mean when they rebel against the limitations of their art in our civilization. They have no desire to deal with nakedness, as painters and sculptors freely do in the worship of beauty; or with certain facts of life, as the stage does, in the service of sensation. But they ask why, when the conventions of the plastic and histrionic arts liberate their followers to the *portrayal* of almost any phase of the physical or of the emotional nature, an American novelist may not write a story on the lines of *Anna Karenina* or *Madame Bovary*. Sappho they put aside, and from Zola's work they avert their eyes. They do not condemn him or Daudet, necessarily, or accuse their motives; they leave them out of the question; they do not want to do that kind of thing. But they do sometimes wish to do another kind, to touch one of the most serious and sorrowful problems of life in the spirit of Tolstoy and Flaubert, and they ask why they may not. At one time, they remind us, the Anglo-Saxon novelist did deal with such problems—Defoe in his spirit, Richardson in his, Goldsmith in his. At what moment did our fiction lose this privilege? In what fatal hour did the Young Girl arise and seal the lips of Fiction, with a touch of her finger, to some of the most vital interests of life?

Whether I wished to oppose them in their aspiration for greater freedom, or whether I wished to encourage them, I should begin to answer them by saying that the Young Girl had never done anything of the kind. The manners of the novel have been improving with those of its readers; that is all. Gentlemen no longer swear or fall drunk under the table, or abduct young ladies and shut them up in lonely country houses, or so habitually set about the ruin of their neighbors' wives, as they once did. Generally, people now call a spade an agricultural implement; they have not grown decent without having also grown a little squeamish, but they have grown comparatively decent; there is no doubt about that. They require of a novelist whom they respect unquestionable proof of his seriousness, if he proposes to deal with certain phases of life; they require a sort of scientific decorum. He can no longer expect to be received on the ground of entertainment only; he assumes a higher function, something like that of a physician or a priest, and they expect him to be bound by laws as sacred as those of such professions; they hold him solemnly pledged not to betray them or abuse their confidence. If he will accept the conditions, they give him their confidence, and he may then treat to his greater honor, and not at all to his disadvantage, of such experiences, such relations of men and women as George Eliot treats in *Adam Bede*, in *Daniel Deronda*, in *Romola*, in almost all her books; such as Hawthrone treats in *The Scarlet Letter*; such as Dickens treats in *David Copperfield*; such as Thackeray treats in *Pendennis*, and glances at in every one of his fictions; such as most of the masters of English fiction have at some time treated more or less openly. It is quite false or quite mistaken to suppose that our novels have left untouched these most important realities of life. They have only not made them their stock in trade; they have kept a true perspective in regard to them; they have relegated them in their pictures of life to the space and place they occupy in life itself, as we know it in England and America. They have kept a correct proportion, knowing perfectly well that unless the novel is to be a map, with everything scrupulously laid down in it, a faithful record of life in far the greater extent could be made to the exclusion of guilty love and all its circumstances and consequences.

I justify them in this view not only because I hate what is cheap and meretricious, and hold in peculiar loathing the cant of the critics who require "passion" as something in itself admirable and desirable in a novel, but because I prize fidelity in the historian of feeling and character. Most of these critics who demand "passion" would seem to have no conception of any passion but one. Yet there are several other passions: the passion of grief, the passion of avarice, the passion of pity, the passion of ambition, the passion of hate, the passion of envy, the passion of devotion, the passion of friendship; and all these have a greater part in the drama of life than the passion of love, and infinitely greater than the passion of guilty love. Wittingly or unwittingly, English fiction and American fiction have recognized this truth, not fully, not in the measure it merits, but in greater degree than most other fiction.

26

Randolph Bourne: HISTORY OF
A LITERARY RADICAL [1918]

For a man of culture, my friend Miro began his literary career in a singularly unpromising way. Potential statesmen in log cabins might miraculously come in touch with all the great books of the world, but the days of Miro's young school life were passed in innocence of Homer or Dante or Shakespeare, or any of the other traditional mind-formers of the race. What Miro had for his nourishment, outside the Bible, which was a magical book that you must not drop on the floor, or his school-readers, which were like lightning flashes of unintelligible scenes, was the literature that his playmates lent him —exploits of British soldiers in Spain and the Crimea, the death-defying adventures of young filibusters in Cuba and Nicaragua. Miro gave them a languid perusing, and did not criticize their literary style. Huckleberry Finn and Tom Sawyer somehow eluded him until he had finished college, and no fresher tale of adventure drifted into his complacent home until the era of "Richard Carvel" and "Janice Meredith" sharpened his wits and gave him a vague feeling that there was such a thing as literary art. The classics were stiffly enshrined behind glass doors that were very hard to open—at least Hawthorne and Irving and Thackeray were there, and Tennyson's and Scott's poems—but nobody ever discussed them or looked at them. Miro's busy elders were taken up with the weekly *Outlook* and *Independent* and *Christian Work,* and felt they were doing much for Miro when they provided him and his sister with *St. Nicholas* and *The Youth's Companion.* It was only that Miro saw the black books looking at him accusingly from the case, and a rudimentary conscience, slipping easily over from Calvinism to culture, forced him solemnly to grapple with *The Scarlet Letter* or *Marmion.* All he remembers is that the writers of these books he browsed among used a great many words and made a great fuss over shadowy offenses and conflicts and passions that did not even stimulate his imagination with sufficient force to cause him to ask his elders what it was all about. Certainly the filibusters were easier.

At school Miro was early impressed with the vast dignity of the literary works and names he was compelled to learn. Shakespeare and Goethe and Dante lifted their plaster heads frowningly above the teacher's, as they perched on shelves about the room. Much was said of the greatness of literature. But the art of phonetics and the complications of grammar swamped Miro's early school years. It was not until he reached high school that literature began really to assume that sacredness which he had heretofore felt only for Holy Scripture. His initiation into culture was made almost a religious mystery by the conscientious and harassed teacher. As the Deadwood Boys and Henty and David Harum slipped away from Miro's soul in the presence of Milton's *Comus* and Burke's *On Conciliation,* a cultural devoutness was engendered in him that never really died. At first it did not take Miro beyond the stage where your conscience is strong enough to make you uncomfortable, but not strong enough to make you do anything about it. Miro did not actually become an omnivorous reader of great books. But he was filled with a rich grief that the millions pursued cheap and vulgar fiction instead of the best that has been thought and said in the world. Miro indiscriminately bought cheap editions of the English classics and read them with a certain patient incomprehension.

As for the dead classics, they came to Miro from the hands of his teachers with a prestige even vaster than the books of his native tongue. No doubt ever entered his head that four years of Latin and three years of Greek, an hour a day, were the important preparation he needed for his future as an American citizen. No doubt ever hurt him that the world into which he would pass would be a world where, as his teacher said, Latin and Greek were a solace to the aged, a quickener of taste, a refreshment after manual labor, and a clue to the general knowledge of all human things. Miro would as soon have doubted the rising of the sun as have doubted the wisdom of these serious, puckered women who had the precious manipulation of his cultural upbringing in their charge. Miro was a bright, if a rather vague, little boy, and a fusion of brightness and docility gave him high marks in the school where we went together.

No one ever doubted that these marks expressed Miro's assimilation of the books we pored over. But he told me later that he had never really known what he was studying. Caesar, Vergil, Cicero, Xenophon, Homer, were veiled and misty experiences to him. His mind was a moving present, obliterating each day what it had read the day before, and piercing into a no more comprehended future. He could at no time have given any intelligible account of Aeneas's wanderings or what Cicero was really inveighing against. The *Iliad* was even more obscure. The only thing which impressed him deeply was an expurgated passage, which he looked up somewhere else and found to be about Mars and Venus caught in the golden bed. Caesar seemed to be at war, and Xenophon wandering somewhere in Asia Minor, with about the same lengthiness and hardship as Miro suffered in reading him. The trouble, Miro thought afterwards, was that these books were to his mind flickering lights in a vast jungle of ignorance. He does not remember marveling at the excessive dullness of the stories themselves. He plodded his faithful way, using them as his conscientious teachers did, as exercises in language. He looked on Vergil and Cicero as essentially problems in disentangling words which had unaccountably gotten into a bizarre order, and in recognizing certain rather amusing and ingenious combinations, known as "constructions." Why these words took so irritating an order Miro never knew, but he always connected the problem with those algebraic puzzles he had elsewhere to unravel. Vergil's words were further complicated by being arranged in lines which one had to "scan." Miro was pleased with the rhythm, and there were stanzas that had a roll of their own. But the inexorable translating that had to go on tore all this fabric of poetry to pieces. His translations were impeccable, but, as he never wrote them down, he had never before his eyes the consecutive story.

Translations Miro never saw. He knew that they were implements of deadly sin that boys used to cheat with. His horror of them was such as a saint might feel towards a parody of the Bible. Just before Miro left school, his sister in a younger class began to read a prose translation of the *Odyssey,* and Miro remembers the scorn with which he looked down on so sneaking an entrance into the temple of light. He knew that not everyone could study Latin and Greek, and he learned to be proud of his knowledge. When at last he had passed his examinations for college—his Latin composition and grammar, his syntax and his sight-reading, and his Greek composition and grammar, his Greek syntax and sight-reading, and his translation of Gallic battles and Anabatic frosts, and Dido's farewell and Cicero's objurgations—his zealous rage did not abate. He even insisted on reading the Bucolics, while he was away on his vacation, and a book or two in the *Odyssey*. His family was a little chilled by his studiousness, but he knew well that he was laying up cultural treasures in heaven, where moth and rust do not corrupt, neither do thieves break in and steal.

Arrived at college, Miro expanded his cultural interests on the approved lines. He read Horace and Plato, Lysias and Terence, impartially, with faithful conscience. Horace was the most exciting because of the parodies that were beginning to appear in the cleverer newspapers. Miro scarcely knew whether to be amused or shocked at *Odi Persicos* or *Integer Vitæ* done into current slang. The professors, mild-mannered men who knew their place and kept it, never mentioned these impudent adventurers, but for Miro it was the first crack in his Ptolemaic system of reverences. There came a time when his mind began to feel replete, when this heavy pushing through the opaque medium of dead language began to fatigue him. He should have been able to read fluently, but there were always turning up new styles, new constructions, to plague him. Latin became to him like a constant diet of beefsteak, and Greek like a constant diet of fine wheaten bread. They lost their taste. These witty poets and ostentatious orators—what were they all about? What was their background? Where did they fit into Miro's life? The professors knew some history, but what did that history mean? Miro found himself surfeited and dissatisfied. He began to look furtively at translations to get some better English than he was able to provide. The hairsplittings of Plato began to bore him when he saw them in crystal-clear English, and not muffled in the original Greek. His apostasy had begun.

It was not much better in his study of English literature. Miro was given a huge anthology, a sort of press-clipping bureau of belles-lettres, from Chaucer to Arthur Symons. Under the direction of a professor who was laying out a career for himself as poet—or "modern singer," as he expressed it—the class went briskly through the centuries sampling their genius and tasting the various literary flavors. The enterprise reminded Miro of those books of woolen samples which one looks through when one is to have a suit of clothes made. But in this case, the student did not even have the pleasure of seeing the suit of clothes. All that was expected of him, apparently, was that he should become familiar, from these microscopic pieces, with the different textures and patterns. The great writers passed before his mind like figures in a crowded street. There was no time for preferences. Indeed the professor strove diligently to give each writer his just due. How was one to appreciate the great thoughts and the great styles if one began to choose violently between them, or attempt any discrimination on grounds of their peculiar congeniality for one's own soul? Criticism had to spurn such subjectivity, scholarship could not be willful. The neatly arranged book of "readings," with its medicinal doses of inspiration, became the symbol of Miro's education.

These early years of college did not deprive Miro of his cultural loyalty, but they deadened his appetite. Although almost inconceivably docile, he found himself being bored. He had come from school a serious boy, with more than a touch of priggishness in him, and a vague inspiration to be a "man of letters." He found himself becoming a collector of literary odds-and-ends. If he did not formulate this feeling clearly, he at least knew. He found that the literary life was not as interesting as he had expected. He sought no adventures. When he wrote, it was graceful lyrics or polite criticisms of William Collins or Charles Lamb. These canonized saints of culture still held the field for Miro, however. There was nothing between them and that popular literature of the day that all good men bemoaned. Classic or popular, "highbrow" or "lowbrow," this was the choice, and Miro unquestioningly took the orthodox heaven. In 1912 the most popular of Miro's English professors had never heard of Galsworthy, and another was creating a flurry of scandal in the department by recommending Chesterton to his classes. It would scarcely have been in college that Miro would have learned of an escape from the closed dichotomy of culture. Bored with the "classic," and frozen with horror at the "popular," his career as a man of culture must have come to a dragging end if he had not been suddenly liberated by a chance lecture which he happened to hear while he was at home for the holidays.

The literary radical who appeared before the Lyceum Club of Miro's village was none other than Professor William Lyon Phelps, and it is to that evening of cultural audacity Miro thinks he owes all his later emancipation. The lecturer grappled with the "modern novel," and tossed Hardy, Tolstoy, Turgenev, Meredith, even Trollope, into the minds of the charmed audience with such effect that the virgin shelves of the village library were ravished for days to come by the eager minds upon whom these great names dawned for the first time. *Jude the Obscure* and *Resurrection* were of course kept officially away from the vulgar, but Miro managed to find *Smoke* and *Virgin Soil* and *Anna Karenina* and *The Warden* and *A Pair of Blue Eyes* and *The Return of the Native*. Later at college he explored the forbidden realms. It was as if some devout and restless saint had suddenly been introduced to the Apocrypha. A new world was opened to Miro that was neither "classic" nor "popular," and yet which came to one under the most unimpeachable auspices. There was, at first, it is true, an air of illicit adventure about the enterprise. The lecturer who made himself the missionary of such vigorous and piquant doctrine had the air of being a heretic, or at least a boy playing out of school. But Miro himself returned to college a cultural revolutionist. His orthodoxies crumbled. He did not try to reconcile the new with the old. He applied pick and dynamite to the whole structure of the canon. Irony, humor, tragedy, sensuality, suddenly appeared to him as literary qualities in forms that he could understand. They were like oxygen to his soul.

If these qualities were in the books he had been reading, he had never felt them. The expurgated sample-books he had studied had passed too swiftly over the Elizabethans to give him a sense of their lustiness. Miro immersed himself voluptuously in the pessimism of Hardy. He fed on the poignant torture of Tolstoy. While he was reading *Resurrection,* his class in literature was making an "intensive" study of Tennyson. It was too much. Miro rose in revolt. He forswore literary courses forever, dead rituals in which anaemic priests mumbled their trite critical commentary. Miro did not know that to naughtier critics even Mr. Phelps might eventually seem a pale and timid Gideon, himself stuck in moral sloughs. He was grateful enough for that blast of trumpets which made his own scholastic walls fall down.

The next stage in Miro's cultural life was one of frank revolt. He became as violent as a heretic as he had been docile as a believer. Modern novels merely started the rift that widened into modern ideas. The professors were of little use. Indeed, when Miro joined a group of radicals who had started a new college paper, a relentless vendetta began with the teachers. Miro and his friends threw over everything that was mere literature. Social purpose must shine from any writing that was to rouse their enthusiasm. Literary flavor was to be permissible only where it made vivid high and revolutionary thought. Tolstoy became their god, Wells their high priest. Chesterton infuriated them. They wrote violent assaults upon him which began in imitation of his cool paradoxicality and ended in incoherent ravings. There were so many enemies to their new fervor that they scarcely knew where to begin. There were not only the old tables of stone to destroy, but there were new and threatening prophets of the eternal verities who had to be exposed. The nineteenth century which they had studied must be weeded of its nauseous moralists. The instructors consulted together how they might put down the revolt and bring these sinners back to the faith of cultural scripture.

It was of no avail. In a short time Miro had been converted from an aspiration for the career of a cultivated "man of letters" to a fiery zeal for artistic and literary propaganda in the service of radical ideas. One of the results of this conversion was the discovery that he really had no standards of critical taste. Miro had been reverential so long that he had felt no preferences. Everything that was classic had to be good to him. But now that he had thrown away the books that were stamped with the mark of the classic mint, and was dealing with the raw materials of letters, he had to become a critic and make selections. It was not enough that a book should be radical. Some of the books he read, though impeccably revolutionary as to ideas, were clearly poor as literature. His muffled taste began to assert itself. He found himself impressionable where before he had been only mildly acquisitive. The literature of revolt and free speculation fired him into a state of spiritual explosiveness. All that he read now stood out in brighter colors and in sharper outlines than before. As he reached a better balance, he began to feel the vigor of literary form, the value of sincerity and freshness of style. He began to look for them keenly in everything he read. It was long before Miro realized that enthusiasm not docility had made him critical. He became a little proud of his sensitive and discriminating reactions to the modern and the unsifted.

This pursuit had to take place without any help from the college. After Miro graduated, it is true that it became the fashion to study literature as the record of ideas and not merely as a canon of sacred books to be analyzed, commented upon, and absorbed. But no dent was made upon the system in Miro's time, and, the inventory of English criticism not going beyond Stevenson, no college course went beyond Stevenson. The Elizabethans had been exhumed and fumigated, but the most popular attention went to the gallery of Victorians, who combined moral soundness with literary beauty, and were therefore considered wholesome food for young men. The instructors all remained in the state of reverence which saw all things good that had been immemorially taught. Miro's own teacher was a fragile, earnest young man, whose robuster parents had evidently seized upon his nature as a fortunate pledge of what the family might produce in the way of an intellectual flower that should surpass in culture and gentility the ambitions of his parents. His studiousness, hopeless for his father's career as grocer, had therefore been capitalized into education.

The product now shone forth as one of the most successful and promising younger instructors in the department. He knew his subject. Card indexes filled his room, covering in detail the works, lives, and deaths of the illustrious persons whom he expounded, as well as everything that had been said about them in the way of appreciation or interpretation. An endless number of lectures and courses could be made from this bountiful store. He never tried to write himself, but he knew all about the different kinds of writing, and when he corrected the boys' themes he knew infallibly what to tell them to avoid. Miro's vagaries scandalized his teacher all the more because during his first year in college Miro had been generally noticed as one with the proper sobriety and scholarly patience to graduate into a similar priestly calling. Miro found scant sympathy in the young man. To the latter, literary studies were a science not an art, and they were to be treated with somewhat the same cold rigor of delimitation and analysis as any other science. Miro felt his teacher's recoil at the idea that literature was significant only as the expression of personality or as interpretation of some social movement. Miro saw how uneasy he became when he was confronted with current literature. It was clear that Miro's slowly growing critical sense had not a counterpart in the scholastic mind.

When Miro and his friends abandoned literary studies, they followed after the teachers of history and philosophy, intellectual arenas of which the literary professors seemed scandalously ignorant. At this ignorance Miro boiled with contempt. Here were the profitable clues that would give meaning to dusty literary scholarship, but the scholars had not the wits to seize them. They lived along, playing what seemed to Miro a rather dreary game, when they were not gaping reverently at ideas and forms which they scarcely had the genuine personality to appreciate. Miro felt once and for all free of these mysteries and reverences. He was to know the world as it has been and as it is. He was to put literature into its proper place, making all "culture" serve its apprenticeship for him as interpretation of things larger than itself, of the course of individual lives and the great tides of society.

Miro's later cultural life is not without interest. When he had finished college and his architectural course, and was making headway in his profession, his philosophy of the intellectual life began to straighten itself out. Rapid as his surrender of orthodoxy had been, it had taken him some time to live down that early education. He found now that he would have to live down his heresies also, and get some coherent system of tastes that was his own and not the fruit of either docility or the zeal of propaganda.

The old battles that were still going on helped Miro to realize his modern position. It was a queer, musty quarrel, but it was enlisting minds from all classes and of all intellectual fibers. The "classics" were dying hard, as Miro recognized whenever he read, in the magazines, attacks on the "new education." He found that professors were still taken seriously who declared in passion that without the universal study of the Latin language in American schools all conceptions of taste, standards, criticism, the historic sense itself, would vanish from the earth. He found that even as late as 1917 professional men were gathering together in solemn conclave and buttressing the "value of the classics" with testimonials from "successful men" in a variety of vocations. Miro was amused at the fact that the mighty studies once pressed upon him so uncritically should now require, like the patent medicines, testimonials as to their virtue. Bank presidents, lawyers, and editors had taken the Latin language regularly for years, and had found its effects painless and invigorating. He could not escape the unconscious satire that such plump and prosperous Americans expressed when they thought it admirable to save their cherished intellectual traditions in any such fashion.

Other conservatives Miro saw to be abandoning the line of opposition to science, only to fall back on the line of a defensive against "pseudo-science," as they seemed to call whatever intellectual interests had not yet become indubitably reputable. It was a line which would hold them rather strongly for a time, Miro thought, because so many of the cultural revolutionists agreed with them in hating some of these arrogant and mechanical psychologies and sociologies that reduced life to figures or organisms. But Miro felt also how obstructive was their fight. If the "classics" had done little for him except to hold his mind in an uncomprehending prison, and fetter his spontaneous taste, they seemed to have done little more for even the thorough scholars. When professors had devoted scholarly lives to the "classics" only to exhibit in their own polemics none of the urbanity and intellectual command which were supposed by the believer somehow to rub off automatically on the faithful student, Miro had to conclude an absence of causal connection between the "classics" and the able modern mind. When, moreover, critical power or creative literary work became almost extinct among these defenders of the "old education," Miro felt sure that a revolution was needed in the materials and attitudes of "culture."

The case of the defenders was all the weaker because their enemies were not wanton infidels, ignorant of the holy places they profaned. They were rather cultural "Modernists," reforming the church from within. They had the classic background, these young vandals, but they had escaped from its flat and unoriented surface. Abreast of the newer objective, impersonal standards of thinking, they saw the weakness of these archaic minds which could only appeal to vested interests in culture and testimonials from successful men.

The older critics had long since disavowed the intention of discriminating among current writers. These men, who had to have an Academy to protect them, lumped the younger writers of verse and prose together as "anarchic" and "naturalistic," and had become, in these latter days, merely peevish and querulous, protesting in favor of standards that no longer represented our best values. Every one, in Miro's time, bemoaned the lack of critics, but the older critics seemed to have lost all sense of hospitality and to have become tired and a little spitefully disconsolate, while the newer ones were too intent on their crusades against puritanism and philistinism to have time for a constructive pointing of the way.

Miro had a very real sense of standing at the end of an era. He and his friends had lived down both their old orthodoxies of the classics and their new orthodoxies of propaganda. Gone were the priggishness and self-consciousness which had marked their teachers. The new culture would be more personal than the old, but it would not be held as a personal property. It would be democratic in the sense that it would represent each person's honest spontaneous taste. The old attitude was only speciously democratic. The assumption was that if you pressed your material long enough and winningly enough upon your culturable public, they would acquire it. But the material was something handed down, not grown in the garden of their own appreciations. Under these conditions the critic and appreciator became a mere impersonal register of orthodox opinion. The cultivated person, in conforming his judgments to what was authoritatively taught him, was really a member of the herd—a cultivated herd, it is true, but still a herd. It was the mass that spoke through the critic and not his own discrimination. These authoritative judgments might, of course, have come—probably had come—to the herd through discerning critics, but in Miro's time judgment in the schools had petrified. One believed not because one felt the original discernment, but because one was impressed by the weight and reputability of opinion. At least so it seemed to Miro.

Now just as the artists had become tired of conventions and were breaking through into new and personal forms, so Miro saw the younger critics breaking through these cultural conventions. To the elders the result would seem mere anarchy. But Miro's attitude did not want to destroy, it merely wanted to rearrange the materials. He wanted no more secondhand appreciations. No one's cultural store was to include anything that one could not be enthusiastic about. One's acquaintance with the best that had been said and thought should be encouraged—in Miro's ideal school—to follow the lines of one's temperament. Miro, having thrown out the old gods, found them slowly and properly coming back to him. Some would always repel him, others he hoped to understand eventually. But if it took wisdom to write the great books, did it not also take wisdom to understand them? Even the Latin writers he hoped to recover, with the aid of translations. But why bother with Greek when you could get Euripides in the marvelous verse of Gilbert Murray? Miro was willing to believe that no education was complete without at least an inoculation of the virus of the two orthodoxies that he was transcending.

As Miro looked around the American scene, he wondered where the critics were to come from. He saw, on the one hand, Mr. Mencken and Mr. Dreiser, and their friends, going heavily forth to battle with the philistines, glorying in pachydermatous vulgarisms that hurt the polite and cultivated young men of the old school. And he saw these violent critics, in their rage against puritanism, becoming themselves moralists, with the same bigotry and tastelessness as their enemies. No, these would never do. On the other hand, he saw Mr. Stuart P. Sherman, in his youthful if somewhat belated ardor, revolting so conscientiously against the "naturalism" and crude expression of current efforts that, in his defense of belles-lettres, of the fine tradition of literary art, he himself became a moralist of the intensest brand, and as critic plumped for Arnold Bennett, because that clever man had a feeling for the proprieties of human conduct. No, Mr. Sherman would do even less adequately. His fine sympathies were as much out of the current as was the specious classicism of Professor Shorey. He would have to look for the critics among the young men who had an abounding sense of life, as well as a feeling for literary form. They would be men who had not been content to live on their cultural inheritance, but had gone out into the modern world and amassed a fresh fortune of their own. They would be men who were not squeamish, who did not feel the delicate differences between "animal" and "human" conduct, who were enthusiastic about Mark Twain and Gorki as well as Romain Rolland, and at the same time were thrilled by Copeau's theater.

Where was a better program for culture, for any kind of literary art? Culture as a living effort, a driving attempt both at sincere expression and at the comprehension of sincere expression wherever it was found! Appreciation to be as far removed from the "I know what I like!" as from the textbook impeccability of taste! If each mind sought its own along these lines, would not many find themselves agreed? Miro insisted on liking Amy Lowell's attempt to outline the tendencies in American poetry in a form which made clear the struggles of contemporary men and women with the tradition and against "every affectation of the mind." He began to see in the new class-consciousness of poets the ending of that old division which "culture" made between the chosen people and the gentiles. We were now to form little pools of workers and appreciators of similar temperaments and tastes. The little magazines that were starting up became voices for these new communities of sentiment. Miro throught that perhaps at first it was right to adopt a tentative superciliousness towards the rest of the world, so that both Mr. Mencken with his shudders at the vulgar Demos and Mr. Sherman with his obsession with the sanely and wholesomely American might be shut out from influence. Instead of fighting the Philistine in the name of freedom, or fighting the vulgar iconoclast in the name of wholesome human notions, it might be better to write for one's own band of comprehenders, in order that one might have something genuine with which to appeal to both the mob of the "bourgeois" and the ferocious vandals who had been dividing the field among them. Far better a quarrel among these intensely self-conscious groups than the issues that had filled *The Atlantic* and *The Nation* with their dreary obsolescence. Far better for the mind that aspired towards "culture" to be told not to conform or worship, but to search out its group, its own temperamental community of sentiment, and there deepen appreciations through sympathetic contact.

It was no longer a question of being hospitable towards the work of other countries. Miro found the whole world open to him, in these days, through the enterprise of publishers. He and his friends felt more sympathetic with certain groups in France and Russia than they did with the variegated "prominent authors" of their own land. Winston Churchill as a novelist came to seem more of an alien than Artzybashev. The fact of culture being international had been followed by a sense of its being. The old cultural attitude had been hospitable enough, but it had imported its alien culture in the form of "comparative literature." It was hospitable only in trying to mold its own taste to the orthodox canons abroad. The older American critic was mostly interested in getting the proper rank and reverence for what he borrowed. The new critic will take what suits his community of sentiment. He will want to link up not with the foreign canon, but with that group which is nearest in spirit with the effort he and his friends are making. The American has to work to interpret and portray the life he knows. He cannot be international in the sense that anything but the life in which he is saturated, with its questions and its colors, can be the material for his art. But he can be international—and must be—in the sense that he works with a certain hopeful vision of a "young world," and with certain ideal values upon which the younger men, stained and revolted by war, in all countries are agreeing.

Miro wonders sometimes whether the direction in which he is tending will not bring him around the circle again to a new classicism. The last stage in the history of the man of culture will be that "classic" which he did not understand and which his mind spent its youth in overthrowing. But it will be a classicism far different from that which was so unintelligently handed down to him in the American world. It will be something worked out and lived into. Looking into the future he will have to do what Van Wyck Brooks calls "inventing a usable past." Finding little in the American tradition that is not tainted with sweetness and light and burdened with the terrible patronage of bourgeois society, the new classicist will yet rescue Thoreau and Whitman and Mark Twain and try to tap through them a certain eternal human tradition of abounding vitality and moral freedom, and so build out the future. If the classic means power with restraint, vitality with harmony, a fusion of intellect and feeling, and a keen sense of the artistic conscience, then the revolutionary world is coming out into the classic. When Miro sees behind the minds of *The Masses* group a desire for form and for expressive beauty, and sees the radicals following Jacques Copeau and reading Chekhov, he smiles at the thought of the American critics, young and old, who do not know yet that they are dead.

27

H. L. Mencken: PURITANISM AS A LITERARY FORCE [1917]

"Calvinism," says Dr. Leon Kellner, in his excellent little history of American literature,● "is the natural theology of the disinherited; it never flourished, therefore, anywhere as it did in the barren hills of Scotland and in the wilds of North America." The learned doctor is here speaking of theology in what may be called its narrow technical sense—that is, as a theory of God. Under Calvinism, in the New World as well as in the Old, it became no more than a luxuriant demonology; even God himself was transformed into a superior sort of devil, ever wary and wholly merciless. That primitive demonology still survives in the barbaric doctrines of the Methodists and Baptists, particularly in the South; but it has been ameliorated, even there, by a growing sense of the divine grace, and so the old God of Plymouth Rock, as practically conceived, is now scarcely worse than the average jail warden or Italian padrone. On the ethical side, however, Calvinism is dying a much harder death, and we are still a long way from the enlightenment. Save where Continental influences have

● *American Literature, tr. by Julia Franklin; New York, Doubleday, Page & Co., 1915.*

measurably corrupted the Puritan idea—e.g., in such cities as New York, San Francisco and New Orleans—the prevailing American view of the world and its mysteries is still a moral one, and no other human concern gets half of the attention that is endlessly lavished upon the problem of conduct, particularly of the other fellow. It needed no official announcement to define the function and office of the republic as that of an international expert in morals, and the mentor and exemplar of the more backward nations. Within, as well as without, the eternal rapping of knuckles and proclaiming of new austerities goes on. The American, save in moments of conscious and swiftly lamented deviltry, casts up all ponderable values, including even the values of beauty, in terms of right and wrong. He is beyond all things else, a judge and a policeman; he believes firmly that there is a mysterious power in law; he supports and embellishes its operation with a fanatical vigilance.

Naturally enough, this moral obsession has given a strong color to American literature. In truth, it has colored it so brilliantly that American literature is set off sharply from all other literatures. In none other will you find so wholesale and ecstatic a sacrifice of aesthetic ideas, of all the fine gusto of passion and beauty, to notions of what is meet, proper and nice. From the books of grisly sermons that were the first American contribution to letters down to that amazing literature of "inspiration" which now flowers so prodigiously, with two literary ex-Presidents among its chief virtuosi, one observes no relaxation of the moral pressure. In the history of every other literature there have been periods of what might be called moral innocence—periods in which a naive *joie de vivre* has broken through all concepts of duty and responsibility, and the wonder and glory of the universe have been hymned with unashamed zest. The age of Shakespeare comes to mind at once: the violence of the Puritan reaction offers a measure of the pendulum's wild swing. But in America no such general rising of the blood has ever been seen. The literature of the nation, even the literature of the enlightened minority, has been under harsh Puritan restraints from the beginning, and despite a few stealthy efforts at revolt—usually quite without artistic value or even common honesty, as in the case of the cheap fiction magazines and that of smutty plays on Broadway, and always very short-lived—it shows not the slightest sign of emancipating itself today. The American, try as he will, can never imagine any work of the imagination as wholly devoid of moral content. It must either tend toward the promotion of virtue, or be suspect and abominable.

If any doubt of this is in your mind, turn to the critical articles in the newspapers and literary weeklies; you will encounter enough proofs in a month's explorations to convince you forever. A novel or a play is judged among us, not by its dignity of conception, its artistic honesty, its perfection of workmanship, but almost entirely by its orthodoxy of doctrine, its platitudinousness, its usefulness as a moral tract. A digest of the reviews of such a book as David Graham Phillips' *Susan Lenox* or of such a play as Ibsen's *Hedda Gabler* would make astounding reading for a Continental European. Not only the childish incompetents who write for the daily press, but also most of our critics of experience and reputation, seem quite unable to estimate a piece of writing as a piece of writing, a work of art as a work of art; they almost inevitably drag in irrelevant gabble as to whether this or that personage in it is respectable, or this or that situation in accordance with the national notions of what is edifying and nice. Fully nine-tenths of the reviews of Dreiser's *The Titan*, without question the best American novel of its year, were devoted chiefly to indigent denunciations of the morals of Frank Cowperwood, its central character. That the man was superbly imagined and magnificently depicted, that he stood out from the book in all the flashing vigor of life, that his creation was an artistic achievement of a very high and difficult order—these facts seem to have made no impression upon the reviewers whatever. They were Puritans writing for Puritans, and all they could see in Cowperwood was an anti-Puritan, and in his creator another. It will remain for Europeans, I daresay, to discover the true stature of *The Titan*, as it remained for Europeans to discover the true stature of *Sister Carrie*.

Just how deeply this corrective knife has cut you may find plainly displayed in Dr. Kellner's little book. He sees the throttling influence of an ever alert and bellicose Puritanism, not only in our grand literature, but also in our petit literature, our minor poetry, even in our humor. The Puritan's utter lack of aesthetic sense, his distrust of all romantic emotion, his unmatchable intolerance of opposition, his unbreakable belief in his own bleak and narrow views, his savage cruelty of attack, his lust for relentless and barbarous persecution— these things have put an almost unbearable burden upon the exchange of ideas in the United States, and particularly upon that form of it which involves playing with them for the mere game's sake. On the one hand, the writer who would deal seriously and honestly with the larger problems of life, particularly in the rigidly partitioned ethical field, is restrained by laws that would have kept a Balzac or a Zola in prison from year's end to year's end; and on the other hand the writer who would proceed against the reigning superstitions by mockery has been silenced by taboos that are quite as stringent, and by an indifference that is even worse. For all our professed delight in and capacity for jocosity, we have produced so far but one genuine wit—Ambrose Bierce—and, save to a small circle, he remains unknown today. Our great humorists, including even Mark Twain, have had to take protective coloration, whether willingly or unwillingly, from the prevailing ethical foliage, and so one finds them leveling their darts, not at the stupidities of the Puritan majority, but at the evidence of lessening stupidity in the anti-Puritan minority. In other words, they have done battle, not against, but *for* Philistinism —and Philistinism is no more than another name for Puritanism. Both wage a ceaseless warfare upon beauty in its every form, from painting to religious ritual, and from the drama to the dance—the first because it holds beauty to be a mean and stupid thing, and the second because it holds beauty to be distracting and corrupting.

Mark Twain, without question, was a great artist; there was in him something of that prodigality of imagination, that aloof engrossment in the human comedy, that penetrating cynicism, which one associates with the great artists of the Renaissance. But his nationality hung around his neck like a millstone; he could never throw off his native Philistinism. One ploughs through *The Innocents Abroad* and through parts of *A Tramp Abroad* with incredulous amazement. Is such coarse and ignorant clowning to be accepted as humor, as great humor, as the best humor that the most humorous of peoples has produced? Is it really the mark of a smart fellow to lift a peasant's cackle over *Lohengrin?* Is Titian's chromo of Moses in the bulrushes seriously to be regarded as the noblest picture in Europe? Is there nothing in Latin Christianity, after all, save petty grafting, monastic scandals and the worship of the knuckles and shinbones of dubious saints? May not a civilized man, disbelieving in it, still find himself profoundly moved by its dazzling history, the lingering remnants of its old magnificence, the charm of its gorgeous and melancholy loveliness? In the presence of all beauty of man's creation—in brief, of what we roughly call art, whatever its form—the voice of Mark Twain was the voice of the Philistine. A literary artist of very high rank himself, with instinctive gifts that lifted him, in *Huckleberry Finn* to kinship with Cervantes and Aristophanes, he was yet so far the victim of his nationality that he seems to have had no capacity for distinguishing between the good and the bad in the work of other men of his own craft. The literary criticism that one occasionally finds in his writings is chiefly trivial and ignorant; his private inclination appears to have been toward such romantic sentimentality as entrances schoolboys; the thing that interested him in Shakespeare was not the man's colossal genius but the absurd theory that Bacon wrote his plays. Had he been born in France (the country of his chief abomination!) instead of in a Puritan village of the American hinterland, I venture that he would have conquered the world. But try as he would, being what he was, he could not get rid of the Puritan smugness and cocksureness, the Puritan distrust of new ideas, the Puritan incapacity for seeing beauty as a thing in itself, and the full peer of the true and the good.

It is, indeed, precisely in the works of such men as Mark Twain that one finds the best proofs of the Puritan influence in American letters, for it is there that it is least expected and hence most significant. Our native critics, unanimously Puritans themselves, are anaesthetic to the flavor, but to Dr. Kellner, with his half-European, half-Oriental culture, it is always distinctly perceptible. He senses it, not only in the harsh Calvinistic fables of Hawthorne and the pious gurglings of Longfellow, but also in the poetry of Bryant, the tea-party niceness of Howells, the "maiden-like reserve" of James Lane Allen, and even in the work of Joel Chandler Harris. What! A Southern Puritan? Well, why not? What could be more erroneous than the common assumption that Puritanism is exclusively a Northern, a New England, madness? The truth is that it is as thoroughly national as the kindred belief in the devil, and runs almost unobstructed from Portland to Portland and from the Lakes to the Gulf. It is in the South, indeed, and not in the North, that it takes on its most bellicose and extravagant form. Between the upper tier of New England and the Potomac River there is not a single prohibition state —but thereafter, alas, they come in huge blocks! And behind that infinitely prosperous Puritanism there is a long and unbroken tradition. Berkeley, the last of the Cavaliers, was kicked out of power in Virginia so long ago as 1650. Lord Baltimore, the Proprietor of Maryland, was brought to terms by the Puritans of the Severn in 1657. The Scotch Covenanter, the most uncompromising and unenlightened of all Puritans, flourished in the Carolinas from the start, and in 1698, or thereabout, he was reinforced from New England. In 1757 a band of Puritans invaded what is now Georgia—and Georgia has been a Puritan barbarism ever since. Even while the early (and half-mythical) Cavaliers were still in nominal control of all these Southern plantations, they clung to the sea-coast. The population that moved down the chain of the Appalachians during the latter part of the eighteenth century, and then swept over them into the Mississippi valley, was composed almost entirely of Puritans— chiefly intransigeants from New England (where Unitarianism was getting on its legs), kirk-crazy Scotch, and that plupious and beauty-hating folk, the Scotch-Irish. "In the South today," said John Fiske a generation ago, "there is more Puritanism surviving than in New

England." In that whole region, an area three times as large as France or Germany, there is not a single orchestra capable of playing Beethoven's C minor symphony, or a single painting worth looking at, or a single public building or monument of any genuine distinction, or a single factory devoted to the making of beautiful things, or a single poet, novelist, historian, musician, painter or sculptor whose reputation extends beyond his own country. Between the Mason and Dixon line and the mouth of the Mississippi there is but one opera house, and that one was built by a Frenchman, and is now, I believe, closed. The only domestic art this huge and opulent empire knows is in the hands of Mexican greasers; its only native music it owes to the despised Negro; its only genuine poet was permitted to die up an alley like a stray dog.

II

In studying the anatomy and physiology of American Puritanism, and its effects upon the national literature, one quickly discerns two main streams of influence. On the one hand, there is the influence of the original Puritans—whether of New England or of the South— who came to the New World with a ready-made philosophy of the utmost clarity, positiveness and inclusiveness of scope, and who attained to such a position of political and intellectual leadership that they were able to force it almost unchanged upon the whole population, and to endow it with such vitality that it successfully resisted alien opposition later on. And on the other hand, one sees a complex of social and economic conditions which worked in countless irresistible ways against the rise of that dionysian spirit, that joyful acquiescence in life, that philosophy of the *Ja-sager,* which offers to Puritanism, today as in times past, its chief and perhaps only effective antagonism. In other words, the American of the days since the Revolution has had Puritanism diligently pressed upon him from without, and at the same time he has led, in the main, a life that has engendered a chronic hospitality to it, or at all events to its salient principles, within.

Dr. Kellner accurately describes the process whereby the aesthetic spirit, and its concomitant spirit of joy, were squeezed out of the original New Englanders, so that no trace of it showed in their literature, or even in their lives, for a century and a half after the first settlements. "Absorption in God," he says, "seems incompatible with the presentation (i.e., aesthetically) of mankind. The God of the Puritans was in this respect a jealous God who brooked no sort of creative rivalry. The inspired moments of the loftiest souls were filled with the thought of God and His designs; spiritual life was wholly dominated by solicitude regarding salvation, the hereafter, grace; how could such petty concerns as personal experience of a lyric nature, the transports or the pangs of love, find utterance? What did a lyric occurrence like the first call of the cuckoo, elsewhere so welcome, or the first sight of the snowdrop, signify compared with the last Sunday's sermon and the new interpretation of the old riddle of evil in the world? And apart from the fact that everything of a personal nature must have appeared so trivial, all the sources of secular lyric poetry were offensive and impious to Puritan theology. . . . One thing is an established fact: up to the close of the eighteenth century America had no belletristic literature."

This Puritan bedevilment by the idea of personal sin, this reign of the God-crazy, gave way in later years, as we shall see, to other and somewhat milder forms of pious enthusiasm. At the time of the Revolution, indeed, the importation of French political ideas was accompanied by an importation of French theological ideas, and such men as Franklin and Jefferson dallied with what, in those days at least, was regarded as downright atheism. Even in New England this influence made itself felt; there was a gradual letting down of Calvinism to the softness of Unitarianism, and that change was presently to flower in the vague temporizing of Transcendentalism. But as Puritanism, in the strict sense, declined in virulence and took deceptive new forms, there was a compensating growth of its brother, Philistinism, and by the first quarter of the nineteenth century, the distrust of beauty, and of the joy that is its object, was as firmly established throughout the land as it had ever been in New England. The original Puritans had at least been men of a certain education, and even of a certain austere culture. They were inordinately hostile to beauty in all its forms, but one somehow suspects that much of their hostility was due to a sense of their weakness before it, a realization of its disarming psychical pull. But the American of the new republic was of a different kidney. He was not so much hostile to beauty as devoid of any consciousness of it; he stood as unmoved before its phenomena as a savage before a table of logarithms. What he had set up on this continent, in brief, was a commonwealth of peasants and small traders, a paradise of the third-rate, and its national philosophy, almost wholly unchecked by the more sophisticated and civilized ideas of an aristocracy, was precisely the philosophy that one finds among peasants and small traders at all times and everywhere. The difference between the United States and any other nation did not lie in any essential difference between American peasants and other peasants, but simply in the fact that here, alone, the voice of the peasant was the single voice of the nation—that here, alone, the only way to eminence and public influence was the way of acquiescence in the opinions and prejudices of the untutored and Philistine mob. Jackson was the *Stammvater* of the new statesmen and philosophers; he carried the mob's distrust of good taste even into the field of conduct; he was the first to put rewards of conformity above the dictates of common decency; he founded a whole hierarchy of Philistine messiahs, the roaring of which still belabors the ear.

Once established, this culture of the intellectually disinherited tended to defend and perpetuate itself. On the one hand, there was no appearance of a challenge from within, for the exigent problems of existence in a country that was yet but half settled and organized left its people with no energy for questioning what at least satisfied their gross needs, and so met the pragmatic test. And on the other hand, there was no critical pressure from without, for the English culture which alone reached over the sea was itself entering upon its Victorian decline, and the influence of the native aristocracy—the degenerating *Junkers* of the great estates and the boorish magnates of the city *bourgeoisie*—was quite without any cultural direction at all. The chief concern of the American people, even above the bread-and-butter question, was politics. They were incessantly hag-ridden by political difficulties, both internal and external, of an inordinate complexity, and these occupied all the leisure they could steal from the sordid work of everyday. More, their new and troubled political ideas tended to absorb all the rancorous certainty of their fading religious ideas, so that devotion to a theory or a candidate became translated into devotion to a revelation, and the game of politics turned itself into a holy war. The custom of connecting purely political doctrines with pietistic concepts of an inflammable nature, then firmly set up by skillful persuaders of the mob, has never quite died out in the United States. There has not been a presidential contest since Jackson's day without its Armageddons, its marching of Christian soldiers, its crosses of gold, its crowns of thorns. The most successful American politicians, beginning with the antislavery agitators, have been those most adept at twisting the ancient gauds and shibboleths of Puritanism to partisan uses. Every campaign that we have seen for eighty years has been, on each side, a pursuit of bugaboos, a denunciation of heresies, a snouting up of immoralities.

But it was during the long contest against slavery, beginning with the appearance of William Lloyd Garrison's *Liberator* in 1831 and ending at Appomattox, that this gigantic supernaturalization of politics reached its most astounding heights. In those days, indeed, politics and religion coalesced in a manner not seen in the world since the Middle Ages, and the combined pull of the two was so powerful that none could quite resist it. All men of any ability and ambition turned to political activity for self-expression. It engaged the press to the exclusion of everything else; it conquered the pulpit; it even laid its hand upon industry and trade. Drawing the best imaginative talent into its service—Jefferson and Lincoln may well stand as examples —it left the cultivation of belles-lettres, and of all the other arts no less, to women and admittedly second-rate men. And when, breaking through this taboo, some chance first-rate man gave himself over to purely aesthetic expression, his reward was not only neglect, but even a sort of ignominy, as if such enterprises were not fitting for males with hair on their chests. I need not point to Poe and Whitman, both disdained as dreamers and wasters, and both proceeded against with the utmost rigors of outraged Philistinism.

In brief, the literature of that whole period, as Algernon Tassin shows in *The Magazine in America,*• was almost completely disassociated from life as men were then living it. Save one counts in such crude politico-puritan tracts as *Uncle Tom's Cabin,* it is difficult to find a single contemporaneous work that interprets the culture of the time, or even accurately represents it. Later on, it found historians and anatomists, and in one work, at least, to wit, *Huckleberry Finn,* it was studied and projected with the highest art, but no such impulse to make imaginative use of it showed itself contemporaneously, and there was not even the crude sentimentalization of here and now that one finds in the popular novels of today. Fenimore Cooper filled his romances, not with the people about him, but with the Indians beyond the sky line, and made them half-fabulous to boot. Irving told fairy tales about the forgotten Knickerbockers; Hawthorne turned backward to the Puritans of Plymouth Rock; Longfellow to the Acadians and the prehistoric Indians; Emerson took flight from earth altogether; even Poe sought refuge in a land of fantasy. It was only the frank second-raters—e.g., Whittier and Lowell—who ventured to turn to the life around them, and the banality of the result is a sufficient indication of the crudeness of the current taste, and the mean position assigned to the art of letters. This was pre-eminently the era of the moral tale, the Sunday-school book. Literature was conceived, not as a thing in itself, but merely as a handmaiden to politics or religion. The great celebrity of Emerson in New England

• *New York, Dodd, Mead & Co., 1916.*

was not the celebrity of a literary artist, but that of a theologian and metaphysician; he was esteemed in much the same way that Jonathan Edwards had been esteemed. Even down to our own time, indeed, his vague and empty philosophizing has been put above his undeniable capacity for graceful utterance, and it remained for Dr. Kellner to consider him purely as a literary artist, and to give him due praise for his skill.

The Civil War brought that era of sterility to an end. As I shall show later on, the shock of it completely reorganized the American scheme of things, and even made certain important changes in the national Puritanism, or, at all events, in its machinery. Whitman, whose career straddled, so to speak, the four years of the war, was the leader—and for a long while, the only trooper—of a double revolt. On the one hand he offered a courageous challenge to the intolerable prudishness and dirty-mindedness of Puritanism, and on the other hand he boldly sought the themes and even the modes of expression of his poetry in the arduous, contentious and highly melodramatic life that lay all about him. Whitman, however, was clearly before his time. His countrymen could see him only as immoralist; save for a pitiful few of them, they were dead to any understanding the manner of Randall's "Maryland, My Maryland."

In the seventies and eighties, with the appearance of such men as Henry James, William Dean Howells, Mark Twain and Bret Harte, of his stature as artist, and even unaware that such a category of men existed. He was put down as an invader of the public decencies, a disturber of the public peace; even his eloquent war poems, surely the best of all his work, were insufficient to get him a hearing; the sentimental rubbish of "The Blue and the Gray" and the ecstatic supernaturalism of "The Battle Hymn of the Republic" were far more to the public taste. Where Whitman failed, indeed, all subsequent explorers of the same field have failed with him, and the great war has left no more mark upon American letters than if it had never been fought. Nothing remotely approaching the bulk and beam of Tolstoy's *War and Peace,* or, to descend to a smaller scale, Zola's *The Attack on the Mill,* has come out of it. Its appeal to the national imagination was undoubtedly of the most profound character; it colored politics for fifty years, and is today a dominating influence in the thought of whole sections of the American people. But in all that stirring up there was no upheaval of artistic consciousness, for the plain reason that there was no artistic consciousness there to heave up, and all we have in the way of Civil War literature is a few conventional melodramas, a few half-forgotten short stories by Ambrose Bierce and Stephen Crane, and a half dozen idiotic popular songs in a better day seemed to be dawning. Here, after a full century of infantile romanticizing, were four writers who at least deserved respectful consideration as literary artists, and what is more, three of them turned from the conventionalized themes of the past to the teeming and colorful life that lay under their noses. But this promise of better things was soon found to be no more than a promise. Mark Twain, after *The Gilded Age,* slipped back into romanticism tempered by Philistinism, and was presently in the era before the Civil War, and finally in the Middle Ages, and even beyond. Harte, a brilliant technician, had displayed his whole stock when he had displayed his technique: his stories were not even superficially true to the life they presumed to depict; one searched them in vain for an interpretation of it; they were simply idle tales. As for Howells and James, both quickly showed that timorousness and reticence which are the distinguishing marks of the Puritan, even in his most intellectual incarnations. The American scene that they depicted with such meticulous care was chiefly peopled with marionettes. They shrunk, characteristically, from those larger, harsher clashes of will and purpose which one finds in all truly first-rate literature. In particular, they shrunk from any interpretation of life which grounded itself upon an acknowledgment of its inexorable and inexplicable tragedy. In the vast combat of instincts and aspirations about them they saw only a feeble jousting of comedians, unserious and insignificant. Of the great questions that have agitated the minds of men in Howells' time one gets no more than a faint and faraway echo in his novels. His investigations, one may say, are carried on *in vacuo;* his discoveries are not expressed in terms of passion, but in terms of giggles.

In the followers of Howells and James one finds little save an empty imitation of their emptiness, a somewhat puerile parodying of their highly artful but essentially personal technique. To wade through the books of such characteristic American fictioneers as Frances Hodgson Burnett, Mary E. Wilkins Freeman, F. Hopkinson Smith, Alice Brown, James Lane Allen, Winston Churchill, Ellen Glasgow, Gertrude Atherton and Sarah Orne Jewett is to undergo an experience that is almost terrible. The flow of words is completely purged of ideas; in place of them one finds no more than a romantic restatement of all the old platitudes and formulas. To call such an emission of graceful poppycock a literature, of course, is to mouth an absurdity, and yet, if the college professors who write treatises on letters are to be believed, it is the best we have to show. Turn, for example, to *A History of American Literature Since 1870,* by Prof. Fred Lewis Pattee, one of the latest and undoubtedly one of the least unintelligent of these books. In it the gifted pedagogue gives extended notice to no less than six of the nine writers I have mentioned, and upon all of them his verdicts are flattering. He bestows high praises, direct and indirect, upon Mrs. Freeman's "grim and austere" manner, her "repression," her entire lack of poetical illumination. He compares Miss Jewett to both Howells and Hawthorne, not to mention Mrs. Gaskell—and Addison! He grows enthusiastic over a hollow piece of fine writing by Miss Brown. And he forgets altogether to mention Dreiser, or Sinclair, or Medill Patterson, or Harry Leon Wilson, or George Ade! . . .

So much for the best. The worst is beyond description. France has her Brieux and her Henry Bordeaux; Germany has her Mühlbach, her stars of the *Gartenlaube;* England contributes Caine, Corelli, Oppenheim and company. But it is in our country alone that banality in letters takes on the proportions of a national movement; it is only here that a work of the imagination is habitually judged by its sheer emptiness of ideas, its fundamental platitudinousness, its correspondence with the imbecility of mob thinking; it is only here that "glad" books run up sales of hundreds of thousands. Richard Harding Davis, with his ideals of a floorwalker; Gene Stratton Porter, with her snuffling sentimentality; Robert W. Chambers, with his "society" romances for shopgirls; Irvin Cobb, with his labored, *Ayers' Almanac* jocosity; the authors of the *Saturday Evening Post* school, with their heroic drummers and stockbrokers, their ecstatic celebration of the stupid, the sordid, the ignoble—these, after all, are our typical *literati.* The Puritan fear of ideas is the master of them all. Some of them, in truth, most of them, have undeniable talent; in a more favorable environment not a few of them might be doing sound work. But they see how small the ring is, and they make their tricks small to fit it. Not many of them ever venture a leg outside. The lash of the ringmaster is swift, and it stings damnably. . . .

I say not many; I surely do not mean none at all. As a matter of fact, there have been intermittent rebellions against the prevailing pecksniffery and sentimentality ever since the days of Irving and Hawthorne. Poe led one of them—as critic more than as creative artist. His scathing attacks upon the Gerald Stanley Lees, the Hamilton Wright Mabies and the George E. Woodberrys of his time keep a liveliness and appositeness that the years have not staled; his criticism deserves to be better remembered. Poe sensed the Philistine pull of a Puritan civilization as none had before him, and combated it with his whole artillery of rhetoric. Another rebel, of course, was Whitman; how he came to grief is too well known to need recalling. What is less familiar is the fact that both the *Atlantic Monthly* and the *Century* (first called *Scribner's*) were set up by men in revolt against the reign of mush, as *Putnam's* and the *Dial* had been before them. The salutatory of the *Dial,* dated 1840, stated the case against the national mugginess clearly. The aim of the magazine, it said, was to oppose "that rigor of our conventions of religion and education which is turning us to stone" and to give expression to "new views and the dreams of youth." Alas, for these brave *révoltés! Putnam's* succumbed to the circumambient rigors and duly turned to stone, and is now no more. The *Atlantic,* once so heretical, has become as respectable as the New York *Evening Post.* As for the *Dial,* it was until lately the very pope of orthodoxy and jealously guarded the college professors who read it from the pollution of ideas. Only the *Century* has kept the faith unbrokenly. It is, indeed, the one first-class American magazine that has always welcomed newcomers, and that maintains an intelligent contact with the literature that is in being, and that consistently tries to make the best terms possible with the dominant Philistinism. It cannot go the whole way without running into danger; let it be said to the credit of its editors that they have more than once braved that danger.

The tale might be lengthened. Mark Twain, in his day, felt the stirrings of revolt, and not all his Philistinism was sufficient to hold him altogether in check. If you want to find out about the struggle that went on within him, read the biography by Albert Bigelow Paine, or, better still, *The Mysterious Stranger* and *What is Man?* Alive, he had his position to consider; dead, he now speaks out. In the preface to *What is Man?* dated 1905, there is a curious confession of his incapacity for defying the taboos which surrounded him. The studies for the book, he says, were begun "twenty-five or twenty-seven years ago"—the period of *A Tramp Abroad* and *The Prince and the Pauper.* It was actually written "seven years ago"—that is, just after *Following the Equator* and *Personal Recollections of Joan of Arc.* And why did it lie so long in manuscript, and finally go out stealthily, under a private imprint?• Simply because, as Mark frankly confesses, he "dreaded (*and could not bear*) the disapproval of the people around" him. He knew how hard his fight for recognition had been; he knew what direful penalties outraged orthodoxy could inflict; he had in him the somewhat pathetic discretion of a respectable family man. But, dead, he is safely beyond reprisal, and so, after a prudent interval, the faithful Paine begins printing books in which, writing knowingly behind six feet of earth, he could set down his true ideas without fear.

• *The first edition for public sale did not appear until June, 1917, and in it the preface was suppressed.*

Some day, perhaps, we shall have his microbe story, and maybe even his picture of the court of Elizabeth.

A sneer in Prof. Pattee's history, before mentioned, recalls the fact that Hamlin Garland was also a rebel in his day and bawled for the Truth with a capital T. That was in 1893. Two years later the guardians of the national rectitude fell afoul of *Rose of Dutchers' Coolly* and Garland began to think it over; today he devotes himself to the safer enterprise of chasing spooks; his name is conspicuously absent from the Dreiser Protest. Nine years before his brief offending John Hay had set off a discreet bomb in *The Bread-Winners*—anonymously because "my standing would be seriously compromised" by an avowal. Six years later Frank Norris shook up the Phelpses and Mores of the time with *McTeague*. Since then there have been assaults timorous and assaults headlong—by Bierce, by Dreiser, by Phillips, by Fuller—by Mary MacLanes and by Upton Sinclairs—by ploughboy poets from the Middle West and by jitney geniuses in Greenwich Village—assaults gradually tapering off to a mere sophomoric brashness and deviltry. And all of them like snowballings of Verdun. All of them petered out and ineffectual. The normal, the typical American book of today is as fully a remouthing of old husks as the normal book of Griswold's day. The whole atmosphere of our literature, in William James's phrase, is "mawkish and dishwatery." Books are still judged among us, not by their form and organization as works of art, their accuracy and vividness as representations of life, their validity and perspicacity as interpretations of it, but by their conformity to the national prejudices, their accordance with set standards of niceness and propriety. The thing irrevocably demanded is a "sane" book; the ideal is a "clean," an "inspiring," a "glad" book. . . .

28

H. L. Mencken: SKETCHES IN CRITICISM:
CREDO [1913]

I believe that *Huckleberry Finn* is one of the great masterpieces of
the world, that it is the full equal of *Don Quixote* and *Robinson
Crusoe,* that it is vastly better than *Gil Blas, Tristam Shandy, Nicholas
Nickleby* or *Tom Jones.* I believe that it will be read by human
beings of all ages, not as a solemn duty but for the honest love of
it, and over and over again, long after every book written in America
between the years 1800 and 1860, with perhaps three exceptions,
has disappeared entirely save as a classroom fossil. I believe that
Mark Twain had a clearer vision of life, that he came nearer to its
elementals and was less deceived by its false appearances, than any
other American who has ever presumed to manufacture generalizations. I believe that, admitting all his defects, he wrote better English,
in the sense of cleaner, straighter, vivider, saner English, than either
Irving or Hawthorne. I believe that four of his books—*Huck, Life
on the Mississippi, Captain Stormfield's Visit to Heaven,* and *A
Connecticut Yankee*—are alone worth more, as works of art and as
criticisms of life, than the whole output of Cooper, Irving, Holmes,
Mitchell, Stedman, Whittier and Bryant. I believe that he ranks well
above Whitman and certainly not below Poe. I believe that he was

the true father of our national literature, the first genuinely American artist of the blood royal.

THE DEAN [1919]

William Dean Howells, during his lifetime, was almost the national ideal of a literary character: an urbane, cleanly and highly respectable gentleman, a sitter on committees, an intimate of professors and the prophets of movements, a placid conformist. The result was that in his last twenty years his successive books were not criticized, nor even adequately reviewed, but merely fawned over; the critics of the newspapers, male and female, could no more bring themselves to question them than they could question Lincoln's Gettysburg speech, or Paul Elmer More, or their own virginity. The dean of American letters in point of years, and in point of published quantity, and in point of public prominence and influence, he was gradually enveloped in a web of superstitutious reverence, and it still grates somewhat harshly to hear his actual achivement discussed in cold blood.

Nevertheless, all this merited respect for an industrious and inoffensive man is bound, soon or late, to yield to a critical examination of the artist within, and that examination will have its bitter moments for those who naïvely accept the Howells legend. It will show, without doubt, a competent journeyman, a contriver of pretty things, a facile stylist—but it will also show a long row of uninspired and hollow books with no more ideas in them than so many volumes of the *Ladies' Home Journal,* and no more deep and contagious feeling than so many reports of autopsies, and no more glow and gusto than so many tables of prices. The profound dread and agony of life, the surge of passion and aspiration, the grand crash and glitter of things, the tragedy that runs eternally under the surface—all this the critic will seek in vain in Howells's elegant and shallow volumes. And seeking it in vain, he will probably dismiss all of them together with fewer words than he gives to *Huckleberry Finn.*

Already, indeed, the Howells legend tends to become a mere legend, and empty of all genuine significance. Who actually reads the Howells novels? Who even remembers their names? *The Minister's Charge, An Imperative Duty, The Unexpected Guests, Out of the Question, No Love Lost*—these titles are already as meaningless as a roll of Sumerian kings. Perhaps *The Rise of Silas Lapham* survives, at least in the colleges—but go read it if you would tumble downstairs. The truth about Howells is that he really had nothing to say, for all the charm he got into saying it. His psychology was superficial, amateurish, often nonsensical; his irony was scarcely more than a polite facetiousness; his characters simply refused to live. No figure even remotely comparable to Norris's McTeague or Dreiser's Frank Cowperwood is to be encountered in his novels. He was quite unequal to any such evocation of the race-spirit, of the essential conflict of forces among us, of the peculiar drift and color of American life. The world he moved in was suburban, caged, flabby. He could no more have written the last chapters of *Lord Jim* than he could have written the Book of Mark.

As a critic he belonged to a measurably higher level, if only because of his eager curiosity, his gusto for minor novelty. He dealt valiant licks for E. W. Howe, Frank Norris, Edith Wharton and William Vaughn Moody. He brought forward the Russians diligently and persuasively, albeit they left no mark upon his own manner. In his ingratiating way, back in the seventies and eighties, he made war upon some of the worst of the prevailing sentimentalities. But his history as a critic is full of errors and omissions. One finds him loosing a fanfare for W. B. Trites, the Philadelphia Zola, and praising Frank A. Munsey—and one finds him leaving the discovery of all the Shaws, George Moores, Dreisers, Synges and Galsworthys to the Pollards and Hunekers. Busy in the sideshows, he didn't see the elephants go by. . . . Here temperamental defects handicapped him. Turn to his *My Mark Twain* and you will see what I mean. The Mark that is exhibited in this book is a Mark whose Himalayan outlines are discerned but hazily through a pink fog of Howells. There is a moral note in the tale—an obvious effort to palliate, to touch up, to excuse. Poor Mark, of course, was charming, and there was talent in him, but what a weakness he had for thinking aloud—and such shocking thoughts! What oaths in his speech! What awful cigars he smoked! How barbarous his contempt for the strict sonata form! It seems incredible that two men so unlike should have found common denominators for a friendship lasting forty-four years. The one derived from Rabelais, Chaucer, the Elizabethans and Benvenuto—buccaneers of the literary high seas, loud laughters, lawbreakers, giants of a lordlier day; the other came down from Jane Austen, Washington Irving and Hannah More. The one wrote English as Michelangelo hacked marble, broadly, brutally, magnificently; the other was a maker of pretty waxen groups. The one was utterly unconscious of the way he achieved his staggering effects; the other was the most toilsome, fastidious and self-conscious of craftsmen. . . .

What remains of Howells is his style. He invented a new harmony of "the old, old words." He destroyed the Johnsonian periods of the Poe tradition, and erected upon the ruins a complex and savory carelessness, full of soft naïvetés that were sophisticated to the last degree. Like Mark, but in a diametrically different way, he loosened the tightness of English, and let a blast of air into it. He achieved, for all his triviality, for all his narrowness of vision, a pungent and often admirable style.

STEPHEN CRANE [1924]

Next to Poe and Walt Whitman, Crane seems destined to go down into history as the most romantic American author of the nineteenth century. Even while he lived legend was busy with him. He was, by one story, a young man of mysterious and probably aristocratic origin, the scion of a Junker family in decay. He was, by another, a practitioner of strange, levantine vices—an opium smoker, a devotee of hashish. He was, by a third, the heaviest drinker known to vital statistics since Daniel Webster. He was, by a fourth, a consorter with harlots and the lover of Sarah Bernhardt. He was, by a fifth, sixth, seventh and eighth, the worst dead beat in New York.

All these yarns were fictions. Crane was actually the son of a respectable burgher in New Jersey and his mother was a member of the Methodist Church. If he drank somewhat freely when he was in funds, then so did all the other newspaper reporters of his era. If he borrowed money when he was out of a job, then ditto. If he took drugs, it was only to relieve his frequent and distressing infirmities, of which the last was the tuberculosis pulmonalis which took him off. As for his offenses against sex hygiene, they were chiefly imaginary. All through his youth he was romantically in love with a lady visibly his senior, and before he was much beyond twenty-five he married another lady still more his senior. In brief, a somewhat banal life. Even his war adventures were far less thrilling in fact than in his florid accounts of them. When he went to the Greek-Turkish War he came to grief because he could speak no language save English; when he went to the Spanish-American War he came down with severe cramps and had to be nursed by his fellow-correspondents.

But Crane could write, so some of his books have outlived their time. It was his distinction that he had an eye for the cold, glittering fact in an age of romantic illusion. The dignified authors of that time were such shallow, kittenish fellows as Howells, F. Hopkinson Smith and Frank R. Stockton, with Richard Watson Gilder as their high priest. The popular authors revolved around Richard Harding Davis. Crane's first writings alarmed Howells and shocked Gilder, but gradually a gang of younger men gathered around him, and before he died he was a national celebrity—in fact, a sort of American Kipling. He was, indeed, the head and forefront of the Young America movement in the middle nineties. No man of that movement was more vastly admired, and none has survived with less damage. How far would he have got if he had lived? It is useless to speculate. He died, like Schubert, at thirty. He left behind him one superlatively excellent book, four or five magnificent short stories, some indifferent poems and a great mass of journalistic trash. The Gilders of his time left only trash.

RING LARDNER [1924]

A few years ago a young college professor, eager to make a name for himself, brought out a laborious "critical" edition of *Sam Slick,* by Judge Thomas C. Halliburton, eighty-seven years after its first publication. It turned out to be quite unreadable—a dreadful series of archaic jocosities about varieties of *Homo americanus* long perished and forgotten, in a dialect now intelligible only to paleophilologists. Sometimes I have a fear that the same fate awaits Ring Lardner. The professors of his own days, of course, were quite unaware of him, save perhaps as a low zany to be enjoyed behind the door. They would no more have ventured to whoop him up publicly and officially than their predecessors of 1880 would have ventured to whoop up Mark Twain, or their remoter predecessors of 1837 would have dared to say anything for Haliburton. In such matters the academic mind, being chiefly animated by a fear of sneers, works very slowly. So slowly, indeed, does it work that it usually works too late. By the time Mark Twain got into the textbooks for sophomores two-thirds of his compositions had already begun to date; by the time Haliburton was served up as a sandwich between introduction and notes he was long dead. As I say, I suspect sadly that Lardner is doomed to go the same route. His stories, it seems to me, are superbly adroit and amusing; no other American of his generation, sober or gay, wrote better. But I doubt that they last: our grandchildren will wonder what they are about. It is not only, or even mainly, that the dialect that fills them will pass, though that fact is obviously a serious handicap in itself. It is principally that the people they depict will pass, that Larner's incomparable baseball players, pugs, song-writers, Elks, small-town Rotarians, and golf caddies were flittering figures of a transient civilization, and are doomed to be as puzzling and soporific, in the year 2000, as Haliburton's Yankee clock peddler is today.

The fact—if I may assume it to be a fact—is certain not to be set against Lardner's account; on the contrary, it is, in its way, highly complimentary to him. For he deliberately applied himself, not to the anatomizing of the general human soul, but to the meticulous histological study of a few salient individuals of his time and nation, and he did it with such subtle and penetrating skills that one must belong to his time and nation to follow him. I doubt that anyone who is not familiar with professional ball players, intimately and at first hand, will ever comprehend the full merit of the amazing sketches in *You Know Me, Al*; I doubt that anyone who has not given close and deliberate attention to the American vulgate will ever realize how magnificently Lardner handled it. He had more imitators, I suppose, than any other American writer of the first third of the century, but had he any actual rivals? If so, I have yet to hear of them. They all tried to write the speech of the streets as adeptly and as amusingly as he wrote it, and they all fell short of him; the next best was miles and miles behind him. And they were all inferior in observation, in sense of character, in shrewdness and insight. His studies, to be sure, are never very profound; he made no attempt to get at the primary springs of human motive; all his people share the same amiable stupidity, the same transparent vanity, the same shallow swinishness; they are all human Fords in bad repair, and alike at bottom. But if he thus confined himself to the surface, it yet remains a fact that his investigations on that surface were extraordinarily alert, ingenious and brilliant—that the character he finally set before us, however roughly articulated as to bones, was so astoundingly realistic as to epidermis that the effect is indistinguishable from that of life itself. The old man in "The Golden Honeymoon" is not merely well done: he is perfect. And so is the girl in "Some Like Them Cold." And so, even, is the idiotic Frank X. Farrell in "Alibi Ike"— an extravagant grotesque and yet quite real from glabella to calcaneus.

Lardner knew more about the management of the short story than all of its professors. His stories are built very carefully, and yet they seem to be wholly spontaneous, and even formless. He grasped the primary fact that no conceivable ingenuity can save a story that fails to show a recognizable and interesting character; he knew that a good character sketch is always a good story, no matter what its structure. Perhaps he got less attention than he ought to have got, even among the antiacademic critics, because his people were all lowly boors. For your reviewer of books, like every other sort of American, is always vastly impressed by fashionable pretensions. He belongs to the white-collar class of labor, and shares its prejudices. He can't rid himself of the feeling that Edith Wharton, whose people have butlers, was a better novelist than Willa Cather, whose people, in the main, dine in their kitchens. He lingers under the spell of Henry James, whose most humble character, at any rate in the later years, was at least an Englishman, and hence superior. Lardner, so to speak, hit such critics under the belt. He not only filled his stories with people who read the tabloids, said "Shake hands with my friend," and bought diamond rings on the installment plan; he also showed them having a good time in the world, and quite devoid of inferiority complexes. They amused him sardonically, but he did not pity them. A fatal error! The moron, perhaps, has a place in fiction, as in life, but he is not to be treated too easily and casually. It must be shown that he suffers tragically because he cannot abandon the plow to write poetry, or the sample-case to study for opera. Lardner was more realistic. If his typical hero has a secret sorrow it is that he is too old to take up osteopathy and too much in dread of his wife to venture into bookmaking.

In his later years a sharply acrid flavor got into Lardner's buffoonery. His baseball players and fifth-rate pugilists, beginning in his first stories as harmless jackasses, gradually converted themselves into loathsome scoundrels. Turn, for example, to the sketches in the volume called *The Love Nest*. The first tells the story of a cinema queen married to a magnate of the films. On the surface she seems to be nothing but a noodle, but underneath there is a sewer; the woman is such a pig that she makes one shudder. Again, he investigated another familiar type: the village practical joker. The fellow, in one form or other, has been laughed at since the days of Aristophanes. But here is a mercilessly realistic examination of his dunghill humor, and of its effects upon decent people. A third figure is a successful theatrical manager: he turns out to have the professional competence of a phrenologist and the honor of a highjacker. A fourth is a writer of popular songs: stealing other men's ideas has become so fixed a habit with him that he comes to believe that he has an actual right to them. A fourth is a trained nurse—but I spare you this dreadful nurse. The rest are bores of the homicidal type. One gets the effect, communing with the whole gang, of visiting a museum of anatomy. They are as shocking as what one encounters there—but in every detail they are unmistakably real.

Lardner concealed his new savagery, of course, beneath his old humor. It did not flag. No man writing among us had greater skill at the more extravagant varieties of jocosity. He saw startling and revelatory likeness between immensely disparate things, and he was full of pawky observations and bizarre comments. Two baseball players are palavering, and one of them, Young Jake, is boasting of his conquests during spring practice below the Potomac. "Down South ain't here!" replies the other. "Those dames in some of those swamps, they lose their head when they see a man with shoes on!" The two proceed to the discussion of a third imbecile, guilty of some obscure tort. "Why," inquires Young Jake, "didn't you break his nose or bust him in the chin?" "His nose was already broke," replied the other, "and he didn't have no chin." Such wise cracks seem easy to devise. Broadway diverts itself by manufacturing them. They constitute the substance of half the town shows. But in those made by Lardner there is something far more than mere facile humor: they are all rigidly in character, and they illuminate that character. Few American novelists, great or small, have had character more firmly in hand. Lardner did not see situations; he saw people. And what people! They are all as revolting as so many Methodist bishops, and they are all as thoroughly American.

29

Alfred Kazin: WILLA CATHER AND
ELLEN GLASGOW [1942]

"It's memory: the memory that goes with the vocation."
—WILLA CATHER on Sarah Orne Jewett

The "new freedom" after the war was not a movement; it was a succession of opportunities for writers who were themselves often in open conflict. To the "middle generation" of writers like Mencken, Anderson, Lewis, Cabell, and Hergesheimer, Willa Cather and Ellen Glasgow, it meant long-delayed triumphs after years of preparation or neglect. To the younger writers who began to come up immediately after the war, like Fitzgerald, Cummings, Hemingway, and Dos Passos, men who felt themselves part of a tougher and disillusioned generation, writing was to seem as much a rejection of what the "middle generation" already represented as it was a testament to their experiences in the war. Emancipation by emancipation, the pattern of a modern American literature took shape out of that simultaneous emergence of so many different educations, talents, and aspirations; and nothing so illuminated the richness and variety of that literature as the fact that everything suddenly seemed to come together in the postwar scene. At the very moment that Fitzgerald was writing his tales of "the flapper age," and Cummings, Hemingway, and Dos Passos were writing their bitter antiwar novels, Anderson and Lewis were leading "the revolt from the village." At the very moment that the younger writers were going to school to Gertrude Stein in Paris and working away at a new American style, two richly gifted women of an older generation, Willa Cather and Ellen Glasgow, had finally achieved recognition, and were just beginning to publish their best works. Ellen Glasgow had published her first novel in 1897, when most of the lost-generation novelists were one year old; and there were whole worlds, as it seemed, between *The Sun Also Rises* and *A Lost Lady,* or between *The Great Gatsby* and *The Romantic Comedians.* Yet it was the famous liberation of the twenties that brought them together, and at the time they even seemed to express a common postwar spirit of revolt and—especially with Ellen Glasgow—of satire.

Like the younger writers, both Willa Cather and Ellen Glasgow had a brilliant sense of style and an instinct for craftsmanship. But their feeling for style demanded none of the formal declarations and laborious experiments that Hemingway and Dos Passos brought to theirs. Like so many women in modern American writing from Emily Dickinson to Katherine Anne Porter, they had a certain dignity of craft from the first, a felicity all their own. In a period so marked by devotional aestheticism in writing, and one when it was easy to slip into the ornamental fancywork of men like Cabell and Hergesheimer, Willa Cather and Ellen Glasgow stood out as examples of serious craftsmanship.

Yet their art had no gestures, no tricks, and—this is less true of Ellen Glasgow—no glitter. They were almost too serenely good; it was always so easy to put them into their placid niches. Yet if they seemed to be off on their own, it was largely because the experience that became the substance of their books now seemed distant and the hold of the past on them so magnetic. Willa Cather soon became a conscious traditionalist, as Ellen Glasgow satirized traditionalism; but what isolated them both was the fact that they brought the resources of the modern novel in America—and frequently not a little of the bitterness of the postwar spirit—to the persistent exploration and evocation of the past. Unlike so many of their postwar contemporaries, they used modernism as a tool; they did not make it their substance. Sharing in the self-consciousness and freedom of the new literature, their minds persistently ranged below and beyond it. Yet unlike writers like Irving Babbitt and Paul Elmer More, who went directly against the current of the new literature, they were wholly a part of it. Indeed, they testified by their very presence, as writers so diverse as F. Scott Fitzgerald and Anderson, Mencken and Van Wyck Brooks, Hemingway and Cabell, had already testified, to the variety and freedom of the new American literature.

II

Willa Cather and Nebraska grew up together. Born in Virginia, she was taken at eight to a country moving in the first great floodtide of Western migration in the eighties. Within a single decade half a million people—Yankee settlers, sod-house pioneers out of the Lincoln country, Danes, Norwegians, Germans, Bohemians, Poles— pulled up stakes or emigrated from the farms of northern and eastern Europe to settle on the plains of a region that had been "a state before there were people in it." Nebraska was the first of the great settlements beyond the Mississippi after the Civil War, and the pace of its settlement and the polyglot character of its people were such that they seemed to mark a whole new society in flower. The successive stages of economic and social development were leaped quickly, but not too quickly; as late as 1885 the state was mostly raw prairie, and for the children of the first pioneers history began with the railroad age roaring in from the East. Nebraska was a bristling new society, proud of its progress and of values and a morality consciously its own. The prairie aristocracy that was to play as triumphant and even didactic a role in Willa Cather's novels as the colonial aristocracy had played in Edith Wharton's may have been composed out of the welter of emigration; but it was a founding class, and Willa Cather never forgot it.

Her enduring values were the values of this society, but they were not merely pioneer and agrarian ones. There was a touch of Europe in Nebraska everywhere during her girlhood, and much of her literary culture was to be drawn from it. The early population numbered so many Europeans among it that as a young girl she would spend Sundays listening to sermons in French, Norwegian, and Danish. There was a Prague in Nebraska as well as in Bohemia. Europe had given many brilliant and restless young men to the West. Amiel wrote letters to a nephew who died among the Nebraska farmers; Knut Hamsun worked on a farm just across the state line in South Dakota; a cousin of Camille Saint-Saëns lived nearby in Kansas. One could walk along the streets of a country seat like Wilber and not hear a word of English all day long. It was in this world, with its accumulation of many cultures, a world full of memories of Grieg and Liszt, of neighbors who taught her Latin and two grandmothers at home with whom she read the English classics, that Willa Cather learned to appreciate Henry James and at the same time to see in the pioneer society of the West a culture and distinction of its own. Her first two years there, she wrote later, were the most important to her as a writer.

All through her youth the West was moving perpetually onward, but it seemed anything but rootless to her; it suggested a distinctive permanence in the midst of change, a prairie culture that imparted to her education a tender vividness. Unconsciously, perhaps, the immigrants came to symbolize a tradition, and that tradition anchored her and gave her an almost religious belief in its sanctity. Growing up in a period of violent disruption and social change, she was thus brought up at the same time to a homely traditionalism. Later she was to elegize it, as all contemporary America was to elegize the tradition of pioneer energy and hardihood; but only because it gave her mind an abiding image of order and—what so few have associated with the pioneer tradition—of humanism. Her love for the West grew from a simple affection for her own kind into a reverence for the qualities they represented; from a patriotism of things and place-names into a patriotism of ideas. What she loved in the pioneer tradition was human qualities rather than institutions—the qualities of Ántonia Shimerda and Thea Kronberg, Alexandra Bergson and Godfrey St. Peter—but as those qualities seemed to disappear from the national life she began to think of them as something more than personal traits; they became the principles which she was to oppose to contemporary dissolution.

Willa Cather's traditionalism was thus anything but the arbitrary or patronizing opposition to contemporary ways which Irving Babbitt personified. It was a candid and philosophical nostalgia, a conviction and a standard possible only to a writer whose remembrance of the world of her childhood and the people in it was so overwhelming that everything after it seemed drab and more than a little cheap. Her distinction was not merely one of cultivation and sensibility; it was a kind of spiritual clarity possible only to those who suffer their loneliness as an act of the imagination and the will. It was as if the pervasive and incommunicable sense of loss felt by a whole modern American generation had become a theme rather than a passing emotion, a dissociation which one had to suffer as well as report. The others were lost in the new materialism, satirized or bewailed it; she seceded, as only a very rare integrity could secede with dignity. Later, as it seemed, she became merely sentimental, and her direct criticism of contemporary types and manners was often petulant and intolerant. But the very intensity of her nostalgia had from the first led her beyond nostalgia; it had given her the conviction that the values of the world she had lost were the primary values, and everything else merely their degradation.

It was this conflict, one that went beyond classes and could be represented only as a struggle between grandeur and meanness, the two poles of her world, that became the great theme of her novels.

She did not celebrate the pioneer as such; she sought his image in all creative spirits●—explorers and artists, lovers, and saints, who seemed to live by a purity of aspiration that represented everything that had gone out of life or had to fight a losing battle for survival in it. "O Eagle of Eagles!" she apostrophized in *The Song of the Lark*. "Endeavor, desire, glorious striving of human art!" The world of her first important novels —*O Pioneers!*, *The Song of the Lark*, *My Ántonia*—was unique in its serenity. Its secret was the individual discovery, the joy of fulfilling oneself in the satisfaction of an appointed destiny. The material Alexandra Bergson and Thea Kronberg worked with was like the naked prairies Jim Burden saw in *My Ántonia* on the night ride to his grandparents' farm. "There was nothing but land: not a country at all, but the material out of which countries are made." It was always the same material and always the same creative greatness impressed upon it. Ántonia was a peasant and Thea a singer, but both felt the same need of a great and positive achievement; Alexandra was a farmer, but her feeling for the land was like Thea's feeling for music. The tenacious ownership of the land, the endless search of its possibilities, became the very poetry of her character.

Yet even as Willa Cather's pale first novel, *Alexander's Bridge*, had been a legend of creative desire and its frustration, so in these novels the ideal of greatness had been subtly transformed into a lesson of endurance. Even in *My Ántonia*, the earliest and purest of her elegies, the significance of achievement had become only a rigid determination to see one's life through. The exultation was there, but it was already a little sad. Her heroines were all pioneers, pioneers on the land and pioneers of the spirit, but something small, cantankerous, and bitter had stolen in. The pioneer quality had thinned, as the pioneer zest had vanished. Ántonia might go on, as Thea might flee to the adobe deserts and cliff cities of the Southwest for refuge, but the new race of pioneers consisted of thousands of farm women suffering alone in their kitchens, living in a strange world amidst familiar scenes, wearing their lives out with endless chores and fears.

On starlight nights I used to pace up and down those long, cold streets,

---

● *"Nothing is far and nothing is dear, if one desires. The world is little, human life is little. There is only one big thing—desire. And before it, when it is big, all is little."—Old Wunsch to Thea Kronberg in* The Song of the Lark.
"Desire is creation."—Godfrey St. Peter in The Professor's House.

scowling at the little, sleeping porches on either side, with their storm-windows and covered back porches. They were flimsy shelters, most of them poorly built of light wood, with spindle porch-posts horribly mutilated by the turning-lathe. Yet for all their frailness, how much jealousy and envy and unhappiness some of them managed to contain! The life that went on in them seemed to me made up of evasions and negations; shifts to save cooking, to save washing and cleaning, devices to propitiate the tongue of gossip.

By 1920, the stories in *Youth and the Bright Medusa* hinted at a growing petulance, and in stories like "A Wagner Matinée" and "The Sculptor's Funeral" there was nothing to indicate that Willa Cather thought any better of small-town life than Sinclair Lewis. Yet by their very bitterness, so much more graphic than the dreary tonelessness of *Miss Lulu Bett,* these stories revealed how sharp her disillusionment had been, and when she developed the theme of small-town boorishness in *One of Ours* into the proverbial story of the sensitive young man, she could only repeat herself lamely. She was writing about an enemy—the oppressively narrow village world—which seemed only one of the many enemies of the creative spirit, but she did not have Zona Gale's inverted sentimentality, or anything like the spirit of Lewis's folksy and fundamentally affectionate satire. *One of Ours* was a temporary position for an artist whose need of an austere ideal was so compelling. Claude Wheeler was only the Midwest *révolté*; her authentic heroes were something more than sensitive young men who "could not see the use of working for money when money brought nothing one wanted. Mrs. Ehrlich said it brought security. Sometimes he thought that this security was what was the matter with everybody: that only perfect safety was required to kill all the best qualities in people and develop the mean ones." The farmer's wife in "A Wagner Matinée" had felt something deeper when, after her few moments of exultation at the concert, she turned and cried: " 'I don't want to go, Clark. I don't want to go!' Outside the concert hall lay the black pond with the cattle-tracked bluffs; the tall, unpainted house with weather-curled boards, naked as a tower; the crook-backed ash seedlings where the dish-cloths hung to dry; the gaunt moulting turkeys picking up refuse about the kitchen door."

The climax in Willa Cather's career came with two short novels she published between 1923 and 1925, *A Lost Lady* and *The Professor's House.* They were parables of the decline and fall of her own great tradition; and they were both so serenely and artfully written that they suggested that she could at last commemorate it quietly and even a little ironically. The primary values had gone, if not the bitterness she felt at their going; but where she had once written with a naively surging affection or irritation, she now possessed a cultivated poise that could express regret without rancor or loss without anguish. She had, in a sense, finally resigned herself to the physical and moral destruction of her ideal in the modern world, but only because she was soon to turn her back on that world entirely in novels like *Death Comes for the Archbishop* and *Shadows on the Rock*. In the person of Captain Forrester dreaming railroads across the prairies, of a Godfrey St. Peter welding his whole spirit into a magnificent history of the Spanish explorers in America, she recaptured the enduring qualities she loved in terms of the world she had at last been forced to accept. These were the last of her pioneers, the last of her great failures; and the story she was now to tell was how they, like all their line, would go down in defeat before commerce and family ties and human pettiness.

Only once in *A Lost Lady* did her submerged bitterness break through, in her portrait of Ivy Peters, the perfect bourgeois:

Now all this vast territory they had won was to be at the mercy of men like Ivy Peters, who had never dared anything, never risked anything. They would drink up the mirage, dispel the morning freshness, root out the great brooding spirit of freedom, the generous, easy life of the great landholders. The space, the color, the princely carelessness of the pioneer they would destroy and cut up into profitable bits, as the match factory splinters the primeval forest. All the way from Missouri to the mountains this generation of shrewd young men, trained to petty economies by hard times, would do exactly what Ivy Peters had done.

The theme was corruption, as it was to be the theme of *The Professor's House*. It was as explicit as Marian Forrester's dependence on her husband's frontier strength and integrity, as brutal as Ivy Peters's acquisition of Marian Forrester herself. And at the very moment that Willa Cather recognized that corruption, gave its name and source, she resigned herself to it. It had been her distinction from the first to lament what others had never missed; she now became frankly the elegist of the defeated, the Amiel of the novel. The conflict between grandeur and meanness, ardor and greed, was more than ever before the great interest of her mind; where she had once propounded that conflict, she now saw nothing but failure in it and submitted her art almost rejoicingly to the subtle exploration of failure. In any other novelist this would have made for sickliness and preciosity; now that she was no longer afraid of failure as a spiritual fact, her work gained a new strength and a keener radiance.

The significance of this new phase in Willa Cather's work is best seen in *The Professor's House*, which has been the most persistently underrated of her novels. Actually it is one of those imperfect and ambitious works whose very imperfections illuminate the quality of an imagination. The story of Godfrey St. Peter is at once the barest and the most elaborately symbolic version of the story of heroic failure she told over and over again, the keenest in insight and the most hauntingly suggestive. The violence with which she broke the book in half to tell the long and discursive narrative of Tom Outland's boyhood in the Southwest was a technical mistake that has damned the book, but the work as a whole is the most brilliant statement of her endeavor as an artist. For St. Peter is the archetype of all her characters and the embodiment of her own beliefs. He is not merely the scholar as artist, the son of pioneer parents who has carried the pioneer passion into the world of art and thought; he is what Willa Cather herself has always been or hoped to be—a pioneer in mind, a Catholic by instinct, French by inclination, a spiritual aristocrat with democratic manners.

The tragedy of St. Peter, though it seems nothing more than a domestic tragedy, is thus the most signal and illuminating of all Willa Cather's tragedies. The enemy she saw in Ivy Peters—the new trading, grasping class—has here stolen into St. Peter's home; it is reflected in the vulgar ambition of his wife and eldest daughter, the lucrative commercial use his son-in-law has made of the invention Tom Outland had developed in scholarly research, the genteel but acquisitive people around him. St. Peter's own passion, so subtle a pioneer passion, had been for the life of the mind. In the long and exhaustive research for his great history, in the writing of it in the attic of his old house, he had known something of the physical exultation that had gone into the explorations he described. As a young man in France, studying for his doctorate, he had looked up from a skiff in the Mediterranean and seen the design of his lifework reflected in the ranges of the Sierra Nevada, "unfolded in the air above him." Now, after twenty years, that history was finished; the money he had won for it had gone into the making of a new and pretentious house. The great creative phase of his life was over. To hold onto the last symbol of his endeavor, St. Peter determined to retain his old house against the shocked protests of his family. It was a pathetic symbol, but he needed some last refuge in a world wearing him out by slow attrition.

In this light the long middle section of the novel, describing Tom Outland's boyhood in the desert, is not a curious interlude in the novel; it becomes the parable of St. Peter's own longing for that remote world of the Southwest which he had described so triumphantly in his book. Willa Cather, too, was moving toward the South, as all her books do: always toward the more primitive in nature and the more traditional in belief. Tom Outland's desert life was thus the ultimate symbol of a forgotten freedom and harmony that could be realized only by a frank and even romantic submission to the past, to the Catholic order and doctrine, and the deserts of California and New Mexico in which the two priests of *Death Comes for the Archbishop* lived with such quiet and radiant perfection. Her characters no longer had to submit to failure; they lived in a charming and almost antediluvian world of their own. They had withdrawn, as Willa Cather now withdrew; and if her world became increasingly recollective and abstract, it was because she had fought a losing battle that no one of her spirit could hope to win. It was a long way from the Catholic Bohemian farmers of Nebraska to the eighteenth-century Catholicism of the Southwest, but she had made her choice, and she accepted it with an almost haughty serenity. As early as 1922, in "The Novel *Démeublé,*" her essay on fiction, she had defined her rejection of modern industrial culture explicitly, and had asked for a pure novel that would throw the "social furniture" out of fiction. Even a social novelist like Balzac, she had insisted, wrote about subjects unworthy of him; for the modern social novelists she had only a very gracious and superior contempt. "Are the banking system and the Stock Exchange worth being written about at all?" she asked. She thought not, and itemized the "social furniture" that had to be thrown out of the novel, among them the factory and a whole realm of "physical sensations." It was now but a step from the colonial New Mexico of *Death Comes for the Archbishop* to old Quebec in *Shadows on the Rock* and the lavender and old lace of *Lucy Gayheart*. Her secession was complete.

III

The significance of Willa Cather's exquisitely futile values was often slurred over or sentimentalized; the felicity of her art was never ignored. Her importance to the older generation—a generation that was now to make room for Hemingway—was a simple and moving one: she was its consummate artist. To critics sated with the folksy satire or bitterness of the village revolt, she suggested a preoccupation with the larger motives; to critics weary of the meretriciousness of Cabell and Hergesheimer, she personified a poised integrity; to critics impatient with the unkempt naturalism of Dreiser and Anderson, she offered purity of style. As an indigenous and finished craftsman, she seemed so native, and in her own way so complete that she restored confidence to the novel in America. There was no need to apologize for her or to "place" her; she had made a place for herself, carved out a subtle and interesting world of her own. If that world became increasingly elegiac and soft, it was riches in a little room.

Ellen Glasgow, in many respects a much stronger and more interesting talent, presented a different problem. She was even more profoundly a traditionalist than Willa Cather, but her tradition was a subject to be explored, often a very comic subject; it was not an attitude of mind to be imposed upon one's material. Willa Cather made her own tradition and suffered for it; Ellen Glasgow was born imprisoned in a social and physical tradition not of her own making, and made her career by satirizing it. She began as the most girlish of Southern romantics and later proved the most biting critic of Southern romanticism; she was at once the most traditional in loyalty to Virginia and its most powerful satirist; the most sympathetic historian of the Southern mind in modern times and a consistent satirist of that mind. She wrote like a dowager and frequently suggested the mind of a nihilist; she was at once the most old-fashioned of contemporary American novelists and frequently the wittiest.

Like Tolstoy, who knew only one society and spent his life quarreling with it, Ellen Glasgow knew only the Virginia which to Virginians of her class is not a state but an idea. She did not quarrel with her heritage; she coated it with ridicule. Yet her conception of life was bound for her by the feudal tastes, the gracious evasions, the inherent kindliness, and the pride of caste that have marked her class from the first. She grew up to be not so much a Southerner as a citizen of the Old Dominion; and the young Sub-Lieutenant Tolstoy in His Imperial Majesty's Crimean Army could have had no more instinctive loyalty to the concept of Holy Russia than Ellen Glasgow had to the social principles of Virginia.

Thrown back on the defensive after the Civil War, Virginia stiffened in its loyalties and grew more charming and vague as its prejudices grew more rigid. It became a society living perpetually in the shadow of the Civil War, a society curiously lacking in the sense of time, but oppressively fanatical when dealing with contemporary problems; obsessed by principle, but living on pluck; dedicated to "culture" and rapidly suspicious of ideas other than its own. It was a culture that Ellen Glasgow once described as a series of "sanctified fallacies." It believed in the chivalric legends of its history, and practiced a withered gentility. It regarded literature, as Virginius Littlepage confessed in *They Stooped to Folly*, "as a pursuit even less profitable, and scarcely more distinguished than crockery, as a business." Mr. Littlepage even told his errant son-in-law, who aspired to be a writer, that "without posing as an authority, I may express the opinion that there isn't much material in Virginia history that hasn't already been exhausted."

Ellen Glasgow's first problem, unlike Willa Cather's, was thus how to become a writer at all. "I grew up," she confessed in later life, "in a charming society, where ideas were accepted as naturally as the universe or the weather, and cards for the old, dancing for the young, and conversation flavored with personalities for the middle-aged, were the only arts practiced." Virginia prided itself on a society that had developed almost a feudal standard of noblesse-oblige neighborliness, of mutual admiration and understanding where feminine virtue set the ideal and complacency was thick. "From the very beginning of its history," Ellen Glasgow wrote in a preface to *The Miller of Old Church,* "the South had suffered less from a scarcity of literature than from a superabundance of living. Soil, scenery, all the color and animation of the external world, tempted a convivial race to an endless festival of the seasons. . . . Life was deficient in those violent contrasts that subdue the natural pomposity of man." The natural pomposity of some Virginians, however, became her great subject. Virginia could not stifle her desire to write, but it was necessary for her to hide her first published book from her family and friends.

As a spectator of the disintegration of the feudal South Ellen Glasgow saw so much of what she was later to call "the triumph in Virginia of idealism over actuality" that her first instinct was to quarrel with the facile myths of Southern romanticism. She revolted passionately—the word is her own—"not only from the school of local color, but also from the current gentility of letters, and more especially from the sentimental elegiac tone this tradition had assumed in Virginia." Her first desire as a writer was to tell the truth about Virginia against a setting of those legendary virtues in which she still believed. Her ambition was a whole series of works recording the history of modern Virginia. She aimed to be a realist in behalf of the great tradition, where so many of her compatriots were writing romance for the sake of romance. Significantly, however, she began, even after her first jejune novels, with a conventional Civil War romance, *The Battle-Ground,* on the ground that "one cannot approach the Confederacy without touching the very heart of romantic tradition. It is the single occasion in American history, and one of the few occasions in the history of the world, when the conflict of actualities was . . . the expiring gesture of chivalry."

Written on these lines, *The Battle-Ground* was a superior sword-

and-cape romance based on the legend that the Civil War was fought between gentlemen and bounders. Yet for all its girlish sentimentality, it was the first of her many comedies of humors. Her most valuable and characteristic insight into Southern life was to see that the old aristocracy fiercely kept to the illusion that theirs was a truly feudal society; they needed to believe, where once they had claimed it as a matter of course, that life as they knew it was divided by inveterate principles of caste, and that in their caste each man had his place and each gentleman his appointed function. If there were lordly privileges, there were knightly obligations. The comedy of Southern life—Ellen Glasgow was the first realist in her time to see it—was thus the waking difference between illusion and truth. The South lived by a fiction: it rationalized failure with such pompous circumlocution that it could ascribe the most sordid tragedies to a defect of manners, and the most violent to bad taste. The great quality of the life she saw all about her was a simple and astonishing refusal to admit reality. That quality did not always seem wrong to her; she thought it even a little charming, though she knew that it was fundamentally ridiculous and even tragic. But where else in modern American society could one man say to another, as Virginius Littlepage said to his saucy brother Marmaduke, "There are occasions when I should think twice before calling you a Southern gentleman"? Even when the South was cruel—and it could be monumentally cruel, as Ellen Glasgow knew perhaps better than William Faulkner—its addiction to illusion was not something to be destroyed; it was one of those qualities on which a culture is grounded, and without which it perishes. And she was a Virginian, and did not want to see it change; least of all would she admit that it could perish, save in the haunting last pages of *The Sheltered Life*. What remained to her was a crisp and epigrammatic irony that could verge on farce—or an inclination to the despair that is beyond all understanding.

In several of her books—notably *Barren Ground*—Ellen Glasgow wrote about other classes in the South, but her main interest was the aristocracy she knew almost too well. She ignored something far more ominous than the intellectual poverty of her class—its paralytic domination over Southern life—but the modulated bitterness of her wit went far to tell how deep her perplexity had been. Hers was a wit raised to the dignity of a style, a wit that peered through her affection for the life she described and summed up her exasperation with it. When she discovered about 1913, the year she published *Virginia,* that the comedy of manners was her work, she made it serve what the very best comedies of manners have always served: as an index to the qualities of a civilization, and as a subtle guide to its covert tragedy. From one point of view, of course, her talent was only the highest expression of the society she lampooned; but her attacks on Southern complacency were never complacent in themselves. She belonged to a tradition and lived out her career in it; and her understanding seemed all the more moving because she was so immovably a participant in the world she scorned.

Virginia, the first of Ellen Glasgow's great tragicomedies, was thus significantly a story of innocence. Of all the chivalric myths she set out to satirize, the most fervid was the religious code of Southern womanhood. It was the crowning unreality. Beneath the hollowed pretensions of the Southern gentleman, the exaggerated and mechanical courtesy, there was sanctimonious cruelty. Pure womanhood, raised in pure ignorance, married off for the purest of motives, came to pure disaster. Young Virginia Pendleton had been educated in the Dinwiddie School for Young Ladies, where Miss Priscilla Batte— "I've always heard that poetry was the ruination of Poe"—indoctrinated the maidenly intelligence. "Just as the town had battled for an idea without understanding it, so she was capable of dying for an idea, but not of conceiving one." In this school Virginia was taught to look for sermons in running brooks and virtue in all men of her class. She ascribed her parents' poverty to their saintliness and her husband's coldness to his superior tastes. Inevitably her marriage disintegrated, while both Virginia and her husband pretended—she out of pure ignorance, he out of loyalty to the genteel code—that proper marriages in their class never failed.

The succeeding novels often kept to this note: they recorded a long succession of frozen and unreal marriages. So Judge Gamaliel Bland, shown burying his wife as *The Romantic Comedians* opens, sighed wistfully over a marriage that was chiefly polite conversation, and straightway outraged his code and himself by falling madly in love with a flapper. So Virginius Littlepage in *They Stooped to Folly,* the very model of a Virginia gentleman, found himself smothered by the massive and imperturbable respectability of his wife. The classic wife in Ellen Glasgow's novels is a woman perfect in energy and grace, rich in quiet affection, a successful hostess, an admirable mother; but never a lover. She thwarts her husband as energetically as she inspires him to rise in their world; she preserves his place in the community and keeps him from enjoying it; she is so good that she bores him, and so possessive that she absorbs him. Beneath those inviolate marriages, frozen into the established order by an endless round of social duties, supported by a tradition capable of destroying any threat to its security, respectable lawyers dream of a world adolescent in its pleasures and overwhelming in its subterranean desire. Like Virginius Littlepage, they may even come to dislike their own children; but their emotion is little more than exasperation.

The scene of Ellen Glasgow's first postwar novels may seem at first to be only the comfortable upper-middle-class world of the twenties; in reality it is the last and most tragic phase of Southern feudalism. "In Queenborough," she wrote in her preface to *The Romantic Comedians,* "where lip-homage was still rendered to the code of beautiful behavior, the long reverberations of violence were felt chiefly under the surface. An increased momentum, a shriller vehemence, a wilder restlessness—these were the visible manifestations of a decayed . . . social order. The comic spirit, an enemy to unreason in any form, was still urbane, though its irony was suddenly spiced with malice." This was the society she described in the text of the novel as one which "had never outgrown an early stage of arrested development." Like Chekhov, she needed to describe a world that seemed to be dying slowly at the roots. Chekhov, who did not know that his world was prerevolutionary, sensed its coming disintegration; Ellen Glasgow, who never believed that the South would be revolutionary, knew that its great tradition was already dead. In the twenties her novels remained comedies, since the illusions by which her characters lived seemed private and vain; but when those illusions became something more than the winsome futility of tired old men like Littlepage and Judge Bland, they came to suggest a sick horror. It was the subtle development of this idea that became the subject of her most moving and penetrating novel, *The Sheltered Life.*

Like Chekhov's *The Cherry Orchard,* which it closely resembles in spirit, *The Sheltered Life* became a haunting study in social decomposition. Its characters were an archetypal gallery of Ellen Glasgow's society: Judge Archbald, married for thirty years to a woman he did not love simply because he had "compromised" her in their youth by being found alone with her in a carriage after midnight; Aunt Etta, the painfully indomitable spinster gentlewoman, the last of that procession of women who stream through Ellen Glasgow's novels quarreling with life and protected from it; George Birdsong, married to a beautiful woman whom he idolized but could not remain faithful to; Isabella, the coquettish rebel against Southern chivalry; and Eva Birdsong, in whom Ellen Glasgow had her triumph. For Eva was the last and the purest embodiment of ideal Southern womanhood, and her agony bespoke the ultimate agony of her tradition. Intelligent enough to grasp the disastrous implications of her code, she was blindly committed to it. Her powerlessness in the face of her husband's philandering, the genteel resignation by which she was condemned to poverty, became the parable of her class in its final distress. Under the impact of the depression the gentility of its traditional manners turned in on itself, and Eva, who had been the town belle, was now the subject of its busiest gossip. She had once been an image of the ideal, and she was now being used to kill it.

Behind the livid tragedy of Eva's invalidism, her sweet-smiling and grotesque patience, the world of which she was so perfect a symbol was now going under. The old families were being smoked out by the nouveaux riches and factories along the countryside. George Birdsong's poverty, which in the first years after Appomattox might have been almost a badge of honor, was now only an inconvenience. "Here they had lived, knit together by ties of kinship and tradition, in the Sabbath peace that comes only to those who have been vanquished in war. Here they resisted chance and adversity and progress; and here at last they were scattered by nothing more tangible than a stench." Reduced by George's poverty, the Birdsongs now live too close to the factory, and their tragedy—emphasized by George's helpless philandering—is only a cold and forlorn indignity. Like the cry from that other world which closes *The Cherry Orchard,* that first ax breaking into the twilight darkness, *The Sheltered Life* ends as the new society that the South has denied and patronized so long encroaches on the old. "After living here all our lives," cries George Birdsong, "shall we at last be driven out by a smell?"

30

Alfred Kazin: THEODORE DREISER AND
HIS CRITICS

> *The impression is simply one of truth, and therein lies*
> *at once the strength and the horror of it.*
> The Newark *Sunday News* on *Sister Carrie,*
> September 1, 1901.

At a time when the one quality which so many American writers
have in common just now is their utter harmlessness, Theodore
Dreiser makes painful reading. The others you can take up without
being involved in the least. They are "literature"—beautiful, stylish
literature. You are left free to think not of the book you are reading
but of the author, and not even of the whole man behind the author
but just of his cleverness, his sensibility, his style. Dreiser gets under
your skin and you can't wait to get him out again; he stupefies with
reality:

> *Carrie looked about her, very much disturbed and quite sure that she*
> *did not want to work here. Aside from making her uncomfortable by*
> *sidelong glances no one paid her the least attention. She waited until the*
> *whole department was aware of her presence. Then some word was sent*
> *around, and a foreman, in an apron and shirt sleeves, the latter rolled*
> *up to his shoulders, approached.*
> *"Do you want to see me?" he asked.*

"Do you need any help?" said Carrie, already learning directness of address.

"Do you know how to stitch caps?" he returned.

"No, sir," she replied.

"Have you ever had any experiences at this kind of work?" he inquired. She answered that she had not.

"Well," said the foreman, scratching his ear meditatively, "we do need a stitcher. We like experienced help, though. We've hardly got time to break people in." He paused and looked away out of the window. "We might, though, put you at finishing," he concluded reflectively.

"How much do you pay a week?" ventured Carrie, emboldened by a certain softness in the man's manner and his simplicity of address.

"Three and a half," he answered.

"Oh," she was about to exclaim, but she checked herself and allowed her thoughts to die without expression.

"We're not exactly in need of anybody," he went on vaguely, looking her over as one would a package.

The city had laid miles and miles of streets and sewers through regions where, perhaps, one solitary house stood out alone—a pioneer of the populous ways to be. There were regions open to the sweeping winds and rain, which were as yet lighted throughout the night with long, blinking lines of gas-lamps, fluttering in the wind. Narrow board walks extended out, passing here a house, and there a store, at far intervals, eventually ending on the open prairie.

"He said that if you married me you would only get ten thousand a year. That if you didn't and still lived with me you would get nothing at all. If you would leave me, or if I would leave you, you would get all of a million and a half. Don't you think you had better leave me now?"

These are isolated passages—the first two from *Sister Carrie,* the third from *Jennie Gerhardt*—and normally it would be as unkind to pick passages from Dreiser as it would be to quote for themselves those frustrated mental exchanges that Henry James's characters hold with each other. For Dreiser works in such detail that you never really feel the force of any phrase until you see the whole structure, while James is preoccupied with an inner meditation that his own characters always seem to be interrupting. But even in these bits from Dreiser there is an overwhelming impression that puzzles and troubles us because we cannot trace it to its source. "One doesn't see how it's made," a French critic once complained about some book he was reviewing. That is the trouble we always have with Dreiser. Carrie measuring herself against the immensity of Chicago, that wonderful night-scene in which we see a generation just off the farms and out of the small towns confronting the modern city for the first time; the scene in which Hurstwood comes on Carrie sitting in the dark; Jennie Gerhardt's growing solitude even after the birth of her child; Clyde Griffiths and Roberta Alden walking along the haunted lakes while he is looking for one where he can kill her—one doesn't see the man writing this. We are too absorbed. Something is happening that tastes of fear, of the bottom loneliness of human existence, that just barely breaks into speech from the depths of our souls; the planet itself seems to creak under our feet and there are long lines of people bitterly walking to work in the morning dark, thinking only of how they can break through the iron circle of their frustration. Every line hurts. It hurts because you never get free enough of anything to ask what a character or a situation "really" means; it hurts because Dresier is not trying to prove anything by it or to change what he sees; it hurts even when you are trying to tell yourself that all this happened in another time, that we are cleverer about life than Dreiser was. It hurts because it is all too much like "reality" to be "art."

It is because we have all identified Dreiser's work with reality that, for more than half a century now, he has been for us not a writer like other writers but a whole chapter of American life. From the very beginning, as one can see in reading over the reviews of *Sister Carrie,* Dreiser was accepted as a whole new class, a tendency, a disturbing movement in American life, an eruption from below. The very words he used, the dreaminess of his prose, the stilted but grim matter-of-fact of his method, which betrayed all the envy and wonder with which he looked at the great world outside—all this seemed to say that it was not art he worked with but *knowledge,* some new and secret knowledge. It was this that the reviewers instantly felt, that shocked the Doubledays so deeply, that explains the extraordinary bitterness toward Dreiser from the first—and that excited Frank Norris, the publisher's reader (Dreiser looked amazingly like the new, "primitive" types that Norris was getting into his own fiction). Dreiser was the man from outside, the man from below, who wrote with the terrible literalness of a child. It is this that is so clearly expressed in the publisher's effort to kill the book, in the fact that most literary and general magazines did not review the book at all, that even some newspapers reviewed the book a year late, and that the tone of those early reviews is plainly that of people trying to accustom themselves to an unpleasant shock.

Sister Carrie did not have a bad press; it had a frightened press, with many of the reviewers plainly impressed, but startled by the concentrated truthfulness of the book. The St. Louis *Mirror* complained that "the author writes with a startling directness. At times this directness seems to be the frankness of a vast unsophistication. The scenes of the book are laid always among a sort of people that is numerous but seldom treated in a serious novel." The general reaction was that of the Newark *Sunday News* which, almost a year after the book had been published, commented: "Told with an unsparing realism and detail, it has all the interest of fact. . . . The possibility of it all is horrible: an appalling arraignment of human society. And there is here no word of preachment; there are scarce any philosophic reflections or deductions expressed. The impression is simply one of truth, and therein lies at once the strength and the horror of it."

This was the new note of the book, the unrelieved seriousness of it—but a seriousness so native, so unselfconscious, that Dreiser undoubtedly saw nothing odd about his vaguely "poetic" and questioning chapter titles, which are his efforts to frame his own knowledge, to fit it into a traditional system of thought, though he could not question any of this knowledge itself. Writing *Sister Carrie,* David Brion Davis comments, "was something like translating the Golden Plates." For Carrie was Dreiser's own sister, and he wrote without any desire to shock, without any knowledge that he could. This is what made the book so important, and so hateful, to many people. Compare this with so "naturalistic" a book as Thomas Hardy's *Tess of the D'Urbervilles,* where the style is itself constantly commenting on the characters, and where the very old-fashioned turns of the prose, in all its complex urbanity, is an effort to interpret the story, to accommodate it to the author's own tradition of thought. Dreiser *could* not comment; it was all his own story; so deeply had he identified himself with the story that there was no place left in it for him to comment *from.* And such efforts as he made to comment, in the oddly invertebrate chapter titles, were like gasps in the face of a reality from which he could not turn away. The book was exactly like a dream that Dreiser had lived through and which in fact, after the failure of *Sister Carrie,* he was to live again, up to the very brink of Hurstwood's suicide.

It was this knowledge, this exclusive knowledge, this *"ich kann nicht anders,"* this absence of alternatives, that led people to resent Dreiser, and at the same time stunned young writers of the period into instant recognition of his symbolic value to them. We never know how much has been missing from our lives until a true writer comes along. Everything which had been missing from American literature, everything which lay in the gap between the generations, everything which Henry James said would belong to an "American Balzac"—that world of industrial capitalism which, James confessed, had been a "closed book" to him from his youth—everything free of "literature" and so free to become literature, now became identified with this "clumsy" and "stupid" ex-newspaperman whose book moved the new writers all the more deeply because they could not see where Dreiser's genius came from. To the young writers of the early twentieth century, Dreiser became, in H. L. Mencken's phrase, the Hindenburg of the novel—the great dumb ox who pushed American life forward for them; who went on, blindly, unchangeably, trampling down the lies of gentility and Victorianism, of Puritanism and academicism. Dreiser was the primitive, the man from the abyss, the stranger who had grown up outside the middle-class Protestant morality and so had no need to accept its sanctions. In Sherwood Anderson's phrase, he could be honored with "an apology for crudity," and in fact the legend that *Sister Carrie* had been suppressed by the publisher's wife now became so dear to the hearts of the rising generation that Mrs. Doubleday became a classic character, the Carrie Nation of the American liberal epos, her axe forever lifted against "the truth of American life." So even writers like Van Wyck Brooks, who had not shared in the bitterness of Dreiser's early years, and who as socialists disapproved of his despair, now defended him as a matter of course—he cleared the way; in the phrase that was to be repeated with increasing meaninglessness through the years, he "liberated the American novel."

Dreiser now embodied the whole struggle of the new American literature. The "elderly virgins of the newspapers," as Mencken called them, never ceased to point out how uncouth he was; the conservative academicians and New Humanists, the old fogeys and the young fogeys—all found in Dreiser everything new, brutal, and alien they feared in American life. Gertrude Atherton was to say during the First World War that Dreiser repesented the "Alpine School of Literature"—"Not a real American could be found among them with a magnifying glass"; Mary Austin was to notice that "our Baltic and Slavic stock will have another way than the English of experiencing love, and possibly a more limited way. . . . All of Theodore Dreiser's people love like the peasants in a novel by Bojer or Knut Hamsun. His women have a cowlike complaisance such as can be found only in people who have lived for generations close to the soil"; Stuart Sherman, in his famous article of 1915 on "The Barbaric Naturalism of Theodore Dreiser," made it clear that Dreiser, "coming from the 'ethnic' element of our mixed population," was thus unable to understand the higher beauty of the American spirit.

So Dreiser stood in no man's land, pushed on like a beast by one camp, attacked by the other. Everything about him made him a polemical figure; his scandals, miseries, and confusions were as well known as his books. The "liberals," the "modernists," defended books like *The "Genius"* because "it told the truth"—and how delighted they must have been when John S. Sumner tried to get the book banned in 1915 and anybody who *was* anybody (including Ezra Pound, John Reed, and David Belasco) rushed to its defense. To the English novelists of the period (and *Sister Carrie* owes its fame to the edition Heinemann brought out in London) he was the raw America they envied amid the doldrums of literary London. How much of that fighting period comes back to you now when you discover Arnold Bennett on his feverish trips to America identifying all the rich, teeming opportunities of American life with Dreiser, or listen to Ford Madox Ford—"Damn it all, it *is* fun to see that poor old language, that vehicle for conveying moderated thoughts, having the guts kicked out of it, like a deflated football, over all the fields of the boundless Middle West." While Mencken, in Dreiser's name slew William Lyon Phelps in his thousands, the young English discovered that Dreiser was the friend of art. Each side in the controversy used Dreiser, and each, in its own way, was embarrassed. How many times did the young Turks have to swallow Dreiser's bad books, to explain away his faults; and how clear it is from reading Paul Elmer More (who was a deeper critic than his opponents and would have been a great critic if he had not always tried to arm himself against American life) that he was always more moved by Dreiser's cosmic doubts than he could confess. More settled the problem of Dreiser, as he settled the problem of every writer he feared, by studying the man's "philosophy"—where he could show up Dreiser to his heart's content, and prove—in a prose that could not have been more removed from the actualities of the subject— that he had disposed forever of this intellectual barbarian.

This pattern remained to the end—Dreiser was the great personifier. When he went to Russia, even the title of the book he wrote had to begin with Dreiser rather than with Russia; when Sinclair Lewis praised Dreiser in his Nobel prize speech, he did so with all the enthusiasm of a Congressman trying for the farm vote; when Dreiser delivered himself of some remarks about Jews, the *Nation* was not so much indignant as bewildered that this son of the common people could express such illiberal sentiments; when he spoke against England at the beginning of the Second World War, there was a similar outcry that Dreiser was letting the masses down. It is typical of Dreiser's symbolic role that a writer now so isolated as James T. Farrell has been able to find support for his own work only in Dreiser's example; that the word *plebeian* has always been used either to blacken Dreiser or to favor him; that the Russians were able to make use of him; that Sergei Eisenstein suffered so long to make a film of *An American Tragedy* that would be the ultimate exposure of American capitalism. When Dreiser joined the Communists, his act was greeted as everything but what it really was —the lonely and confused effort of an individual to identify himself with the one group that had taken him up in his decline; when he died in 1945, in the heyday of American-Soviet friendship, one left-wing poet announced that Dreiser's faults had always been those of America anyway, that he was simply America writ large—"Much as we wish he had been surer, wiser, we cannot change the fact. The man was great in a way Americans uniquely understand who know the uneven contours of their land, its storms, its droughts, its huge and turbulent Mississippi, where his youth was spent." Even Dreiser's sad posthumous novels, *The Bulwark* and *The Stoic,* each of which centers around a dying old man, were written about with forced enthusiasm, as if the people attacking them were afraid of being called reactionary, while those who honestly liked them reported that they were *surprisingly* good. And how F. O. Matthiessen suffered all through the last year of his life to do justice to Dreiser as if that would fulfill an *obligation* to the cause of "progressivism" in America.

But soon after the war all this changed—Dreiser was now simply an embarrassment. The reaction against him was only partly literary, for much of it was founded on an understandable horror of the fraudulent "radicals" who had been exploiting Dreiser before his death. And thanks not a little to the cozy prosperity of a permanent war economy, America, it seemed, no longer required the spirit of protest with which Dreiser had been identified. The writers were now in the universities, and they all wrote about writing. No longer hoary sons of toil, a whole intelligentsia, post-Communist, post-Marxist, which could not look at Alger Hiss in the dock without shuddering at how near they had come to his fate, now tended to find their new ideology in the good old middle-class virtues. A new genteel tradition had come in. Writing in America had suddenly become very conscious that literature is made with words, and that these words should look nice on the page. It became a period when fine writing was everything; when every anonymous smoothie on *Time* could write cleaner prose about God's alliance with America than poor old Dreiser could find for anything; when even the *Senior Scholastic,* a magazine intended for high school students, complained of Dreiser that "some of the writing would shock an English class." It is of this period, in which we live, that Saul Bellow has noted: "I think that the insistence on neatness and correctness is one of the signs of a modern nervousness and irritability. When has clumsiness in composition been felt as so annoying, so enraging? The 'good' writing of the *New Yorker* is such that one experiences a furious anxiety, in reading it, about errors and lapses from taste; finally what emerges is a terrible hunger for conformity and uniformity. The smoothness of the surface and its high polish must not be marred. One has a similar anxiety in reading a novelist like Hemingway and comes to feel that in the end Hemingway wants to be praised for the offenses he does not commit. He is dependable; he never names certain emotions or ideas, and he takes pride in that—it is a form of honor. In it, really, there is submissiveness, acceptance of restriction."

The most important expression of the reaction against Dreiser is Lionel Trilling's "Reality in America" (the opening chapter in *The Liberal Imagination*). This essay expresses for a great many people in America just now their impatience with the insurgency that dominated our famously realistic fiction up to the war, and not since Paul Elmer More's essay of 1920 has anyone with so much critical insight made out so brilliant a case against Dreiser. Not since William Dean Howells supported Stephen Crane's *Maggie,* but not *Sister Carrie,* has anyone contrasted so sharply those notorious faults of style and slovenly habits of thought, which our liberal criticism has always treated as "essentially social and political virtues," with the wonderful play of mind and fertility of resource one finds in Henry James. Never has the case against the persistent identification of Dreiser with "reality" in America—coarse, heavy, external reality —been put with so much intellectual passion. For Trilling is writing against the decay of a liberal movement ruined largely by its flirtation with totalitarianism, by its disregard of human complexity and its fear of intellect. No one who has followed the extent to which our liberal critics have always acknowledged that Dreiser *is* a bad thinker—and have excused on the grounds that the poor man at least "told the truth about American life"—can help but share Mr. Trilling's impatience with what has always passed in this country for liberal "imagination."

But may it not be suggested that Henry James as a culture hero serves us as badly as Dreiser once did? What happens whenever we convert a writer into a symbol is that we lose the writer himself in all his indefeasible singularity, his particular inimitable genius. A literature that modeled itself on Dreiser would be unbearable; a literature that saw all the virtues of literature in Henry James would be preposterous. If one thing is clear about our addiction to Henry

James just now, it is that most of our new writing has nothing in common with James whatever. For James's essential quality is his intellectual appetite—"all life belongs to you"—his unending inner meditation, and not the air of detachment which so misleads us whenever we encounter it on the surface of the society James wrote about—the only society he knew, and one he despaired of precisely because it was never what it seemed. Just now, however, a certain genteel uninvolvement is dear to us, while Dreiser's bread lines and streetcar strikes, his suffering inarticulate characters, his Chicago, his "commonness," are that bad dream from which we have all awakened. As Dreiser's faults were once acclaimed as the virtues of the common man, so now we are ashamed of him because he brings up everything we should like to leave behind us.

There is no "common man"—though behind this fiction wait those who may yet prepare all too common a fate for us all. Literary people, as a class, can get so far away from the experience of other classes that they tend to see them only symbolically. Dreiser as "common man" once served a purpose; now he serves another. The basic mistake of all the liberal critics was to think that Dreiser could ever see this world as something to be ameliorated. They misjudged the source of Dreiser's strength, and misunderstood what Dreiser and the early naturalists really believed. For these writers and painters were "naturalist" only in the stark sense that the world had suddenly come down to them divested of its supernatural sanctions. They were actually obsessed with the transcendental possibilities of this "real" world; like Whitman, they gloried in the beauty of the iron city. In their contemplative acceptance of this world, in their indifference to social reform, in their awe before life itself, they were actually in the tradition not of political "liberalism" but in that deeper American strain which leads from the early pietists through Whitman to the first painters of the modern city.

This gift of contemplativeness, of wonder, of reverence, even, is at the center of Dreiser's world. Who can forget the image of the rocking chair in *Sister Carrie,* where from *this* cradle endlessly rocking man stares forever at a world he is not too weak but too bemused to change? And it is this lack of smartness, this puzzled lovingness for the substance of all our mystery, that explains why we do not know what to *do* with Dreiser today. For Dreiser is in a very old, a very difficult, a very lonely American tradition. It is no longer "transcendentalist" but always it seeks to transcend. This does not mean that Dreiser's philosophy is valuable in itself, or that his excursions into philosophy and science—fields for which he was certainly not well equipped—have to be excused. It does mean that this vision is always in Dreiser's work, and makes it possible. Just as the strength of his work is that he got into it those large rhythms of wonder, of curiosity, of amazement before the power of the universe, that give such largeness to his characters and such unconscious majesty to life itself, so the weakness and instability of his work is that he could become almost too passive before the great thing he saw out there, always larger than man himself. The truth is, as Eliseo Vivas says, that Dreiser is "not only an American but a universal novelist, in the very literal sense of the word. The mystery of the universe, the puzzle of destiny, haunts him; and he, more than any other of his contemporaries, has responded to the need to relate the haunting scene of puzzlement and mystery to the human drama. No other American novelist of his generation has so persistently endeavored to look at men under the aspect of eternity. It is no . . . paradox, therefore, that . . . while Dreiser tries to demonstrate that man's efforts are vain and empty, by responding to the need to face the problem of destiny, he draws our attention to dimensions of human existence, awareness of which is not encouraged by current philosophic fashions. . . ." To understand how this gets into Dreiser's work one must look not back of it but into it for that sense of "reality" which he thirsted for—that whole reality, up to the very shores of light, that made him cry out in *Jennie Gerhardt*: "We turn our faces away from the creation of life as if that were the last thing that man should dare to interest himself in, openly."

This is what makes Dreiser so painful—in his "atheism," his cosmology; this is what dismays us in our sensible literary culture, just as it bothered a generation that could never understand Dreiser's special bitterness against orthodox religion, against the churches; this is what drove Dreiser to look for God in the laboratories, to write essays on "My Creator." He may have been a "naturalist," but he was certainly not a materialist. What sticks in our throats is that Dreiser is outside the agreed boundaries of our concern, that he does not accept our "society" as the whole of reality, that he may crave after its fleshpots, but does not believe that getting along is the ultimate reach of man's effort. For we live in a time when traditionalists and "progressives" and ex-progressives alike are agreed that the man not to be trusted is the man who does not fit in, who has no "position," who dares to be distracted—when this great going machine, this prig's paradise in which we live just now, is the best of all possible worlds. Dreiser committed the one sin that a writer can commit in our society: he would not accept this society itself as wholly real.

It is here, I think, that we get perspective on his famous awkwardness. For what counts with a writer is that his reach should be felt as well as his grasp; that words should be his means, not his ends. It is this that Malcolm Cowley noticed when he wrote that "there are moments when Dreiser's awkwardness in handling words contributes to the force of his novels, since he seems to be groping in them for something on a deeper level than language." This is what finally disturbs us about Dreiser in a period when fine writing is a polished mirror that gives back our superficiality. Dreiser hurts because he is always looking for the source; to that which broke off into the mysterious halves of man's existence; to that which is behind language and sustains it; to that which is not ourselves but gives life to our words.

31

Delmore Schwartz: T. S. ELIOT AS
THE INTERNATIONAL HERO [1945]

A culture hero is one who brings new arts and skills to mankind. Prometheus was a culture hero and the inventors of the radio may also be said to be culture heroes, although this is hardly to be confounded with the culture made available by radio.

The inventors of the radio made possible a new range of experience. This is true of certain authors; for example, it is true of Wordsworth in regard to nature, and Proust in regard to time. It is not true of Shakespeare, but by contrast it is true of Surrey and the early Elizabethan playwrights who invented blank verse. Thus the most important authors are not always culture heroes, and thus no rank, stature, or scope is of necessity implicit in speaking of the author as a culture hero.

When we speak of nature and of a new range of experience, we may think of a mountain range: some may make the vehicles by means of which a mountain is climbed, some may climb the mountain, and some apprehend the new view of the surrounding countryside which becomes possible from the heights of the mountain. T. S. Eliot is a culture hero in each of these three ways. This becomes clear when we study the relationship of his work to the possible experiences of modern life. The term, possible, should be kept in mind, for many human beings obviously disregard and turn their backs upon much of modern life, although modern life does not in the least cease to circumscribe and penetrate their existence.

The reader of T. S. Eliot by turning the dials of his radio can hear the capitals of the world, London, Vienna, Athens, Alexandria, Jerusalem. What he hears will be news of the agony of war. Both the agony and the width of this experience are vivid examples of how the poetry of T. S. Eliot has a direct relationship to modern life. The width and the height and the depth of modern life are exhibited in his poetry; the agony and the horror of modern life are represented as inevitable to any human being who does not wish to deceive himself with systematic lies. Thus it is truly significant that E. M. Forster, in writing of Eliot, should recall August 1914 and the beginning of the First World War; it is just as significant that he should speak of first reading Eliot's poems in Alexandria, Egypt, during that war, and that he should conclude by saying that Eliot was one who had looked into the abyss and refused henceforward to deny or forget the fact.

We are given an early view of the international hero in the quasi-autobiographical poem which Eliot entitles: "*Mélange Adultère de Tout.*" The title, borrowed from a poem by Corbière, is ironic, but the adulterous mixture of practically everything, every time and every place, is not ironic in the least: a teacher in America, the poem goes, a journalist in England, a lecturer in Yorkshire, a literary nihilist in Paris, overexcited by philosophy in Germany, a wanderer from Omaha to Damascus, he has celebrated, he says, his birthday at an African oasis, dressed in a giraffe's skin. Let us place next to this array another list of names and events as heterogeneous as a circus or America itself: St. Louis, New England, Boston, Harvard, England, Paris, the First World War, Oxford, London, the Russian Revolution, the Church of England, the postwar period, the world crisis and depression, the Munich Pact, and the Second World War. If this list seems farfetched or forced, if it seems that such a list might be made for any author, the answer is that these names and events are *presences* in Eliot's work in a way which is not true of many authors, good and bad, who have lived through the same years.

Philip Rahv has shown how the heroine of Henry James is best understood as the heiress of all the ages. So, in a further sense, the true protagonist of Eliot's poems is the heir of all the ages. He is the descendant of the essential characters of James in that he is the American who visits Europe with a Baedeker in his hand, just like

Isabel Archer. But the further sense in which he is the heir of all the ages is illustrated when Eliot describes the seduction of a typist in a London flat from the point of view of Tiresias, a character in a play by Sophocles. To suppose that this is the mere exhibition of learning or reading is banal misunderstanding. The important point is that the presence of Tiresias illuminates the seduction of the typist just as much as a description of her room. Hence Eliot writes in his notes to *The Waste Land* "what Tiresias *sees* is the substance of the poem." The illumination of the ages is available at any moment, and when the typist's indifference and boredom in the act of love must be represented, it is possible for Eliot to invoke and paraphrase a lyric from a play by Oliver Goldsmith. Literary allusion has become not merely a Miltonic reference to Greek gods and Old Testament geography, not merely the citation of parallels, but a powerful and inevitable habit of mind, a habit which issues in judgment and the representation of different levels of experience, past and present.

James supposed that his theme was the international theme: would it not be more precise to speak of it as the transatlantic theme? This effort at a greater exactness defines what is involved in Eliot's work. Henry James was concerned with the American in Europe. Eliot cannot help but be concerned with the whole world and all history. Tiresias sees the nature of love in all times and all places and when Sweeney outwits a scheming whore, the fate of Agamemnon becomes relevant. So too, in the same way exactly, Eliot must recognize and use a correspondence between St. Augustine and Buddha in speaking of sensuality. And thus, as he writes again in his notes to *The Waste Land,* "The collocation of these two representatives of eastern and western asceticism as the culmination of this part of the poem is not an accident." And it is not an accident that the international hero should have come from St. Louis, Missouri, or at any rate from America. Only an American with a mind and sensibility which is cosmopolitan and expatriated could have seen Europe as it is seen in *The Waste Land.*

A literary work may be important in many ways, but surely one of the ways in which it is important is in its relationship to some important human interest or need, or in its relationship to some new aspect of human existence. Eliot's work is important in relationship to the fact that experience has become international. We have become an international people, and hence an international hero is possible. Just as the war is international, so the true causes of many of the things in our lives are world-wide, and we are able to understand the character of our lives only when we are aware of all history, of the philosophy of history, of primitive peoples and the Russian Revolution, of ancient Egypt and the unconscious mind. Thus again it is no accident that in *The Waste Land* use is made of *The Golden Bough,* and a book on the quest of the Grail; and the way in which images and associations appear in the poem illustrates a new view of consciousness, the depths of consciousness and the unconscious mind.

The protagonist of *The Waste Land* stands on the banks of the Thames and quotes the Upanishads, and this very quotation, the command to "give, sympathize, and control," makes possible a comprehensive insight into the difficulty of his life in the present. But this emphasis upon one poem of Eliot's may be misleading. What is true of much of his poetry is also true of his criticism. When the critic writes of tradition and the individual talent, when he declares the necessity for the author of a consciousness of the past as far back as Homer, when he brings the reader back to Dante, the Elizabethans and Andrew Marvell, he is also speaking as the heir of all the ages.

The emphasis on a consciousness of literature may also be misleading, for nowhere better than in Eliot can we see the difference between being merely literary and making the knowledge of literature an element in vision, that is to say, an essential part of the process of seeing anything and everything. Thus, to cite the advent of Tiresias again, the literary character of his appearance is matched by the unliterary actuality by means of which he refers to himself as being "like a taxi throbbing waiting." In one way, the subject of *The Waste Land* is the sensibility of the protagonist, a sensibility which is literary, philosophical, cosmopolitan and expatriated. But this sensibility is concerned not with itself as such, but with the common things of modern life, with two such important aspects of existence as religious belief and making love. To summon to mind such profound witnesses as Freud and D. H. Lawrence is to remember how often, in modern life, love has been the worst sickness of human beings.

The extent to which Eliot's poetry is directly concerned with love is matched only by the extent to which it is concerned with religious belief and the crisis of moral values. J. Alfred Prufrock is unable to make love to women of his own class and kind because of shyness, self-consciousness, and fear of rejection. The protagonists of other poems in Eliot's first book are men or women laughed at or rejected in love, and a girl deserted by her lover seems like a body deserted by the soul.

In Eliot's second volume of poems, an old man's despair issues in part from his inability to make love, while Sweeney, an antithetical character, is able to make love, but is unable to satisfy the woman with whom he copulates. In *The Waste Land,* the theme of love as a failure is again uppermost. Two lovers return from a garden after a moment of love, and the woman is overcome by despair or pathological despondency. A lady, perhaps the same woman who has returned from the garden in despair, becomes hysterical in her boudoir because her lover or her husband has nothing to say to her and cannot give her life any meaning or interest: "What shall I do now?" she says, "what shall I ever do?" The neurasthenic lady is succeeded in the poem by cockney women who gossip about another cockney woman who has been made ill by contraceptive pills taken to avoid the consequences of love; which is to say that the sickness of love has struck down every class in society: "What you get married for, if you don't want children?" And then we witness the seduction of the typist; and then other aspects of the sickness of love appear when, on the Thames bank, three girls ruined by love rehearse the sins of the young men with whom they have been having affairs. In the last part of the poem, the impossibility of love, the gulf between one human being and another, is the answer to the command to give, that is to say, to give oneself or surrender oneself to another human being in the act of making love.

Elsewhere love either results in impotence, or it is merely copulation. In "The Hollow Men," the hollow men are incapable of making love because there is a shadow which falls between the desire and the spasm. The kinship of love and belief is affirmed when the difficulty of love and of religious belief are expressed in the same way and as parallels, by means of a paraphrase and parody of the Lord's Prayer. In "Sweeney Agonistes," Sweeney returns to say that there is nothing in love but copulation, which, like birth and death, is boring. Sweeney's boredom should be placed in contrast with the experience of Burbank, who encountered the Princess Volupine in Venice, and found himself impotent with her. A comparison ought also to be made between Sweeney and the protagonist of one of Eliot's poems in French who harks back to a childhood experience of love: "I tickled her to make her laugh. I experienced a moment of power and delirium." Eliot's characters when they make love either suffer from what the psychoanalysts term "psychic impotence," or they make love so inadequately that the lady is left either hysterical or indifferent when the episode is over. The characters who are potent and insensitive are placed in contrast with the characters who are impotent and sensitive. Grishkin has a bust which promises pneumatic bliss, while Burbank's kind, the kind of a man who goes to

Europe with a Baedeker, has to crawl between the dry ribs of metaphysics because no contact possible to flesh is satisfactory. The potent and the insensitive, such as Sweeney, are not taken in by the ladies, the nightingales and the whores; but Burbank, like Agamemnon, is betrayed and undone.

This synoptic recitation might be increased by many more examples. Its essence is expressed perfectly in "Little Gidding": "Love is the unfamiliar name." But we ought to remember that the difficulty of making love, that is to say, of entering into the most intimate of relationships, is not the beginning but the consequence of the whole character of modern life. That is why the apparatus of reference which the poet brings to bear upon failure in love involves all history ("And I Tiresias have foresuffered all") and is international. So too the old man who is the protagonist of "Gerontion" must refer to human beings of many nationalities, to Mr. Silvero at Limoges, Hakagawa, Madame de Tornquist, Fräulein von Kulp and Christ [the tiger] and he finds it necessary to speak of all history as well as his failure in love. History is made to illuminate love and love is made to illuminate history. In modern life, human beings are whirled beyond the circuit of the constellations: their intimate plight is seen in connection or relation with the anguish of the Apostles after Calvary, the murder of Agamemnon, the insanity of Ophelia and children who chant that London bridge is falling down. In the same way, the plight of Prufrock is illuminated by means of a rich, passing reference to Michelangelo, the sculptor of the strong and heroic man. Only when the poet is the heir of all the ages can he make significant use of so many different and distant kinds of experience. But conversely, only when experience becomes international, only when many different and distant kinds of experience are encountered by the poet, does he find it necessary to become the heir of all the ages.

Difficulty in love is inseparable from the deracination and the alienation from which the international man suffers. When the traditional beliefs, sanctions and bonds of the community and of the family decay or disappear in the distance like a receding harbor, then love ceases to be an act which is in relation to the life of the community, and in immediate relation to the family and other human beings. Love becomes purely personal. It is isolated from the past and the future, and since it is isolated from all other relationships, since it is no longer celebrated, evaluated and given a status by the community, love does become merely copulation. The protagonist of "Gerontion" uses one of the most significant phrases in Eliot's work when he speaks of himself as living in a *rented* house; which is to say, not in the house where his forebears lived. He lives in a rented house, he is unable to make love, and he knows that history has many cunning, deceptive, and empty corridors. The nature of the house, of love and of history are interdependent aspects of modern life.

When we compare Eliot's poetry to the poetry of Valéry, Yeats and Rilke, Eliot's direct and comprehensive concern with the essential nature of modern life gains an external definition. Yeats writes of Leda and he writes of the nature of history; Valéry writes of Narcissus and the serpent in the Garden of Eden; Rilke is inspired by great works of art, by Christ's mother and by Orpheus. Yet in each of these authors the subject is transformed into a timeless essence. The heritage of Western culture is available to these authors and they use it many beautiful ways; but the fate of Western culture and the historical sense as such does not become an important part of their poetry. And then if we compare Eliot with Auden and with Pound, a further definition becomes clear. In his early work, Auden is inspired by an international crisis in a social and political sense; in his new work, he writes as a teacher and preacher and secular theologian. In neither period is all history and all culture a necessary part of the subject or the sensibility which is dealing with the subject. With Pound, we come closer to Eliot and the closeness sharpens the difference. Pound is an American in Europe too, and Pound, not Eliot, was the first to grasp the historical and international dimension of experience, as we can see in an early effort of his to explain the method of the *Cantos* and the internal structure of each Canto: "All times are contemporaneous," he wrote, and in the *Cantos,* he attempts to deal with all history as if it were part of the present. But he fails; he remains for the most part an American in Europe, and the *Cantos* are never more than a book of souvenirs of a tour of the world and a tour of culture.

To be international is to be a citizen of the world and thus a citizen of no particular city. The world as such is not a community and it has no constitution or government: it is the turning world in which the human being, surrounded by the consequences of all times and all places, must live his life as a human being and not as the citizen of any nation. Hence, to be the heir of all the ages is to inherit nothing but a consciousness of how all heirlooms are rooted in the past. Dominated by the historical consciousness, the international hero finds that all beliefs affect the holding of any belief (he cannot think of Christianity without remembering Adonis); he finds that many languages affect each use of speech (*The Waste Land* concludes with a passage in four languages).

When nationalism attempts to renew itself, it can do so only through the throes of war. And when nationalism in America attempts to become articulate, when a poet like Carl Sandburg writes that "The past is a bucket of ashes," or when Henry Ford makes the purely American remark that "History is the bunk," we have only to remember such a pilgrimage as that of Ford in the Peace Ship in which he attempted to bring the First World War to an end in order to see that anyone can say whatever he likes: no matter what anyone says, existence has become international for everyone.

Eliot's political and religious affirmations are at another extreme, and they do not resemble Ford's quixotic pilgrimage except as illustrating the starting point of the modern American, and his inevitable journey to Europe. What should be made explicit here is that only one who has known fully the deracination and alienation inherent in modern life can be moved to make so extreme an effort at returning to the traditional community as Eliot makes in attaching himself to Anglo-Catholicism and Royalism. Coming back may well be the same thing as going away; or at any rate, the effort to return home may exhibit the same predicament and the same topography as the fact of departure. Only by going to Europe, by crossing the Atlantic and living thousands of miles from home, does the international hero conceive of the complex nature of going home.

Modern life may be compared to a foreign country in which a foreign language is spoken. Eliot is the international hero because he has made the journey to the foreign country and described the nature of the new life in the foreign country. Since the future is bound to be international, if it is anything at all, we are all the bankrupt heirs of the ages, and the moments of the crisis expressed in Eliot's work are a prophecy of the crises of our own future in regard to love, religious belief, good and evil, the good life and the nature of the just society. *The Waste Land* will soon be as good as new.

32

Randall Jarrell: INTRODUCTION TO
W. C. WILLIAMS [1949]

An introduction to these poems can be useful to the reader in the way that an introduction to Peirce or William James can be: the reader is entering a realm that has some of the confusion and richness of the world, and any sort of summary is useful that keeps him reassured for a while—after that the place is its own justification. But most readers will automatically make any adjustments they need to make for writers so out-spoken, good-hearted, and largely generous as Peirce and James and Williams. Just their voices are introduction enough: if an American doesn't understand these men, what will he understand?

Anyone would apply to Williams—besides *outspoken, good-hearted,* and *generous*—such words as *fresh, sympathetic, enthusiastic, spontaneous, open, impulsive, emotional, observant, curious, rash, courageous, undignified, unaffected, humanitarian, experimental, empirical, liberal, secular, democratic.* Both what he keeps and what he rejects are unusual: how many of these words would fit the other good poets of the time? He was born younger than they, with more of the frontier about him, of the this-worldly optimism of the eighteenth century; one can imagine his reading *Rameau's Nephew* with delighted enthusiasm, but wading along in Karl Barth with a dour blank frown. (I don't mean to dissociate myself from these responses.) And he is as Pelagian as an obstetrician should be: as he points to the poor red thing mewling behind plate glass, he says with professional, observant disbelief: "You mean you think *that's* full of Original Sin?" He has the honesty that consists in writing down the way things seem to you yourself, not the way that they really must be, that they *are,* that everybody but a misguided idealist or shallow optimist or bourgeois sentimentalist *knows* they are. One has about him the amused, admiring, and affectionate certainty that one has about Whitman: *Why, he'd say anything!*—creditable or discreditable, sayable or unsayable, so long as he believes it. There is something particularly willing and generous about the man in and behind the poems: one is attracted to him so automatically that one is "reminded of a story" of how S—— was defined as the only man in the universe who didn't like William James.

A *Selected Poems* like this does far less than justice to Williams. Any fair selection would have to include his wonderful *Paterson* (Part I), which is itself a book; and Williams is one of those poets, like Hardy, whose bad or mediocre poems do repay reading and do add to your respect for the poet. Williams' bad poems are usually rather winning machine-parts minus their machine, irrepressible exclamations about the weather of the world, interesting but more or less autonomous and irrelevant entries in a Lifetime Diary. But this is attractive; the usual bad poem in somebody's *Collected Works* is a learned, mannered, valued habit—a habit a little more careful than, and a little emptier than, brushing one's teeth.

The first thing one notices about Williams' poetry is how radically sensational and perceptual it is: "Say it! No ideas but in things." Williams shares with Marianne Moore and Wallace Stevens a feeling that almost nothing is more important, more of a true delight, than the way things look. Reading their poems is one long shudder of recognition; their reproduction of things, in its empirical gaiety, its clear abstract refinement of presentation, has something peculiarly and paradoxically American about it—English readers usually talk about their work as if it had been produced by three triangles fresh from Flatland. All three of these poets might have used, as an epigraph for their poetry, Goethe's beautiful saying that it is nicer to think than to do, to feel than to think, but nicest of all merely to look. Williams' poems, so far as their spirit is concerned, remind one of Marianne Moore's "It is not the plunder,/but 'accessibility to experience' "; so far as their letter is concerned, they carry scrawled all over them Stevens' "The greatest poverty is not to live/In a physical world"—and Stevens continues, quite as if he were Williams looking with wondering love at all the unlikely beauties of the poor:

> One might have thought of sight, but who could think
> Of what it sees, for all the ill it sees.

All three poets did their first good work in an odd climate of poetic opinion. Its expectations of behavior were imagist (the poet is supposed to see everything, to feel a great deal, and to think and to do and to make hardly anything), its metrical demands were minimal, and its ideals of organization were mosaic. The subject of poetry had changed from the actions of men to the reactions of poets—*reactions* being defined in a way that left the poet almost without motor system or cerebral cortex. This easily led to a strange kind of abstraction: for what is more abstract than a fortuitous collocation of sensations? Stevens, with his passion for philosophy, order, and blank verse, was naturally least affected by the atmosphere of the time, in which he was at most a tourist; and Marianne Moore synthesized her own novel organization out of syllabic verse, extravagantly elaborated, half-visual patterns, and an extension of moral judgment, feeling, and generalization to the whole world of imagist perception. Williams found his own sort of imagism considerably harder to modify. He had a boyish delight and trust in Things: there is always on his lips the familiar, pragmatic, American *These are the facts*—for he is the most pragmatic of writers, and so American that the adjective itself seems inadequate . . one exclaims in despair and delight: He is the America of poets. Few of his poems had that pure crystalline inconsequence that the imagist poem ideally has—the world and Williams himself kept breaking into them; and this was certainly their salvation.

Williams' poetry is more remarkable for its empathy, sympathy, its muscular and emotional identification with its subjects, than any other contemporary poetry except Rilke's. When you have read *Paterson* you know for the rest of your life what it is like to be a waterfall; and what other poet has turned so many of his readers into trees? Occasionally one realizes that this latest tree of Williams' is considerably more active than anybody else's grizzly bear; but usually the identification is so natural, the feel and rhythm of the poem so hypnotic, that the problem of belief never arises. Williams' knowledge of plants and animals, our brothers and sisters in the world, is surprising for its range and intensity; and he sets them down in the midst of the real weather of the world, so that the reader is full of an innocent lyric pleasure just in being out in the open, in feeling the wind tickling his skin. The poems are full of "Nature": Williams has reproduced with exact and loving fidelity both the illumination of the letter and the movement of the spirit. In these poems emotions, ideals, whole attitudes are implicit in a tone of voice, in the feel of his own overheard speech; or are expressed in terms of plants, animals, the landscape, the weather. You see from his instructions "To a Solitary Disciple" that it is what the landscape *does*—its analogical, anthropomorphized life—that matters to Williams; and it is only as the colors and surfaces reveal this that they are important.

At first people were introduced into the poems mainly as overheard or overlooked landscape; they spread. Williams has the knowledge of people one expects, and often does not get, from doctors; a knowledge one does not expect, and almost never gets, from contemporary poets. (For instance, what is probably the best poem of our time, *Four Quartets,* has only one real character, the poet, and a recurrent state of that character which we are assured is God; even the ghostly mentor encountered after the air raid is half Eliot himself, a sort of Dostoevsky double.) One believes in and remembers the people in Williams' poems, though they usually remain behavioristic, sharply observed, sympathetic and empathetic sketches, and one cannot expect from these sketches the knowledge of a character that one gets from some of Frost's early dramatic monologues and narratives, from a number of Hardy's poems, or from Williams' detailed and conclusive treatment of the most interesting character in his poems, himself. Some of the narrative and dramatic elements of his poetry seem to have drained off into his fiction. Williams' attitude toward his people is particularly admirable: he has neither that condescending, impatient, Pharisaical dismissal of the illiterate mass of mankind, nor that manufactured, mooing awe for an equally manufactured Little or Common Man, that disfigures so much contemporary writing. Williams loves, blames, and yells despairingly at the Little Men just as naturally and legitimately as Saint-Loup got angry at the servants: because he *feels,* not just says, that the differences between men are less important than their similarities—that he and you and I, together, are the Little Men.

Williams has a real and unusual dislike of, distrust in, Authority; and the Father-surrogate of the average work of art has been banished from his Eden. His ability to rest (or at least to thrash happily about) in contradiction, doubts, and general guesswork, without ever climbing aboard any of the monumental certainties that go perpetually by, perpetually on time—this ability may seem the opposite of Whitman's gift for boarding every certainty and riding off into every infinite, but the spirit behind them is the same. Williams' range (it is roughly Paterson, that microcosm which he has half-discovered, half-invented) is narrower than Whitman's, and yet there too one is reminded of Whitman: Williams has much of the freeness of an earlier America, though it is a freedom haunted about by desperation and sorrow. The little motto one could invent for him—*In the sub-urbs, there one feels free*—is particularly ambiguous when one considers that those suburbs of his are overshadowed by, are a part of, the terrible industrial landscape of northeastern New Jersey. But the ambiguity is one that Williams himself not only understands but insists upon: if his poems are full of what is clear, delicate, and beautiful, they are also full of what is coarse, ugly, and horrible. There is no optimistic blindness in Williams, though there is a fresh gaiety, a stubborn or invincible joyousness. But when one thinks of the poems, of Williams himself, in the midst of these factories, dumps, subdivisions, express highways, patients, children, weeds, and flowers of theirs—with the city of New York rising before them on the horizon, a pillar of smoke by day, a pillar of fire by night; when one thinks of this, one sees in an ironic light, the flat matter-of-fact light of the American landscapes, James's remark that America "has no ruins." America is full of ruins, the ruins of hopes.

There are continually apparent in Williams that delicacy and subtlety which are sometimes so extraordinarily present, and sometimes so extraordinarily absent, in Whitman; and the hair-raising originality of some of Whitman's language is another bond between the two—one thinks of Williams as one reads

The orchestra whirls me wider than Uranus flies,
It wrenches such ardors from me I did not know I possessed them.
It sails me, I dab with bare feet, they are lick'd by the indolent waves,
I am cut by bitter and angry hail, I lose my breath,
Steep'd amid honey'd morphine, my windpipe throttled in fakes of death,
At length let up again to feel the puzzle of puzzles. . . .

In spite of their faults—some of them obvious to, and some of them seductive to, the most foolish reader—poets like Whitman and Williams have about them something more valuable than any faultlessness: a wonderful largeness, a quantitative and qualitative generosity.

Williams' imagist-objectivist background and bias have helped his poems by their emphasis on truthfulness, exactness, concrete "presentation"; but they have harmed the poems by their underemphasis on organization, logic, narrative, generalization—and the poems are so short, often, that there isn't time for much. Some of the poems seem to say, "Truth is enough"—*truth* meaning *data brought back alive*. But truth isn't enough. Our crudest demand for excitement, for "the actions of men," for the "real story" of something "important," something strange—this demand is legitimate because it is the nature of the animal, man, to make it; and the demand can hardly be neglected so much as a great deal of the poetry of our time—of the good poetry of our time—has neglected it. The materials of Williams' unsuccessful poems have as much reality as the brick one stumbles over on the sidewalk; but how little has been done to them! —the poem is pieces or, worse still, a piece. But sometimes just enough, exactly as little as is necessary, has been done; and in these poems the Nature of the edge of the American city—the weeds, clouds, and children of vacant lots—and its reflection in the minds of its inhabitants, exist for good.

One accepts as a perfect criticism of his own insufficiently organized (i.e., insufficiently living) poems Williams' own lines: "And we thought to escape rime/by imitation of the senseless/unarrangement of wild things—the stupidest rime of all"; and one realizes at the same time, with a sense of assurance, that few people know better than Williams how sensible the arrangement of wild things often is. Williams' good poems are in perfect agreement with his own intelligent and characteristic explanation of what a poem is:

"A poem is a small (or large) machine made of words. When I say there's nothing sentimental about a poem I mean that there can be no part, as in any other machine, that is redundant. . . . Its movement is intrinsic, undulant, a physical more than a literary character. Therefore each speech having its own character, the poetry it engenders will be peculiar to that speech also in its own intrinsic form. The effect is beauty, what in a single object resolves our complex feelings of propriety. . . . When a man makes a poem, makes it, mind you, he takes words as he finds them interrelated about him and composes them—without distortion which would mar their exact significances—into an intense expression of his perceptions and ardors that they may constitute a revelation in the speech that he uses. It isn't what he *says* that counts as a work of art, it's what he makes, with such intensity of perception that it lives with an intrinsic movement of its own to verify its authenticity."

One is rather embarrassed at the necessity of calling Williams original; it is like saying that a Cheshire Cat smiles. Originality is one of his major virtues and minor vices. One thinks about some of his best poems, *I've never read or imagined anything like this;* and one thinks about some of his worst, *I wish to God this were a little more like ordinary poetry.* He is even less logical than the average good poet—he is an "intellectual" in neither the good nor the bad sense of the word—but loves abstractions for their own sakes, and makes accomplished, characteristic, inveterate use of them, exactly as if they were sensations or emotions; there is no "dissociation of sensibility" in Williams. Both generalizations and particulars are handled with freshness and humor and imagination, with a delicacy and fantasy that are especially charming in so vigorous, realistic, and colloquial a writer.

The mosaic organization characteristic of imagism or "objectivism" develops naturally into the musical, thematic organization of poems like *Paterson* (Part I); many of its structural devices are interestingly close to those of *Four Quartets* and "Coriolan," though Eliot at the same times utilizes a good many of the traditional devices that Williams dislikes. A large-scale organization which is neither logical, dramatic, nor narrative is something that contemporary poetry has particularly desired; such an organizaiton seems possible but improbable, does not exist at present, and is most nearly approached in *Four Quartets* and *Paterson* (Part I).

Williams' poems are full of imperatives, exclamations, trochees— the rhythms and dynamics of their speech are being insisted upon as they could not be in any prose: it is this insistence upon dynamics that is fundamental in Williams' reading of his own poems. You've never heard a Williams poem until you've heard him read it; the listener realizes with astonished joy that he is hearing a method of reading poetry that is both excellent and completely unlike anything he has ever heard before. About Williams' meters one remark might be enough, here: that no one has written more accomplished and successful free verse. It seems to me that ordinary accentual-syllabic verse, in general, has tremendous advantages over "free," accentual, or syllabic verse. But that these other kinds of verse, in some particular situations or with some particular materials, can work out better for some poets, is so plain that any assertion to the contrary seems obstinate dogmatism. We want to explain *why* Williams' free verse or Marianne Moore's syllabic verse is successful, not to make fools of ourselves by arguing that it isn't. The verse form of one of their poems, as anyone can see, is essential to its success; and it is impossible to produce the same effect by treating their material in accentual-syllabic verse. Anyone can invent the genius who might have done the whole thing even better in ordinary English verse, but he is the most fruitless of inventions.

Contemporary criticism has not done very well by Williams; most of the good critics of poetry have not written about him, and one or two of the best, when they did write, just twitched as if flies were crawling over them. Yvor Winters has been Williams' most valuable advocate, and has written extremely well about one side of Williams' poetry; but his praise has never had enough effect on the average reader, who felt that Williams came as part of the big economy-sized package that included Elizabeth Daryush, Jones Very, and Winters' six best students. The most important thing that criticism can do for a contemporary poet is to establish that amosphere of interested respect which gets his poems a reasonably careful reading; it is only in the last couple of years that any such atmosphere has been established for Williams.

Williams' most impressive single piece is certainly *Paterson* (Part I): a reader has to be determinedly insensitive to modern poetry not to see that it has an extraordinary range and reality, a clear rightness that sometimes approaches perfection. I imagine that almost any list of Williams' best poems would include the extremely moving, completely realized "The Widow's Lament in Springtime"; that terrible poem which begins, "The pure products of America/ go crazy"; "The Yachts," a poem that is a paradigm of all the unjust beauty, the necessary and unnecessary injustice of the world; "These," a poem that is pure deprivation; "Burning the Christmas Greens"; the long poem (called "Paterson: Episode 17" in Williams' *Collected Poems*) that uses for a refrain the phrase "Beautiful Thing"; the unimaginably delicate "To Waken an Old Lady"; the poem that begins "By the road to the contagious hospital"; the wonderful "A Unison," in which Nature once again becomes for us both ritual and myth; and, perhaps, "The Sea-Elephant," "The Semblables," and "The Injury." And how many other poems there are that one never comes on without pleasure!

That Williams' poems are honest, exact, and original, that some of them are really *good* poems, seems to me obvious. But in concluding I had rather mention something even more obvious: their generosity and sympathy, their moral and human attractiveness.

33

G. S. Fraser: E. E. CUMMINGS AND
WALLACE STEVENS• [1955]

Here are two beautiful books,• to handle and look at, and books, for
their contents, that anybody who cares about modern poetry will
want to possess. The sight of them is also a little unnerving; what
they demand of the reviewer is not a progress report but an attempt
at a total judgment, a final placing. It is like a party, after the visitors
have left: set it out of your world, in my shabby autumnal Chelsea.
"How very amusing Mr. Cummings was!" "Yes, and so direct and
touching, too." "I couldn't quite follow all the jokes—that peculiar
dialect, is it *Bronx?*" "And he does go on a bit about *sex,* doesn't he
—about the machinery of it, I mean?" "Oh, that's the 1920s, my
dear. Rather charmingly old-world, in its way." "Yes, of course, but
isn't he rather *sentimental* sometimes?" "Oh, I would say mainly
very innocent and sincere. What are his politics, do you think?" "Oh,
what we would call an old-fashioned Tory-anarchist. American politics are so very difficult; they do that in a kind of radical tone of
voice." "Yes, but didn't you get the impression that he has mixed

• Poems, *1923-1954. By E. E. Cummings. Harcourt, Brace, 1954;* The
Collected Poems of Wallace Stevens. *Alfred A. Knopf, 1954.*

feelings about Jews—mixed feelings about Negroes, possibly—and then, of course, one must take it for granted most Americans don't like *us.*" "Oh, I think you're quite wrong. There's a natural tendency toward emotional impatience and violence, but nothing Fascist. Fundamentally, he's an anarchist and a pacifist." "Is that why he seems to hate so many people?" "Oh, yes, he believes in love. Don't you remember what a lot he had to say about love? That must make you hate a lot of people. And he's very much of an individual, a kind of metropolitan Thoreau, and so he dislikes ordinary, conventional people—you do remember your Tocqueville, and all that, about America, the extraordinary pressure of the urge to social conformity on the American with ideas?" "*I* thought he was lively, but to some extent he did seem to be saying the same thing over and over again." "I think poor Aunt Nelly was quite embarrassed by that anecdote, lively as it was, about the girls in the whorehouse. Though, of course, she's very broad-minded." "It was a little *anatomical,* I did think." "But what about Mr. Stevens?" "Much more cultured, certainly. I must say when Americans go in for culture they go in for it regardless of time, trouble, and expense." "I found it hard sometimes to catch his drift. He's rather shut up in himself, would you say?" "I don't know; we had a long conversation, over there in the corner, about the nature of poetry—I don't know if I could quite summarize the upshot for you, but it seemed very deep at the time." "Oh, deep, he is deep!" "*I* thought he talked wonderfully about painting and landscape and music and things, though, mind you, I found it hard to *pin him down.*" "I thought sometimes of a remote Chinese hermitsage in his mountain hut, and then I thought, it would be a very *natty* hut, wouldn't it? I think Mr. Cummings has been a bit more battered by life." "What a good thing they can't hear us. They are right, really, to dislike us on the whole. We *are* cats. . . ."

Mr. Cummings and Mr. Stevens have, in fact, for an English reader, an extra-poetic fascination—for the light they throw on the roots of American culture—that might easily, for us, deflect discussion of them into the kind of gossipy guesswork, in twittering birdlike voices, I have parodied above. Roughly, of course, we find ourselves fitting Mr. Cummings into a tough and native, Mr. Stevens into a cosmopolitan and sophisticated American tradition. Mr. Cummings has a crude and forceful directness which it would be hard to match in a contemporary English poet; Mr. Stevens a conscious refinement which it would be equally hard to match. It is, however, an Alexandrian rather than an Attic refinement. Mr. Robert Graves is an English poet (an early and late admirer of Cummings) who shares Cummings' cult of what, in a large and loose sense, can be called romantic love; but in his passionate propriety and fastidiousness of diction he is quite unlike Mr. Cummings, and yet equally, when one looks for counterbalancing resemblances, unlike Mr. Stevens. Mr. Graves is an Atticizing writer, he wants words and phrases to be apt, discreetly so, rather than showy; color and showiness are indispensable instruments for Mr. Stevens, his language is opulent, *recherché,* queen of its own mode; every poem might have stepped long-legged and starry-eyed, with tempting shadows on its thighs, wearing this year's lightest and most expensive girdle, from a poetry fashion magazine, an aesthetic equivalent of *Vogue.* There *are* American poets—Mr. Robert Frost is one—of whom it can be claimed (as Bagehot claimed for Wordsworth, as against Tennyson and Browning) that they use language classically. Bagehot, who tagged the epithet "grotesque" onto Browning and the epithet "ornate" onto Tennyson might have used these respectively for Mr. Cummings and Mr. Stevens. It would be fairer to describe Mr. Cummings' use of language as *sensationalist* (and therefore occasionally sentimental, occasionally brutal); and Mr. Stevens' use of language as *aesthetic* (and therefore occasionally precious, occasionally vacuous). Thus, these are two very good and important poets, but judging them by the very highest standards (Chaucer, Shakespeare, Donne, Milton, Pope, Wordsworth, Blake, Yeats, say) one is forced to point out that some element of human experience or range within it traditionally thought of as central, is left out. Mr. Cummings and Mr. Stevens do not fulfill Matthew Arnold's function for the poet of strengthening and uplifting the heart; the very genuine stimulation they offer us is mixed with temptations to evasiveness and relaxation, to various kinds of self-flattery. And that comes out in the off-center language.

What does Mr. Cummings leave out? For one thing (and this may appear a rash statement, for Mr. Cummings, in his more lyrical poems, might be thought to write about almost nothing else), the complex personal relationships of men and women. What Mr. Cummings seems to me to substitute for this fine traditional theme is, firstly, a celebration of the sexual appetites and achievements of the hearty male animal; and, secondly, the celebration of a kind of mystical attitude toward life in general that may indeed spring from a happy and stable relationship between a man and woman, but need not always do so, and is something quite different as a theme. Mr. Cummings' love poetry is, in a bad sense, *impersonal;* and I would connect this impersonality of the love poetry with a general characteristic of the poetry as a whole, its steadily sustained youthful strident energy, of which the dark shadow is its almost complete failure to mature. Mr. Cummings wrote in 1923 as well as he does now, and not very differently. The marks of permanent adolescence in his work are many. Let me list some: (1) an almost entirely uncritical devotion to parents, lovers, and a few chosen friends combined with an attitude of suspicion and dislike toward "outsiders": (2) a general tendency to think of *all* political and economic activities as in the main a sinister conspiracy against the young: (3) a wholehearted universalistic pacifism, deeply emotional, not argued out, combined with a natural violent irascibility: (4) the instinctive generosity of youth (always side emotionally with the rioters against the police) combined with an equally deeply rooted provincial intolerance (unless I am obtuse in finding this intolerance in the dialect parodies and in some of the references to people with Jewish or German names): (5) the violent capacity of the young for disgust (recurrent references to drunkenness, vomit, and so on) which can itself, uncriticized, become disgusting: (6) a youthful, not very well-balanced religiousness, a "reverence for life" combined with a youthful refusal to accept death as a fact ("No young man thinks that he will ever die. . . ."), leading, of course, to a morbid preoccupation with death: (7) indecency, scatology, even here and there something that strikes me as very like pornography—physical frustration leading to emotional frustration, and making even physical fulfillment finally emotionally frustrating, and final emotional fulfillment the object of a kind of private religion. To sum all this up: Mr. Cummings' sense of life is the "lyrical" rather than the "tragic" or "comic" sense. The poet who has not learned to accept "society," "others," the idea of the City in some sense, will never become sufficiently mature for tragedy or comedy. Mr. Cummings' satire is an aggressive-defensive maneuver on behalf of his small private corner in a, for him, still unsullied Garden of Eden; salesmen, politicians, generals, the late President Harding and the late S. S. Van Dine must keep out. Some such drastic preliminary "limiting judgment" is necessary if we are to do justice to Mr. Cummings' achievement within his limits.

Part of that achievement is readability. *Poems, 1923-1954* is a volume of 468 pages and can be read straight through like an American novel of the 1920s, or a volume of essays by Mencken. It is, indeed, of Mencken, Scott Fitzgerald, early Dos Passos that I think when I read Cummings and not—except for turns and tricks, and moods, that sometimes remind me of Pound—of other poets. If Mr. Cummings were a less raw and vulnerable, a more balanced and integrated person his poems would not be such a magnificent documentation of the stresses of the American scene. Some of them have value, perhaps, *merely* as documentation:

yoozwiddupoimnuntwaiv un duyyookusumpnruddur givusuhtoonundup-
hugnting
(*anglice:* youse with the permanent wave and the yuke or somethin' or
other
give us a tune on the ****ing thing!)

Others, like the deliciously funny epitaph on President Harding (a
footnote to Mencken's essays), call up in us a tolerant nostalgia for
the simpler stupidities of yesterday:

> . . . if he wouldn't have eaten them Yapanese Craps
> somebody might hardly never not have been unsorry, perhaps

As a clown, Cummings can make us laugh aloud. But he is at his
best (as in some of the war poems, the one about the conscientious-
objector conscript, the one about the Yale boy marching off to war,
and "My sweet old etcetera") as an angry and tender clown. Angry
and tender clowning begins to pivot over to lyricism in some of the
poems about whores: what begin as half-mockery,

> should i entirely ask of god why
> on the alert neck of this brittle whore
> delicately wobbles an improbably distinct face,

end with intense sinister and pathetic dramatization,

> or why her tiniest whispered invitation
> is like a clock striking in a dark house.

The anger is never purged from even the most purely lyrical poems:
with their recurrent theme that love, love is the only real thing and
damn—damn and hate and torture—any evidence to the contrary.
The finest explicit statement of this is the long, very beautiful poem
beginning,

> my father moved through dooms of love,

and ending magnificently, in a noble, almost "metaphysical" paradox:

> and nothing quite so least as truth
> i— say though hate were why men breathe—
> because my father lived his soul
> love is the whole and more than all

The later lyricism is gentler, the "real world"—so, crudely and inadequately in both directions to call it—held more safely at a distance.

o by the by
has anybody seen
little you-i
who stood on a green
hill and threw
his wish at blue. . . .

So what shall one say, on the whole? There is some of the matter of life here; there is an extraordinary technical dexterity; there is an unurbane wit of a very savagely effective sort; a disturbing gift for evoking sexual situations below head-level; one of the most notable talents for direct and simple lyrical utterance of this century: and, over and above all these, there is something which, however narrow and callow, has been held to obstinately enough to deserve the honorary title of "a philosophy of life." It is the philosophy, say, of the adolescent who wants the moon down out of the sky, but wants it to stay up there and shine on him, too. But far deeper even than this there is the fact that Mr. Cummings' comparative undevelopment as a civilized human being does not, any more than the wrong-headed, peevish, or illogical remarks he makes, prevent one from feeling that in some way he is in close direct touch—in a way that the rest of us, the denizens of the "unreal city" are not—with a source and justification of being. His silliness in a sense is locally traditional, it is in the line of Thoreau's silliness or Emerson's, and carries with it its counterbalance of raw insight. In an orthodox age, like the early seventeenth century, the insight would have been chastened and civilized by a social background; it has had to fight grimly to maintain its right to existence against a social background that seemed to make nonsense of it. That accounts for the stridencies. But a tough, temperamental consistency holds Mr. Cummings' book together; and lust, disgust, highjinks, and despair do not manage to crowd out the impression that love and joy, precariously defended, are what this poet understands most profoundly.

There are no stridencies in Mr. Stevens. And to the question about what is the central thing lacking the answer might be, in his case, just that "matter of life" which is there, for all his faults, in the work of Mr. Cummings. And, indeed, again, the crude and obvious thing to say about Mr. Stevens—yet like many crude and obvious things, the centrally just one—is that, not having wanted to cope with that "matter of life," he has tried to substitute for it a "matter of mind." His poems, to continue on this crude level, are about perception and reflection on perception. They are about what the mind can make of experience, not about experience as raw. They become more and more not only reflective but self-reflective, poems about what the poem is, poems in which the poet asks himself what he is doing, and in answering is still writing the same poem, and so indefinitely can or indeed has to extend his answer. Thus, many of Mr. Stevens' later poems are like commentaries on themselves that could be added to forever, section by section, like expanding bookcases. Something of a similar sort is true of earlier and shorter poems; there are thirteen ways of looking at a blackbird, but there might be fifteen, or twenty, or any number. What the mind picks out from perceptual experience is always one of many possible aspects, and one of many possible ways of presenting that aspect, and about the choosing of the aspect, and the choosing of the mode, there must always be something arbitrary. The whole tone of polite irony, of urbane mystification that pervades Mr. Stevens' work stems, I think, from this central predicament of the reflective aesthete who, philosophically, is a kind of pragmatic solipsist. The world, for Mr. Stevens, that the poet lives in is the world that he chooses to shape by the arbitrary emphases of a detached attention—an attention not itself shaped by the compulsions, for instance, of hunger or love. We feel continually, in reading Mr. Stevens, that his actual *gifts* are comparable with those of the very greatest poets (we do not feel this, about Mr. Cummings, when reading him). Probably no modern poet has a more supple, rich, commanding, and evocative vocabulary; within certain limits—Mr. Stevens would be incapable of achieving the changes of pace, and the suddenings, slackenings and concentrations, of *The Waste Land* or *Ash Wednesday*—few modern poets are more notable masters of rhythm; very few contemporary poets, again, combine as Mr. Stevens does the three apparently disparate gifts of evoking impressions with imagistic vividness, shaping long poems with musical care, and pursuing through a long poem a single, very abstruse, metaphysical argument. Yet in one's heart one does not quite think he is a "great" poet in the sense that, say, Yeats and Eliot are "great" poets. What is it that one misses? Partly, or perhaps mainly, the whole area of life that lies between detached aesthetic perception and philosophical reflection on it; and, as a chief corollary to that, the urgency of ordinary human passion, the sense of commitment and the moment of final concentration. In one crude human sense, Mr. Stevens' enormous talents are being exploited a little frivolously; in all one's continuing pleasure and admiration, while reading him, there is the sense all the time of a lack of the highest tension. It would be impertinent to illustrate the merits of such a distinguished and famous writer by quotation; but here and there Mr. Stevens does seem to me to show an awareness of this lack, in his work, of human grasp, of human contact:

> I cannot bring a world quite round,
> Although I patch it as I can.
>
> I sing a hero's head, large eye
> And breaded bronze, but not a man,
>
> Although I patch him as I can
> And reach through him almost to man,
>
> If to serenade almost to man
> Is to miss, by that, things as they are,
>
> Say that it is the serenade
> Of a man that plays a blue guitar.

A society gets the poets it deserves, and America has obviously deserved very well to get a poet of the painful, raw honesty of Mr. Cummings and such a first-rate artist in verse, and profoundly interesting reflective poet, as Mr. Stevens. The gaps that one finds in them are gaps also which (in England today, as much as in America) one finds in oneself. It is not enough to "plunge into" life or enough, aesthetically and intellectually, to "transcend" it. Saying that, is not saying that anybody else could, set in the perspective of these two poets, have done better. Only a more humane society than we have seen for a long time or are likely to see soon will prove a proper stamping ground for the fully humanist poet.

34

Philip Rahv: THE CULT OF EXPERIENCE
IN AMERICAN WRITING [1940]

Every attentive reader of Henry James remembers that highly dramatic scene in *The Ambassadors*—a scene singled out by its author
as giving away the "whole case" of his novel—in which Lambert
Strether, the elderly New England gentleman who had come to Paris
on a mission of business and duty, proclaims his conversion to the
doctrine of experience. Caught in the spell of Paris, the discovery of
whose grace and form is marked for him by a kind of meaning and
intensity that can be likened only to the raptures of a mystic vision,
Strether feels moved to renounce publicly the morality of abstention
he had brought with him from Woollett, Mass. And that mellow
Sunday afternoon, as he mingles with the charming guests assembled
in the garden of the sculptor Gloriani, the spell of the world capital
of civilization is so strong upon the sensitive old man that he trembles
with happiness and zeal. It is then that he communicates to little
Bilham his newly acquired piety toward life and the fruits thereof.
The worst mistake one can make, he admonishes his youthful inter-
locutor, is not to live all one can.—"Do what you like so long as you
don't make my mistake, . . . Live! . . . It doesn't so much matter
what you do in particular, so long as you have your life. If you

haven't had that, what *have* you had? . . . This place and these impressions . . . have had their abundant message for me, have just dropped *that* into my mind. I see it now . . . and more than you'd believe or I can express. . . . The right time is now yours. The right time is any *time* that one is still so lucky as to have. . . . Live, Live!"

To an imaginative European, unfamiliar with the prohibitive American past and the long-standing national habit of playing hide and seek with experience, Strether's pronouncements in favor of sheer life may well seem so commonplace as scarcely to be worth the loving concentration of a major novelist. While the idea that one should "live" one's life came to James as a revelation, to the contemporary European writers this idea had long been a thoroughly assimilated and natural assumption. Experience served them as the concrete medium for the testing and creation of values, whereas in James's work it stands for something distilled or selected from the total process of living; it stands for romance, reality, civilization—a self-propelling autonomous "presence" inexhaustibly alluring in its own right. That is the "presence" which in the imagination of Hyacinth Robinson, the hero of *The Princess Casamassima,* takes on a form at once "vast, vague, and dazzling—an irradiation of light from objects undefined, mixed with the atmosphere of Paris and Venice."

The significance of this positive approach to experience and identification of it with life's "treasures, felicities, splendors and successes" is that it represents a momentous break with the then dominant American morality of abstention. The roots of this morality are to be traced on the one hand to the religion of the Puritans and, on the other, to the inescapable need of a frontier society to master its world in sober practice before appropriating it as an object of enjoyment. Such is the historical content of that native "innocence" which in James's fiction is continually being ensnared in the web of European "experience." And James's tendency is to resolve this drama of entanglement by finally accepting what Europe offers on condition that it cleanse itself of its taint of evil through an alliance with New World virtue.

James's attitude toward experience is sometimes overlooked by readers excessively impressed (or depressed) by his oblique methods and effects of remoteness and ambiguity. Actually, from the standpoint of the history of the national letters, the lesson he taught in *The Ambassadors,* as in many of his other works, must be understood as no less than a revolutionary appeal. It is a veritable declaration of the rights of man—not, to be sure, of the rights of the public, of the social man, but of the rights of the private man, of the rights of personality, whose openness to experience provides the sole effective guaranty of its development. Already in one of his earliest stories we find the observation that "in this country the people have rights but the person has none." And in so far as any artist can be said to have had a mission, his manifestly was to brace the American individual in his moral struggle to gain for his personal and subjective life that measure of freedom which, as a citizen of a prosperous and democratic community, he had long been enjoying in the sphere of material and political relations.

Strether's appeal, in curiously elaborated, varied, as well as ambivalent forms, pervades all of James's work; and for purposes of critical symbolization it might well be regarded as the compositional key to the whole modern movement in American writing. No literature, it might be said, takes on the qualities of a truly national body of expression unless it is possessed by a basic theme and unifying principle of its own. Thus the German creative mind has in the main been actuated by philosophical interests, the French by the highest ambitions of the intelligence unrestrained by system or dogma, the Russian by the passionately candid questioning and shaping of values. And since Whitman and James the American creative mind, seizing at last upon what had long been denied to it, has found the terms and objects of its activity in the urge toward and immersion in experience. It is this search for experience, conducted on diverse and often conflicting levels of consciousness, which has been the dominant, quintessential theme of the characteristic American literary productions—from *Leaves of Grass* to *Winesburg, Ohio* and beyond; and the more typically American the writer—a figure like Thomas Wolfe is a patent example—the more deeply does it engulf him.

It is through this preoccupation, it seems to me, that one can account, perhaps more adequately than through any other factor, for some of the peculiarities of American writing since the close of its classic period. A basis is thus provided for explaining the unique indifference of this literature to certain cultural aims implicit in the aesthetic rendering of experience—to ideas generally, to theories of value, to the wit of the speculative and problematical, and to that new-fashioned sense of irony which at once expresses and modulates the conflicts in modern belief. In his own way even a writer as intensely aware as James shares this indifference. He is the analyst of fine consciences, and fine minds too, but scarcely of minds capable of grasping and acting upon those ineluctable problems that enter so prominently and with such significant results into the literary art developed in Europe during the past hundred years. And the question is not whether James belonged among the "great thinkers"— very few novelists do—but whether he is "obsessed" by those universal problems, whether, in other words, his work is vitally associated with that prolonged crisis of the human spirit to which the concept of modernity is ultimately reducible. What James asks for, primarily, is the expansion of life beyond its primitive needs and elementary standards of moral and material utility; and of culture he conceives as the reward of this expansion and as its unfailing means of discrimination. Hence he searches for the whereabouts of "Life" and for the exact conditions of its enrichment. This is what makes for a fundamental difference between the inner movement of the American and that of the European novel, the novel of Tolstoy and Dostoyevsky, Flaubert and Proust, Joyce, Mann, Lawrence, and Kafka, whose problem is invariably posed in terms of life's intrinsic worth and destiny.

The intellectual is the only character missing in the American novel. He may appear in it in his professional capacity—as artist, teacher, or scientist—but very rarely as a person who thinks with his entire being, that is to say, as a person who transforms ideas into actual dramatic motives instead of merely using them as ideological conventions or as theories so externally applied that they can be dispensed with at will. Everything is contained in the American novel except ideas. But what are ideas? At best judgments of reality and at worst substitutes for it. The American novelist's conversion to reality, however, has been so belated that he cannot but be baffled by judgments and vexed by substitutes. Thus his work exhibits a singular pattern consisting, on the one hand, of a disinclination to thought and, on the other, of an intense predilection for the real: and the real appears in it as a vast phenomenology swept by waves of sensation and feeling. In this welter there is little room for the intellect, which in the unconscious belief of many imaginative Americans is naturally impervious, if not wholly inimical, to reality.

Consider the literary qualities of Ernest Hemingway, for example. There is nothing Hemingway dislikes more than experience of a make-believe, vague, or frigid nature, but in order to safeguard himself against the counterfeit he consistently avoids drawing upon the more abstract resources of the mind, he snubs the thinking man and mostly confines himself to the depiction of life on its physical levels. Of course, his rare mastery of the sensuous element largely compensates for whatever losses he may sustain in other spheres. Yet the fact remains that a good part of his writing leaves us with a sense of situations unresolved and with a picture of human beings tested by values much too simplified to do them justice. Cleanth Brooks and Robert Penn Warren have recently remarked on the interrelation between qualities of Hemingway's style and his bedazzlement by sheer experience. The following observation in particular tends to bear out the point of view expressed in this essay: "The short simple rhythms, the succession of coordinate clauses, the general lack of subordination—all suggest a dislocated and ununified world. The figures which live in this world live a sort of hand-to-mouth existence perceptually, and conceptually, they hardly live at all. Subordination implies some exercise of discrimination—the sifting of reality through the intellect. But Hemingway has a romantic anti-intellectualism which is to be associated with the premium which he places upon experience as such."

But Hemingway is only a specific instance. Other writers, less gifted and not so self-sufficiently and incisively one-sided, have come to grief through this same creative psychology. Under its condiitoning some of them have produced work so limited to the recording of the unmistakably and recurrently real that it can truly be said of them that their art ends exactly where it should properly begin.

"How can one make the best of one's life?" André Malraux asks in one of his novels. "By converting as wide a range of experience as possible into conscious thought." It is precisely this reply which is alien to the typical American artist, who all too often is so absorbed in experience that he is satisfied to let it "write its own ticket"—to carry him, that is, to its own chance or casual destination.

In the first part of *Faust* Goethe removes his hero, a Gothic dreamer, from the cell of scholastic devotion in order to embroil him in the passions and high-flavored joys of "real life." But in the second part of the play this hero attains a broader stage of consciousness, reconciling the perilous freedom of his newly released personality with the enduring interests of the race, with high art, politics, and the constructive labor of curbing the chaotic forces in man and nature alike. This progress of Faust is foreshadowed in an early scene, when Mephisto promises to reveal to him "the little and then the great world."—*Wir sehen die kleine, dann die grosse Welt.*— The little world is the world of the individual bemused by his personal experience, and his sufferings, guilt feelings, and isolation are to be understood as the penality he pays for throwing off the traditional bonds that once linked him to God and his fellow-men. Beyond the little world, however, lies the broader world of man the inhabitant of his own history, who in truth is always losing his soul in order to gain it. Now the American drama of experience constitutes a kind of half-*Faust,* a play with the first part intact and the second part missing. And the Mephisto of this shortened version is the familiar demon of the Puirtan morality-play, not at all the Goethian philosopher-sceptic driven by the nihilistic spirit of the modern epoch. Nor is the plot of this half-*Faust* consistent within itself. For its protagonist, playing Gretchen as often as he plays Faust, is evidently unclear in his own mind as to the role he is cast in—that of the seducer or the seduced?

It may be that this confusion of roles is the inner source of the famous Jamesian ambiguity and ever recurring theme of betrayal. James's heroines—his Isabel Archers and Milly Theales and Maggie Ververs—are they not somehow always being victimized by the "great world" even as they succeed in mastering it? Gretchen-like in their innocence, they none the less enact the Faustian role in their uninterrupted pursuit of experience and in the use of the truly Mephistophelean gold of their millionaire fathers to buy up the brains and beauty and nobility of the civilization that enchants them. And the later heroes of American fiction—Hemingway's young man, for instance, who invariably appears in each of his novels, a young man posing his virility against the background of continents and nations so old that, like Tiresias, they have seen all and suffered all —in his own way he, too, responds to experience in the schizoid fashion of the Gretchen-Faust character. For what is his virility if not at once the measure of his innocence and the measure of his aggression? And what shall we make of Steinbeck's fable of Lennie, that mindless giant who literally kills and gets killed from sheer desire for those soft and lovely things of which fate has singularly deprived him? He combines an unspeakable innocence with an unspeakable aggression. Perhaps it is not too farfetched to say that in this grotesque creature Steinbeck has unconsciously created a symbolic parody of a figure such as Thomas Wolfe, who likewise crushed in his huge caresses the delicate objects of the art of life.

II

The disunity of American literature, its polar division into above and below or paleface and redskin writing, I have noted elsewhere. Whitman and James, who form a kind of fatal antipodes, have served as the standard examples of this dissociation. There is one sense, however, in which the contrast between these two archetypal Americans may be said to have been overdrawn. There is, after all, a common ground on which they finally, though perhaps briefly, meet —an essential Americanism subsuming them both that is best defined by their mutual affirmation of experience. True, what one affirmed the other was apt to negate; still it is not in their attitudes toward experience as such that the difference between them becomes crucial but rather in their contradictory conceptions of what constitutes experience. One sought its ideal manifestations in America, the other in Europe. Whitman, plunging with characteristic impetuosity into the turbulent, formless life of the frontier and the big cities, accepted experience in its total ungraded state, whereas James, insisting on a precise scrutiny of its origins and conditions, was endlessly discriminatory, thus carrying forward his ascetic inheritance into the very act of reaching out for the charms and felicities of the great European world. But the important thing to keep in mind here is that this plebeian and patrician are historically associated, each in his own incomparable way, in the radical enterprise of subverting the puritan code of stark utility in the conduct of life and in releasing the long compressed springs of experience in the national letters. In this sense, Whitman and James are the true initiators of the American line of modernity.

If a positive approach to experience is the touchstone of the modern, a negative approach is the touchstone of the classic in American writing. The literature of early America is a sacred rather than a profane literature. Immaculately spiritual at the top and local and anecdotal at the bottom, it is essentially, as the genteel literary historian Barrett Wendell accurately noted, a "record of the national inexperience" marked by "instinctive disregard of actual fact." For this reason it largely left untouched the two chief experimental media —the novel and the drama. Brockden Brown, Cooper, Hawthorne, and Melville were "romancers" rather than novelists. They were incapable of apprehending the vitally new principle of realism by virtue of which the art of fiction in Europe was in their time rapidly evolving toward a hitherto inconceivable condition of objectivity and familiarity with existence. Not until James did a fiction writer appear in America who was able to sympathize with and hence to take advantage of the methods of George Eliot, Balzac, and Turgenev. Since the principle of realism presupposes a thoroughly secularized relationship between the ego and experience, Hawthorne and Melville could not possibly have apprehended it. Though not religious men themselves, they were nevertheless held in bondage by ancestral conscience and dogma, they were still living in the afterglow of a religious faith that drove the ego, on its external side, to aggrandize itself by accumulating practical sanctions while scourging and inhibiting its intimate side. In Hawthorne the absent or suppressed experience reappears in the shape of spectral beings whose function is to warn, repel, and fascinate. And the unutterable confusion that reigns in some of Melville's narratives (*Pierre, Mardi*) is primarily due to his inability either to come to terms with experience or else wholly and finally to reject it.

Despite the featureless innocence and moral-enthusiastic air of the old American books, there is in some of them a peculiar virulence, a feeling of discord that does not easily fit in with the general tone of the classic age. In such worthies as Irving, Cooper, Bryant, Longfellow, Whittier, and Lowell there is scarcely anything more than meets the eye, but in Poe, Hawthorne, and Melville there is an incandescent symbolism, a meaning within meaning, the vitality of which is perhaps only now being rightly appreciated. D. H. Lawrence was close to the truth when he spoke of what serpents they were, of the "inner diabolism of their underconsciousness." Hawthorne, "that blue-eyed darling," as well as Poe and Melville, insisted on a subversive vision of human nature at the same time as cultivated Americans were everywhere relishing the orations of Emerson who, as James put it, was helping them "to take a picturesque view of one's internal possibilities and to find in the landscape of the soul all sorts of fine sunrise and moonlight effects." Each of these three creative men displays a healthy resistance to the sentimentality and vague idealism of his contemporaries; and along with this resistance they display morbid qualities that, aside from any specific biographical factors, might perhaps be accounted for by the contradiction between the poverty of the experience provided by the society they lived in and the high development of their moral, intellectual, and affective natures—though in Poe's case there is no need to put any stress on his moral character. And the curious thing is that whatever faults their work shows are reversed in later American literature, the weaknesses of which are not to be traced to poverty of experience but to an inability to encompass it on a significant level.

The dilemma that confronted these early writers chiefly manifests itself in their frequent failure to integrate the inner and outer elements of their world so that they might stand witness for each other by way of the organic linkage of object and symbol, act and meaning. For that is the linkage of art without which its structure cannot stand. Lawrence thought that *Moby Dick* is profound *beyond* human feeling —which in a sense says as much against the book as for it. Its further defects are dispersion, a divided mind: its real and transcendental elements do not fully interpenetrate, the creative tension between them is more fortuitous than organic. In *The Scarlet Letter* as in a few of his shorter fictions, and to a lesser degree in *The Blithedale Romance,* Hawthorne was able to achieve an imaginative order that otherwise eluded him. A good deal of his writing, despite his gift for precise observation, consists of fantasy unsupported by the conviction of reality.

Many changes had to take place in America before its spiritual and material levels could fuse in a work of art in a more or less satisfactory manner. Whitman was already in the position to vivify his democratic ethos by an appeal to the physical features of the country, such as the grandeur and variety of its geography, and to the infinite detail of common lives and occupations. And James too, though sometimes forced to resort to makeshift situations, was on the whole successful in setting up a lively and significant exchange between the moral and empiric elements of his subject matter. Though he was, in a sense, implicitly bound all his life by the morality of Hawthorne, James none the less perceived what the guilt-tossed psyche of the author of *The Marble Faun* prevented him from seeing—that it is not the man trusting himself to experience but the one fleeing from it who suffers the "beast in the jungle" to rend him.

The Transcendentalist movement is peculiar in that it expresses the native tradition of inexperience in its patriculars and the revolutionary urge to experience in its generalities. (Perhaps that is what Van Wyck Brooks meant when, long before prostrating himself at his shrine, he wrote. that Emerson was habitually abstract where he should be concrete, and vice versa.) On a purely theoretical plane, in ways curiously inverted and idealistic, the cult of experience is patently prefigured in Emerson's doctrine of the uniqueness and infinitude, as well as in Thoreau's equally steep estimate, of the private man. American culture was then unprepared for anything more drastic than an affirmation of experience in theory alone, and even the theory was modulated in a semiclerical fashion so as not to set it in too open an opposition to the dogmatic faith that, despite the decay of its theology, still prevailed in the ethical sphere. "The love which is preached nowadays," wrote Thoreau, "is an ocean of new milk for a man to swim in. I hear no surf nor surge, but the winds coo over it." No wonder, then, that Transcendentalism declared itself most clearly and dramatically in the form of the essay—a form in which one can preach without practicing.

III

Personal liberation from social taboos and conventions was the war cry of the group of writers that came to the fore in the second decade of the century. They employed a variety of means to formulate and press home this program. Dreiser's tough-minded though somewhat arid naturalism, Anderson's softer and spottier method of articulating the protest of shut-in people, Lewis's satires of Main Street, Cabell's florid celebrations of pleasure, Edna Millay's emotional expansiveness, Mencken's worldly wisdom and assaults on the provincial pieties, the early Van Wyck Brook's high-minded though bitter evocations of the inhibited past, his ideal of creative self-fulfillment—all these were weapons brought to bear by the party of rebellion in the struggle to gain free access to experience. And the secret of energy in that struggle seems to have been the longing for what was then called "sexual freedom"; for at the time Americans seeking emancipation were engaged in a truly elemental discovery of sex whose literary expression on some levels, as Randolph Bourne remarked, easily turned into "caricatures of desire." The novel, the poem, the play—all contributed to the development of a complete symptomatology of sexual frustration and release. In his *Memoirs,* written toward the end of his life, Sherwood Anderson recalled the writers of that period as "a little band of soldiers who were going to free life . . . from certain bonds." Not that they wanted to overplay sex, but they did want "to bring it back into real relation to the life we lived and saw others living. We wanted the flesh back in our literature, wanted directly in our literature the fact of men and women in bed together, babies being born. We wanted the terrible importance of the flesh in human relations also revealed again." In retrospect much of this writing seems but a naive inversion of the dear old American innocence, a turning inside out of inbred fear and reticence, but the qualities one likes in it are its positiveness of statement, its zeal and pathos of the limited view.

The concept of experience was then still an undifferentiated whole. But as the desire for personal liberation, even if only from the less compulsive social pressures, was partly gratified and the tone of the literary revival changed from eagerness to disdain, the sense of totality gradually wore itself out. Since the nineteen twenties a process of atomization of experience has forced each of its spokesmen into a separate groove from which he can step out only at the risk of utterly disorienting himself. Thus, to cite some random examples, poetic technique became the special experience of Ezra Pound, language that of Gertrude Stein, the concrete object was appropriated by W. C. Williams, super-American phenomena by Sandburg and related nationalists, Kenneth Burke experienced ideas (which is by no means the same as thinking them), Archibald MacLeish experienced public attitudes, F. Scott Fitzgerald the glamour and sadness of the very rich, Hemingway death and virile sports, and so on and so forth. Finally Thomas Wolfe plunged into a chaotic recapitulation of the cult of experience as a whole, traversing it in all directions and ending nowhere.

Though the crisis of the nineteen thirties arrested somewhat the progress of the experiential mode, it nevertheless managed to put its stamp on the entire social-revolutionary literature of the decade. A comparison of European and American left-wing writing of the same period will at once show that whereas Europeans like Malraux and Silone enter deeply into the meaning of political ideas and beliefs, Americans touch only superficially on such matters, as actually their interest is fixed almost exclusively on the class war as an experience which, to them at least, is new and exciting. They succeed in representing incidents of oppression and revolt, as well as sentimental conversions, but conversions of the heart and mind they merely sketch in on the surface or imply in a gratuitous fashion. (What does a radical novel like *The Grapes of Wrath* contain, from an ideological point of view, that agitational journalism cannot communicate with equal heat and facility. Surely its vogue cannot be explained by its radicalism. Its real attraction for the millions who read it lies elsewhere—perhaps in its vivid recreation of "a slice of life" so horridly unfamiliar that it can be made to yield an exotic interest.) The sympathy of these ostensibly political writers with the revolutionary cause is often genuine, yet their understanding of its inner movement, intricate problems, and doctrinal and strategic motives is so deficient as to call into question their competence to deal with political material. In the complete works of the so-called "proletarian school" you will not find a single viable portrait of a Marxist intellectual or of any character in the revolutionary drama who, conscious of his historical role, is not a mere automaton of spontaneous class force or impulse.

What really happened in the nineteen thirties is that due to certain events the public aspects of experience appeared more meaningful than its private aspects, and literature responded accordingly. But the subject of political art is *history,* which stands in the same relation to experience as fiction to biography; and just as surely as failure to generalize the biographical element thwarts the aspirant to fiction, so the ambition of the literary left to create a political art was thwarted by its failure to lift experience to the level of history. (For the benefit of those people who habitually pause to insist on what they call "strictly literary values," I might add that by "history" in this connection I do not mean "history books" or anything resembling what is known as the "historical novel" or drama. A political art would succeed in lifting experience to the level of history if its perception of life—any life—were organized around a perspective relating the artist's sense of the *society* of the dead to his sense of the *society* of the living and the as yet unborn.)

Experience, in the sense of "felt life" rather than as life's total practice, is the main but by no means the total substance of literature. The part experience plays in the aesthetic sphere might well be compared to the part that the materialist conception of history assigns to economy. Experience, in the sense of this analogy, is the substructure of literature above which there rises a superstructure of values, ideas, and judgments—in a word, of the multiple forms of consciousness. But this base and summit are not stationary: they continually act and react upon each other.

It is precisely this superstructural level which is seldom reached by the typical American writer of the modern era. Most of the well-known reputations will bear out my point. Whether you approach a poet like Ezra Pound or novelists like Steinbeck and Faulkner, what is at once noticeable is the uneven, and at times quite distorted, development of the various elements that constitute literary talent. What is so exasperating about Pound's poetry, for example, is its peculiar combination of a finished technique (his special share in the distribution of experience) with amateurish and irresponsible ideas. It could be maintained that for sheer creative power Faulkner is hardly excelled by any living novelist, yet diversity and wonderful intensity of the experience represented in his narratives cannot entirely make up for their lack of order, of a self-illuminating structure, and obscurity of value and meaning. One might naturally counter this criticism by stating that though Faulkner rarely or never sets forth values directly, they none the less exist in his work by implication. Yes, but implications incoherently expressed are not better than mystifications, and nowadays it is values that we can least afford to take on faith. Moreover, in a more striking manner perhaps than any of his contemporaries, Faulkner illustrates the tendency of the experiential mode, if pursued to its utmost extreme, to turn into its opposite through unconscious self-parody. In Faulkner the excess, the systematic inflation of the horrible is such a parody of experience. In Thomas Wolfe the same effect is produced by his swollen rhetoric and compulsion to repeat himself—and repetition is an obvious form of parody. This repetition compulsion has plagued a good many American writers. Its first and most conspicuous victim, of course, was Whitman, who occasionally slipped into unintentional parodies of himself.

Yet there is a positive side to the primacy of experience in late American literature. For this primacy has conferred certain benefits upon it, of which none is more bracing than its relative immunity from abstraction and otherworldliness. The stream of life, unimpeded by the rocks and sands of ideology, flows through it freely. If inept in coping with the general, it particularizes not at all badly; and the assumptions of sanctity that so many European artists seem to require as a kind of guaranty of their professional standing are not readily conceded in the lighter and clearer American atmosphere. "Whatever may have been the case in years gone by," Whitman wrote in 1888, "the true use for the imaginative faculty of modern times is to give ultimate vivification to facts, to science, and to common lives, endowing them with glows and glories and final illustriousness which belong to every real thing, and to real things only." As this statement was intended as a prophecy, it is worth noting that while the radiant endowments that Whitman speaks of—the "glows and glories and final illustriousness"—have not been granted, the desired and predicted vivification of facts, science, and common lives has in a measure been realized, though in the process Whitman's democratic faith has as often been belied as confirmed.

IV

It is not the mere recoil from the inhibitions of puritan and neopuritan times that instigated the American search for experience. Behind it is the extreme individualism of a country without a long past to brood on, whose bourgeois spirit had not worn itself out and been debased in a severe struggle against an old culture so tenacious as to retain the power on occasion to fascinate and render impotent even its predestined enemies. Moreover, in contrast to the derangements that have continually shaken Europe, life in the United States has been relatively fortunate and prosperous. It is possible to speak of American history as "successful" history. Within the limits of the capitalist order—and until the present period the objective basis for a different social order simply did not exist here—the American people have been able to find definitive solutions for the great historical problems that faced them. Thus both the Revolutionary and the Civil War were complete actions that abolished the antagonisms which had initially caused the breakdown of national equilibrium. In Europe similar actions have usually led to festering compromises that in the end reproduced the same conflicts in other forms.

It is plain that until very recently there has really been no urgent need in America for high intellectual productivity. Indeed, the American intelligentsia developed very slowly as a semi-independent grouping; and what is equally important, for more than a century now and especially since 1865, it has been kept at a distance from the machinery of social and political power. What this means is that insofar as it has been deprived of certain opportunities, it has also been sheltered and pampered. There was no occasion or necessity for the intervention of the intellectuals—it was not mentality that society needed most in order to keep its affairs in order. On the whole the intellectuals were left free to cultivate private interests, and, once the moral and aesthetic ban on certain types of exertion had been removed, uninterruptedly to solicit individual experience. It is this lack of a sense of extremity and many-sided involvement which explains the peculiar shallowness of a good deal of American literary expression. If some conditions of insecurity have been known to retard and disarm the mind, so have some conditions of security. The question is not whether Americans have suffered less than Europeans, but of the quality of whatever suffering and happiness have fallen to their lot.

The consequence of all this has been that American literature has tended to make too much of private life, to impose on it, to scour it for meanings that it cannot always legitimately yield. Henry James was the first to make a cause, if not a fetish, of personal relations; and the justice of his case, despite his vaunted divergence from the pioneer type, is that of a pioneer too, for while Americans generally were still engaged in "gathering in the preparations and necessities" he resolved to seek out "the amenities and consummations." Furthermore, by exploiting in a fashion altogether his own the contingencies of private life that fell within his scope, he was able to dramatize the relations of the new world to the old, thus driving the wedge of historical consciousness into the very heart of the theme of experience. Later not a few attempts were made to combine experience with consciousness, to achieve the balance of thought and being characteristic of the great traditions of European art. But except for certain narratives of James and Melville, I know of very little American fiction which can unqualifiedly be said to have attained this end.

Since the decline of the regime of gentility many admirable works have been produced, but in the main it is the quantity of felt life comprised in them that satisfies, not their quality of belief or interpretive range. In poetry there is evidence of more distinct gains, perhaps because the medium has reached that late stage in its evolution when its chance of survival depends on its capacity to absorb ideas. The modern poetic styles—metaphysical and symbolist—depend on a conjunction of feeling and idea. But, generally speaking, bare experience is still the *leitmotiv* of the American writer, though the literary depression of recent years tends to show that this theme is virtually exhausted. At bottom it was the theme of the individual transplanted from an old culture taking inventory of himself and of his new surroundings. This inventory, this initial recognition and experiencing of oneself and one's surroundings, is all but complete now, and those who persist in going on with it are doing so out of mere routine and inertia.

The creative power of the cult of experience is almost spent, but what lies beyond it is still unclear. One thing, however, is certain: whereas in the past, throughout the nineteenth and well into the twentieth century, the nature of American literary life was largely determined by national forces, now it is international forces that have begun to exert a dominant influence. And in the long run it is in the terms of this historic change that the future course of American writing will define itself.

35

Edmund Wilson: HEMINGWAY:
GAUGE OF MORALE [1941]

Ernest Hemingway's *In Our Time* was an odd and original book. It had the appearance of a miscellany of stories and fragments; but actually the parts hung together and produced a definite effect. There were two distinct series of pieces which alternated with one another: one a set of brief and brutal sketches of police shootings, bullfight crises, hangings of criminals, and incidents of the war; and the other a set of short stories dealing in its principal sequence with the growing-up of an American boy against a landscape of idyllic Michigan, but interspersed also with glimpses of American soldiers returning home. It seems to have been Hemingway's intention—*In Our Time* —that the war should set the key for the whole. The cold-bloodedness of the battles and executions strikes a discord with the sensitiveness and candor of the boy at home in the States; and presently the boy turns up in Europe in one of the intermediate vignettes as a soldier in the Italian army, hit in the spine by machine-gun fire and trying to talk to a dying Italian: *"Senta,* Rinaldi. *Senta,"* he says, "you and me, we've made a separate peace."

But there is a more fundamental relationship between the pieces of the two series. The shooting of Nick in the war does not really connect two different worlds: has he not found in the butchery abroad the same world that he knew back in Michigan? Was not life in the Michigan woods equally destructive and cruel? He had gone once with his father, the doctor, when he had performed a Caesarean operation on an Indian squaw with a jackknife and no anaesthetic and had sewed her up with fishing leaders, while the Indian hadn't been able to bear it and had cut his throat in his bunk. Another time, when the doctor had saved the life of a squaw, her Indian had picked a quarrel with him rather than pay him in work. And Nick himself had sent his girl about her business when he had found out how terrible her mother was. Even fishing in Big Two-Hearted River— away and free in the woods——he had been conscious in a curious way of the cruelty inflicted on the fish, even of the silent agonies endured by the live bait, the grasshoppers kicking on the hook.

Not that life isn't enjoyable. Talking and drinking with one's friends is great fun; fishing in Big Tow-Hearted River is a tranquil exhilaration. But the brutality of life is always there, and it is somehow bound up with the enjoyment. Bullfights are especially enjoyable. It is even exhilarating to build a simply priceless barricade and pot the enemy as they are trying to get over it. The condition of life is pain; and the joys of the most innocent surface are somehow tied to its stifled pangs.

The resolution of this dissonance in art made the beauty of Hemingway's stories. He had in the process turned a marvelous prose. Out of the colloquial American speech, with its simple declarative sentences and its strings of Nordic monosyllables, he got effects of the utmost subtlety. F. M. Ford has found the perfect simile for the impression produced by this writing: "Hemingway's words strike you, each one, as if they were pebbles fetched fresh from a brook. They live and shine, each in its place. So one of his pages has the effect of a brook-bottom into which you look down through the flowing water. The words form a tessellation, each in order beside the other."

Looking back, we can see how this style was already being refined and developed at a time—fifty years before—when it was regarded in most literary quarters as hopelessly nonliterary and vulgar. Had there not been the nineteenth chapter of *Huckleberry Finn?*—"Two or three nights went by; I reckon I might say they swum by; they slid along so quick and smooth and lovely. Here is the way we put in the time. It was a monstrous big river down there—sometimes a mile and a half wide," and so forth. These pages, when we happen to meet them in Carl Van Doren's anthology of world literature, stand up in a striking way beside a passage of description from

Turgenev; and the pages which Hemingway was later to write about American wood and water are equivalents to the transcriptions by Turgenev—the *Sportsman's Notebook* is much admired by Hemingway—of Russian forests and fields. Each has brought to an immense and wild country the freshness of a new speech and a sensibility not yet conventionalized by literary associations. Yet it *is* the European sensibility which has come to Big Two-Hearted River, where the Indians are now obsolescent; in those solitudes it feels for the first time the cold current, the hot morning sun, sees the pine stumps, smells the sweet fern. And along with the mottled trout, with its "clear water-over-gravel color," the boy from the American Middle West fishes up a nice little masterpiece.

In the meantime there had been also Ring Lardner, Sherwood Anderson, Gertrude Stein, using this American language for irony, lyric poetry or psychological insight. Hemingway seems to have learned from them all. But he is now able to change this naive accent with a new complexity of emotion, a new shade of emotion: a malaise. The wholesale shattering of human beings in which he has taken part has given the boy a touch of panic.

II

The next fishing trip is strikingly different. Perhaps the first had been an idealization. Is it possible to attain to such sensuous bliss merely through going alone into the woods: smoking, fishing, and eating, with no thought about anyone else or about anything one has ever done or will ever be obliged to do? At any rate, today, in *The Sun Also Rises,* all the things that are wrong with human life are there on the holiday, too—though one tries to keep them back out of the foreground and to occupy one's mind with the trout, caught now in a stream of the Pyrenees, and with the kidding of the friend from the States. The feeling of insecurity has deepened. The young American now appears in a seriously damaged condition: he has somehow been incapacitated sexually through wounds received in the war. He is in love with one of those international sirens who flourished in the cafés of the postwar period and whose ruthless and uncontrollable infidelities, in such a circle as that depicted by Hemingway, have made any sort of security impossible for the relations between women and men. The lovers of such a woman turn upon and rend one another because they are powerless to make themselves felt by *her.*

The casualties of the bullfight at Pamplona, to which these young people have gone for the *fiesta,* only reflect the blows and betrayals of demoralized human beings out of hand. What is the tiresome lover with whom the lady has just been off on a casual escapade, and who is unable to understand that he has been discarded, but the man who, on his way to the bull ring, has been accidentally gored by the bull? The young American who tells the story is the only character who keeps up standards of conduct, and he is prevented by his disability from dominating and directing the woman, who otherwise, it is intimated, might love him. Here the membrane of the style has been stretched taut to convey the vibrations of these qualms. The dry sunlight and the green summer landscapes have been invested with a sinister quality which must be new in literature. One enjoys the sun and the green as one enjoys suckling pigs and Spanish wine, but the uneasiness and apprehension are undruggable.

Yet one can catch hold of a code in all the drunkenness and the social chaos. "Perhaps as you went along you did learn something," Jake, the hero, reflects at one point. "I did not care what it was all about. All I wanted to know was how to live in it. Maybe if you found out how to live in it you learned from that what it was all about." "Everybody behaves badly. Give them the proper chance," he says later to Lady Brett.

" 'You wouldn't behave badly.' Brett looked at me." In the end, she sends for Jake, who finds her alone in a hotel. She has left her regular lover for a young bullfighter, and this boy has for the first time inspired her with a respect which has restrained her from "ruining" him: "You know it makes one feel rather good deciding not to be a bitch." We suffer and we make suffer, and everybody loses out in the long run; but in the meantime we can lose with honor.

This code still markedly figures, still supplies a dependable moral backbone, in Hemingway's next book of short stories, *Men Without Women.* Here Hemingway has mastered his method of economy in apparent casualness and relevance in apparent indirection, and has turned his sense of what happens and the way in which it happens into something as hard and clear as a crystal but as disturbing as a great lyric. Yet it is usually some principle of courage, of honor, of pity—that is, some principle of sportsmanship in its largest human sense—upon which the drama hinges. The old bullfighter in "The Undefeated" is defeated in everything except the spirit which will not accept defeat. You get the bull or he gets you: if you die, you can die game; there are certain things you cannot do. The burlesque show manager in "A Pursuit Race" refrains from waking his advance publicity agent when he overtakes him and realizes that the man has just lost a long struggle against whatever anguish it is that has driven him to drink and dope. "They got a cure for that," the manager had said to him before he went to sleep; " 'No,' William Campbell said, 'they haven't got a cure for anything.' " The burned major in "A Simple Enquiry"—that strange picture of the bedrock stoicism compatible with the abasement of war—has the decency not to dismiss the orderly who has rejected his proposition. The brutalized Alpine peasant who has been in the habit of hanging a lantern in the jaws of the stiffened corpse of his wife, stood in the corner of the woodshed till the spring will make it possible to bury her, is ashamed to drink with the sexton after the latter has found out what he has done. And there is a little sketch of Roman soldiers just after the Crucifixion: "You see me slip the old spear into him?—You'll get into trouble doing that some day.—It was the least I could do for him. I'll tell you he looked pretty good to me in there today."

This Hemingway of the middle twenties—*The Sun Also Rises* came out in 1926—expressed the romantic disillusion and set the favorite pose for the period. It was the moment of gallantry in heartbreak, grim and nonchalant banter, and heroic dissipation. The great watchword was "Have a drink"; and in the bars of New York and Paris the young people were getting to talk like Hemingway.

III

The novel, *A Farewell to Arms,* which followed *Men Without Women,* is in a sense not so serious an affair. Beautifully written and quite moving of course it is. Probably no other book has caught so well the strangeness of life in the army for an American in Europe during the war. The new places to which one was sent of which one had never heard, and the things that turned out to be in them; the ordinary people of foreign countries as one saw them when one was quartered among them or obliged to perform some common work with them; the pleasures of which one managed to cheat the war, intensified by the uncertainty and horror—and the uncertainty, nevertheless, almost become a constant, the horror almost taken for granted; the love affairs, always subject to being suddenly broken up and yet carried on while they lasted in a spirit of irresponsible freedom which derived from one's having forfeited control of all one's other actions—this Hemingway got into his book, written long enough after the events for them to present themselves under an aspect fully idyllic.

But *A Farewell to Arms* is a tragedy, and the lovers are shown as innocent victims with no relation to the forces that torment them. They themselves are not tormented within by that dissonance between personal satisfaction and the suffering one shares with others which it has been Hemingway's triumph to handle. *A Farewell to Arms,* as the author once said, is a *Romeo and Juliet.* And when Catherine and her lover emerge from the stream of action—the account of the Caporetto retreat is Hemingway's best sustained piece of narrative—when they escape from the alien necessities of which their romance has been merely an accident, which have been writing their story for them, then we see that they are not in themselves convincing as human personalities. And we are confronted with the paradox that Hemingway, who possesses so remarkable a mimetic gift in getting the tone of social and national types and in making his people talk appropriately, has not shown any very solid sense of character, or, indeed, any real interest in it. The people in his short stories are satisfactory because he has only to hit them off: the point of the story does not lie in personalities, but in the emotion to which a situation gives rise. This is true even in *The Sun Also Rises,* where the characters are sketched with wonderful cleverness. But in *A Farewell to Arms,* as soon as we are brought into real intimacy with the lovers, as soon as the author is obliged to see them through a searching personal experience, we find merely an idealized relationship, the abstractions of a lyric emotion.

With *Death in the Afternoon,* three years later, a new development for Hemingway commences. He writes a book not merely in the first person, but in the first person in his own character as Hemingway, and the results are unexpected and disconcerting. *Death in the Afternoon* has its value as an exposition of bullfighting; and Hemingway is able to use the subject as a text for an explicit statement of his conception of man eternally pitting himself—he thinks the bullfight a ritual of this—against animal force and the odds of death. But the book is partly infected by a queer kind of maudlin emotion, which sounds at once neurotic and drunken. He overdoes his glorification of the bravery and martyrdom of the bullfighter. No doubt the professional expert at risking his life single-handed is impressive in contrast to the flatness and unreality of much of the business of the modern world; but this admirable miniaturist in prose has already made the point perhaps more tellingly in the little prose poem called "Banal Story." Now he offsets the virility of the bullfighters by anecdotes of the male homosexuals that frequent the Paris cafés, at the same time that he puts his chief celebration of the voluptuous excitement of the spectacle into the mouth of an imaginary old lady. The whole thing becomes a little hysterical.

The master of that precise and clean style now indulges in purple patches which go on spreading for pages. I am not one of those who admire the last chapter of *Death in the Afternoon,* with its rich, all too rich, unrollings of memories of good times in Spain, and with its what seem to me irrelevant reminiscences of the soliloquy of Mrs. Bloom in *Ulysses.* Also, there are interludes of kidding of a kind which Hemingway handles with skill when he assigns them to characters in his stories, but in connection with which he seems to become incapable of exercising good sense or good taste as soon as he undertakes them in his own person (the burlesque *Torrents of Spring* was an early omen of this). In short, we are compelled to recognize that, as soon as Hemingway drops the burning-glass of the disciplined and objective art with which he has learned to concentrate in a story the light of the emotions that flood in on him, he straightway becomes befuddled, slops over.

This befuddlement is later to go further, but in the meantime he publishes another volume of stories—*Winner Take Nothing*—which is almost up to its predecessor. In this collection he deals much more effectively than in *Death in the Afternoon* with that theme of contemporary decadence which is implied in his panegyric of the bullfighter. The first of these stories, "After the Storm," is another of his variations—and one of the finest—on the theme of keeping up a code of decency among the hazards and pains of life. A fisherman goes out to plunder a wreck: he dives down to break in through a porthole, but inside he sees a woman with rings on her hands and her hair floating loose in the water, and he thinks about the passengers and crew being suddenly plunged to their deaths (he has almost been killed himself in a drunken fight the night before). He sees the cloud of sea birds screaming around, and he finds that he is unable to break the glass with his wrench and that he loses the anchor grapple with which he next tries to attack it. So he finally goes away and leaves the job to the Greeks, who blow the boat open and clean her out.

But in general the emotions of insecurity here obtrude themselves and dominate the book. Two of the stories deal with the hysteria of soldiers falling off the brink of their nerves under the strain of the experiences of the war, which here no longer presents an idyllic aspect; another deals with a group of patients in a hospital, at the same time crippled and hopeless; still another (a five-page masterpiece) with a waiter, who, both on his own and on his customers' account, is reluctant to go home at night, because he feels the importance of a "clean well-lighted café" as a refuge from the "nothing" that people fear. "God Rest You Merry, Gentlemen" repeats the theme of castration of *The Sun Also Rises;* and four of the stories are concerned more or less with male or female homosexuality. In the last story, "Fathers and Sons," Hemingway reverts to the Michigan forest, as if to take the curse off the rest: young Nick had once enjoyed a nice Indian girl with plump legs and hard little breasts on the needles of the hemlock woods.

These stories and the interludes in *Death in the Afternoon* must have been written during the years that followed the stock-market crash. They are full of the apprehension of losing control of oneself which is aroused by the getting out of hand of a social-economic system, as well as of the fear of impotence which seems to accompany the loss of social mastery. And there is in such a story as "A Clean Well-Lighted Place" the feeling of having got to the end of everything, of having given up heroic attitudes and wanting only the illusion of peace.

IV

And now, in proportion as the characters in his stories run out of fortitude and bravado, he passes into a phase where he is occupied with building up his public personality. He has already now become a legend, as Mencken was in the twenties; he is the Hemingway of the handsome photographs with the sportsman's tan and the outdoor grin, with the ominous resemblance to Clark Gable, who poses with giant marlin which he has just hauled in off Key West. And unluckily —but for an American inevitably—the opportunity soon presents itself to exploit this personality for profit: he turns up delivering Hemingway monologues in well-paying and trashy magazines; and the Hemingway of these loose disquisitions, arrogant, belligerent and boastful, is certainly the worst-invented character to be found in the author's work. If he is obnoxious, the effect is somewhat mitigated by the fact that he is intrinsically incredible.

There would be no point in mentioning this journalism at all, if it did not seem somewhat to have contributed to the writing of certain unsatisfactory books. *Green Hills of Africa* (1935) owes its failure to falling between the two genres of personal exhibitionism and fiction. "The writer has attempted," says Hemingway, "to write an absolutely true book to see whether the shape of a country and the pattern of a month's action can, if truly presented, compete with a work of the imagination." He does try to present his own role objectively, and there is a genuine Hemingway theme—the connection between success at big-game hunting and sexual self-respect—involved in his adventures as he presents them. But the sophisticated technique of the fiction writer comes to look artificial when it is applied to a series of real happenings; and the necessity of sticking to what really happened makes impossible the typical characters and incidents which give point to a work of fiction. The monologues by the false, the publicity, Hemingway with which the narrative is interspersed are almost as bad as the ones that he has been writing for the magazines. He inveighs with much scorn against the literary life and against the professional literary man of the cities; and then manages to give the impression that he himself is a professional literary man of the touchiest and most self-conscious kind. He delivers a self-confident lecture on the high possibilities of prose writing; and then produces such a sentence as the following: "Going downhill steeply made these Spanish shooting boots too short in the toe and there was an old argument, about the length of boot and whether the bootmaker, whose part I had taken, unwittingly first, only as interpreter, and finally embraced his theory patriotically as a whole and, I believed, by logic, had overcome it by adding onto the heel." As soon as Hemingway begins speaking in the first person, he seems to lose his bearings, not merely as a critic of life, but even as a craftsman.

In another and significant way, *Green Hills of Africa* is disappointing. *Death in the Afternoon* did provide a lot of data on bullfighting and build up for us the bullfighting world; but its successor tells us little about Africa. Hemingway keeps affirming—as if in accents of defiance against those who would engage his attention for social problems—his passionate enthusiasm for the African country and his perfect satisfaction with the hunter's life; but he has produced what must be one of the only books ever written which make Africa and its animals seem dull. Almost the only thing we learn about the animals is that Hemingway wants to kill them. And as for the natives, though there is one fine description of a tribe of marvelous trained runners, the principal impression we get of them is that they were simple and inferior people who enormously admired Hemingway.

It is not only that, as his critics of the left had been complaining, he shows no interest in political issues, but that his interest in his fellow beings seems actually to be drying up. It is as if he were throwing himself on African hunting as something to live for and believe in, as something through which to realize himself; and as if, expecting of it too much, he had got out of it abnormally little, less than he is willing to admit. The disquiet of the Hemingway of the twenties had been, as I have said, undruggable—that is, in his books themselves, he had tried to express it, not drug it, had given it an appeasement in art; but now there sets in, in the Hemingway of the thirties, what seems to be a deliberate self-drugging. The situation is indicated objectively in "The Gambler, the Nun and the Radio," one of the short stories of 1933, in which everything from daily bread to "a belief in any new form of government" is characterized as "the opium of the people" by an empty-hearted patient in a hospital.

But at last there did rush into this vacuum the blast of the social issue, which had been roaring in the wind like a forest fire.

Out of a series of short stories that Hemingway had written about a Florida waterside character he decided to make a little epic. The result was *To Have and Have Not,* which seems to me the poorest of all his stories. Certainly some deep agitation is working upon Hemingway the artist. Craftsmanship and style, taste and sense, have all alike gone by the board. The negative attitude toward human beings has here become definitely malignant: the hero is like a woodenheaded Punch, always knocking people on the head (inferiors—Chinamen or Cubans); or, rather, he combines the characteristics of Punch with those of Popeye the Sailor in the animated cartoon in the movies. As the climax to a series of prodigies, this stupendous pirate-smuggler named Harry Morgan succeeds, alone, unarmed, and with only a hook for a hand—though at the cost of a mortal wound—in outwitting and destroying with their own weapons four men carrying revolvers and a machine gun, by whom he has been shanghaied in a launch. The only way in which Hemingway's outlaw suffers by comparison with Popeye is that his creator has not tried to make him plausible by explaining that he does it all on spinach.

The impotence of a decadent society has here been exploited deliberately, but less successfully than in the earlier short stories. Against a background of homosexuality, impotence and masturbation among the wealthy holiday-makers in Florida, Popeye-Morgan is shown gratifying his wife with the same indefatigable dexterity which he has displayed in his other feats; and there is a choral refrain of praise of his *cojones,* which wells up in the last pages of the book when the abandoned Mrs. Popeye regurgitates Molly Bloom's soliloquy.

To be a man in such a world of maggots is noble, but it is not enough. Besides the maggots, there are double-crossing rats, who will get you if they are given the slightest chance. What is most valid in *To Have and Have Not* is the idea—conveyed better, perhaps, in the first of the series of episodes than in the final scenes of massacre and agony—that in an atmosphere (here revolutionary Cuba) in which man has been set against man, in which it is always a question whether your companion is not preparing to cut your throat, the most sturdy and straightforward American will turn suspicious and cruel. Harry Morgan is made to realize as he dies that to fight this bad world alone is hopeless. Again Hemingway, with his barometric accuracy, has rendered a moral atmosphere that was prevalent at the moment he was writing—a moment when social relations were subjected to severe tensions, when they seemed sometimes already disintegrating. But the heroic Hemingway legend has at this point invaded his fiction and, inflaming and inflating his symbols, has produced an implausible hybrid, half Hemingway character, half nature myth.

Hemingway had not himself particularly labored this moral of individualism *versus* solidarity, but the critics of the left labored it for him and received his least creditable piece of fiction as the delivery of a new revelation. The progress of the Communist faith among our writers since the beginning of the depression has followed a peculiar course. That the aims and beliefs of Marx and Lenin should have come through to the minds of intellectuals who had been educated in the bourgeois tradition as great awakeners of conscience, a great light, was quite natural and entirely desirable. But the conception of the dynamic Marxist will, the exaltation of the Marxist religion, seized the members of the professional classes like a capricious contagion or hurricane, which shakes one and leaves his neighbor standing, then returns to lay hold on the second after the first has become quiet again. In the moment of seizure, each one of them saw a scroll unrolled from the heavens, on which Marx and Lenin and Stalin, the Bolsheviks of 1917, the Soviets of the Five-Year Plan, and the GPU of the Moscow trials were all a part of the same great purpose. Later the convert, if he were capable of it, would get over his first phase of snow blindness and learn to see real people and conditions, would study the development of Marxism in terms of nations, periods, personalities, instead of logical deductions from abstract propositions or—as in the case of the more naive or dishonest—of simple incantatory slogans. But for many there was at least a moment when the key to all the mysteries of human history seemed suddenly to have been placed in their hands, when an infallible guide to thought and behavior seemed to have been given them in a few easy formulas.

Hemingway was hit pretty late. He was still in *Death in the Afternoon* telling the "world-savers," sensibly enough, that they should "get to see" the world "clear and as a whole. Then any part you make will represent the whole, if it's made truly. The thing to do is work and learn to make it." Later he jibed at the literary radicals, who talked but couldn't take it; and one finds even in *To Have and*

Have Not a crack about a "highly paid Hollywood director, whose brain is in the process of outlasting his liver so that he will end up calling himself a Communist, to save his soul." Then the challenge of the fight itself—Hemingway never could resist a physical challenge—the natural impulse to dedicate oneself to something bigger than big-game hunting and bullfighting, and the fact that the class war had broken out in a country to which he was romantically attached, seem to have combined to make him align himself with the Communist as well as the Spanish Loyalists at a time when the Marxist philosophy had been pretty completely shelved by the Kremlin, now reactionary as well as corrupt, and when the Russians were lending the Loyalists only help enough to preserve, as they imagined would be possible, the balance of power against Fascism while they acted at the same time as a police force to beat down the real social revolution.

Hemingway raised money for the Loyalists, reported the battle fronts. He even went so far as to make a speech at a congress of the League of American Writers, an organization rigged by the supporters of the Stalinist regime in Russia and full of precisely the type of literary revolutionists that he had been ridiculing a little while before. Soon the Stalinists had taken him in tow, and he was feverishly denouncing as Fascists other writers who criticized the Kremlin. It has been one of the expedients of the Stalin administration in maintaining its power and covering up its crimes to condemn on trumped-up charges of Fascist conspiracy, and even to kidnap and murder, its political opponents of the left; and, along with the food and munitions, the Russians had brought to the war in Spain what the Austrian journalist Willi Schlamm called that diversion of doubtful value for the working class: "Herr Vyshinsky's Grand Guignol."

The result of this was a play, *The Fifth Column,* which, though it is good reading for the way the characters talk, is an exceedingly silly production. The hero, though an Anglo-American, is an agent of the Communist secret police, enaged in catching Fascist spies in Spain; and his principal exploit in the course of the play is clearing out, with the aid of a single Communist, an artillery post manned by seven Fascists. The scene is like a pushover and getaway from one of the cruder Hollywood Westerns. It is in the nature of a small boy's fantasy, and would probably be considered extravagant by most writers of books for boys.

The tendency on Hemingway's part to indulge himself in these boyish daydreams seems to begin to get the better of his realism at the end of *A Farewell to Arms,* where the hero, after many adventures of fighting, escaping, love-making and drinking, rows his lady thirty-five kilometers on a cold and rainy night; and we have seen what it could do for Harry Morgan. Now, as if with the conviciton that the cause and the efficiency of the GPU have added several cubits to his stature, he has let this tendency loose; and he has also found in the GPU's grim duty a pretext to give rein to the appetite for describing scenes of killing which has always been a feature of his work. He has progressed from grasshoppers and trout through bulls and lions and kudus to Chinamen and Cubans, and now to Fascists. Hitherto the act of destruction has given rise for him to complex emotions: he has identified himself not merely with the injurer but also with the injured; there has been a masochistic complement to the sadism. But now this paradox which splits our natures, and which has instigated some of Hemingway's best stories, need no longer present perplexities to his mind. The Fascists are dirty bastards, and to kill them is a righteous act. He who had made a separate peace, who had said farewell to arms, has found a reason for taking them up again in a spirit of rabietic fury unpleasantly reminiscent of the spy mania and the sacred anti-German rage which took possession of so many civilians and staff officers under the stimulus of the last war.

Not that the compensatory trauma of the typical Hemingway protagonist is totally absent even here. The main episode is the hero's brief love affair and voluntary breaking off with a beautiful and adoring girl whose acquaintance he has made in Spain. As a member of the Junior League and a graduate of Vassar, she represents for him—it seems a little hard on her—that leisure-class playworld from which he is trying to get away. But in view of the fact that from the very first scenes he treats her with more or less open contempt, the action is rather lacking in suspense as the sacrifice is rather feeble in moral value. One takes no stock at all in the intimation that Mr. Philip may later be sent to mortify himself in a camp for training Young Pioneers. And in the meantime he has fun killing Fascists.

In *The Fifth Column,* the drugging process has been carried further still: the hero, who has become finally indistinguishable from the false or publicity Hemingway, has here dosed himself not only with whiskey, but with a seductive and desirous woman, for whom he has the most admirable reasons for not taking any responsibility, with sacred rage, with the excitement of a bombardment, and with indulgence in that headiest of sports, for which he has now the same excellent reasons: the bagging of human beings.

V

You may fear, after reading *The Fifth Column,* that Hemingway will never sober up; but as you go on to his short stories of this period, you find that your apprehensions were unfounded. Three of these stories have a great deal more body—they are longer and more complex—than the comparatively meager anecdotes collected in *Winner Take Nothing.* And here are his real artistic successes with the material of his adventures in Africa, which make up for the miscarried *Green Hills:* "The Short Happy Life of Francis Macomber" and "The Snows of Kilimanjaro," which disengage, by dramatizing them objectively, the themes he had attempted in the earlier book but that had never really got themselves presented. And here is at least a beginning of a real artistic utilization of Hemingway's experience in Spain: an incident of the war in two pages which outweighs the whole of *The Fifth Column* and all his Spanish dispatches, a glimpse of an old man, "without politics," who has so far occupied his life in taking care of eight pigeons, two goats and a cat, but who has now been dislodged and separated from his pets by the advance of the Fascist armies. It is a story which takes its place among the war prints of Callot and Goya, artists whose union of elegance with sharpness has already been recalled by Hemingway in his earlier battle pieces: a story which might have been written about almost any war.

And here—what is very remarkable—is a story, "The Capital of the World," which finds an objective symbol for, precisely, what is wrong with *The Fifth Column.* A young boy who has come up from the country and waits on table in a pension in Madrid gets accidentally stabbed with a meat knife while playing at bullfighting with the dishwasher. This is the simple anecdote, but Hemingway has built in behind it all the life of the pension and the city: the priesthood, the working-class movement, the grown-up bullfighters who have broken down or missed out. "The boy Paco," Hemingway concludes, "had never known about any of this nor about what all these people would be doing on the next day and on other days to come. He had no idea how they really lived nor how they ended. He did not realize they ended. He died, as the Spanish phrase has it, full of illusions. He had not had time in his life to lose any of them, or even, at the end, to complete an act of contrition." So he registers in this very fine piece the discrepancy between the fantasies of boyhood and the realities of the grown-up world. Hemingway the artist, who feels things truly and cannot help recording what he feels, has actually said good-bye to these fantasies at a time when the war correspondent is making himself ridiculous by attempting to hang on to them still.

The emotion which principally comes through in "Francis Macomber" and "The Snows of Kilimanjaro"—as it figures also in *The Fifth Column*—is a growing antagonism to women. Looking back, one can see at this point that the tendency has been there all along. In "The Doctor and the Doctor's Wife," the boy Nick goes out squirrel-hunting with his father instead of obeying the summons of his mother; in "Cross Country Snow," he regretfully says farewell to male companionship on a skiing expedition in Switzerland, when he is obliged to go back to the States so that his wife can have her baby. The young man in "Hills Like White Elephants" compels his girl to have an abortion contrary to her wish; another story, "A Canary for One," bites almost unbearably but exquisitely on the loneliness to be endured by a wife after she and her husband shall have separated; the peasant of "An Alpine Idyll" abuses the corpse of his wife (these last three appear under the general title *Men Without Women*). Brett in *The Sun Also Rises* is an exclusively destructive force: she might be a better woman if she were mated with Jake, the American; but actually he is protected against her and is in a sense revenging his own sex through being unable to do anything for her sexually. Even the hero of *A Farewell to Arms* eventually destroys Catherine—after enjoying her abject devotion—by giving her a baby, itself born dead. The only women with whom Nick Adams' relations are perfectly satisfactory are the little Indian girls of his boyhood who are in a position of hopeless social disadvantage and have no power over the behavior of the white male—so that he can get rid of them the moment he has done with them. Thus in *The Fifth Column* Mr. Philip brutally breaks off with Dorothy—he has been rescued from her demoralizing influence by his enlistment in the Communist crusade, just as the hero of *The Sun Also Rises* has been saved by his physical disability—to revert to a little Moorish whore. Even Harry Morgan, who is represented as satisfying his wife on the scale of a Paul Bunyan, deserts her in the end by dying and leaves her racked by the cruelest desire. •

___

• *There would probably be a chapter to write on the relation between Hemingway and Kipling, and certain assumptions about society which they share. They have much the same split attitude toward women. Kipling anticipates Hemingway in his beliefs that "he travels the fastest that travels alone" and that "the female of the species is more deadly than the male"; and Hemingway seems to reflect Kipling in the submissive infra-Anglo-*

And now this instinct to get the woman down presents itself frankly as a fear that the woman will get the man down. The men in both these African stories are married to American bitches of the most soul-destroying sort. The hero of "The Snows of Kilimanjaro" loses his soul and dies of futility on a hunting expedition in Africa, out of which he has failed to get what he had hoped. The story is not quite stripped clean of the trashy moral attitudes which have been coming to disfigure the author's work: the hero, a seriously intentioned and apparently promising writer, goes on a little sloppily over the dear early days in Paris when he was earnest, happy and poor, and blames a little hysterically the rich woman whom he has married and who has debased him. Yet it is one of Hemingway's remarkable stories. There is a wonderful piece of writing at the end when the reader is made to realize that what has seemed to be an escape by plane, with the sick man looking down on Africa, is only the dream of a dying man. The other story, "Francis Macomber," perfectly realizes its purpose. Here the male saves his soul at the last minute, and then is actually shot down by his woman, who does not want him to have a soul. Here Hemingway has at last got what Thurber calls the war between men and women right out into the open and has written a terrific fable of the impossible civilized woman who despises the civilized man for his failure in initiative and nerve and then jealously tries to break him down as soon as he begins to exhibit any. (It ought to be noted, also, that whereas in *Green Hills of Africa* the descriptions tended to weigh down the narrative with their excessive circumstantiality, the landscapes and animals of "Francis Macomber" are alive and unfalteringly proportioned.)

Going back over Hemingway's books today, we can see clearly what an error of the politicos it was to accuse him of an indifference to society. His whole work is a criticism of society: he has responded

---

Saxon women that make his heroes such perfect mistresses. The most striking example of this is the amoebalike little Spanish girl, Maria, in For Whom the Bell Tolls. *Like the docile native "wives" of English officials in the early stories of Kipling, she lives only to serve her lord and to merge her identity with his; and this love affair with a woman in a sleeping-bag, lacking completely the kind of give and take that goes on between real men and women, has the all-too-perfect felicity of a youthful erotic dream. One suspects that* "Without Benefit of Clergy" *was read very early by Hemingway and that it made on him a lasting impression. The pathetic conclusion of this story of Kipling's seems unmistakably to be echoed at the end of* A Farewell to Arms.

to every pressure of the moral atmosphere of the time, as it is felt at the roots of human relations, with a sensitivity almost unrivaled. Even his preoccupation with licking the gang in the next block and being known as the best basketball player in high school has its meaning in the present epoch. After all, whatever is done in the world, political as well as athletic, depends on personal courage and strength. With Hemingway, courage and strength are always thought of in physical terms, so that he tends to give the impression that the bullfighter who can take it and dish it out is more of a man than any other kind of man, and that the sole duty of the revolutionary socialist is to get the counterrevolutionary gang before they get him.

But ideas, however correct, will never prevail by themselves: there must be people who are prepared to stand or fall with them, and the ability to act on principle is still subject to the same competitive laws which operate in sporting contests and sexual relations. Hemingway has expressed with genius the terrors of the modern man at the danger of losing control of his world, and he has also, within his scope, provided his own kind of antidote. This antidote, paradoxically, is almost entirely moral. Despite Hemingway's preoccupation with physical contests, his heroes are almost always defeated physically, nervously, practically: their victories are moral ones. He himself, when he trained himself stubbornly in his unconventional unmarketable art in a Paris which had other fashions, gave the prime example of such a victory; and if he has sometimes, under the menace of the general panic, seemed on the point of going to pieces as an artist, he has always pulled himself together the next moment. The principle of the Bourdon gauge, which is used to measure the pressure of liquids, is that a tube which has been curved into a coil will tend to straighten out in proportion as the liquid inside it is subjected to an increasing pressure.

The appearance of *For Whom the Bell Tolls* since this essay was written in 1939 carries the straightening process further. Here Hemingway has largely sloughed off his Stalinism and has reverted to seeing events in terms of individuals pitted against specific odds. His hero, an American teacher of Spanish who has enlisted on the side of the Loyalists, gives his life to what he regards as the cause of human liberation; but he is frustrated in the task that has been assigned him by the confusion of forces at cross purposes that are throttling the Loyalist campaign. By the time that he comes to die, he has little to sustain him but the memory of his grandfather's record as a soldier in the American Civil War. The psychology of this young man is presented with a certain sobriety and detachment in comparison with Hemingway's other full-length heroes; and the author has here succeeded as in none of his earlier books in externalizing in plausible characters the elements of his own complex personality. With all this, there is an historical point of view which he has learned from his political adventures: he has aimed to reflect in this episode the whole course of the Spanish War and the tangle of tendencies involved in it.

The weaknesses of the book are its diffuseness—a shape that lacks the concision of his short stories, that sometimes sags and sometimes bulges; and a sort of exploitation of the material, an infusion of the operatic, that lends itself all too readily to the movies.

36

John Peale Bishop: THE SORROWS OF
THOMAS WOLFE [1939]

Thomas Wolfe is dead. And that big work which he was prepared to write, which was to have gone to six long volumes and covered in the course of its narrative the years between 1781 and 1933, with a cast of characters whose numbers would have run into the hundreds, will never be finished. The title which he had chosen for it, *Of Time and the River,* had already been allowed to appear on the second volume. There its application is not altogether clear; how appropriate it would have been to the work as a whole we can only conjecture. No work of such magnitude has been projected by another of his generation in America; Wolfe's imagination, it appears, could conceive on no smaller scale. He was, he confesses, devoted to chance; he had no constant control over his faculties; but his fecundity was nothing less than prodigious. He had, moreover, a tenacity which must, but for his dying, have carried him through to the end.

Dying, he left behind him a mass of manuscript; how much of it can be published there is now no knowing. Wolfe was the most wasteful of writers.

His aim was to set down America as far as it can belong to the experience of one man. Wolfe came early on what was for him the one available truth about this continent—that it was contained in himself. There was no America which could not be made out—mountains, rivers, trains, cities, people—in the memory of an American. If the contours were misty, then they must be made clear. It was in flight from a certain experience of America, as unhappy as it had been apparently sterile, it was in Paris, in an alien land, that Wolfe first understood with hate and with love the horror and the wonder of his native country. He had crossed the seas from West to East only to come upon the North Carolina hills where he had been born. "I had found out," he says, "during those years that the way to discover one's own country was to leave it; that the way to find America was to find it in one's own heart, one's memory, and one's spirit, and in a foreign land. I think I may say that I discovered America during those years abroad out of my very need of her."

This is not an uncommon experience, but what made it rewarding in Wolfe's case was that his memory was anything but common. He could—and it is the source of what is most authentic in his talents—displace the present so completely by the past that its sights and sounds all but destroyed surrounding circumstances. He then lost the sense of time. For Wolfe, sitting at a table on a terrace in Paris, contained within himself not only the America he had known; he also held, within his body, both his parents. They were there, not only in his memory, but more portentously in the make-up of his mind. They loomed so enormous to him that their shadows fell across the Atlantic, their shade was on the café table under which he stretched his long American legs.

"The quality of my memory," he said in his little book, *The Story of a Novel,* "is characterized, I believe, in a more than ordinary degree by the intensity of its sense impressions, its power to evoke and bring back the odors, sounds, colors, shapes and feel of things with concrete vividness." That is true. But readers of Wolfe will remember that the mother of Eugene Gant was afflicted with what is known as total recall. Her interminable narratives were the despair of her family. Wolfe could no more than Eliza Gant suppress any detail, no matter how irrelevant; indeed, it was impossible for him to feel that any detail was irrelevant to his purpose. The readers of *Look Homeward, Angel* will also remember that Eugene's father had a gift, unrivalled among his associates, of vigorous utterance. Nobody, they said, can tie a knot in the tail of the English language like old W. O. But the elder Gant's speech, for all that it can on occasion sputter into fiery intensity, more often than not runs off into a homespun rhetoric. It sounds strong, but it has very little connection with any outer reality and is meaningless, except in so far as it serves to convey his rage and frustration. We cannot avoid supposing that

Wolfe drew these two characters after his own parents. At the time he began writing *Look Homeward, Angel,* he stood far enough apart from them to use the endlessness of Eliza's unheard discourses, the exaggerated violence of old Gant's objurgations, for comic effect. He makes father and mother into something at once larger and less than human. But in his own case, he could not, at least so long as he was at his writing, restrain either the course of his recollections or their outcome in words. He wrote as a man possessed. Whatever was in his memory must be set down—not merely because he was Eliza's son, but because the secret end of all his writing was expiation—and it must be set down in words to which he constantly seems to be attaching more meaning than they can properly own. It was as though he were aware that his novel would have no meaning that could not be found in the words. The meaning of a novel should be in its structure. But in Wolfe's novel, as far as it has gone, it is impossible to discover any structure at all.

II

It is impossible to say what Wolfe's position in American letters would have been had he lived to bring his work to completion. At the moment he stands very high in the estimation both of the critics and of the common reader. From the time of *Look Homeward, Angel,* he was regarded, and rightly, as a young man of incomparable promise. *Of Time and the River* seemed to many to have borne out that promise and, since its faults were taken as due merely to an excess of fecundity, it was met with praise as though it were the consummation of all Wolfe's talents. Yet the faults are fundamental. The force of Wolfe's talents is indubitable; yet he did not find for that novel, nor do I believe he could ever have found, a structure of form which would have been capable of giving shape and meaning to his emotional experience. He was not without intelligence; but he could not trust his intelligence, since for him to do so would have been to succumb to conscience. And it was conscience, with its convictions of guilt, that he was continually trying to elude.

His position as an artist is very like that of Hart Crane. Crane was born in 1899, Wolfe in 1900, so that they were almost of an age. Both had what we must call genius; both conceived that genius had been given them that they might celebrate, the one in poetry, the other in prose, the greatness of their country. But Wolfe no more than Crane was able to give any other coherence to his work than that which comes from the personal quality of his writing. And he found, as Crane did before him, that the America he longed to celebrate did not exist. He could record, and none better, its sights, its sounds and its odors, as they can be caught in a moment of time; he could try, as the poet of *The Bridge* did, to absorb that moment and endow it with the permanence of a myth. But he could not create a continuous America. He could not, for all that he was prepared to cover one hundred and fifty of its years, conceive its history. He can record what comes to his sensibility, but he cannot give us the continuity of experience. Everything for Wolfe is in the moment; he can so try to impress us with the immensity of the moment that it will take on some sort of transcendental meaning. But what that meaning is, escapes him, as it does us. And once it has passed from his mind, he can do nothing but recall another moment, which as it descends into his memory seems always about to deliver itself, by a miracle, of some tremendous import.

Both Crane and Wolfe belonged to a world that is indeed living from moment to moment. And it is because they voice its breakdown in the consciousness of continuity that they have significance for it.

Of the two, Wolfe, I should say, was the more aware of his plight. He was, he tells us, while writing *Of Time and the River,* tormented by a dream in which the sense of guilt was associated with the forgetting of time. "I was unable to sleep, unable to subdue the tumult of these creative energies, and, as a result of this condition, for three years I prowled the streets, explored the swarming web of the million-footed city and came to know it as I had never done before. . . . Moreover, in this endless quest and prowling of the night through the great web and jungle of the city, I saw, lived, felt and experienced the full weight of that horrible human calamity. [The time was that of the bottom of the depression, when Wolfe was living in Brooklyn.] And from it all has come as a final deposit, a burning memory, a certain evidence of the fortitude of man, his ability to suffer and somehow survive. And it is for this reason now that I think I shall always remember this black period with a kind of joy that I could not at that time have believed possible, for it was during this time that I lived my life through to a first completion, and through the suffering and labor of my own life came to share those qualities in the lives of the people around me."

This passage is one of extreme interest, not only for what it tells us of Wolfe at this time, but for the promise it contains of an emotional maturity. For as far as Wolfe had carried the history of Eugene Gant, he was dealing with a young man whose isolation from his fellow-men was almost complete. Eugene, and we must suppose the young Wolfe, was incarcerated in his own sensibility. Locked in his cell, he awaits the coming of every moment, as though it would bring the turning of a releasing key. He waits like Ugolino, when he woke uncertain because of his dream and heard not the opening, but the closing of the lock. There is no release. And the place of Wolfe's confinement, no less than that of Ugolino, deserves to be called Famine.

It can be said of Wolfe, as Allen Tate has said of Hart Crane, that he was playing a game in which any move was possible, because none was compulsory. There is no idea which would serve as discipline to the event. For what Wolfe tells us was the idea that furiously pursued him during the composition of *Of Time and the River,* the search for a father, can scarcely be said to appear in the novel, or else it is so incidentally that it seems to no purpose. It does not certainly, as the same search on the part of Stephen Dedalus does in *Ulysses,* prepare a point toward which the whole narrative moves. There was nothing indeed in Wolfe's upbringing to make discipline acceptable to him. He acts always as though his own capacity for feeling, for anguished hope and continual frustration, was what made him superior, as no doubt, along with his romantic propensity for expression, it was. But he was wrong in assuming that those who accept any form of discipline are therefore lacking in vigor. He apparently did not understand that there are those who might say with Yeats, "I could recover if I shrieked my heart's agony," and yet like him are dumb "from human dignity." And his failure to understand was due to no fault of the intelligence, but to a lack of love. The Gant family always strikes us, with its howls of rage, its loud Hah-hahs of hate and derision, as something less than human. And Eugene is a Gant. While in his case we are ready to admit that genius is a law unto itself, we have every right to demand that it discover its own law.

Again like Crane, Wolfe failed to see that at the present time so extreme a manifestation of individualism could not but be morbid. Both came too late into a world too mechanic; they lacked a wilderness and constantly tried to create one as wild as their hearts. It was all very well for them, since both were in the way of being poets, to start out to proclaim the grandeur of America. Such a task seemed superb. But both were led at last, on proud romantic feet, to Brooklyn. And what they found there they abhorred.

They represent, each in his way, a culmination of the romantic spirit in America. There was in both a tremendous desire to impose the will on experience. Wolfe had no uncommon will. And Crane's was strong enough to lead him deliberately to death by drowning. For Wolfe the rewards of experience were always such that he was turned back upon himself. Isolated in his sensations, there was no way out. He continually sought for a door, and there was really none, or only one, the door of death.

III

The intellectual labor of the artist is properly confined to the perception of relations. The conscience of the craftsman must see that these relations are so presented that in spite of all complications they are ultimately clear. It is one of the conditions of art that they cannot be abstractly stated, but must be presented to the senses.

What we have at the center of all Wolfe's writing is a single character, and it was certainly the aim of that writing to present this character in all his manifold contacts with the world of our time. Eugene has, we are told, the craving of a Faust to know all experience, to be able to record all the races and all the social classes which may be said to exist in America. Actually Eugene's experience is not confined to America.

But when we actually come to consider Eugene closely, we see that, once he is beyond the overwhelming presence of his family, his contacts with other people are all casual. The perfect experience for Eugene is to see someone in the throes of an emotion which he can imagine, but in which he has no responsible part. From one train, he sees people passing in another train, which is moving at a faster speed than his own.

And they looked at one another for a moment, they passed and vanished and were gone forever, yet it seemed to him that he had known these people, that he knew them far better than the people in his own train, and that, having met them for an instant under immense and timeless skies, as they were hurled across the continent to a thousand destinations, they had met, passed, vanished, yet would remember this forever. And he thought the people in the two trains felt this, also: slowly they passed each other now, and their mouths smiled and their eyes grew friendly, but he thought there was some sorrow and regret in what they felt. For having lived together as strangers in the immense and swarming city, they had now met upon the everlasting earth, hurled past each other for a moment between two points of time upon the shining rails; never to meet, to speak, to know each other any more, and the briefness of their days, the destiny of man, was in that instant greeting and farewell.

He sees from a train a boy trying to decide to go after a girl; wandering the streets of New York, he sees death come to four men; through one of his students at the university, he comes in contact with an old Jewess wailing a son dead for a year. Each of these moments is completely done; most of them, indeed, overwrought. From the country seen from a train he derives "a wild and solemn joy—the sense of nameless hope, impossible desire, and man's tragic brevity." He reacts to most circumstances, it must seem to us, excessively. But to men and women he does not really answer. The old Jewess's grief fills him "with horror, anger, a sense of cruelty, disgust, and pity." The passion aroused returns to himself. And it is precisely because his passions cannot attain their object, and in one person know peace, that he turns in rage and desire toward the millions. There is in Eugene every emotion you wish but one; there is no love.

The most striking passages in Wolfe's novels always represent these moments of comprehension. For a moment, but a moment only, there is a sudden release of compassion, when some aspect of suffering and bewildered humanity is seized, when the other's emotion is in a timeless completion known. Then the moment passes, and compassion fails. For Eugene Gant, the only satisfactory relationship with another human creature is one which can have no continuity. For the boy at the street corner, seen in the indecision of youthful lust, he has only understanding and pity; the train from which he looks moves on and nothing more is required of Eugene. But if he should approach that same boy on the street, if he should come close enough to overhear him, he would hear only the defilement of language, words which would awaken in him only hate and disgust. He would himself become lonely, strange and cruel. For emotions such as these, unless they can be used with the responsibility of the artist, must remain a torment to the man.

The only human relationship which endures is that of the child to his family. And that is inescapable; once having been, it cannot cease to be. His father is still his father, though dying; and his brother Ben, though dead, remains his brother. He loves and he hates and knows why no more than the poet he quotes. What he does know is that love has been forbidden him.

The only contemporary literary influence on Wolfe which was at all strong is that of Joyce. I shall consider it here only to note that while we know that Joyce could only have created Stephen Dedalus out of the conflicts of his own youth, we never think of Stephen simply as the young Joyce, any more than we think of Hamlet as Shakespeare. He is a creation. But in Wolfe's novels it is impossible to feel that the central figure has any existence apart from the author. He is called Eugene Gant, but that does not deceive anyone for a moment; he is, beyond all doubt, Thomas Wolfe. There is, however, one important distinction to be made between them, and one which we should not allow ourselves to forget: Eugene Gant is always younger, by at least ten years, than Thomas Wolfe.

Wolfe described *Of Time and the River* as being devoted to "the period of wandering and hunger in a man's youth." And in it we are meant to take Eugene as every young man. The following volume would, Wolfe said, declare "a period of greater certitude, which would be dominated by a single passion." That, however, still remains to be seen. So far, Eugene has shown no capacity as a lover, except in casual contact with whores. When for a moment he convinces himself that he is in love with Ann, who is a nice, simple, conventional girl from Boston, he can only shriek at her and call her a bitch and a whore, which she certainly is not. The one contact which lasts for any time—leaving aside the blood ties which bind him to the Pentlands, his mother's people, and the Gants—is that with Starwick. Starwick is the only friend he makes in his two years at Harvard, and in Paris, some years later, he still regards his friendship with Stawick as the most valuable he has ever known.

It ends when he discovers that Starwick is a homosexual. And it has usually been assumed that the violence and bitterness with which it ends are due to disillusionment; the sudden turn in Eugene's affections for the young man may well be taken as a natural reaction to his learning, first that Ann is in love with Starwick, and only a little later how hopelessly deep is Starwick's infatuation with the young tough he has picked up, by apparent chance, one night in a Paris bar. But that is, I think, to take too simple a view of the affair. There is more to it than that. What we have been told about Starwick from his first appearance in the book is that, despite a certain affection and oddity of manner, he is, as Eugene is not, a person capable of loving and being loved. What is suddenly revealed in Paris is that for him, too, love is a thing the world has forbidden. In Starwick's face Eugene sees his own fate. Just as in his brother Ben's complaint at his neglect, he had looked back through another's sight at his own neglected childhood and in his brother's death foremourned his own, so now, when he beats Starwick's head against the wall, he is but raging against his own frustration and despair.

In his father's yard, among the tombstones, stood for years a marble angel. Old Gant curses it, all hope he thinks lost that he will ever get his money back for it. It stands a magnificent reminder of the time when as a boy, with winged ambition, he had wanted to be not merely a stone cutter but a sculptor. Then, unexpectedly, a customer comes for it. The one symbol of the divine in the workshop is sold to adorn the grave of a prostitute; what the boy might have been the man lets go for such a purpose. It cannot be said that Thomas Wolfe ever sold his angel. But the faults of the artist are all of them traceable to the failures of the man. He achieved probably the utmost intensity of which incoherent writing is capable; he proved that an art founded solely on the individual, however strong his will, however vivid his sensations, cannot be sound, or whole, or even passionate, in a world such as ours, in which "the integrity of the individual consciousness has been broken down." How far it has broken down, I do not believe he ever knew, yet all that he did is made of its fragments.

37

Lionel Trilling: F. SCOTT FITZGERALD [1945]

" 'So be it! I die content and my destiny is fulfilled,' said Racine's Orestes; and there is more in his speech than the insanely bitter irony that appears on the surface. Racine, fully conscious of this tragic grandeur, permits Orestes to taste for a moment before going mad with grief the supreme joy of a hero; to assume his *exemplary* role." The heroic awareness of which André Gide speaks in his essay on Goethe was granted to Scott Fitzgerald for whatever grim joy he might find in it. It is a kind of seal set upon his heroic quality that he was able to utter his vision of his own fate publicly and aloud and in *Esquire* with no lessening of his dignity, even with an enhancement of it. The several essays in which Fitzgerald examined his life in crisis have been gathered together by Edmund Wilson—who is for many reasons the most appropriate editor possible—and published, together with Fitzgerald's notebooks and some letters, as well as certain tributes and memorabilia, in a volume called, after one of the essays, *The Crack-Up.* It is a book filled with the grief of the lost and the might-have-been, with physical illness and torture of mind. Yet the heroic quality is so much here, Fitzgerald's assumption of the "exemplary role" is so proper and right that it occurs to us to say, and not merely as a piety but as the most accurate expression of what we really do feel, that

Nothing is here for tears, nothing to wail
Or knock the breast, no weakness, no contempt,
Dispraise, or blame, nothing but well and fair,
And what may quiet us in a death so noble.

This isn't what we may fittingly say on all tragic occasions, but the original occasion for these words has a striking aptness to Fitzgerald. Like Milton's Samson, he had the consciousness of having misused the power with which he had been endowed. "I had been only a mediocre caretaker . . . of my talent," he said. And the parallel carries further, to the sojourn among the Philistines and even to the maimed hero exhibited and mocked for the amusement of the crowd —on the afternoon of September 25, 1936, the New York *Evening Post* carried on its front page a feature story in which the triumphant reporter tells how he managed to make his way into the Southern nursing home where the sick and distracted Fitzgerald was being cared for and there "interviewed" him, taking all due note of the contrast between the present humiliation and the past glory. It was a particularly gratuitous horor, and yet in retrospect it serves to augment the moral force of the poise and fortitude which marked Fitzgerald's mind in the few recovered years that were left to him.

The root of Fitzgerald's heroism is to be found, as it sometimes is in tragic heroes, in his power of love. Fitzgerald wrote much about love, he was preoccupied with it as between men and women, but it is not merely where he is being explicit about it that his power appears. It is to be seen where eventually all a writer's qualities have their truest existence, in his style. Even in Fitzgerald's early, cruder books, or even in his commercial stories, and even when the style is careless, there is a tone and pitch to the sentences which suggest his warmth and tenderness, and, what is rare nowadays and not likely to be admired, his gentleness without softness. In the equipment of the moralist and therefore in the equipment of the novelist, aggression plays an important part, and although it is of course sanctioned by the novelist's moral intention and by whatever truth of moral vision he may have, it is often none the less fierce and sometimes even cruel. Fitzgerald was a moralist to the core and his desire to "preach at people in some acceptable form" is the reason he gives for not going the way of Cole Porter and Rodgers and Hart—we must always remember in judging him how many real choices he was free and forced to make—and he was gifted with the satiric eye; yet we feel that in his morality he was more drawn to celebrate the good than to denounce the bad. We feel of him, as we cannot feel of all moralists, that he did not attach himself to the good because this attachment would sanction his fierceness toward the bad—his first impulse was to love the good, and we know this the more surely because we perceive that he loved the good not only with his mind but also with his quick senses and his youthful pride and desire.

He really had but little impulse to blame, which is the more remarkable because our culture peculiarly honors the act of blaming, which it takes as the sign of virtue and intellect. "Forbearance, good word," is one of the jottings in his notebook. When it came to blame, he preferred, it seems, to blame himself. He even did not much want to blame the world. Fitzgerald knew where "the world" was at fault. He knew that it was the condition, the field, of tragedy. He is conscious of "what preyed on Gatsby, what foul dust floated in the wake of his dreams." But he never made out that the world imposes tragedy, either upon the heroes of his novels, whom he called his "brothers," or upon himself. When he speaks of his own fate, he does indeed connect it with the nature of the social world in which he had his early flowering, but he never finally lays it upon that world, even though at the time when he was most aware of his destiny it was fashionable with minds more pretentious than his to lay all personal difficulty whatever at the door of the "social order." It is, he feels, *his* fate—and as much as to anything else in Fitzgerald, we respond to the delicate tension he maintained between his idea of personal free will and his idea of circumstance: we respond to that moral and intellectual energy. "The test of a first-rate intelligence," he said, "is the ability to hold two opposed ideas in the mind, at the same time, and still retain the ability to function."

The power of love in Fitzgerald, then, went hand in hand with a sense of personal responsibility and perhaps created it. But it often happens that the tragic hero can conceive and realize a love that is beyond his own prudence or beyond his powers of dominance or of self-protection, so that he is destroyed by the very thing that gives him his spiritual status and stature. From Proust we learn about a love that is destructive by a kind of corrosiveness, but from Fitzgerald's two mature novels, *The Great Gatsby* and *Tender Is the Night,* we learn about a love—perhaps it is peculiarly American—that is destructive by reason of its very tenderness. It begins in romance, sentiment, even "glamour"—no one, I think, has remarked how innocent of mere "sex," how charged with sentiment is Fitzgerald's description of love in the jazz age—and it takes upon itself reality, and permanence, and duty discharged with an almost masochistic scrupulousness of honor. In the bright dreams begins the responsibility which needs so much prudence and dominance to sustain; and Fitzgerald was anything but a prudent man and he tells us that at a certain point in his college career "some old desire for personal dominance was broken and gone." He connects that loss of desire for dominance with his ability to write; and he set down in his notebook the belief that "to record one must be unwary." Fitzgerald, we may say, seemed to feel that both love and art needed, a sort of personal defenselessness.

The phrase from Yeats, the derivation of the "responsibility" from the "dreams," reminds us that we must guard against dismissing, with easy words about its immaturity, Fitzgerald's preoccupation with the bright charm of his youth. Yeats himself, a wiser man and wholly fulfilled in his art, kept to the last of his old age his connection with his youthful vanity. A writer's days must be bound each to each by his sense of his life, and Fitzgerald the undergraduate was father of the best in the man and the novelist.

His sojourn among the Philistines is always much in the mind of everyone who thinks about Fitzgerald, and indeed it was always much in his own mind. Everyone knows the famous exchange between Fitzgerald and Ernest Hemingway—Hemingway refers to it in his story, "The Snows of Kilimanjaro" and Fitzgerald records it in his notebook—in which, to Fitzgerald's remark, "The very rich are different from us," Hemingway replied, "Yes, they have more money." It is usually supposed that Hemingway had the better of the encounter and quite settled the matter. But we ought not be too sure. The novelist of a certain kind, if he is to write about social life, may not brush away the reality of the differences of class, even though to do so may have the momentary appearance of a virtuous social avowal. The novel took its rise and its nature from the radical revision of the class structure in the eighteenth century, and the novelist must still live by his sense of class differences, and must be absorbed by them, as Fitzgerald was, even though he despise them, as Fitzgerald did.

No doubt there was a certain ambiguity in Fitzgerald's attitude toward the "very rich"; no doubt they were for him something more than the mere object of his social observation. They seem to have been the nearest thing to an aristocracy that America could offer him, and we cannot be too simple about what a critic has recently noted, the artist's frequent "taste for aristocracy, his need—often quite open—of a superior social class with which he can make some fraction of common cause—enough, at any rate, to account for his own distinction." Every modern reader is by definition wholly immune from all ignoble and social considerations, and, no matter what his own social establishment or desire for it may be, he knows that in literature the interest in social position must never be taken seriously. But not all writers have been so simple and virtuous—what are we to make of those risen gentlemen, Shakespeare and Dickens, or those fabricators of the honorific "de," Voltaire and Balzac? Yet their snobbery—let us call it that—is of a large and generous kind and we are not entirely wrong in connecting their peculiar energies of mind with whatever it was they wanted from gentility or aristocracy. It is a common habit of writers to envision an actuality of personal life which shall have the freedom and the richness of detail and the order of form that they desire in art. Yeats, to mention him again, spoke of the falseness of the belief that the "inherited glory of the rich" really holds richness of life. This, he said, was a mere dream; and yet, he goes on, it is a necessary illusion—

> Yet Homer had not sung
> Had he not found it certain beyond dreams
> That out of life's own self-delight had sprung
> The abounding glittering jet. . . .

And Henry James, at the threshold of his career, allegorized in his story "Benvolio" the interplay that is necessary for some artists between their creative asceticism and the bright, free, gay life of worldliness, noting at the same time the desire of worldliness to destroy the asceticism.•

With a man like Goethe the balance between the world and his asceticism is maintained, and so we forgive him his often absurd feelings—but perhaps absurd as well as forgivable only in the light of our present opinion of his assured genius—about aristocracy. Fitzgerald could not always keep the balance true; he was not, as we know, a prudent man. And no doubt he deceived himself a good deal in his youth, but certainly his self-deception was not in the interests of vulgarity, for aristocracy meant to him a kind of disciplined distinction of personal existence which, presumably, he was so humble as not to expect from his art. What was involved in that notion of distinction can be learned from the use which Fitzgerald makes of the word "aristocracy" in one of those serious moments which occur in his most frivolous *Saturday Evening Post* stories; he says of the life of the young man of the story, who during the war was on duty behind the lines, that "it was not so bad—except that when the infantry came limping back from the trenches he wanted to be one

---

• *George Moore's comment on Æ's having spoken in reproof of Yeats's pride in a quite factitious family line is apposite; "Æ, who is usually quick-witted, should have guessed that Yeats's belief in his lineal descent from the great Duke of Ormonde was part of his poetic equipment."*

of them. The sweat and mud they wore seemed only one of those ineffable symbols of aristocracy that were forever eluding him." Fitzgerald was perhaps the last notable writer to affirm the Romantic fantasy, descended from the Renaissance, of personal ambition and heroism, of life committed to, or thrown away for, some ideal of self. To us it will no doubt come more and more to seem a merely boyish dream; the nature of our society requires the young man to find his distinction through cooperation, subordination, and an expressed piety of social usefulness, and although a few young men have made Fitzgerald into a hero of art, it is likely that even to these admirers the whole nature of his personal fantasy is not comprehensible, for young men find it harder and harder to understand the youthful heroes of Balzac and Stendhal, they increasingly find reason to blame the boy whose generosity is bound up with his will and finds its expression in a large, strict, personal demand upon life.

I am aware that I have involved Fitzgerald with a great many great names and that it might be felt by some that this can do him no service, the disproportion being so large. But the disproportion will seem large only to those who think of Fitzgerald chiefly through his early public legend of heedlessness. Those who have a clear recollection of the mature work or who have read *The Crack-Up* will at least not think of the disproportion as one of kind. Fitzgerald himself did not, and it is by a man's estimate of himself that we must begin to estimate him. For all the engaging self-depreciation which was part of his peculiarly American charm, he put himself, in all modesty, in the line of greatness, he judged himself in a large way. When he writes of his depression, of his "dark night of the soul" where "it is always three o'clock in the morning," he not only derives the phrase from St. John of the Cross but adduces the analogous black despairs of Wordsworth, Keats, and Shelley. A novel with Ernest Hemingway as the model of its hero suggests to him Stendhal portraying the Byronic man, and he defends *The Great Gatsby* from some critical remark of Edmund Wilson's by comparing it with *The Brothers Karamazov*. Or again, here is the stuff of his intellectual pride at the very moment that he speaks of giving it up, as years before he had given up the undergraduate fantasies of valor: "The old dream of being an entire man in the Goethe-Byron-Shaw tradition . . . has been relegated to the junk heap of the shoulder pads worn for one day on the Princeton freshman football field and the overseas cap never worn overseas." And was it, that old dream, unjustified? To take but one great name, the one that on first thought seems the least relevant of all—between Goethe at twenty-four the author of *Werther,* and Fitzgerald, at twenty-four the author of *This*

Side of Paradise, there is not really so entire a difference as piety and textbooks might make us think; both the young men so handsome, both winning immediate and notorious success, both rather more interested in life than in art, each the spokesman and symbol of his own restless generation.

It is hard to overestimate the benefit which came to Fitzgerald from his having consciously placed himself in the line of the great. He was a "natural," but he did not have the contemporary American novelist's belief that if he compares himself with the past masters, or if he takes thought—which, for a writer, means really knowing what his predecessors have done—he will endanger the integrity of his natural gifts. To read Fitzgerald's letters to his daughter—they are among the best and most affecting letters I know—and to catch the tone in which he speaks about the literature of the past, or to read the notebooks he faithfully kept, indexing them as Samuel Butler had done, and to perceive how continuously he thought about literature, is to have some clue to the secret of the continuing power of Fitzgerald's work.

The Great Gatsby, for example, after a quarter-century is still as fresh as when it first appeared; it has even gained in weight and relevance, which can be said of very few American books of its time. This, I think, is to be attributed to the specifically intellectual courage with which it was conceived and executed, a courage which implies Fitzgerald's grasp—both in the sense of awareness and of appropriation—of the traditional resources available to him. Thus, *The Great Gatsby* has its interest as a record of contemporary manners, but this might only have served to date it, did not Fitzgerald take the given moment of history as something more than a mere circumstance, did he not, in the manner of the great French novelists of the nineteenth century, seize the given moment as a moral fact. The same boldness of intellectual grasp accounts for the success of the conception of its hero—Gatsby is said by some to be not quite credible, but the question of any literal credibility he may or may not have becomes trivial before the large significance he implies. For Gatsby, divided between power and dream, comes inevitably to stand for America itself. Ours is the only nation that prides itself upon a dream and gives its name to one, "the American dream." We are told that "the truth was that Jay Gatsby of West Egg, Long Island, sprang from his Platonic conception of himself. He was a son of God—a phrase which, if it means anything, means just that—and he must be about His Father's business, the service of a vast, vulgar, and meretricious beauty." Clearly it is Fitzgerald's intention that our mind should turn to the thought of the nation that has sprung from its "Platonic conception" of itself. To the world it is anomalous in America, just as in the novel it is anomalous in Gatsby, that so much raw power should be haunted by envisioned romance. Yet in that anomaly lies, for good or bad, much of the truth of our national life, as, at the present moment, we think about it.

Then, if the book grows in weight of significance with the years, we can be sure that this could not have happened had its form and style not been as right as they are. Its form is ingenious—with the ingenuity, however, not of craft but of intellectual intensity. The form, that is, is not the result of careful "plotting"—the form of a good novel never is—but is rather the result of the necessities of the story's informing idea, which require the sharpness of radical fore-shortening. Thus, it will be observed, the characters are not "developed": the wealthy and brutal Tom Buchanan, haunted by his "scientific" vision of the doom of civilization, the vaguely guilty, vaguely homosexual Jordan Baker, the dim Wolfsheim, who fixed the World Series of 1919, are treated, we might say, as if they were ideographs, a method of economy that is reinforced by the ideographic use that is made of the Washington Heights flat, the terrible "valley of ashes" seen from the Long Island Railroad, Gatsby's incoherent parties, and the huge sordid eyes of the oculist's advertising sign. (It is a technique which gives the novel an affinity with *The Waste Land,* between whose author and Fitzgerald there existed a reciprocal admiration.) Gatsby himself, once stated, grows only in the understanding of the narrator. He is allowed to say very little in his own person. Indeed, apart from the famous "Her voice is full of money," he says only one memorable thing, but that remark is overwhelming in its intellectual audacity: when he is forced to admit that his lost Daisy did perhaps love her husband, he says, "In any case it was just personal." With that sentence he achieves an insane greatness, convincing us that he really is a Platonic conception of himself, really some sort of Son of God.

What underlies all success in poetry, what is even more important than the shape of the poem or its wit of metaphor, is the poet's voice. It either gives us confidence in what is being said or it tells us that we do not need to listen; and it carries both the modulation and the living form of what is being said. In the novel no less than in the poem, the voice of the author is the decisive factor. We are less consciously aware of it in the novel, and, in speaking of the elements of a novel's art, it cannot properly be exemplified by quotation because it is continuous and cumulative. In Fitzgerald's work the voice of his prose is of the essence of his success. We hear in it at once the tenderness toward human desire that modifies a true firmness of moral judgment. It is, I would venture to say, the normal or ideal voice of the novelist. It is characteristically modest, yet it has in it, without apology or self-consciousness, a largeness, even a stateliness, which derives from Fitzgerald's connection with tradition and with mind, from his sense of what has been done before and the demands which this past accomplishment makes. ". . . I became aware of the old island here that flowered once for Dutch sailors' eyes—a fresh green breast of the new world. Its vanished trees, the trees that had made way for Gatsby's house, had once pandered in whispers to the last and greatest of all human dreams; for a transitory and enchanted moment man must have held his breath in the presence of this continent, compelled into an aesthetic contemplation he neither understood nor desired, face to face for the last time in history with something commensurate to his capacity for wonder." Here, in the well-known passage, the voice is a little dramatic, a little *intentional,* which is not improper to a passage in climax and conclusion, but it will the better suggest in brief compass the habitual music of Fitzgerald's seriousness.

Fitzgerald lacked prudence, as his heroes did, lacked that blind instinct of self-protection which the writer needs and the American writer needs in double measure. But that is all he lacked—and it is the generous fault, even the heroic fault. He said of his Gatsby, "If personality is an unbroken series of successful gestures, there was something gorgeous about him, some heightened sensitivity to the promises of life, as if he were related to one of those intricate machines that register earthquakes ten thousand miles away. This responsiveness had nothing to do with that flabby impressionability which is dignified under the name of 'the creative temperament'—it was an extraordinary gift for hope, a romantic readiness such as I have never found in any other person and which it is not likely I shall ever find again." And it is so that we are drawn to see Fitzgerald himself as he stands in his exemplary role.

38

Irving Howe: FAULKNER AND
THE SOUTHERN TRADITION [1952]

Until very recently, regional consciousness has remained stronger in
the South than in any other part of the United States. This "historical"
lag" is the source of whatever is most distinctive in Southern thought
and feeling. After its defeat in the Civil War, the South could not
participate fully and freely in the "normal" development of American society—that is, industrialism and large-scale capitalism arrived
there later and with far less force than in the North or West. By the
Reconstruction period ⸴New England regional consciousness was in
decline and by the turn of the century the same was probably true for
the Midwest; but the South, because it was a pariah region or because
its recalcitrance in defeat forced the rest of the nation to treat it as
such, felt its sectional identity most acutely during the very decades
when the United States was becoming a self-conscious nation. While
the other regions meekly submitted to dissolution, the South worked
desperately to keep itself intact. Through an exercise of the will, it
insisted that the regional memory be the main shaper of its life.

Perhaps because it had so little else to give its people, the South
nurtured in them a generous and often obsessive sense of the past.
The rest of the country might be committed to commercial expansion

or addicted to the notion of progressive optimism, but the South, even if it cared to, was unable to accept these dominant American values; it had been left behind, it was living on the margin of history —a position that often provides the sharpest perspective on history. Some decades after the defeat of the South, its writers could maintain a relation to American life comparable, in miniature, to the relation in the nineteenth century between Russian writers and European life. For while nineteenth-century Russia was the most backward country on the continent, its writers managed to use that backwardness as a vantage point from which to observe West-European life and thereby to arrive at a profound and withering criticism of bourgeois morality. Precisely because Russia was trailing the capitalist West, the Russian writers could examine the bourgeois code without hesitation or illusion. It was this crucial advantage of distance, this perspective from the social rear, that was the major dispensation the South could offer its writers.

And it gave them something else: a compact and inescapable subject. The Southern writer did not have to cast about for his materials; he hardly enjoyed a spontaneous choice in his use of them, for they welled within him like a dream recurrent since childhood. Faulkner has given a vivid if somewhat romantic description of this subject in *Intruder in the Dust:*

For every Southern boy fourteen years old, not once but whenever he wants it, there is the instance when it's still not two o'clock on that July afternoon in 1863, the brigades are in position behind the rail fence, the guns are laid and ready in the woods and the furled flags are already loosened to break out and Pickett himself with his long oiled ringlets and his hat in one hand probably and his sword in the other looking up the hill waiting for Longstreet to give the word and it's all in the balance, it hasn't happened yet, it hasn't even begun. . . .

But of course it has happened, it must begin. The basic Southern subject is the defeat of the homeland, though its presentation can vary from the magnolia romancing of *The White Rose of Memphis* to the despairing estimate of social loss in *The Sound and the Fury*. Nor does it matter, for the moment, whether one defines the Southern subject, in Allen Tate's words, as "the destruction by war and the later degradation by carpetbaggers and scalawags, and a consequent lack of moral force and imagination in the cynical materialism of the New South," or as the defeat of a reactionary slave-owning class followed by its partial recapture of power through humiliating alliances with Northern capital and a scrofulous commercial class of local origin. Regardless of which interpretation one accepts, the important point is that this subject, like a thick cloud of memory, has been insistently and implacably *there*. The Southern writer could romanticize it, reject it, enlarge it into an image of the general human situation; he could not escape it. And precisely this ubiquity of subject matter provided him with some very considerable advantages. Not so long before the Civil War Hawthorne had remarked that "No author can conceive of the difficulty of writing a romance about a country where there is no shadow, no antiquity, no picturesque and gloomy wrong, nor anything but a commonplace prosperity." But now the War and Reconstruction gave the Southern writers all that Hawthorne had found lacking—all but antiquity. And there were ruins to take its place.

It was not until the First World War, however, that serious Southern writing began to appear—that is, not until Southern regional consciousness began to decay. One reason for this lag was simply that before the 1910's and 1920's there had not been enough money in the South to send many young people to college or to encourage them in such social luxuries as literary careers. A land bent by defeat was not likely to turn to letters with an urgent passion or enthusiasm. Nor could the South look back upon a serious literary tradition of its own, certainly none comparable to that of New England; antebellum Southern writing had for the most part been sentimental, genteel and insipid. Its talented men had given themselves to politics and oratory, and had looked upon literature as a minor pastime hardly sufficient to engage their intellectual capacities. Only some decades later, when the most sensitive minds of the South would be appalled by the Snopesian vulgarity of its politics, would they turn to the arts half in hope, half in desperation.

For it was the reality of twentieth-century life, in all its coarse provocation, which drove so many Southern writers to a regional past that in happier circumstances they might have peaceably neglected. The mottoes of Southern agrarianism were hardly to be taken seriously as social proposals for the most industrialized country in the world; but as signs of a fundamental quarrel with modern life, an often brilliant criticism of urban anonymity, they very much deserved to be taken seriously.

Before the Southern writers could make imaginative statements about their own past, they had to be exposed to intellectual drafts from beyond their regional horizon. Southern literature at its best— the work of Faulkner, Caldwell, Ransom, Tate, Warren—was conceived in an explosive mixture of provincialism and cosmopolitanism, tradition and modernity. To measure the stature of their ancestor Poe, the Southern writers had first to understand what he had meant to Baudelaire, and for that they had to possess a sophisticated awareness of the European literary past. For the Southern imagination to burst into high flame it had to be stimulated, or irritated, by the pressures of European and Northern ideas and literary modes. Left to itself, a regional consciousness is not likely to result in anything but a tiresome romanticizing of the past and thereby a failure to understand the present. Once, however, the South reached the point at which it still remained a distinct region but was already cracking under alien influences, it could begin to produce serious works of art. As Allen Tate has shrewdly remarked, the distinctive Southern "consciousness is quite temporary. It has made possible the curious burst of intelligence that we get at the crossing of the ways, not unlike, on an infinitesimal scale, the outburst of poetic genius at the end of the sixteenth century when commercial England had already begun to crush feudal England." What Tate seems to be saying here is that Southern literature assumed a dimension of seriousness and grandeur only when the South as a region began to die, when its writers were forced to look back upon a past that was irretrievable and forward to a future that seemed intolerable.

It is therefore insufficient to say, as some critics do, that Faulkner is a traditional moralist drawing his creative strength from the Southern myth; the truth is that he writes in opposition to his tradition as well as in acceptance, that he struggles with the Southern myth even as he acknowledges and celebrates it. His relation to his own beliefs is far more ambivalent and difficult than was the case for most nineteenth-century American writers. We may safely assume that Melville and Whitman, in their major work, were moved by the democratic yearnings of ninetenth-century America; one feels of *Moby Dick* and *Leaves of Grass* that they are books written with the resources of an entire age behind them. Melville's epic conceptions and Whitman's rolling declamations follow, in part, from their adherence to a myth that is still viable and therefore likely to stir men to dedicated action. Faulkner, however, is working with the decayed fragments of a myth, the somewhat soured pieties of regional memory, and that is why his language is so often tortured, forced and even incoherent. Unquestionably Faulkner has been influenced by Melville, but in their uses of language one can see reflected the difference between a belief still vigorous and a belief picking at its own bones. Yeats's definition of rhetoric as the will doing the work of the imagination is pertinent to both Melville and Faulkner, but particularly to Faulkner. For what is the soft shapeless rhetoric of *Sartoris* but the sign of a strained will floundering in sentimentality, and what is the agonized rhetoric of *Absalom, Absalom!* but the sign of a strained will confronted with its own intolerably acute awareness?

What then *is* the Southern myth? Like any other myth, it is a story or cluster of stories that expresses the deepest attitudes and reflects the most fundamental experiences of a people. And its subject, in this case, is the fate of a ruined homeland. The homeland—so the story goes—had proudly insisted that it alone should determine its destiny; provoked into a war impossible to win, it had nevertheless fought to its last strength, and had fought this war with a reckless gallantry and a superb heroism that, as Faulkner might say, made of its defeat not a shame but almost a vindication. But the homeland fell, and from this fall came misery and squalor: the ravaging by the conquerors, the loss of faith among the descendants of the defeated, and the rise of a new breed of faceless men who would batten on their neighbors' humiliation.

From these stories there follows that pride in ancestral glory and that mourning over the decline of the homeland which constitute the psychology of the "lost cause." Thus, for one intermittently Southern writer, John Peale Bishop, the South found its highest distinction in "a manner of living somewhat more amiable than any other that has ever been known on the continent." And for another Southern writer, Allen Tate, the South is the one place that "clings blindly to forms of European feeling and conduct that were crushed by the French Revolution." Where else, he asks, "outside of the South, is there a society that believes even covertly in the Code of Honor?"

A myth which pervades a people's imagination is hardly open to rational attack or defense, particularly when it is considered as part of a work of literature. The historian, no doubt, would have to compare the claims of the Southern myth with the actual course of Southern history. He would evaluate the tradition and order so often ascribed to the old South; inquire exactly for whom its way of living could be somewhat more amiable; speculate on the extent to which the Southern emphasis on honor and heroism may often have been a means of salvaging pride from defeat or a token of uncertainty about the moral value of its cause. And if our historian were inclined to moral reflection he might ask the one question that by its very nature the myth cannot tolerate: Granted heroism, granted honor, was the homeland defending a just cause? For the critic these questions, while important, are not the crux of the matter, since it is hardly necessary to take at face value or even give substantial credence to the claims of the Southern myth—I certainly do not—in order to acknowledge the powerful uses to which it can be put by a sympathetic imagination. The Southern myth, like any other, is less an attempt at historical description than a voicing of the collective imagination, perhaps of the collective will. The old South over which it chants in threnody is an ideal image—a buried city, Allen Tate has called it. Both the violence and the poignancy with which this ideal image has been employed suggest an awareness that the buried city can never be found.

Such myths form the raw material of literature. The writer often comes to a myth eager for acquiescence, but after articulating its assumptions he may begin to wonder about its meaning, its value. During the past few decades Northern writers have been engaged in a large-scale examination of the myths of industrial capitalism, of enterprise, accumulation and success; the rejection of these myths has motivated a great many contemporary writers. Somewhat similarly, Faulkner in his stories and novels has been conducting a long, sometimes painful and at other times heroic examination of the Southern myth. He has set his pride in the past against his despair over the present, and from this counterpointing has come much of the tension in his work. He has investigated the myth itself; wondered about the relation between the Southern tradition he admires and that memory of Southern slavery to which he is compelled to return; tested not only the present by the past, but also the past by the myth, and finally the myth by that morality which has slowly emerged from his entire process of exploration. The testing of the myth, though by no means the only important activity in Faulkner's work, is basic to the Yoknapatawpha novels and stories, and from it comes his growing vision as an artist.

39

Robert Penn Warren: WILLIAM FAULKNER [1946]

Malcolm Cowley's editing of *The Portable Faulkner* is remarkable on two counts. First, the selection from Faulkner's work is made not merely to give a cross section or a group of good examples but to demonstrate one of the principles of integration in the work. Second, the introductory essay is one of the few things ever written on Faulkner which is not hagridden by prejudice or preconception and which really sheds some light on the subject.

The selections here are made to describe the place, Yoknapatawpha County, Mississippi, which is, as Cowley puts it, "Faulkner's mythical kingdom," and to give the history of that kingdom. The place is the locale of most of Faulkner's work. Its 2,400 square miles lie between the hills of north Mississippi and the rich, black bottom lands. It has a population of 15,611 persons, composing a society with characters as different as the Bundrens, the Snopeses, Ike McCaslin, Percy Grimm, Temple Drake, the Compsons, Christmas, Dilsey, and the tall convict of *The Wild Palms*. No land in all fiction lives more vividly in its physical presence than this mythical county —the "pine-winey" afternoons, the nights with "a thin sickle of moon like the heel print of a boot in wet sand," the tremendous reach of the big river in flood, "yellow and sleepy in the afternoon," and the "little piddling creeks, that run backward one day and forward the next and come busting down on a man full of dead mules and hen houses," the ruined plantation which was Popeye's hangout, the swamps and fields and hot, dusty roads of the Frenchman's Bend section, and the remnants of the great original forests, "green with gloom" in summer, "if anything actually dimmer than they had been in November's gray dissolution, where even at noon the sun fell only in windless dappling upon the earth which never completely dried."

And no land in all fiction is more painstakingly analyzed from the sociological standpoint. The descendants of the old families, the descendants of bushwhackers and carpetbaggers, the swamp rats, the Negro cooks and farm hands, bootleggers and gangsters, peddlers, college boys, tenant farmers, country storekeepers, county-seat lawyers are all here. The marks of class, occupation, and history are fully rendered and we know completely their speech, dress, food, houses, manners, and attitudes. Nature and sociology, geography and human geography, are scrupulously though effortlessly presented in Faulkner's work, and their significance for his work is very great; but the significance is of a conditioning order. They are, as it were, aspects of man's "doom"—a word of which Faulkner is very fond— but his manhood in the face of that doom is what is important.

Cowley's selections are made to give the description of the mythical kingdom, but more important, they are made to give its history. Most critics, even those who have most naively or deliberately misread the meaning of the fact, have been aware that the sense of the past is crucial in Faulkner's work. Cowley has here set up selections running in date of action from 1820 to 1940. The first, "A Justice," is a story about Ikkemotubbe, the nephew of a Chickasaw chief who went to New Orleans, where he received the name of du Homme, which became Doom; who came back to the tribe to poison his way to the Man-ship; and who, in the end (in Faulkner's "history" though not in "A Justice" itself) swaps a mile square of "virgin north Mississippi dirt" for a racing mare owned by Jason Lycurgus Compson, the founder of the Compson family in Mississippi. The last selection, "Delta Autumn," shows us Isaac McCaslin, the man who brings the best of the old order, philosopher, aristocrat, woodsman, into the modern world and who gives the silver-mounted horn which General Compson had left him to a mulatto woman for her bastard son by a relative of McCaslin's. In between "A Justice" and "Delta Autumn" fall such pieces as the magnificent "Red Leaves," the profoundly symbolic story called "The Bear," the Civil War and Reconstruction stories, "Rain" (from *The Unvanquished*) and "Wash," "Old Man" (the story of the tall convict from *The Wild Palms*), and the often anthologized "That Evening Sun" and "A Rose for Emily," and the brilliant episode of "Percy Grimm" (from *Light in August*). There are other pieces included, but these are the best, and the best for showing high points in the history of Yoknapatawpha County.

Cowley's introduction undertakes to define the significance of place and history in Faulkner's work, that "labor of imagination that has not been equaled in our time." That labor is, as he points out, a double labor: "first, to invent a Mississippi county that was like a mythical kingdom, but was complete and living in all its details; second, to make his story of Yoknapatawpha County stand as a parable or legend of all the Deep South." The legend—called a legend "because it is obviously no more intended as a historical account of the country south of the Ohio than *The Scarlet Letter* was intended as a history of Massachusetts"—is, as Cowley defines it, this:

The South was settled by Sartorises (aristocrats) and Sutpens (nameless, ambitious men) who, seizing the land from the Indians, were determined to found an enduring and stable order. But despite their strength and integrity their project was, to use Faulkner's word, "accursed" by slavery, which, with the Civil War as an instrument, frustrated their design. Their attempt to rebuild according to the old plan and old values was defeated by a combination of forces—the carpetbaggers and Snopeses ("a new exploiting class descended from the landless whites"). Most of the descendants of the old order are in various ways incompetent: They are prevented by their code from competing with the codeless Snopeses, they cling to the letter and forget the spirit of their tradition, they lose contact with the realities of the present and escape into a dream world of alcohol or rhetoric or gentility or madness, they fall in love with defeat or death, they lose nerve and become cowards, or they, like the last Jason in *The Sound and the Fury*, adopt Snopesism and become worse than any Snopes. Figures like Popeye (eyes like "rubber knobs," a creature having "that vicious depthless quality of stamped tin," the man "who made money and had nothing he could do with it, spend it for, since he knew that alcohol would kill him like poison, who had no friends and had never known a woman") are in their dehumanized quality symbols of modernism, for the society of finance capitalism. The violence of some of Faulkner's work is, according to Cowley, "an example of the Freudian method turned backward, being full of sexual nightmares that are in reality social symbols. It is somehow connected in the author's mind with what he regards as the rape and corruption of the South."

This is, in brief, Cowley's interpretation of the legend, and it provides an excellent way into Faulkner; it exactly serves the purpose which an introduction should serve. The interpretation is indebted, no doubt, to that of George Marion O'Donnell (the first and still an indispensable study of Faulkner's theme), but it modifies O'Donnell's tendency to read Faulkner with an allegorical rigidity and with a kind of doctrinal single-mindedness.

It is possible that the present view, however, should be somewhat modified, at least in emphasis. Although no writer is more deeply committed to a locality than Faulkner, the emphasis on the Southern elements may blind us to other elements, or at least other applications, of deep significance. And this is especially true in so far as the work is interpreted merely as Southern apologetics or, as it is by Maxwell Geismar, as the "extreme hallucinations" of a "cultural psychosis."

It is important, I think, that Faulkner's work be regarded not in terms of the South against the North, but in terms of issues which are common to our modern world. The legend is not merely a legend of the South, but is also a legend of our general plight and problem. The modern world is in moral confusion. It does suffer from a lack of discipline, of sanctions, of community of values, of a sense of a mission. It is a world in which self-interest, workableness, success, provide the standards. It is a world which is the victim of abstraction and of mechanism, or at least, at moments, feels itself to be. It can look back nostalgically upon the old world of traditional values and feel loss and perhaps despair—upon the world in which, as one of Faulkner's characters puts it, men "had the gift of living once or dying once instead of being diffused and scattered creatures drawn blindly from a grab bag and assembled"—a world in which men were, "integer for integer," more simple and complete.

If it be objected that Faulkner's view is unrealistic, that had the old order satisfied human needs it would have survived, and that it is sentimental to hold that it was killed from the outside, the answer is clear in the work: the old order did not satisfy human needs—the Southern old order or any other—for it, not being founded on justice, was "accursed" and held the seeds of its own ruin in itself. But even in terms of the curse the old order, as opposed to the new order (in so far as the new is to be equated with Snopesism), allowed the traditional man to define himself as human by setting up codes, concepts of virtue, obligations, and by accepting the risks of his humanity. Within the traditional order was the notion of truth, even if man in the flow of things did not succeed in realizing that truth. Take, for instance, the passage from "The Bear":

"All right," he said. "Listen," and read again, but only one stanza this time and closed the book and laid it on the table. "She cannot fade, though thou hast not thy bliss," McCaslin said: "Forever wilt thou love, and she be fair."

"He's talking about a girl," he said.

"He had to talk about something," McCaslin said. Then he said, "He was talking about truth. Truth is one. It doesn't change. It covers all things which touch the heart—honor and pride and pity and justice and courage and love. Do you see now?"

The human effort is what is important, the capacity to make the effort to rise above the mechanical process of life, the pride to endure, for in endurance there is a kind of self-conquest.

When it is said, as it is often said, that Faulkner's work is "backward-looking," the answer is that the constant ethical center is to be found in the glorification of the human effort and of human endurance, which are not in time, even though in modernity they seem to persist most surely among the despised and rejected. It is true that Faulkner's work contains a savage attack on modernity, but it is to be remembered that Elizabethan tragedy, for instance, contained just such an attack on its own special "modernity." (Ambition is the most constant tragic crime, and ambition is the attitude special to an opening society; all villains are rationalists and appeal to "nature" beyond traditional morality for justification, and rationalism is, in the sense implied here, the attitude special to the rise of a secular and scientific order before a new morality can be formulated.)

It is not ultimately important whether the traditional order (Southern or other) as depicted by Faulkner fits exactly the picture which critical historical method provides. Let it be granted, for the sake of discussion, that Faulkner does oversimplify the matter. What is ultimately important, both ethically and artistically, is the symbolic function of that order in relation to the world which is set in opposition to it. The opposition between the old order and the new does not, however, exhaust the picture. What of the order to come? "We will have to wait," old Ike McCaslin says to the mulatto girl who is in love with a white man. A curse may work itself out in time; and in such glimpses, which occur now and then, we get the notion of a grudging meliorism, a practical supplement to the idealism, like Ike McCaslin's, which finds compensation in the human effort and the contemplation of "truth."

The discussion, even at a larger scope and with more satisfactory analysis, of the central theme of Faulkner would not exhaust the interest of his work. In fact, the discussion of this question always runs the risk of making his work appear too schematic, too dry and too complacent when in actual fact it is full of rich detail, of shadings and complexities of attitude, of ironies and ambivalences. Cowley's introduction cautions the reader on this point and suggests various fruitful topics for investigation and thought. But I shall make bold —and in the general barrenness of criticism on Faulkner it does not require excessive boldness—to list and comment on certain topics which seem to me to demand further critical study.

Nature. The vividness of the natural background is one of the impressive features of Faulkner's work. It is accurately observed, but observation only provides the stuff from which the characteristic effects are gained. It is the atmosphere which counts, the poetry, the infusion of feeling, the symbolic weight. Nature provides a backdrop—of lyric beauty (the meadow in the cow episode of *The Hamlet*), of homely charm (the trial scene of the "Spotted Horses" story from the same book), of sinister, brooding force (the river in "Old Man" from *The Wild Palms*), of massive dignity (the forest in "The Bear")—for the human action and passion. The indestructible beauty is there: "God created man," Ike McCaslin says in "Delta Autumn," "and He created the world for him to live in and I reckon He created the kind of world He would have wanted to live in if He had been a man."

Ideally, if man were like God, as Ike McCaslin puts it, man's attitude toward nature would be one of pure contemplation, pure participation in its great forms and appearances; the appropriate attitude is love, for with Ike McCaslin the moment of love is equated with godhood. But since man "wasn't quite God himself," since he lives in the world of flesh, he must be a hunter, user, and violator. To return to McCaslin: God "put them both here: man and the game he would follow and kill, foreknowing it. I believe He said, 'So be it.' I reckon He even foreknew the end. But He said, 'I will give him his chance. I will give him warning and foreknowledge too, along with the desire to follow and the power to slay. The woods and the fields he ravages and the game he devastates will be the consequence and signature of his crime and guilt, and his punishment.' "

There is, then, a contamination implicit in the human condition —a kind of Original Sin, as it were—but it is possible, even in the contaminating act, the violation, for man to achieve some measure of redemption, a redemption through love. For instance, in "The Bear," the great legendary beast which is pursued for years to the death is also an object of love and veneration, and the symbol of virtue, and the deer hunt of "Delta Autumn" is for Ike McCaslin a ritual of renewal. Those who have learned the right relationship to nature—"the pride and humility" which young Ike McCaslin learns from the half-Negro, half-Indian Sam Fathers—are set over against those who have not. In "The Bear," General Compson speaks up to

Cass McCaslin to defend the wish of the boy Ike McCaslin to stay an extra week in the woods:

> You got one foot straddled into a farm and the other foot straddled into a bank; you ain't even got a good hand-hold where this boy was already an old man long before you damned Sartorises and Edmondses invented farms and banks to keep yourselves from having to find out what this boy was born knowing and fearing too maybe, but without being afraid, that could go ten miles on a compass because he wanted to look at a bear none of us had ever got near enough to put a bullet in and look at the bear and came the ten miles back on the compass in the dark; maybe by God that's the why and wherefore of farms and banks.

Those who have the wrong attitude toward nature are the pure exploiters, the apostles of abstractionism, the truly evil men. For instance, the very opening of *Sanctuary* presents a distinction on this ground between Benbow and Popeye. While the threat of Popeye keeps Benbow crouching by the spring, he hears a Carolina wren sing, and even under these circumstances tries to recall the local name for it. And he says to Popeye: "And of course you don't know the name of it. I don't suppose you'd know a bird at all, without it was singing in a cage in a hotel lounge, or cost four dollars on a plate." Popeye, as we may remember, spits in the spring (he hates nature and must foul it), is afraid to go through the woods ("Through all them trees?" he demands when Benbow points out the short cut), and when an owl whisks past them in the twilight, claws at Benbow's coat with almost hysterical fear ("It's just an owl," Benbow says. "It's nothing but an owl.")

The pure exploiters, though they may gain ownership and use of a thing, never really have it; like Popeye, they are impotent. For instance, Flem Snopes, the central character and villain of *The Hamlet*, who brings the exploiter's mentality to Frenchman's Bend, finally marries Eula Varner, a kind of fertility goddess or earth goddess; but his ownership is meaningless, for she always refers to him as "that man" (she does not even have a name for him), and he has only got her after she has given herself willingly to one of the bold, hot-blooded boys of the neighborhood. In fact, nature can't, in one sense, be "owned." Ike McCaslin, in "The Bear," says of the land which has come down to him:

> It was never Father's and Uncle Buddy's to bequeath me to repudiate, because it was never Grandfather's to bequeath them to bequeath me to repudiate, because it was never old Ikkemotubbe's to sell to Grandfather for bequeathment and repudiation. Because it was never Ikkemotubbe's father's father's to bequeath Ikkemotubbe to sell to Grandfather or any man because on the instant when Ikkemotubbe discovered, realized, that

he could sell it for money, on that instant it ceased ever to have been his forever, father to father, to father, and the man who bought it bought nothing.

The right attitude toward nature is, as a matter of fact, associated with the right attitude toward man, and the mere lust for power over nature is associated with the lust for power over other men, for God gave the earth to man, we read in "The Bear," not "to hold for himself and his descendants inviolable title forever, generation after generation, to the oblongs and squares of the earth, but to hold the earth mutual and intact in the communal anonymity of brotherhood, and all the fee He asked was pity and humility and sufferance and endurance and the sweat of his face for bread." It is the failure of this pity which curses the earth (the land in Faulkner's particular country is "accursed" by chattel slavery, but slavery is simply one of the possible forms of the failure). But the rape of nature and the crime against man are always avenged. The rape of nature, the mere exploitation of it without love, is always avenged because the attitude which commits that crime also commits the crime against men which in turn exacts vengence, so that man finally punishes himself. It is only by this line of reasoning that one can, I think, read the last page of "Delta Autumn":

This land which man has deswamped and denuded and derivered in two generations so that white men can own plantations and commute every night to Memphis and black men own plantations and ride in jim crow cars to Chicago to live in millionaires' mansions on Lake Shore Drive; where white men rent farms and live like niggers and niggers crop on shares and live like animals; where cotton is planted and grows man-tall in the very cracks of the sidewalks, and usury and mortgage and bankruptcy and measureless wealth, Chinese and African and Aryan and Jew, all breed and spawn together until no man has time to say which one is which nor cares. . . . No wonder the ruined woods I used to know don't cry for retribution! he thought: The people who have destroyed it will accomplish its revenge.

The attitude toward nature in Faulkner's work, however, does not involve a sinking into nature. In Faulkner's mythology man has "suzerainty over the earth," he is not of the earth, and it is the human virtues which count—"pity and humility and sufferance and endurance." If we take even the extreme case of the idiot Snopes and his fixation on the cow in *The Hamlet* (a scene whose function in the total order of the book is to show that even the idiot pervert is superior to Flem), a scene which shows the human being as close as possible to the "natural" level, we find that the scene is the most lyrical in Faulkner's work: even the idiot is human and not animal,

for only human desires, not animal, clothe themselves in poetry. I
think that George Marion O'Donnell is right in pointing to the
humanism-naturalism opposition in Faulkner's work, and over and
over again we find that the point of some novel or story has to do
with the human effort to find or create values in the mechanical
round of experience—"not just to eat and evacuate and sleep warm,"
as Charlotte Rittenmeyer says in *The Wild Palms*, "so we can get
up and eat and evacuate in order to sleep warm again," or not just
to raise cotton to buy niggers to raise cotton to buy niggers, as it
is put in another place. Even when a character seems to be caught
in the iron ring of some compulsion, of some mechanical process
(the hunted Negro of "Red Leaves," the tall convict of *The Wild
Palms*, Christmas of *Light in August*), the effort may be discernible.
And in Quentin's attempt, in *The Sound and the Fury*, to persuade
his sister Caddy, who is pregnant by one of the boys of Jefferson,
to confess that she has committed incest with him, we find among
other things the idea that "the horror" and "the clean flame" would
be preferable to the meaninglessness of the "loud world."

Humor. One of the most important remarks in Cowley's introduction is that concerning humor. There is, especially in the later
books, "a sort of homely and sober-sided frontier humor that is
seldom achieved in contemporary writing." Cowley continues: "In
a curious way, Faulkner combines two of the principal traditions in
American letters: the tradition of psychological horror, often close
to symbolism, that begins with Charles Brockden Brown, our first
professional novelist, and extends through Poe, Melville, Henry
James (in his later stories), Stephen Crane and Hemingway; and
the other tradition of frontier humor and realism, beginning with
Augustus Longstreet's *Georgia Scenes* and having Mark Twain as its
best example." The observation is an acute one, for the distortions
of humor and the distortions of horror in Faulkner's work are closely
akin and frequently, in a given instance, can scarcely be disentangled.

It is true that the most important strain of humor in Faulkner's
work is derived from the tradition of frontier humor (though it is
probable that he got it from the porches of country stores and the
courthouse yards of county-seat towns and not from any book), and
it is true that the most spectacular displays of Faulkner's humor are
of this order—for example, the "Spotted Horses" episode from *The
Hamlet* or the story "Was." But there are other strains which might
be distinguished and investigated. For example, there is a kind of
Dickensian humor; the scene in the Memphis brothel from *Sanctuary*,
which is reprinted here under the title "Uncle Bud and the Three
Madams," is certainly more Dickensian than frontier. There is a sub-

dued humor, sometimes shading into pathos, in the treatment of some of the Negro characters and in their dialogue. And there is an irony ranging from that in the scene in *Sanctuary* where Miss Reba, the madam, in offended decency keeps telling Temple, "Lie down and cover up your nekkidness," while the girl talks with Benbow, to that in the magnificently sustained monologue of Jason at the end of *The Sound and the Fury.*

In any case, humor in Faulkner's work is never exploited for its own sake. It is regularly used as an index, as a lead, to other effects. The humor in itself may be striking, but Faulkner is not a humorist in the sense, say, that Mark Twain is. His humor is but one perspective on the material and it is never a final perspective, as we can see from such an example as the episode of "Spotted Horses." Nothing could be more wide of the point than the remark in Maxwell Geismar's essay on Faulkner to the effect that Faulkner in *The Hamlet* "seems now to accept the antics of his provincial morons, to enjoy the chronicle of their low-grade behavior; he submerges himself in their clownish degradation." All the critic seems to find in Mink Snopes' victim with his lifelong devotion to the memory of his dead wife, and in Ratliff with his good heart and ironical mind and quiet wisdom, is comic "descendants of the gangling and giggling Wash Jones."

The Poor White. The above remark leads us to the not uncommon misconception about the role of the poor white in Faulkner's work. It is true that the Snopeses are poor whites, descendants of bushwhackers (and therefore outside society, as the bushwhacker was outside society, had no "side" in the Civil War but tried to make a good thing of it), and it is true that Snopesism represents a special kind of villainy and degradation, the form that the pure doctrine of exploitation and degradation takes in the society of which Faulkner writes, but any careful reader realizes that a Snopes is not to be equated with a poor white. For instance, the book most fully about the poor white, *As I Lay Dying,* is full of sympathy and poetry. There are a hundred touches like that in Cash's soliloquy about the phonograph: "I reckon it's a good thing we ain't got ere a one of them. I reckon I wouldn't never get no work done a-tall for listening to it. I don't know if a little music ain't about the nicest thing a fellow can have. Seems like when he comes in tired of a night, it ain't nothing could rest him like having a little music played and him resting." Or like the long section toward the middle of the book devoted to Addie Bundren, a section which is full of eloquence like that of this paragraph: "And then he died. He did not know he was dead. I would lie by him in the dark, hearing the dark land talking of God's love and His beauty and His sin; hearing the dark voicelessness in which the words are the deeds, and the other words that are not deeds, that are just the gaps in people's lacks, coming down like the cries of geese out of the wild darkness in the old terrible nights, fumbling at the deeds like orphans to whom are pointed out in a crowd two faces and told, That is your father, your mother." Do these pages indicate a relish in the "antics of his provincial morons"?

The whole *As I Lay Dying* is based on the heroic effort of the Bundren family to fulfill the promise to the dead mother, to take her body to Jefferson; and the fact that Anse Bundren, after the heroic effort has been completed, immediately gets him a new wife, the "duck-shaped woman" with the "hard-looking pop-eyes," does not negate the heroism of the effort nor the poetry and feeling which give flesh to the book. We are told by one critic that "what should have been the drama of the Bundrens thus becomes in the end a sort of brutal farce," and that we are "unable to feel the tragedy because the author has refused to accept the Bundrens, as he did accept the Compsons, as tragic." Rather, I should say, the Bundrens may come off a little better than the latter-day Compsons, the whining mother, the promiscuous Caddy, the ineffectual Quentin, and the rest. The Bundrens, at least, are capable of the heroic effort, and the promise is fulfilled. What the conclusion indicates is that even such a fellow as Anse Bundren (who is not typical of his family, by the way), in the grip of an idea, in terms of promise or code, is capable of rising out of his ordinary level; Anse falls back at the end, but only after the prop of the idea and obligation have been removed. And we may recall that even the "gangling and giggling Wash Jones" has always been capable of some kind of obscure dream and aspiration (his very attachment to Sutpen indicates that), and that in the end he achieves dignity and manhood.

The final and incontrovertible evidence that Snopes is not to be equated with poor white comes in *The Hamlet* (though actually most of the characters in the book, though they may be poor, are not, strictly speaking, "poor whites" at all, but rather what uninstructed reviewers choose to call by that label). The point of the book is the assault made on a solid community of plain, hard-working small farmers by Snopeses and Snopesism. Ratliff is not rich, but he is not Flem Snopes. And if the corruption of Snopesism does penetrate into the community, there is no one here who can be compared in degradation and vileness to Jason of *The Sound and the Fury,* the Compson who has embraced Snopesism. In fact, Popeye and Flem, Faulkner's best advertised villains, cannot, for vileness and ultimate meanness, touch Jason.

The Negro. In one of Faulkner's books it is said that every white child is born crucified on a black cross. Remarks like this have led to a gross misconception of the place of the Negro in Faulkner's work, to the notion that Faulkner "hates" Negroes. For instance, we find Maxwell Geismar exclaiming what a "strange inversion" it is to take the Negro, who is the "tragic consequence," and to exhibit him as the "evil cause" of the failure of the old order in the South.

This is a misreading of the text. It is slavery, not the Negro, which is defined, quite flatly, as the curse, over and over again, and the Negro is the black cross in so far as he is the embodiment of the curse, the reminder of the guilt, the incarnation of the problem. That is the basic point. But now and then, as a kind of tangential irony, we have the notion, not of the burden of the white on the black, but of the burden of the black on the white, the weight of obligation, inefficiency, and so on, as well as the weight of guilt (the notion we find in the old story of the plantation mistress who, after the Civil War, said: "Mr. Lincoln thought he was emancipating those slaves, but he was really emancipating me").

For instance, we get hints of this notion in "Red Leaves": one of the Indians, sweating in the chase of the runaway Negro who is to be killed for the Man's funeral, says, "Damn that Negro," and the other Indian replies, "Yao. When have they ever been anything but a trial and a care to us?" But the black cross is, fundamentally, the weight of the white man's guilt, the white man who now sells salves and potions to "bleach the pigment and straighten the hair of Negroes that they might resemble the very race which for two hundred years had held them in bondage and from which for another hundred years not even a bloody civil war would have set them completely free." The curse is still operative, as the crime is still compounded.

The actual role of the Negro in Faulkner's fiction is consistently one of pathos or heroism. It is not merely, as has been suggested more than once, that Faulkner condescends to the good and faithful servant, the "white folks' nigger." There are figures like Dilsey, but they are not as impressive as the Negro in "Red Leaves" or Sam Fathers, who, with the bear, is the hero of "The Bear." The fugitive, who gains in the course of the former story a shadowy symbolic significance, is told in the end by one of the Indians who overtake him, "You ran well. Do not be ashamed," and when he walks among the Indians, he is "the tallest there, his high, close, mud-caked head looming above them all." And Sam Fathers is the fountainhead of wisdom which Ike McCaslin finally gains, and the repository of the virtues which are central for Faulkner—"an old man, son of a Negro slave and an Indian king, inheritor on the one hand of the long chronicle of a people who had learned humility through suffering and learned pride through the endurance which survived suffering, and on the other side the chronicle of a people even longer in the land than the first, yet who now existed there only in the solitary brotherhood of, an old and childless Negro's alien blood and the wild and invincible spirit of an old bear."

Even Christmas in *Light in August,* though he is sometimes spoken of as a villain, is a mixture of heroism and pathos. He is the lost, suffering, enduring creature (the figure like Sam Fathers, the tall convict of *The Wild Palms,* or Dilsey in *The Sound and the Fury*), and even the murder he commits at the end is a fumbling attempt to define his manhood, is an attempt to break out of the iron ring of mechanism, to lift himself out of "nature," for the woman whom he kills has become a figure of the horror of the human which has surrendered the human attributes. (We may compare Christmas to Mink Snopes in *The Hamlet* in this respect: Mink, mean and vicious as he is, kills out of a kind of warped and confused pride, and by this affirmation is set off against his kinsman Flem, whose only values are those of pure Snopesism.)

Even such a brief comment on the Negro in Faulkner's work cannot close without this passage from "The Bear":

"Because they will endure. They are better than we are. Stronger than we are. Their vices are vices aped from white men or that white men and bondage have taught them: improvidence and intemperance and evasion —not laziness: evasion: of what white men had set them to, not for their aggrandizement or even comfort but his own—" and McCaslin

"All right. Go on: Promiscuity. Violence. Instability and lack of control. Inability to distinguish between mine and thine—" and he

"How distinguish when for two hundred years mine did not even exist for them?" and McCaslin

"All right. Go on. And their virtues—" and he

"Yes. Their own. Endurance—" and McCaslin

"So have mules:" and he

"—and pity and tolerance and forbearance and fidelity and love of children—" and McCaslin

"So have dogs:" and he

"—whether their own or not or black or not. And more: what they got not only from the white people but not even despite white people because they had it already from the old free fathers a longer time free than us because we have never been free—"

And there is a single comment under Dilsey's name in the annotated genealogy of the Compsons which Faulkner has prepared for the present volume: "They endured."

Technique. There are excellent comments on this subject by

Cowley, Conrad Aiken, Warren Beck, Joseph Warren Beach, and Alfred Kazin, but the subject has not been fully explored. One difficulty is that Faulkner is an incorrigible and restless experimenter, is peculiarly sensitive to the expressive possibilities of shifts in technique and has not developed (like Hemingway or Katherine Anne Porter—lyric rather than dramatic writers, artists with a great deal of self-certainty) in a straight line.

Provisionally, we may distinguish in Faulkner's work three basic methods of handling a narrative. One is best typified in *Sanctuary,* where there is a tightly organized plot, a crisp, laconic style, an objective presentation of character—an impersonal method. Another is best typified by *As I Lay Dying* or *The Sound and the Fury,* where each character unfolds in his own language or flow of being before us—a dramatic method in that the author does not obtrude, but a method which makes the subjective reference of character the medium of presentation. Another is best typified by "Was," "The Bear," or the story of the tall convict in *The Wild Palms,* where the organization of the narrative is episodic and the sense of a voice, a narrator's presence (though not necessarily a narrator in the formal sense), is almost constantly felt—a method in which the medium is ultimately a "voice" as index to sensibility. The assumptions underlying these methods, and the relations among them, would provide a study.

Cowley's emphasis on the unity of Faulkner's work, the fact that all the novels and stories are to be taken as aspects of a single, large design, is very important. It is important, for one thing, in regard to the handling of character. A character, Sutpen, for instance, may appear in various perspectives, so that from book to book we move toward a final definition much as in actual life we move toward the definition of a person. The same principle applies to event, as Conrad Aiken has pointed out, the principle of the spiral method which takes the reader over and over the same event from a different altitude, as it were, and a different angle. In relation to both character and event this method, once it is understood by the reader, makes for a kind of realism and a kind of suspense (in the formal not the factual sense) not common in fiction.

The emphasis on the unity of Faulkner's work may, however, lead to an underrating of the degree of organization within individual works. Cowley is right in pointing out the structural defect in *Light in August,* but he may be putting too much emphasis on the overall unity and not enough on the organization of the individual work when he says that *The Hamlet* tends to resolve into a "series of episodes resembling beads on a string." I think that in that novel we have a type of organization in which the thematic rather than the narrative emphasis is the basic principle, and once we grasp that fact the unity of the individual work may come clear. In fact, the whole subject of the principle of thematic organization in the novels and long stories, "The Bears," for instance, needs investigation. In pieces which seem disjointed, or which seem to have the mere tale-teller's improvisations, we may sometimes discover the true unity if we think of the line of meaning, the symbolic ordering, and surrender ourselves to the tale-teller's "voice." And it may be useful at times to recall the distinction between the formal, forensic realism of Ibsen as opposed to the fluid, suggestive realism of Chekhov.

Symbol and Image. Cowley and O'Donnell have given acute readings of the main symbolic outline of Faulkner's fiction, but no one has yet devoted himself to the study of symbolic motifs which, though not major, are nevertheless extremely instructive. For instance, the images of the hunt, the flight, the pursuit, such as we have in "Red Leaves," *The Wild Palms,* the episode of "Percy Grimm" in *Light in August,* "The Bear," "Delta Autumn," "Was," and (especially in the hordes of moving Negroes) in *The Unvanquished.* Or there is the important symbolic relationship between man and earth. Or there is the contrast between images of compulsion and images of will or freedom. Or there is the device of what we might call the frozen moment, the arrested action which becomes symbolic, as in the moment when, in "An Odor of Verbena" (from *The Unvanquished*), Drusilla offers the pistols to the hero.

Polarity. To what extent does Faulkner work in terms of polarities, oppositions, paradoxes, inversions of roles? How much does he employ a line of concealed (or open) dialectic progression as a principle for his fiction? The study of these questions may lead to the discovery of principles of organization in his work not yet defined by criticism.

The study of Faulkner is the most challenging single task in contemporary American literature for criticism to undertake. Here is a novelist who, in mass of work, in scope of material, in range of effect, in reportorial accuracy and symbolic subtlety, in philosophical weight can be put beside the masters of our own past literature. Yet this accomplishment has been effected in what almost amounts to critical isolation and silence, and when the silence has been broken it has usually been broken by someone (sometimes one of our better critics) whose reading has been hasty, whose analysis unscholarly and whose judgments superficial. The picture of Faulkner presented to the public by such criticism is a combination of Thomas Nelson Page, a fascist and a psychopath, gnawing his nails. Of course, this picture is usually accompanied by a grudging remark about genius.

Cowley's book, for its intelligence, sensitivity, and sobriety in the introduction, and for the ingenuity and judgment exhibited in the selections, would be valuable at any time. But it is especially valuable at this time. Perhaps it can mark a turning point in Faulkner's reputation. That will be of slight service to Faulkner, who, as much as any writer of our place and time, can rest in confidence. He can afford to wait. But can we?

40

Henry Bamford Parkes: METAMORPHOSES OF
LEATHERSTOCKING [1956]

Popular fiction and the other popular arts have considerable sociological interest in that they illustrate the attitudes and expectations
shared by the large mass audiences. Since they take the form largely
of wish-fulfillments, they show what kind of wishes are current in a
particular society at a particular period. Popular fiction is largely
built around stock characters whom audiences can either dream
about or identify themselves with, and when the same type of character reappears in fiction over a period of several generations, one
can presumably conclude that some pervasive and deeply rooted
emotional attitude is finding expression. Two obvious examples from
the American tradition are the superman type, originally represented
by personalities like Mike Fink and David Crockett and still popular
in the comics, and the protective mother-figure who was so prominent in nineteenth-century sentimental fiction and is today the central
character in the daytime soap opera of the radio. But the most significant of such types is the kind of frontier hero who may be defined
as a fugitive from civilization. First presented in the Leatherstocking
novels of Fenimore Cooper, he was immediately taken over by
writers for the masses and, under different names and in different

milieus, has reappeared again and again in fiction over the last hundred and thirty years.

It seems to me, therefore, that a study of the implications of the Leatherstocking type can tell us a good deal about American culture in general. I may remark, however, that I can by no means agree with those recent critics, such as Yvor Winters and Marius Bewley, who have tried to claim major literary importance for Cooper. Cooper had some of the potentialities of a great writer, since he was a complex person whose sympathies pulled him in opposite directions. While he felt the appeal of the frontier individualism represented by Leatherstocking, he also had a deep respect for the conservative ideals of social order and discipline. As Henry Nash Smith remarks, "his conflict of allegiances was truly ironic, and if he had been able—as he was not—to explore to the end the contradictions in his ideas and emotions, the Leatherstocking series might have been a major work of art." Unfortunately he was too extraverted and too belligerent to penetrate below the surface of his subject matter. Preferring to quarrel with his contemporaries rather than with himself, he produced (to borrow Yeats's phraseology) rhetoric rather than poetry. His characters are two-dimensional, and he describes every scene and every action at inordinate length, in a style which never achieved any degree of complexity or intensity.

Leatherstocking's major characteristics may be summarized as follows:

In the first place, he is a simple person—illiterate, in fact—of obscure origin, who is capable of extraordinary achievements because he has acquired special technical skills as a hunter and a pathfinder. These skills are physical rather than intellectual; and as is shown in his conversations with Dr. Obed Battius in *The Prairie,* he has a good deal of contempt for academic learning and intellectualism. He also has great physical toughness and the kind of courage which shows itself most typically not in any positive acts of daring but in the stoical endurance of suffering.

In the second place, he has (at least in the later novels) an unerring moral sense, exhibited particularly in his belief in justice for everybody, even the Indians, and in his loyalty to his friends, especially to his Delaware Indian partner, Chingachgook. His morality seems to be natural rather than acquired, fostered by the life of the wilderness and unconnected with any particular system of religious or social dogmas. It is true that in the Preface to *The Deerslayer* Cooper suggests that Leatherstocking may have retained memories of an early Christian education acquired before he went to live among the Indians; but this interpretation is not supported by anything in the novels themselves, in which Leatherstocking is consistently presented as an example of Rousseauistic natural virtue and natural religion.

In the third place, Leatherstocking prefers to live alone, without social or family ties. He hates what he calls in *The Prairie* "the waste and wickedness of the settlements and the villages"; and in his old age, after a life spent in the forests of upstate New York, actually migrates westward to the prairies beyond the Mississippi where he can no longer hear the sound of the woodman's axe and need not surrender his independence. In his attitudes toward women he is not wholly consistent. In *The Pathfinder* he considers marriage with Mabel Dunham, though he is very ready to give up the notion when he finds that she loves somebody else. But in *The Deerslayer* he refuses to marry Judith Hutter, chiefly because he prefers his solitary life in the forests, though he seems also to be influenced by Judith's reputation for unchastity. In general, he reverences women but is determined to remain aloof from marital entanglements, and his elemental ties of loyalty to male comrades weigh more heavily than sexual emotion.

In the fourth place, he is unsympathetic to all that is implied by civilization and its laws and institutions. It is true that Cooper endows him with some of his own respect for established rank and authority, so that Leatherstocking does not forget his humble background or presume to claim equality with his social betters. But these attitudes are inconsistent with the main outlines of his character. In general, Leatherstocking shows a marked tendency to contrast natural goodness with social corruption. As he declares in *The Deerslayer,* "when the colony's laws, or even the king's laws, run agin the laws of God, they get to be onlawful and ought not to be obeyed." In *The Pioneers* he actually comes into conflict with the laws of society by failing to obey the game regulations which have resulted from the establishment of property rights over forest lands. In his protest to Judge Temple against the regulations, he declares that "it's a hard case to a man to have his honest calling for a livelihood stopped by laws, and that, too, when if right was done, he mought hunt or fish on any day in the week or on the best flat in the Patent." Leatherstocking believes that it is precisely because of his isolation from organized society that he has been able to preserve his virtue; and this conviction, in spite of its inconsistency with Cooper's own conservative social philosophy, is corroborated by the structure of two of the novels. In *The Deerslayer* and *The Prairie* Leatherstocking's moral sense is contrasted with the depravity of other frontier types, but it is clearly indicated that their depravity

is a product not of the wilderness but of society. In *The Deerslayer*
Hurry Harry and Tom Hutter are guilty of the wanton shooting of
an Indian woman; but whereas Leatherstocking condemns their behavior on the basis of natural virtue, Harry and Hutter point out
that, in denying elemental human rights to the savages, they are
complying with the laws of the colony of New York and the practices of white society. In *The Prairie* Leatherstocking comes into
conflict with the squatter Ishmael Bush and his family; and although
Bush is represented as belonging to the dregs of society, he is—unlike Leatherstocking—definitely a forerunner of civilization; he and
his sons are agricultural settlers and not hunters, they commit the
cardinal crime of felling trees, and—in imposing capital punishment
upon a member of the family who has committed murder—they
even represent the embryonic beginnings, in patriarchal form, of
organized law and order.

Technical skill, along with physical courage and endurance; simplicity of character, with a distrust of intellectualism; an innate sense
of justice; freedom from all social or family ties except those of
loyalty to male comrades; and above all a claustrophobic compulsion
to escape from civilization, supported by a belief that social organization destroys natural virtue and by a generally critical attitude toward
all established institutions—these are the main qualities of the
Leatherstocking type. Once Cooper had fixed the pattern and demonstrated its immense popular appeal, it was picked up by writers
for the masses and became the main staple of the fiction turned out
during the later nineteenth century by the house of Beadle and Adams
and other publishers of dime novels. Leatherstocking's qualities
were transferred to a later frontier type, the mountain man who
gathered furs and opened trails in the Far West; but despite the
change of milieu, there was no essential change of character. As
Smith points out, "the strongest link connecting the Beadle Westerns
with Cooper is the representation of a benevolent hunter without a
fixed place of abode, advanced in age, celibate, and of unequalled
prowess in trailing, marksmanship and Indian fighting. . . . Of
seventy-nine dime novels selected as a sample of those dealing with
the West between 1860 and 1893, forty contain one or more hunters
or trappers whose age, costume, weapons and general functions en-
title them to be considered lineal descendants of the great original."

On the whole the purveyors of popular fiction continued to cling
to Leatherstocking until the end of the century although they showed
some tendency to modify the original characterization for the sake
of a more sensational appeal. While the essential qualities of natural
virtue and flight from civilization were always retained, some per-

formers of the Leatherstocking role had a tendency to become younger and more attractive to women, occasionally succumbing to marriage at the end of the book in spite of their dislike of entanglements, and in some instances, especially after dime novelists discovered the mining frontier, they acquired past lives carrying an aura of criminality and became benevolent outlaws of the Robin Hood variety. Occasionally Leatherstocking may have borrowed qualities from other well-established folk symbols of the frontier spirit: from the superman of the Fink and Crockett type, and also from the humorist who made shrewd comments on national affairs and thereby showed the superiority of simple Western folk wisdom to Eastern and European sophistication.

In sucession to the forest hunter and the mountain man, the third frontier type to be celebrated in popular fiction was the cowboy of the Great Plains, who began to become a dime-novel hero in the 1880's. This necessitated some change of characterization. The cowboy lived not in solitude but as a member of a group, and his way of life had a flavor of chivalry derived partly from Spanish Mexico and partly from the Old South. The type was set chiefly by Owen Wister's *The Virginian,* published in 1902. Wister's hero conforms to the frontier tradition in his obscure origin, his freedom from ties, his loyalty to male comrades, his physical prowess, and his moral sense; standing for justice in a community where the law courts have become corrupt, he puts cattle thieves to death by lynch law. But his carefree gaiety, shown especially in his love of practical joking, is a new element; and in spite of his independence he is ultimately on the side of civilization, or what Wister regarded as such. Wister drenches his hero in a nauseating mixture of snobbery and sentimentality, and ends by marrying him to a Vermont schoolteacher and making him a wealthy mine-owner and businessman. The fulsome dedication to Theodore Roosevelt is in keeping with the whole tone of the book.

Later cowboy heroes, however, do not normally succumb to respectability. The gaiety and nonchalance of the Virginian have become permanent features of the tradition, and make a pleasing contrast with the propensity for pious sermonizing displayed by Cooper's forest moralist. As David Davis has suggested, one of the main reasons for the popularity of the cowboy hero in modern big-city society is probably that he represents the wish-fulfillment of an ideal self-assurance and freedom from anxiety. But folk characters like Hopalong Cassidy and The Lone Ranger do not marry schoolteachers or become owners of coal mines. Having shot the cattle thieves and seen justice done in a corrupt society, they usually ride away toward the horizon with their primeval independence still intact. Leatherstocking's flight from civilization is still a common feature of the Western folk heroes of paperbacks, movies, and radio.

One of the best of recent Hollywood movies, *High Noon,* is a good example of the continued appeal of the Leatherstocking myth. Virtuosos of Westerns have complained that it does not conform to the established conventions of the genre; but despite some innovations of plot and locale, the main theme is traditional. It was appropriate that the central character should have been played by Gary Cooper, the actor who most closely fits the Leatherstocking type and who had also portrayed Wister's Virginian. The significant features about the hero of *High Noon* are that he is a simple character with an intuitive sense of right and wrong which he does not quite understand himself; he can face danger and stand up under punishment; he meets his crisis alone, deserted even by his girl; and his moral sense is not supported by the judge, the minister, and the other official authorities. In the last shot of the movie he contemptuously flings his sheriff's badge in the dust, in front of the townspeople who have refused to help him in his lonely battle for justice, and drives away.

One can find the same ingredients in other forms of popular fiction. Consider, for example, the structure of the American detective novel, particularly the hard-boiled variety developed by Dashiell Hammett and continued by such writers as Raymond Chandler and Mickey Spillane. The private eye is an urban rather than a rural type, with a big-city callousness and sophistication; and although he declines all offers of marriage, the Leatherstocking reverence for women has been replaced by an unromantic receptivity to sexual invitations. The most effective movie portrayer of the type is Humphrey Bogart. But the cynicism is only a veneer, and like Leatherstocking, the private eye fights a lonely battle for morality, unsupported by a corrupt society. Sam Spade in *The Maltese Falcon* appears to be completely disillusioned, but he stands for justice, though he gets little cooperation from the official exponents of law and order, and his loyalty to his murdered partner, even though he had personally disliked him, takes precedence over the sexual attractions of Bridget O'Shaugnessy and the financial offers of the fat man. Raymond Chandler—incidentally much inferior to Hammett in literary quality—conforms even more closely to the tradition. The Chandler detective is a simple, harassed and nonintellectual character who is perpetually taking a terrific series of beatings; he prefers to live alone, in spite of the fact that southern California is—according to Chandler—filled with seductive females; he is governed by an innate honesty, though he never quite knows himself what always prevents him from taking tainted money; and in his pursuit of justice he gets little help from anybody else, the police in particular being usually corrupt. Spillane, as inferior to Chandler as Chandler is to Hammett, doubles the sadism and triples the sex, but conforms to the same basic formula: the solitary individual fighting for justice in an evil society.

It may be suggested that it is unnecessary to invoke the American spirit in order to explain the popularity of this type of hero, since the emphasis on escape from social discipline has an obvious and universal appeal, especially to adolescents. It is significant, however, that the popular literature of other countries does not specialize in the same character type. For example, the equivalent stock character of English adventure and detective fiction produced by writers like John Buchan and Dornford Yates, Sapper and Dorothy Sayers, represents very different attitudes. Whereas the American exists in a social void, being of obscure origin and guided only by an instinctive sense of right and wrong, the English hero is definitely a gentleman from the public-school class; and even though he may be temporarily operating alone, often in disguise, in some remote part of the world, he has behind him the moral support of the public-school ethical code and a complex of upper-class social ties and traditions. And while the American battles for a justice which is not supported by official authorities, and is therefore potentially a radical critic of society, the Englishman is always a conservative engaged in the defense of the established order and can count on the cooperation of Scotland Yard. In English detective novels the police are always on the right side, whereas with the American hard-boiled school the honest cop is a rare exception and the town authorities are often tools of the gangsters. After he has disposed of the criminals or the revolutionaries, the Englishman will marry into his own class and settle down as a member of a county family; but no such happy consummation can be predicted for the American. Like the original Leatherstocking, he seems destined always to be moving on lest civilization should catch up with him.

It may also be suggested that the essential features of the American frontier hero were derived from historical reality and hence that it is unnecessary to postulate some bias of the American ·imagination. In view of the intrinsic sensational possibilities of the frontier experience, it is, of course, easy to understand why so many writers of adventure fiction should have turned to it for material; and there can be no doubt that some of Leatherstocking's qualities' were actually displayed by forest hunters like Daniel Boone and by mountain men like Jim Bridger, Jedediah Smith, and Kit Carson. The obscure origin, the technical skills, the anti-intellectualism, and the independence of the frontier hero of fiction really existed. But his most important quality was his combination of an innate moral sense with a hatred of organized society, and the fact that this has been extended to a different milieu in detective fiction suggests that it conforms to some basic wish or expectation of American audiences. This quality, I suggest, was mythical. Cooper himself was explicit on this point. "In a physical sense," he said of Leatherstocking in the preface to *The Deerslayer,* "different individuals known to the writer in early life, certainly presented themselves as models, through recollection; but in a moral sense this man of the forests is purely a creation." In general, it is probable that those historical frontier characters who, like Leatherstocking, fled from civilization were motivated by a psychopathic desire to escape from social discipline into the moral freedom of savagery, while those who retained a sense of morality regarded themselves as forerunners of civilization's westward march. The Leatherstocking character is an expression not of reality but of some deep compulsion of the American spirit. As Smith has shown, this compulsion was manifested, even before Cooper wrote the first of the Leatherstocking novels, in popular conceptions of the character of Daniel Boone. Boone himself held a number of official positions in early Kentucky, and seems to have thought of himself as a kind of empire-builder, his move later in life across the river to Missouri being motivated by nothing more romantic than the failure of his land speculations. Certainly this is how he was portrayed by his earliest biographers. Yet as early as 1816 journalists had begun to create a mythical Boone perpetually retreating westward to escape from the advance of civilization, and by the time that Timothy Flint came to write his biography, in 1833, he had become a standard symbol of Rousseauism. Boone, according to Flint, preferred to live in the forests in order that "the beautiful influence of the indulgence of none but natural desires and pure affections would not be deadened by the selfishness, vanity and fear of ridicule, that are the harvest of what is called civilization and cultivated life." There was a similar discrepancy between the reality and the popular representation in the case of Kit Carson, while later in the nineteenth century the myth actually began to create its own embodiments. This imitation of art by nature was most strikingly exemplified by Buffalo Bill, who may be said to have been invented by the dime-novelist Ned Buntline and who devoted himself to portraying, and cashing in on, the role of frontier hero which Buntline had created for him.

As the quotation from Timothy Flint suggests, what is most obviously expressed in Leatherstocking is the doctrine of natural goodness. He is the embodiment of Thomas Jefferson's belief that man is "endowed with a sense of right and wrong" which is "as much a part of his nature as the senses of hearing, seeing, feeling." "This sense," Jefferson went on to say, "is submitted, indeed, in some degree, to the guidance of reason; but it is a small stock which is required for this; even a less one than what we call common sense. State a moral case to a ploughman and a professor. The former will decide it as well, and often better than the latter, because he has not been led astray by artificial rules." Unquestionably some kind of trust in human virtue is an essential element in the democratic faith; American ideals of freedom and equality probably depend on the optimistic view of man introduced by the Enlightenment. But the Leatherstocking ideal, and Jefferson's preference for the ploughman over the professor, imply something more; they imply that man's natural goodness is best preserved in isolation from organized society and is not expressed through institutions, which for some obscure reason generally become corrupt. Organized society appears as a repressive force tending to pervert the spontaneous virtues of its individual members—a degeneration which Jefferson attributed to the wickedness of kings, priests and aristocrats who—mysteriously —had lost their moral sense.

I have mentioned some of the expressions in popular art of the belief that organized society is somehow antagonistic to individual integrity. This belief also pervades much of the higher literature of the United States. It is significant, for example, that in each of the two greatest works of fiction written by Americans during the nineteenth century the central figure is, like Leatherstocking, a refugee from civilization. But whereas popular novelists have presented the wish-fulfillment of an ideal individualist capable of defending virtue without any support from institutions, more serious writers have felt that the flight from civilization can have no positive goal and that the individual who fights his society is doomed to failure. Emerson could assert his independence without leaving Concord, and Thoreau could successfully demonstrate it by flying only as far as Walden Pond; but Melville and Mark Twain, presenting forms of flight which may be described as extensive rather than intensive, ended in frustration, as have almost all of their twentieth-century successors. The pessimism of modern American literature is, in fact, its most striking characteristic, making a baffling contrast with the optimistic tone of American society. I suggest that it is due to the continued identification of goodness and reality with the self-governing resistance of the ego to the world and the realization that such resistance can end only in defeat.

Melville's Ishmael flies to the ocean instead of to the forest, taking passage in a ship which is "not so much bound to any haven ahead as rushing from all havens astern"; and in the crew of the Pequod he finds many of the qualities which Cooper attributed to his frontiersman. There is a similar emphasis on technical skill, on the virtues of simple men, and on a male comradeship which, as with Leatherstocking's relations with Chingachgook, transcends racial differences, and there is a similar absence of women and of family and social ties. The flight from civilization, indeed, pervades all of Melville's early writings, throughout which emotional fulfillment can be found only by membership in a ship's crew or among the Marquesan savages, never in any marital or social relationship ashore. When Melville deserts the sea, as in *Pierre, The Confidence Man,* and the last chapters of *Israel Potter,* the gloom is unmitigated. But he was too profound a writer to remain content with Rousseauistic nature-worship. Men carry their civilization with them, the Pequod representing in microcosm the whole endeavor of mankind to dominate the natural world; and *Moby Dick* ends with the triumph of natural malevolence. Unlike the serene and pious Leatherstocking, Ishmael learns that "the invisible spheres were formed in fright." It is interesting that this sentence comes at the conclusion of a long passage dealing not with the white whale but with a white horse on the Western prairies, almost as though Melville were directly replying to Cooper.

Melville realized that the hope of escape was an illusion, and the same bitter knowledge was shared by Mark Twain. In *Huckleberry Finn* can be found most of the same ingredients: the flight from civilization to nature, the male comradeship, the contrast between the natural virtue of simple people and social corruption. Adult life is presented as mostly cruelty and folly, whereas Huck's moral intuitions, when he is not led astray by what society has taught him, are unerring. But by making his central character a small boy Twain set the whole theme of escape in a new perspective and exposed it as an adolescent fantasy. We know that Huckleberry Finn will grow up, that—like Twain himself—he must learn to conform to what society requires, and that his natural moral sense will probably be stifled.

The major novelists of the twentieth century have not dealt so directly with the theme of escape, yet most of them have continued to express similar attitudes. The individual can still preserve his integrity only by flight or resistance to society; rarely, if ever, is it suggested that he can find emotional and moral fulfillment in conformity to institutional mores and disciplines. But the closing of the frontier, the rise of the big corporation as the central institution of modern society, and the growth of complex mass organizations of all kinds have made both flight and resistance less easy than in the nineteenth century, and the individual has usually gone down more quickly to inevitable defeat. These generalizations do not seem to apply to the Southerners, who have been dealing with a situation not duplicated elsewhere in the United States; but they can be illustrated from the work of almost all other leading novelists. One might cite, as obvious examples, Babbitt's attempt at self-assertion against the mores of a midwestern business community and his final surrender; the flight of a series of Sherwood Anderson characters in search of some kind of emotional fulfillment which remains always unrealized; Willa Cather's idealization of pioneer virtues, her inability to find any place for them in modern America, and her final retreat back to the values of French and Spanish Catholicism; the choice between escape and corruption in the early novels of Dos Passos; and the metamorphosis of the frontier hero into Fitzgerald's Gatsby, the bootlegger from Dakota, with the contrast between his naive idealism and the heartlessness of all the upper-class characters. But of all modern writers, it is probably Hemingway who conforms most closely to the theme I am discussing. The Hemingway hero, as Philip Young has suggested, can be regarded as a grown-up Huckleberry Finn, and he displays most of the essential Leatherstocking qualities. This is most obvious with the boxers, bullfighters, and other simple characters who maintain a stoical integrity in defiance of all social pressures; but it is also true of the heroes of several of the novels, who remain simple people in spite of the education and sophistication which the author attributes to them. The similarity was underlined when, in the Hollywood versions of *A Farewell to Arms* and *For Whom the Bell Tolls,* the leading roles were played by Gary Cooper.

One other generalization may be ventured about American novelists. By contrast with Europeans, they rarely deal with the kind of love that may be expected to culminate in a happy marriage. In the major writers of the nineteenth century, except rather mildly in Hawthorne and Henry James, normal sexuality is, in fact, remarkably absent. Sexual emotion either appears in morbid forms, as in Poe, Melville, and probably Whitman, or else it is nonexistent, as in Emerson and Thoreau and in Mark Twain. Since 1900 literature has been less reticent; but any sexual fulfillment is mostly extramarital and therefore an aspect of the resistance to society, the most notable example being in the Hemingway novels. The frontier hero's view of marriage as a trap by which civilization tames and corrupts the individual still pervades the world of the novelist. One can cite again Lewis's *Babbitt* and several Anderson novels, Fitzgerald's

Tender Is the Night, and Hemingway's "The Short Happy Life of Francis Macomber" and "The Snows of Kilimanjaro."

These American attitudes are not duplicated in modern European literature, though the difference is much less acute than in popular fiction. It is true that European writers of the past two centuries have been generally critical of social institutions, and one must go back before the Romantic movement to find major writers who seem to be unequivocally committed to support of the established order. But most European novelists place their characters within a social milieu and present them as illustrations of social tendencies. It is difficult to think of many comparable European examples of the dichotomy between individual integrity and social corruption and the consequent emphasis on flight or resistance.

I turn now to the question of how this dichotomy originated and what it means.

Its most obvious source is, of course, the frontier experience. America came into being through a long series of migrations, the participants· in which generally knew what they were escaping *from* more clearly than what they were escaping *to;* and as long as this process continued, individuals could normally respond to emotional or economic pressures by physically removing themselves. To a large extent the United States was settled by groups who, like Melville's Pequod, were "not so much bound to any havens ahead as rushing from all havens astern." If, however, one looks more closely at the frontier experience and its symbolic embodiment in the frontier hero, one finds a basic ambiguity, the exploration of which can lead only to the pessimism exemplified in the novelists. Did the frontier really mean an escape from civilization, or did it mean its expansion? Leatherstocking hated the life of the settlements, and Daniel Boone was portrayed by journalists in the same fashion. Yet the actual historic function of the frontiersman was not to repudiate settled society but to act as the vanguard of its advance. The myth embodied in the frontier hero was engendered by the subjective attitude of escape to freedom, but this was destined to be constantly negated by the objective reality of an expanding civilization. There is a similar ambiguity in the heroes of later popular fiction, since they both stand for order and justice and are, at the same time, markedly antisocial. The Virginian stops cattle-thieving, but since juries are corrupt, he acts by lynch law. The hero of *High Noon* shoots the gangsters and then flings his sheriff's badge in the dust and drives away. The private eye avenges crime, but is invariably regarded as a suspicious character by the district attorney and the officers of the homicide bureau. Objectively, the hero is defending civilization, yet at the same time civilization is repressive and corrupting.

The same dilemma can be found in historical interpretations of the frontier experience, especially that of Frederick Jackson Turner. According to Turner, the frontier promoted individual freedom and democracy and produced a new type of society fundamentally different from that of Europe, yet on the other hand it represented merely a primitive stage through which each segment of American society must pass in its evolution toward civilization. These propositions implied that with the closing of the frontier American society would lose its democratic virtues. It will be recalled that a century earlier Thomas Jefferson had predicted that when the public land was exhausted and Americans became piled up in cities, as in Europe, they would become corrupt like the Europeans. Turner's efforts to evade the pessimism which his thesis implied were unremitting but never very convincing.

The dilemma, moreover, has larger applications. Insofar as all American society has been the product of a westward movement from the original centers of Western civilization, the whole history of America has been the history of a frontier; and the ambivalence represented by the frontier hero has always been manifested, on a broader scale, in American attitudes toward Europe. How far does the United States represent the extension to a New World of the heritage of Western civilization, and how far is it an escape from Old World corruption to a purer and more natural way of life? In some sense all American intellectual history has been a long exploration of this question, and insofar as the American mind has wished to differentiate itself from its European matrix, it has usually insisted that in flying from European sophistication, the American has become more virtuous. This is conspicuously true not only of such belligerent redskins as Mark Twain but also of palefaces like Henry James. Balancing simple-minded integrity against cultivated corruption, James achieved the kind of density and complexity which is so lacking in Cooper; but he had a similar conflict of allegiances, and the contrast between the purity of his American characters and the double-dealing of his Europeans conforms to the Leatherstocking pattern. If one considers the realities with which he was dealing, the extent to which his view of life was shaped by the Leatherstocking myth immediately becomes apparent. Could a businessman make millions in the age of the robber barons and retain the naive nobility which James ascribes to Christopher Newman and Adam Verver? Were all upper-class Europeans interested so exclusively in taking advantage of American heiresses?

Whether American society has been fairly represented in its literature and thought is, of course, a debatable question. Nonliterary evidence, however, can be adduced for the prevalence of similar attitudes. As a small but significant example, one might consider the use of the word "sincerity." This is probably the most popular American virtue. Even chain stores like the A. and P. claim that they treat their customers sincerely. When confronted by the more elaborate manners of European or Latin American society, the average American is likely to complain of insincerity. This may be regarded as a healthy protest against the stifling of individuality by traditional ceremonial, but in demanding sincerity the American often fails to recognize that all human beings, himself included, observe certain social forms and that civilization is impossible without them. This is precisely the attitude that finds symbolic expression in the frontier hero.

The physical process of migration, however, provides only a superficial explanation of American characteristics. As the more extreme exponents of the Turner thesis failed to recognize, the frontier was occasion rather than cause; it produced the effects which Turner attributed to it only because they were already present in the germ before the migration. Where the germ was lacking, as in Latin America and in parts of the Deep South, there was no comparable development. Perhaps the most difficult problem for students of American civilization is to determine which of its qualities are due to the American environment and which belong to Western civilization as a whole but have developed further and faster in America because of the lack of conflicting traditions. The main intellectual influence in the shaping of American attitudes and institutions was the eighteenth-century Enlightenment; and if Americans have preferred to interpret the frontier experience as an escape from civilization rather than as its expansion, this has been largely because the Enlightenment taught them that nature was good and civilization corrupt. It was the Enlightenment that caused Crèvecoeur to depict the life of the American farmer as a utopian idyll and that encouraged Franklin and Jefferson to make such sharp contrast between American virtue and European corruption. The American political heritage, with its suspicion of all organized government as at best a necessary evil and the almost total lack of that exaltation of communal authority and tradition which one finds in European thinkers like Burke and Coleridge, is closely related to the cultural attitudes which I have been discussing; and American political beliefs are derived mainly from the liberalism of the Enlightenment.

The Enlightenment was a necessary movement of liberation against a political and social system that had no longer satisfied human needs, but its faith in individual virtue has long ceased to be a tenable attitude. In the twentieth century the myth of man's natural goodness finds expression not in the piety of Leatherstocking but in the sadism of Mike Hammer. I would suggest that such major changes as the closing of the frontier, the rise of the corporate economy, and the rise of the United States from a peripheral to a central position in the Western world make a change in American cultural attitudes unavoidable; and that the persistence of the kind of individualism that identifies virtue with flight or resistance, while the forces making for collective unity appear only as restricting and repressive, can result only in the baffled frustration that has pervaded the American literature of the twentieth century.

I do not, of course, wish to imply that the Leatherstocking myth has pervaded the whole of the American literary heritage. Hawthorne, who never believed in man's natural goodness, may be cited as a writer whose work, on the whole, was critical of individualism. In its more obvious meaning Melville's *Billy Budd* affirms the need for institutions, culminating in the assertion that "with mankind forms, measured forms, are everything," though, as Richard Chase has demonstrated, a close reading reveals a number of equivocal elements. But for the most usable statement of the problem, expressed in the most elemental terms, I suggest *Democratic Vistas*. Moving beyond Transcendentalist individualism, Whitman recognized that democracy required not one positive but two, not only "the pride and centripetal isolation of the human being by himself," but also the union of the individual with the group: two principles, which were "confronting and ever modifying the other, often clashing, paradoxical, yet neither of highest avail without the other."

SOURCES AND ACKNOWLEDGMENTS

Acknowledgments and thanks are due to the publishers listed below for permission to reprint copyrighted material.

"Literary Characteristics of Democratic Times" by Alexis de Tocqueville is Chapter XIII of Volume II of *Democracy in America* in the Henry Reeve text as revised by Francis Bowen and further corrected and edited by Phillips Bradley (Alfred A. Knopf, Inc., New York, 1945).

"American Literature" by James Fenimore Cooper is an abridged text of Letter XXIII in *Notions of the Americans* (1828).

"Emerson" by John Jay Chapman is the first section of the essay of that title; text from *Emerson and Other Essays* (1898).

"Nationality in Literature" by E. A. Duyckinck is an abridged version of text in *Democratic Review*, Vol. XX, pp. 264-272.

"Nationality in Literature" by James Russell Lowell is an abridged version of text in *North American Review*, 1849, pp. 196-215.

"Hawthorne: Early Manhood" by Henry James is Chapter II of *Hawthorne* (1879).

"Hawthorne: Looking Before and After" by Paul Elmer More is taken from *Shelburne Essays*, Second Series, 1905.

"The Poe Centenary" by V. S. Pritchett is taken from *Books in General* (Harcourt, Brace & Co., New York, 1952).

"Poe's Influence" by F. O. Matthiessen is the last section (pp. 340-342) of essay on Poe in Vol. I of *The Literary History of the United States*, edited by Robert E. Spiller, Willard Thorp, Thomas H. Johnson and Henry Seidel Canby (The Macmillan Company, New York, 1948).

"Our Poets" by Van Wyck Brooks comprises the first six sections of the chapter of that title in *America's Coming-of-Age* (B. W. Huebsch, New York, 1915).

"One's Self I Sing" by Richard Chase is a selection (pp. 58-82) from *Walt Whitman Reconsidered* (William Sloane Associates, New York, 1955).

"The Whale" by Newton Arvin is a selection (pp. 165-193) from *Herman Melville* (William Sloane Associates, New York, 1950).

"Emily Dickinson" by Allen Tate is taken from *The Man of Letters in the Modern World: Selected Essays 1928:1955* (Meridian Books, New York, 1955).

"Introduction to Mark Twain" by Bernard de Voto is the text, slightly abridged, of the introduction to *The Portable Mark Twain* (The Viking Press, New York, 1946).

"Henry James" by T. S. Eliot is taken from *The Little Review*, August, 1918.

"Henry James" by Ezra Pound is a selection (pp. 295-306) from the essay of that title, first published in *The Little Review*, August, 1918, and reprinted in *Literary Essays of Ezra Pound*, edited by T. S. Eliot (New Directions, New York, 1954).

"James and 'the Rights of Personality'" by F. W. Dupee is a selection (pp. 121-130) from *Henry James* (William Sloane Associates, New York, 1951).

"Henry Adams and the Hand of the Fathers" by Ferner Nuhn is a chapter from *The Wind Blew from the East: A Study in the Orientation of American Culture* (Harper & Brothers, New York, 1942).

"Realism and the American Novel" by William Dean Howells is taken from *Criticism and Fiction* (Harper & Brothers, New York, 1892).

"History of a Literary Radical" by Randolph Bourne is the title essay of *History of a Literary Radical and Other Essays*, edited with an introduction by Van Wyck Brooks (B. W. Huebsch, New York, 1920).

"Puritanism as a Literary Force" by H. L. Mencken comprises the first two sections of the essay of that title; text is from *A Book of Prefaces* (Alfred A. Knopf, Inc., New York, 1917).

"Credo," "The Dean," "Stephen Crane," and "Ring Lardner" by H. L. Mencken are taken from *A Mencken Chrestomathy* (Alfred A. Knopf, Inc., New York, 1949).

"Elegy and Satire: Willa Cather and Ellen Glasgow" by Alfred Kazin is Chapter 9 of *On Native Grounds: A Study of American Prose Literature from 1890 to the Present* (Harcourt, Brace & Co., New York, 1942).

"Theodore Dreiser and His Critics" by Alfred Kazin is taken from *The Stature of Theodore Dreiser*, edited by Alfred Kazin and Charles Shapiro (Indiana University Press, Bloomington, 1955).

"T. S. Eliot as the International Hero" by Delmore Schwartz first appeared in *Partisan Review*, Spring, 1945.

"Introduction to W. C. Williams" by Randall Jarrell, first published as an introduction to *Selected Poems* by W. C. Williams (New Directions, 1949), is taken from *Poetry and the Age* (Alfred A. Knopf, Inc., New York, 1953).

"E. E. Cummings and Wallace Stevens" by G. S. Fraser first appeared in *Partisan Review*, Spring, 1955.

"The Cult of Experience in American Writing" by Philip Rahv, first published in *Partisan Review*, November-December 1940, is taken from *Image and Idea: Fourteen Essays on Literary Themes* (New Directions, New York, 1949).

"Hemingway: the Gauge of Morale" by Edmund Wilson is taken from *The Wound and the Bow: Seven Studies in Literature* (Houghton, Mifflin Co., Boston, 1941).

"The Sorrows of Thomas Wolfe" by John Peale Bishop Copyright 1939 Kenyon College. Reprinted from *The Collected Essays of John Peale Bishop*, by permission of Charles Scribner's Sons, New York.

"F. Scott Fitzgerald" by Lionel Trilling is taken from *The Liberal Imagination* (The Viking Press, New York, 1950).

"Faulkner and the Southern Tradition" by Irving Howe is a chapter from *William Faulkner* (Random House, New York, 1951).

"William Faulkner" by Robert Penn Warren first appeared in *The New Republic*, August 12 and 26, 1946.

"Metamorphoses of Leatherstocking" by Henry Bamford Parkes first appeared in *Modern Writing* No. 3, edited by William Phillips and Philip Rahv (Berkeley Publishing Co., New York, 1956).

"Fenimore Cooper's Leatherstocking Novels" by D. H. Lawrence is reprinted from *Studies in Classic American Literature* by D. H. Lawrence copyright 1923 by Thomas Seltzer, Inc., 1951 by Frieda Lawrence, by permission of The Viking Press, Inc., New York.

"Our Poets" by Van Wyck Brooks is reprinted from *Three Essays on America* by Van Wyck Brooks, copyright 1934 by E. P. Dutton & Company, Inc., New York.

SELECTED BIBLIOGRAPHY

Arvin, Newton. *Hawthorne* (1929); *Whitman* (1938); *Herman Melville* (1950).

Beach, Joseph Warren. *The Method of Henry James* (1918); *American Fiction, 1920-1940* (1941).

Berryman, John. *Stephen Crane* (1953).

Blackmur, Richard P. *Language as Gesture: Essays in Poetry* (1952). Contains essays on Emily Dickinson, Pound, Eliot, Crane, Moore, and other American poets.

Bogan, Louise. *Achievement in American Poetry* (1951).

Bourne, Randolph. *The History of a Literary Radical,* edited by Van Wyck Brooks (1920).

Boynton, Percy Holmes. *Literature and American Life* (1936).

Brooks, Van Wyck. *The Wine of the Puritans* (1909); *America's Coming-of-Age* (1915); *Letters and Leadership* (1918); *The Ordeal of Mark Twain* (1920); *The Pilgrimage of Henry James* (1925); *Emerson and Others* (1927); *Three Essays on America* (1934); *The Flowering of New England* (1936); *New England: Indian Summer* (1940); *The World of Washington Irving* (1944); *The Times of Melville and Whitman* (1947); *The Writer in America* (1953).

Brownell, William Cary. *American Prose Masters* (1909).

Cargill, Oscar. *Intellectual America: Ideas on the March* (1941).

Chapman, John Jay. *Emerson and Other Essays* (1898).

Chase, Richard. *Herman Melville: A Critical Study* (1949); *Emily Dickinson* (1951); *Walt Whitman Reconsidered* (1955).

Cowley, Malcolm. *Exile's Return: A Narrative of Ideas* (1934); editor, *After the Genteel Tradition* (1937); *The Literary Situation* (1954).

De Voto, Bernard. *Mark Twain's America* (1932).

Dupee, F. W. *Henry James* (1951); editor, *The Question of Henry James* (1945).

Foerster, Norman. *Toward Standards: A Study of the Present Critical Movement in American Letters* (1930); editor, *Humanism and America* (1930).

Frank, Waldo. *The Rediscovery of America* (1928); *In the American Jungle* (1937).

Gregory, Horace (with Zaturenska, Marya). *A History of American Poetry: 1900-1940* (1946).

Hoffman, Frederick J. *The Twenties: American Writing in the Post-War Decade* (1955).

Horton, Philip. *Hart Crane: The Life of an American Poet* (1937).

Howe, Irving. *Sherwood Anderson* (1951); *William Faulkner* (1952).

Howells, William Dean. *Literary Friends and Acquaintance* (1900); *Literature and Life* (1902); *My Mark Twain* (1910).

James, Henry. *Hawthorne* (1879); *The American Essays,* edited by Leon Edel (1956).

Jarrell, Randall. *Poetry and the Age* (1953). Contains essays on Whitman, Frost, Ransom, Stevens, and other American poets.

Jones, Howard Mumford. *The Theory of American Literature* (1948).

Josephson, Matthew. *Portrait of the Artist as an American* (1930).

Kazin, Alfred. *On Native Grounds: An Interpretation of Modern American Prose Literature* (1942); *The Inmost Leaf* (1956).

Krutch, Joseph Wood. *Edgar Allan Poe: A Study in Genius* (1926); *Henry David Thoreau* (1948).

Lewisohn, Ludwig. *Expression in America* (1932).

Macy, John. *The Spirit of American Literature* (1913).

Masters, Edgar Lee. *Vachel Lindsay: A Poet in America* (1935).

Matthiessen, Francis Otto. *Sarah Orne Jewett* (1929); *American Renaissance: Art and Expression in the Age of Emerson and Whitman* (1941); *Henry James: The Major Phase* (1944); *Theodore Dreiser* (1951).

Mencken, Henry Louis. *A Book of Prefaces* (1917); *Prejudices* (six series, 1919-1927); *A Mencken Chrestomathy* (1949); *The American Language* (1918, fourth revised edition, 1936).

Miller, Perry. *The New England Mind: The Seventeenth Century* (1939); *Jonathan Edwards* (1949); editor, *The Transcendentalists* (1950); *The Raven and the Whale* (1956).

Mizener, Arthur. *The Far Side of Paradise: Biography of F. Scott Fitzgerald* (1951).

More, Paul Elmer. *Shelburne Essays* (1904-1921), eleven volumes containing a number of essays on American themes.

Muller, Herbert J. *Thomas Wolfe* (1947).

Mumford, Lewis. *The Golden Day: A Study of American Experience and Culture* (1926); *Herman Melville* (1929).

Nuhn, Ferner. *The Wind Blew from the East: A Study in the Orientation of American Culture* (1942).

Parrington, Vernon Louis. *Main Currents in American Thought: An Interpretation of American Thought from the Beginnings to 1920* (in three volumes, 1927-1930).

Pound, Ezra. *Patria Mia* (1950); *The Letters of Ezra Pound* (1950).

Quinn, Arthur Hobson. *Edgar Allan Poe: A Critical Biography* (1941).

Rahv, Philip. *Image and Idea: Fourteen Essays on Literary Themes* (1949, revised edition, 1957); editor, *Discovery of Europe: The Story of American Experience in the Old World* (1947).

Ransom, John Crowe. *The World's Body* (1938).

Rourke, Constance. *American Humor: A Study of the National Character* (1951); *The Roots of American Culture* (1942).

Santayana, George. *Character and Opinion in the United States* (1920); *The Genteel Tradition at Bay* (1931).

Sherman, Stuart P. *The Genius of America: Studies in Behalf of the Younger Generation* (1923); *The Emotional Discovery of America and Other Essays* (1932).

Stafford, John. *The Literary Criticism of "Young America"* (1952).

Tate, Allen. *On the Limits of Poetry: Selected Essays* (1948); *The Man of Letters in the Modern World: Selected Essays 1928-1955.* Contains studies of Poe, Pound, Crane, Robinson, MacLeish and other American writers.

Trilling, Lionel. *The Liberal Imagination: Essays on Literature and Society* (1950); *The Opposed Self: Nine Essays in Criticism* (1955). Includes studies of W. D. Howells and of James' *The Bostonians*.

Van Doren, Mark. *Henry David Thoreau: A Critical Study* (1916); *Edwin Arlington Robinson* (1927); *Nathaniel Hawthorne* (1949).

Warren, Austin. *The Elder Henry James* (1934); *New England Saints* (1956).

Whipple, T. K. *Spokesmen: Modern Writers and American Life* (1928); *Study Out the Land* (1943).

Wilson, Edmund. *The Triple Thinkers* (1938, revised edition, 1948), includes studies of James, Chapman, and Paul Elmer More; *The Wound and the Bow: Seven Studies in Literature* (1941), includes a valuable essay on Edith Wharton; *The Boys in the Back Room* (1941); editor, *The Shock of Recognition* (1943); *The Shores of Light: A Literary Chronicle of the Twenties and Thirties* (1952).

Winters, Yvor. *Maule's Curse: Seven Studies in the History of American Obscurantism* (1938); *In Defence of Reason* (1947).

Zabel, Morton Dauwen. editor, *Literary Opinion in America* (revised edition, 1951).